D1536381

JUL 06

The South

A Tour of Its Battlefields and Ruined Cities,

A Journey Through the Desolated States, and Talks with the People:

being a description of the

present state of the country—its agriculture—railroads—business
and
finances—giving and accounting of confederate misrule, and of the
sufferings, necessities and mistakes, political views,
social condition and prospectus, of the aristocracy,
middle class, poor whites and
negroes

including visits to patriot graves and rebel prisons—and embracing
special notes on the free labor system—education
and moral elevation of the freedmen—also, on plans of
reconstruction and inducements to emigration.

From personal observations and experience during months of
southern travel.

By J. T. Trowbridge

1867

THE PUBLICATION OF THIS BOOK IS DUE IN PART TO A GENEROUS GIFT BY THE WATSON-BROWN FOUNDATION.

John Townsend Trowbridge

The South

ATour of its Battlefields and Ruined
Cities, A Journey Through the Desolated
States, and Talks with the People 1867

J. H. Segars, editor

Mercer University Press
Macon, Georgia 2006

ISBN 0-86554-969-9
MUP/P310

The paper used in this publication meets the minimum requirements of American National Standard for Information Sciences—Permanence of Paper for Printed Library Materials, ANSI Z39.48-1992.

Library of Congress Cataloging-in-Publication Data

Library of Congress Cataloging-in-Publication Data

Trowbridge, J. T. (John Townsend), 1827-1916.
The South : a tour of its battlefields and ruined cities, a journey through the desolated states, and talks with the people, 1867 / John Townsend Trowbridge ; J.H. Segars, editor.—1st ed.
p. cm.
Includes bibliographical references.
ISBN-13: 978-0-86554-969-2 (pbk. : alk. paper)
ISBN-10: 0-86554-969-9 (pbk. : alk. paper)
1. Southern States—Description and travel. 2. Reconstruction (U.S. history, 1865-1877) 3. United States--History—Civil War, 1861-1865--Battlefields. 4. United States—History—Civil War, 1861-1865—Destruction and pillage. 5. United States—History—Civil War, 1861-1865—Personal narratives. 6. Trowbridge, J. T. (John Townsend), 1827-1916—Travel—Southern States. I. Segars, J. H. (Joe Henry), 1949-
II. Title.
F216.T8624 2006
917.50444—dc22
2006006619

Editor's Introduction

In September 2001, Americans became unwitting spectators to unbelievable acts of terrorism that extended from the heart of New York City to the Pentagon in Washington, DC, and, finally, to a solitary field in rural Pennsylvania. Television viewers from across the globe were exposed to grim images that are most often associated with natural disasters and acts of warfare: grim scenes of explosive fires, screaming fire trucks, ruined structures, and injured victims. The chaos of these historic moments cannot be forgotten and, for the moment, the sheer destruction of property and the human anguish of lives lost seemed to be without parallel in American history.

Upon further reflection, however, we know that there have been periods of United States history where large numbers of casualties and great loss of life took place as, for example, during World Wars I and II, and the Korean and Vietnam conflicts. Yet, the American people have faced no greater national calamity than the one occurring during 1861–1865, the years of the Civil War. This fratricidal holocaust claimed the lives of over 600,000 soldiers and countless numbers of civilians; and, today, the property damages would total in the billions of dollars.

If we consider the earliest years after the Civil War, the South continued to lie prostrate under the continuing burden of economic ruin and social upheaval; former Confederates faced days that were seemingly without hope. To make matters even worse, the US government seemed paralyzed by an inability to deal with a victory marred by the death of Abraham Lincoln. And federal military occupation and the subsequent reconstruction program did little to alleviate sectional poverty or bitterness. Consequently, Southerners remained marginalized from the rest of the nation and economic distress plagued the populace for several generations—perhaps until the end of World War II.

During Reconstruction, few Southern publishers were in a position to publish books about their defeated region, especially sociological and anthropological studies. Furthermore, journalists from outside the South were equally fatigued and were most eager to return to peaceful homes and more prosperous endeavors; visiting the war-ravaged South was not a priority for most. Fortunately, there existed a New Englander who could be persuaded to undertake the daunting mission of traveling and reporting on the South: John Townsend Trowbridge (1827–1916). This journalist, born on 18 September 1827, in Ogden, New York, was of literary renown and, during his lifetime, made acquaintance with many of America's greatest authors, including Ralph Waldo Emerson, Walt Whitman, Oliver Wendell Holmes, Henry Wadsworth Longfellow, and Harriet Beecher Stowe.

John Trowbridge spent much of his life in Boston and Arlington, Massachusetts, and developed a literary following from writing adult fiction, contemporary poetry, and children's books. In addition, the author contributing to the *Atlantic Monthly* and other important periodicals of the day and, following the better-known Harriett Beecher Stowe, became a prolific writer of anti-slavery novels. Overall, he produced over forty books, including such popular titles as *Neighbor Jackwood* (1857), *The Vagabonds* (1863), *Cudjo's Cave* (1864), and *The Three Scouts* (1865). Today, however, outside of literary aficionados who study American authors of the nineteenth century and antiquarian book dealers who buy and sell notable books, few readers are familiar with John Trowbridge or his books. Students researching nineteenth- and twentieth-century authors might encounter one or more of his timeless articles, as, for example, his "Reminiscences of Walt Whitman" that appeared in the February 1902 edition of the *Atlantic Monthly*.

A publisher, identified as L. Stebbins of Hartford, Connecticut (mentioned in Trowbridge's book, *My Own Story: With Recollections of Noted Persons*), visited John Trowbridge in fall 1865 with a business proposition. Stebbins was seeking a skilled journalist to tour the desolate South and to produce a volume of work that could be sold as subscription purchases and magazine installments. At first, Trowbridge refused the offer because he was already obligated to produce articles for two monthly magazines and had only recently moved into a new home. Stebbins, however, was persistent: he immediately countered with incentives that included a good salary with an expense account and Trowbridge realized that with the increased income, months—and perhaps, years—could be taken off the home mortgage. This project would also be a grand opportunity for Trowbridge to be among the first journalists to write about the defeated South and he soon acquired letters of introduction from prominent officials to make the journey easier. Within a week, Trowbridge was happily heading south.

John Townsend Trowbridge traveled the Old Confederacy with the specific purpose of interviewing a broad spectrum of the struggling society: old aristocrats, ordinary citizens, Confederate veterans, freed slaves, traveling vagabonds, and an assortment from the poorer classes—all profoundly affected by this greatest of American tragedies. The New Englander was already conversant with such political and military notables as Chief Justice Chase, General Phil Sheridan, Major General Thomas, Governor Brownlow (Tennessee), and numbers of federal officials stationed in the military districts of the occupied South. Letters of introduction would lend access to horses, supplies, and guides and, in a relatively short period of time (four months), the journalist would complete two major journeys covering ten Southern states. The project would yield a 590-page manuscript with one of the longest titles in American literary history: *The South: A Tour of Its Battlefields and Ruined Cities, A Journey Through the Desolated States and Talks With the People: Being a Description of the Present State of the Country—Its' Agriculture—Railroads—Business and Finances—Giving an Account of Confederate Misrule, and of the Sufferings Necessities and Mistakes, Political Views, Social Conditions and Prospects, Of the Aristocracy, Middle Class, Poor Whites and Negroes. Including Visits to Patriot Graves and Rebel Prisons—And Embracing Special Notes on the Free*

Labor System—Education and Moral Elevation of the Freedmen—Also, on Plans of Reconstruction and Inducements to Emigration. From Personal Observations and Experience During Months of Southern Travel.

The lengthy title provides readers with a description of the book's contents to include firsthand glimpses of historic battlefields, war torn cities, and desolate landscapes. Initially, this book was sold on a subscription (door-to-door) basis and several of the chapters were later featured in popular journals. Over the years, there have been few reprints—most notably Gordon Carroll's 1956 edited version entitled *The Desolate South 1865–1866*. Nevertheless, John Trowbridge's historic travelogue has yet to receive the full acclaim that it deserves. In fact, the value of this "American Iliad" is quite extraordinary since Trowbridge—as reporter turned anthropologist, psychologist and sociologist—effectively explores not only the impoverished landscape, but also the mindset of his fellow countrymen who were suffering the most from the effects of a cruel war.

The author's previous experience writing books of fiction and poetry served him well in this endeavor of producing a readable adaptation. The old cliché that "history dramatically unfolds" really holds true for this book; the witnessed accounts, lively stories, and colorful vignettes are arranged in such a way that we are reminded of storylines and characters that can only be found in nineteenth-century novels. For example, one of the most fascinating stories in Trowbridge's *The South* emerging from Civil War lore—and now often repeated—is the account of John Burns, "the old man who took up his gun and went into the first day's fight" at Gettysburg. Trowbridge's documentation of this event may have been the first recorded and published account of the gallant and elderly volunteer. Amazingly, "the old hero" led the author on a tour of the forlorn battlefield covered with graves. Burns gave a first hand explanation about his involvement and provided many surprises: he provided revelations about Rebel sympathizers in Gettysburg and gave stark descriptions of mass burials and views of "wagon loads of [military] arms, haversacks, knapsacks, and clothing…strewn over the country."

During another part of the journey, Trowbridge spoke with residents of Chambersburg about the infamous "torching" of their town by Confederate troops. A ransom demand ($400,000 in gold or $500,000 in United States currency) was to be paid in fifteen minutes—the ransom was not paid and the town was burned. And, in another scene, an elderly plowman accompanies the author to one of the nation's bloodiest battlefields, Antietam. Here, the guide has tilled among the graves of 8,000–10,000 soldiers who lie "on this farm, Rebels and Union together." Trowbridge—in, perhaps, the most poignant moment of the journey—picks up a loose skull and reflects upon the man who is "no longer a perishable mortal." Whether traveling by horse, buggy, wagon, steamer, or on foot, our journalist is astounded by what he sees: "farms and plantations laid waste! Complete paralysis of business, [the] rich reduced to poverty…" and, at the hallowed grounds of the Battle of the Wilderness, human skulls were flung "over the paling into the cemetery where they blanching among the graves." Other scenes were equally disturbing; shallow graves with uncovered bodies, and one where the diggers "had left the feet of one of the poor fellows sticking out."

Trowbridge seems to be comfortable interviewing countrymen from all walks of life and was skilled in drawing quotations from a wide variety of ordinary folk from the lowly to the mighty: veterans, patriots, deserters, illiterates, the young and the old, the weak and the mighty. Former slaves and newly freed men are questioned and recorded in their dialects. Moreover, the reporter does not shrink away from describing distasteful scenes (to include Yankee vandalism) and from mentioning heartfelt sentiments. For example, in one episode he writes: "skeletons, uprooted by hogs…on the open fields are a sight not becoming a country that calls itself Christian."

Our traveling journalist is also adept at describing geography and historical landmarks, and in providing commentary on economic, social, and labor issues. Along the way he takes time to visit Arlington and the tombs of George and Martha Washington and, then, to cross over into Washington, DC, to conduct a lively interview with President Andrew Johnson. Trowbridge is also interested in the opinions of ordinary folk and stops to find out if citizens had been adequately compensated for damages in the war and about their feelings on the role of African Americans in the new society. On the old Frederickburg battlefield, he asks a young Confederate "if the South would be better off without slavery?" When the young man responds in the affirmative, the ever-vigilant reporter replies, "Then why did you fight for it?"

Surprisingly, John Trowbridge, an avowed abolitionist and Yankee sympathizer, does not avoid reporting accounts of the reckless misdeeds of Union soldiers. He witnessed the firsthand effects of plundering and vandalism and writes about the desecration of churches along Sherman's route and the sacking of Columbia, South Carolina. Before the war, this writer had never visited the South and his political perspectives were strongly cultivated by a New England upbringing. Nevertheless, personal and political opinions are offered with a sense of fairness and sympathy unlike other journalists who portrayed Southerners with a measure of disdain and derision.

Trowbridge does not appear vengeful or spiteful in his writings; nor does he ridicule those interviewed or pull statements out of context in order to make a partisan point. In short, his goal is not to sensationalize the trivial or demean those being interviewed; instead, he chooses to maintain a degree of journalistic and human dignity while revealing a measure of empathy towards his former enemies. On one battlefield, for example, someone suggests that Northern residents might object to Rebels being buried alongside Union troops; Trowbridge—in honest fashion—answers, "I do not."

Civil War historians will not agree with every opinion issued by Trowbridge and many of his views were no doubt influenced by Northern newspapers; in particular, the explanations about the POW situation at Andersonville and about John Brown's raid. On the other hand, there are some opinions, such as those about

Sherman's atrocities in Georgia and South Carolina that could have been spoken from the Southern perspectives. Nevertheless, Trowbridge covers a wide range of topics—from discussions about death of Stonewall Jackson to debate over the reasons why a general charged as he did in a given battle. There are also conversations ranging from the lighthearted (the importance of mules) to the serious (an analysis of the plight of newly freed slaves).

Today, historians are constantly searching for reliable eyewitness accounts and first person narrative. With the proliferation of published material on the Civil War, it is not always easy to find trustworthy sources; errors, omissions, and embellishments are to be encountered. Readers will find Trowbridge's travelogue to be straightforward, plainspoken, and entertaining: a picturesque portrayal of life in America during some of our darkest times. And, suffice it to say, because of the era it was penned, *The South: 1865 to 1867* may be, arguably, without parallel. Indeed, this book holds great value to those interested in an unvarnished Southern—and American—history.

J. H. Segars

Sources
Sloane, David E. E. "John Townsend Trowbridge," in *Nineteenth-Century American Fiction Writers* Volume 202 of *The Dictionary of Literary Biography*. Edited by Kent P. Ljungquist. The Gale Group, 1999. pp. 271–78.

Trowbridge, John Townsend. *My Own Story With Recollections of Noted Persons*. Boston: Houghton, Mifflin, 1893.

Note: The *John Townsend Trowbridge Papers* are archived in the Houghton Library, Harvard University Library, Cambridge MA 02138.

PREFACE.

In the summer of 1865, and in the following winter, I made two visits to the South, spending four months in eight of the principal States which had lately been in rebellion. I saw the most noted battle-fields of the war. I made acquaintance with officers and soldiers of both sides. I followed in the track of the destroying armies. I travelled by railroad, by steamboat, by stage-coach, and by private conveyance ; meeting and conversing with all sorts of people, from high State officials to "low-down" whites and negroes ; endeavoring, at all times and in all places, to receive correct impressions of the country, of its inhabitants, of the great contest of arms just closed, and of the still greater contest of principles not yet terminated.

This book is the result. It is a record of actual observations and conversations, free from fictitious coloring. Such stories as were told me of the war and its depredations would have been spoiled by embellishment ; pictures of existing conditions, to be valuable, must be faithful ; and what is now most desirable, is not hypothesis or declamation, but the light of plain facts upon the momentous question of the hour, which must be settled, not according to any political or sectional bias, but upon broad grounds of Truth and Eternal Right.

I have accordingly made my narrative as ample and as literally faithful as the limits of these pages, and of my own opportunities, would allow. Whenever practicable, I have stepped aside and let the people I met speak for themselves. Notes taken on the spot, and under all sorts of circumstances, — on horseback, in jolting wagons, by the firelight of a farm-house, or negro camp, sometimes in the dark, or in the rain, — have enabled me to do this in many cases with absolute fidelity. Conversations which could not be reported in this way, were written out as soon as possible after they took place, and while yet fresh in my memory. Idiomatic peculiarities, which are often so expressive of character, I have reproduced without exaggeration. To intelligent and candid men it was my habit to state frankly my intention to publish an account of my journey, and then, with their permission, to jot down such views and facts as they saw fit to impart. Sometimes I was requested not to report certain statements of an important nature, made in the glow of conversation ; these, not without regret, I have suppressed : and I trust that in no instance have I violated a confidence that was reposed in me.

I may add that the conversations recorded are generally of a representative character, being selected from among hundreds of such ; and that if I have given seemingly undue prominence to any subject, it has been because I found it an absorbing and universal topic of discussion.

MAY, 1866.

TABLE OF CONTENTS.

——◆——

LIST OF ILLUSTRATIONS.

THE SOUTH.

CHAPTER I.

THE START.

In the month of August, 1865, I set out to visit some of the scenes of the great conflict through which the country had lately passed.

On the twelfth I reached Harrisburg, — a plain, prosaic town of brick and wood, with nothing especially attractive about it except its broad-sheeted, shining river, flowing down from the Blue Ridge, around wooded islands, and between pleasant shores.

It is in this region that the traveller from the North first meets with indications of recent actual war. The Susquehanna, on the eastern shore of which the city stands, forms the northern limit of Rebel military operations. The "high-water mark of the Rebellion" is here: along these banks its uttermost ripples died. The bluffs opposite the town are still crested with the hastily constructed breastworks, on which the citizens worked night and day in the pleasant month of June, 1863, throwing up, as it were, a dike against the tide of invasion. These defences were of no practical value. They were unfinished when the Rebels appeared in force in the vicinity: Harrisburg might easily have been taken, and a way opened into the heart of the North. But a Power greater than man's ruled the event. The Power that lifted these azure hills, and spread out the green valleys, and hollowed a passage for the stream, appointed to treason also a limit and a term. "Thus far and no farther."

The surrounding country is full of lively reminiscences of those terrible times. Panic-stricken populations flying at the approach of the enemy; whole families fugitive from homes none thought of defending; flocks and herds, horses, wagon-loads of promiscuously heaped household stuffs and farm prod-uce, — men, women, children, riding, walking, running, driving or leading their bewildered four-footed chattels, — all rushing forward with clamor and alarm under clouds of dust, crowding every road to the river, and thundering across the long bridges, regardless of the " five-dollars-fine " notice, (though it is to be hoped that the toll-takers did their duty ;) — such were the scenes which occurred to render the Rebel invasion memorable. The thrifty Dutch farmers of the lower counties did not gain much credit either for courage or patriot-ism at that time. It was a panic, however, to which almost any community would have been liable. Stuart's famous raid of the previous year was well remembered. If a small cavalry force had swept from their track through a circuit of about sixty miles over two thousand horses, what was to be expected from Lee's whole army? Resistance to the formidable advance of one hundred thousand disciplined troops was of course out of the question. The slowness, however, with which the people responded to the State's almost frantic calls for volunteers was in singular contrast with the alacrity each man showed to run off his horses and get his goods out of Rebel reach.

From Harrisburg I went, by the way of York and Hanover, to Gettysburg. Having hastily secured a room at a hotel in the Square, (the citizens call it the " Di'mond,") I inquired the way to the battle-ground.

" You are on it now," said the landlord, with proud satis-faction, — for it is not every man that lives, much less keeps a tavern, on the field of a world-famous fight. " I tell you the truth," said he ; and, in proof of his words, (as if the fact were too wonderful to be believed without proof,) he showed me a Rebel shell imbedded in the brick wall of a house close by. (N. B. The battle-field was put into the bill.)

Gettysburg is the capital of Adams County : a town of about three thousand souls,— or fifteen hundred, according to John Burns, who assured me that half the population were Copperheads, and that they had no souls. It is pleasantly situated on the swells of a fine undulating country, drained by the headwaters of the Monocacy. It has no especial natural advantages ; owing its existence, probably, to the mere fact that several important roads found it convenient to meet at this point, to which accident also is due its historical renown. The circumstance which made it a burg made it likewise a battle-field.

About the town itself there is nothing very interesting. It consists chiefly of two-story houses of wood and brick, in dull rows, with thresholds but little elevated above the street. Rarely a front yard or blooming garden-plot relieves the dreary monotony. Occasionally there is a three-story house, comfortable, no doubt, and sufficiently expensive, about which the one thing remarkable is the total absence of taste in its construction. In this respect Gettysburg is but a fair sample of a large class of American towns, the builders of which seem never once to have been conscious that there exists such a thing as beauty.

John Burns, known as the "hero of Gettysburg," was almost the first person whose acquaintance I made. He was sitting under the thick shade of an English elm in front of the tavern. The landlord introduced him as " the old man who took his gun and went into the first day's fight." He rose to his feet and received me with sturdy politeness ; his evident delight in the celebrity he enjoys twinkling through the veil of a naturally modest demeanor.

" John will go with you and show you the different parts of the battle-ground," said the landlord. " Will you, John ? "

" Oh, yes, I 'll go," said John, quite readily ; and we set out.

2

CHAPTER II.

THE FIELD OF GETTYSBURG.

A MILE south of the town is Cemetery Hill, the head and front of an important ridge, running two miles farther south to Round Top, — the ridge held by General Meade's army during the great battles.   The Rebels attacked on three sides, — on the west, on the north, and on the east; breaking their forces in vain upon this tremendous wedge, of which Cemetery Hill may be considered the point.   A portion of Ewell's Corps had passed through the town several days before, and neglected to secure that very commanding position.   Was it mere accident, or something more, which thus gave the key to the country into our hands, and led the invaders, alarmed by Meade's vigorous pursuit, to fall back and fight the decisive battle here ?

With the old " hero " at my side pointing out the various points of interest, I ascended Cemetery Hill.   The view from the top is beautiful and striking.   On the north and east is spread a finely variegated farm country ; on the west, with woods and valleys and sunny slopes between, rise the summits of the Blue Ridge.

It was a soft and peaceful summer day.   There was scarce a sound to break the stillness, save the shrill note of the locust, and the perpetual click-click of the stone-cutters at work upon the granite headstones of the soldiers' cemetery.   There was nothing to indicate to a stranger that so tranquil a spot had ever been a scene of strife.   We were walking in the time-hallowed place of the dead, by whose side the martyr-soldiers who fought so bravely and so well on those terrible first days of July, slept as sweetly and securely as they.

"It don't look here as it did after the battle," said John Burns. "Sad work was made with the tombstones. The ground was all covered with dead horses, and broken wagons, and pieces of shells, and battered muskets, and everything of that kind, not to speak of the heaps of dead." But now the tombstones have been replaced, the neat iron fences have been mostly repaired, and scarcely a vestige of the fight remains. Only the burial-places of the slain are there. *Thirty-five hundred and sixty slaughtered Union soldiers lie on the field of Gettysburg.* This number does not include those whose bodies have been claimed by friends and removed.

The new cemetery, devoted to the patriot slain, and dedicated with fitting ceremonies on the 19th of November, 1863, adjoins the old one. In the centre is the spot reserved for the monument, the corner-stone of which was laid on the 4th of July, 1865. The cemetery is semicircular, in the form of an amphitheatre, except that the slope is reversed, the monument occupying the highest place. The granite headstones resemble rows of semicircular seats. Side by side, with two feet of ground allotted to each, and with their heads towards the monument, rest the three thousand five hundred and sixty. The name of each, when it could be ascertained, together with the number of the company and regiment in which he served, is lettered on the granite at his head. But the barbarous practice of stripping such of our dead as fell into their hands, in which the Rebels indulged here as elsewhere, rendered it impossible to identify large numbers. The headstones of these are lettered "Unknown." At the time when I visited the cemetery, the sections containing most of the unknown had not yet received their headstones, and their resting-places were indicated by a forest of stakes. I have seen few sadder sights.

The spectacle of so large a field crowded with the graves of the slain brings home to the heart an overpowering sense of the horror and wickedness of war. Yet, as I have said, not all our dead are here. None of the Rebel dead are here. Not one of those who fell on other fields, or died in hospitals an.l prisons in those States where the war was chiefly waged, — not one out of those innumerable martyred hosts lies on this pleasant hill. The bodies of once living and brave men, slowly mouldering to dust in this sanctified soil, form but a small, a single sheaf from that great recent harvest reaped by Death with the sickle of war.

Once living and brave! How full of life, how full of un- flinching courage and fiery zeal they marched up hither to fight the great fight, and to give their lives! And each man had his history; each soldier resting here had his interests, his loves, his darling hopes, the same as you or I. All were laid down with his life. It was no trifle to him : it was as great a thing to him as it would be to you, thus to be cut off from all things dear in this world, and to drop at once into a vague eternity. Grown accustomed to the waste of life through years of war, we learn to think too lightly of such sacrifices. " So many killed," — with that brief sentence we glide over the unimaginably fearful fact, and pass on to other details. We indulge in pious commonplaces, — " They have gone to a better world; they have their reward," and the like. No doubt this is true; if not, then life is a mockery, and hope a lie. But the future, with all our faith, is vague and uncer- tain. It lies before us like one of those unidentified heroes, hidden from sight, deep-buried, mysterious, its headstone let- tered " Unknown." Will it ever rise? Through trouble, toils, and privations, — not insensible to danger, but braving it, — these men — and not these only, but the uncounted thou- sands represented by these — confronted, for their country's sake, that awful uncertainty. Did they believe in your better world? Whether they did or not, this world was a reality, and dear to them.

I looked into one of the trenches, in which workmen were laying foundations for the headstones, and saw the ends of the coffins protruding. It was silent and dark down there. Side by side the soldiers slept, as side by side they fought. I chose out one coffin from among the rest, and thought of him whose dust it contained, — your brother and mine, althougr

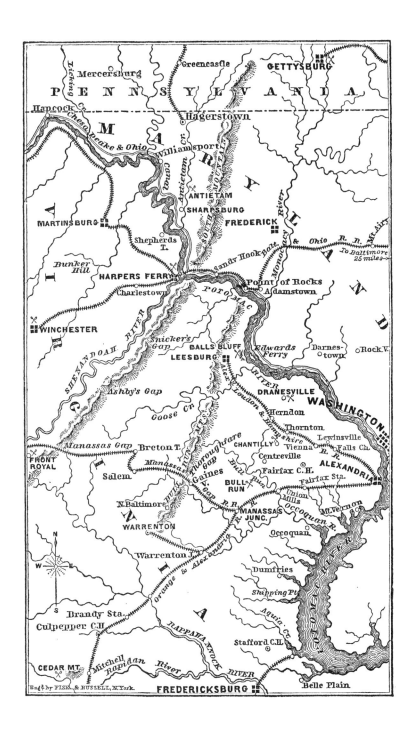

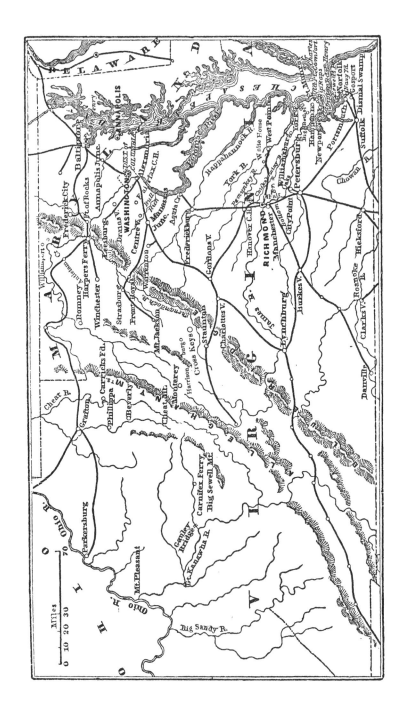

we never knew him. I thought of him as a child, tenderly
reared up — for this. I thought of his home, his heart-life : —

> " Had he a father ?
> Had he a mother ?
> Had he a sister ?
> Had he a brother ?
> Or was there a nearer one
> Still, and a dearer one
> Yet, than all other ? "

I could not know ; in this world, none will ever know. He
sleeps with the undistinguishable multitude, and his headstone
is lettered " Unknown."

Eighteen loyal States are represented by the tenants of
these graves. New York has the greatest number, — upwards of eight hundred ; Pennsylvania comes next in order,
having upwards of five hundred. Tall men from Maine,
young braves from Wisconsin, heroes from every State between, met here to defend their country and their homes.
Sons of Massachusetts fought for Massachusetts on Pennsylvania soil. If they had not fought, or if our armies had been
annihilated here, the whole North would have been at the
mercy of Lee's victorious legions. As Cemetery Hill was the
pivot on which turned the fortunes of the battle, so Gettysburg itself was the pivot on which turned the destiny of the
nation. Here the power of aggressive treason culminated ;
and from that memorable Fourth of July, when the Rebel invaders, beaten in the three days' previous fight, stole away
down the valleys and behind the mountains on their ignominious retreat, — from that day, signalized also by the fall of
Vicksburg in the West, it waned and waned, until it was
swept from the earth.

Cemetery Hill should be first visited by the tourist of the
battle-ground. Here a view of the entire field, and a clear
understanding of the military operations of the three days, are
best obtained. Looking north, away on your left lies Seminary Ridge, the scene of the first day's fight, in which the gallant Reynolds fell, and from which our troops were driven back

in confusion through the town by overwhelming numbers in the afternoon. Farther south spread the beautiful woods and vales that swarmed with Rebels on the second and third day, and from which they made such desperate charges upon our lines. On the right as you stand is Culp's Hill, the scene of Ewell's furious but futile attempts to flank us there. You are in the focus of a half-circle, from all points of which was poured in upon this now silent hill such an artillery fire as has seldom been concentrated upon one point of an open field in any of the great battles upon this planet. From this spot extend your observations as you please.

Guided by the sturdy old man, I proceeded first to Culp's Hill, following a line of breastworks into the woods. Here are seen some of the soldiers' devices, hastily adopted for defence. A rude embankment of stakes and logs and stones, covered with earth, forms the principal work ; aside from which you meet with little private breastworks, as it were, consisting of rocks heaped up by the trunk of a tree, or beside a larger rock, or across a cleft in the rocks, where some sharpshooter stood and exercised his skill at his ease.

The woods are of oak chiefly, but with a liberal sprinkling of chestnut, black-walnut, hickory, and other common forest-trees. Very beautiful they were that day, with their great, silent trunks, all so friendly, their clear vistas and sun-spotted spaces. Beneath reposed huge, sleepy ledges and boulders, their broad backs covered with lichens and old moss. A more fitting spot for a picnic, one would say, than for a battle.

Yet here remain more astonishing evidences of fierce fighting than anywhere else about Gettysburg. The trees in certain localities are all scarred, disfigured, and literally dying or dead from their wounds. The marks of balls in some of the trunks are countless. Here are limbs, and yonder are whole tree-tops, cut off by shells. Many of these trees have been hacked for lead, and chips containing bullets have been carried away for relics.

Past the foot of the hill runs Rock Creek, a muddy, sluggish stream, " great for eels," said John Burns. Big boulders an d blocks of stone lie scattered along its bed. Its low shores are covered with thin grass, shaded by the forest-trees. Plenty of Rebel knapsacks and haversacks lie rotting upon the ground ; and there are Rebel graves near by in the woods. By these I was inclined to pause longer than John Burns thought it worth the while. I felt a pity for these unhappy men, which he could not understand. To him they were dead Rebels, and nothing more ; and he spoke with great disgust of an effort which had been made by certain " Copperheads " of the town to have all the buried Rebels now scattered about in the woods and fields gathered together in a cemetery near that dedicated to our own dead.

" Yet consider, my friend," I said, " though they were altogether in the wrong, and their cause was infernal, these, too, were brave men ; and, under different circumstances, with no better hearts than they had, they might have been lying in honored graves up yonder, instead of being buried in heaps, like dead cattle, down here."

Is there not a better future for these men also ? The time will come when we shall at least cease to hate them.

The cicada was singing, insects were humming in the air, crows were cawing in the tree-tops, the sunshine slept on the boughs or nestled in the beds of brown leaves on the ground, — all so pleasant and so pensive, I could have passed the day there. But John reminded me that night was approaching, and we returned to Gettysburg.

That evening I walked alone to Cemetery Hill, to see the sun set behind the Blue Ridge. A quiet prevailed there still more profound than during the day. The stone-cutters had finished their day's work and gone home. The katydids were singing, and the shrill, sad chirp of the crickets welcomed the cool shades. The sun went down, and the stars came out and shone upon the graves, — the same stars which were no doubt shining even then upon many a vacant home and mourning heart left lonely by the husbands, the fathers, the dear brothers and sons, who fell at Gettysburg.

The next morning, according to agreement, I went to call

on the old hero. I found him living in the upper part of a little whitewashed two-story house, on the corner of two streets west of the town. A flight of wooden steps outside took me to his door. He was there to welcome me. John Burns is a stoutish, slightly bent, hale old man, with a light-blue eye, a long, aggressive nose, a firm-set mouth expressive of determination of character, and a choleric temperament. His hair, originally dark-brown, is considerably bleached with age ; and his beard, once sandy, covers his face (shaved once or twice a week) with a fine crop of silver stubble. A short, massy kind of man ; about five feet four or five inches in height, I should judge. He was never measured but once in his life. That was when he enlisted in the War of 1812. He was then nineteen years old, and stood five feet in his shoes. " But I 've growed a heap since," said John.

At my request he told his story.

On the morning of the first day's fight he sent his wife away, telling her that he would take care of the house. The firing was near by, over Seminary Ridge. Soon a wounded soldier came into the town and stopped at an old house on the opposite corner. Burns saw the poor fellow lay down his musket, and the inspiration to go into the battle seems then first to have seized him. He went over and demanded the gun.

" What are you going to do with it ? " asked the soldier.

" I 'm going to shoot some of the damned Rebels ! " replied John.

He is not a swearing man, and the strong adjective is to be taken in a strictly literal, not a profane, sense.

Having obtained the gun, he pushed out on the Chambersburg Pike, and was soon in the thick of the skirmish.

" I wore a high-crowned hat and a long-tailed blue ; and I was seventy year old."

The sight of so old a man, in such costume, rushing fearlessly forward to get a shot in the very front of the battle, of course attracted attention. He fought with the Seventh Wisconsin Regiment ; the Colonel of which ordered him back, and questioned him, and finally, seeing the old man's patriotic determination, gave him a good rifle in place of the musket he had brought with him.

" Are you a good shot ? "

" Tolerable good," said John, who is an old fox-hunter.

" Do you see that Rebel riding yonder ? "

" I do."

" Can you fetch him ? "

" I can try."

The old man took deliberate aim and fired. He does not say he killed the Rebel, but simply that his shot was cheered by the Wisconsin boys, and that afterwards the horse the Rebel rode was seen galloping with an empty saddle.

" That 's all I know about it."

He fought until our forces were driven back in the afternoon. He had already received two slight wounds, and a third one through the arm, to which he paid little attention ; " only the blood running down my hand bothered me a heap." Then, as he was slowly falling back with the rest, he received a final shot through the leg. " Down I went, and the whole Rebel army run over me." Helpless, nearly bleeding to death from his wounds, he lay upon the field all night. " About sun-up, next morning, I crawled to a neighbor's house, and found it full of wounded Rebels." The neighbor afterwards took him to his own house, which had also been turned into a Rebel hospital. A Rebel surgeon dressed his wounds ; and he says he received decent treatment at the hands of the enemy, until a Copperhead woman living opposite " told on him."

" That 's the old man who said he was going out to shoot some of the damned Rebels ! "

Some officers came and questioned him, endeavoring to convict him of bushwhacking. But the old man gave them little satisfaction. This was on Friday, the third day of the battle ; and he was alone with his wife in the upper part of the house. The Rebels left ; and soon after two shots were fired. One bullet entered the window, passed over Burns's head, and penetrated the wall behind the lounge on which he was lying.

The other shot fell lower, passing through a door. Burns is certain that the design was to assassinate him. That the shots were fired by the Rebels there can be no doubt; and as they were fired from their own side, towards the town, of which they held possession at the time, John's theory seems the true one. The hole in the window, and the bullet-marks in the door and wall, remain.

Burns went with me over the ground where the first day's fight took place. He showed me the scene of his hot day's work, — pointed out two trees behind which he and one of the Wisconsin boys stood and "picked off every Rebel that showed his head," and the spot where he fell and lay all night under the stars and dew.

This act of daring on the part of so aged a citizen, and his subsequent sufferings from wounds, naturally called out a great deal of sympathy, and caused him to be looked upon as a hero. But a hero, like a prophet, has not all honor in his own country. There is a wide-spread, violent prejudice against Burns among that class of the townspeople termed "Copperheads." The young men especially, who did *not* take their guns and go into the fight as this old man did, but who ran, when running was possible, in the opposite direction, dislike Burns; some averring that he did not have a gun in his hand that day, but that he was wounded by accident, happening to get between the two lines.

Of his going into the fight and *fighting*, there is no doubt whatever. Of his bravery, amounting even to rashness, there can be no reasonable question. He is a patriot of the most zealous sort; a hot, impulsive man, who meant what he said when he started with the gun to go and shoot some of the Rebels qualified with the strong adjective. A thoroughly honest man, too, I think; although some of his remarks are to be taken with considerable allowance. His temper causes him to form immoderate opinions, and to make strong statements. "*He always goes beyant*," said my landlord.

Burns is a sagacious observer of men and things, and makes occasionally such shrewd remarks as this:

" Whenever you see the marks of shells and bullets on a house all covered up, and painted and plastered over, that 's the house of a Rebel sympathizer. But when you see them all preserved and kept in sight, as something to be proud of, that 's the house of a true Union man ! "

Well, whatever is said or thought of the old hero, he is *what he is*, and has satisfaction in that, and not in other people's opinions ; for so it must finally be with all. *Character* is the one thing valuable. *Reputation*, which is a mere shadow of the man, what his character is *reputed* to be, is, in the long run, of infinitely less importance.

I am happy to add that the old man has been awarded a pension.

The next day I mounted a hard-trotting horse and rode to Round Top. On the way I stopped at the historical peach-orchard, known as Sherfy's, where Sickles's Corps was repulsed, after a terrific conflict, on Thursday, the second day of the battle. The peaches were green on the trees then ; but they were ripe now, and the branches were breaking down with them. One of Mr. Sherfy's girls — the youngest she told me — was in the orchard. She had in her basket rareripes to sell. They were large and juicy and sweet, — all the redder, no doubt, for the blood of the brave that had drenched the sod. So calm and impassive is Nature, silently turning all things to use. The carcass of a mule, or the godlike shape of a warrior cut down in the hour of glory, — she knows no difference between them, but straightway proceeds to convert both alike into new forms of life and beauty.

Between fields made memorable by hard fighting I rode eastward, and, entering a pleasant wood, ascended Little Round Top. The eastern slope of this rugged knob is covered with timber. The western side is steep, and wild with rocks and bushes. Near by is the Devil's Den, a dark cavity in the rocks, interesting henceforth on account of the fight that took place here for the possession of these heights. A photographic view, taken the Sunday morning after the battle, shows eight dead Rebels tumbled headlong, with their guns, among the rocks below the Den.

A little farther on is Round Top itself, a craggy tusk of the rock-jawed earth pushed up there towards the azure. It is covered all over with broken ledges, boulders, and fields of stones. Among these the forest-trees have taken root, — thrifty Nature making the most of things even here. The serene leafy tops of ancient oaks tower aloft in the bluish-golden air. It is a natural fortress, which our boys strengthened still further by throwing up the loose stones into handy breastworks.

Returning, I rode the whole length of the ridge held by our troops, realizing more and more the importance of that extraordinary position. It is like a shoe, of which Round Top represents the heel, and Cemetery Hill the toe. Here all our forces were concentrated on Thursday and Friday, within a space of two miles. Movements from one part to another of this compact field could be made with celerity. Lee's forces, on the other hand, extended over a circle of seven miles or more around, in a country where all their movements could be watched by us and anticipated.

At a point well forward on the foot of this shoe, Meade had his headquarters. I tied my horse at the gate, and entered the little square box of a house which enjoys that historical celebrity. It is scarcely more than a hut, having but two little rooms on the ground-floor, and I know not what narrow, low-roofed chambers above. Two small girls, with brown German faces, were paring wormy apples under the porch; and a round-shouldered, bareheaded, and barefooted woman, also with a German face and a strong German accent, was drawing water at the well. I asked her for drink, which she kindly gave me, and invited me into the house.

The little box was whitewashed outside and in, except the floor and ceilings and inside doors, which were neatly scoured. The woman sat down to some mending, and entered freely into conversation. She was a widow, and the mother of six children. The two girls cutting wormy apples at the door were the youngest, and the only ones left to her. A son in the army was expected home in a few days. She did not know how old her children were ; she did not know how old she was herself, " she was so forgetful."

She ran away at the time of the fight, but was sorry afterwards she did not stay at home. " She lost a heap." The house was robbed of almost everything ; " coverlids and sheets, and some of our own clo'es, all carried away. They got about two ton of hay from me. I owed a little on my land yit, and thought I 'd put in two lots of wheat that year, and it was all trampled down, and I did n't git nothing from it. I had seven pieces of meat yit, and them was all took. All I had when I got back was jist a little bit of flour yit. The fences was all tore down, so that there wa'n't one standing, and the rails was burnt up. One shell come into the house and knocked a bedstead all to pieces for me. One come in under the roof and knocked out a rafter for me. The porch was all knocked down. There was seventeen dead horses on my land. They burnt five of 'em around my best peach-tree, and killed it ; so I ha'n't no peaches this year. They broke down all my young apple-trees for me. The dead horses sp'iled my spring, so I had to have my well dug."

I inquired if she had ever got anything for the damage.

" Not much. I jist sold the bones of the dead horses. I could n't do it till this year, for the meat had n't rotted off yit. I got fifty cents a hundred. There was seven hundred and fifty pounds. You can reckon up what they come to. That 's all I got."

Not much, indeed !

This poor woman's entire interest in the great battle was, I found, centred in her own losses. What the country lost or gained, she did not know nor care, never having once thought of that side of the question.

The town is full of similar reminiscences ; and it is a subject which everybody except the " Copperheads " likes to talk with you about. There were heroic women here, too. On the evening of Wednesday, as our forces were retreating, an exhausted Union soldier came to Mr. Culp's house, near Culp's Hill, and said, as he sank down, —

"If I can't have a drink of water, I must die."

Mrs. Culp, who had taken refuge in the cellar, — for the house was now between the two fires, — said, —

"I will go to the spring and get you some water."

It was then nearly dark. As she was returning with the water, a bullet whizzed past her. It was fired by a sharpshooter on our own side, who had mistaken her for one of the advancing Rebels. Greatly frightened, she hurried home, bringing the water safely. One poor soldier was made eternally grateful by this courageous, womanly deed. A few days later the sharpshooter came to the house and learned that it was a ministering angel in the guise of a woman he had shot at. Great, also, must have been his gratitude for the veil of darkness which caused him to miss his aim.

Shortly after the battle, sad tales were told of the cruel inhospitality shown to the wounded Union troops by the people of Gettysburg. Many of these stories were doubtless true; but they were true only of the more brutal of the Rebel sympathizers. The Union men threw open their hearts and their houses to the wounded. One afternoon I met a soldier on Cemetery Hill, who was in the battle; and who, being at Harrisburg for a few days, had taken advantage of an excursion train to come over and revisit the scene of that terrible experience. Getting into conversation, we walked down the hill together. As we were approaching a double house with high wooden steps, he pointed out the farther one, and said, –

"Saturday morning, after the fight, I got a piece of bread at that house. A man stood on the steps and gave each of our fellows a piece. We were hungry as bears, and it was a godsend. I should like to see that man and thank him."

Just then the man himself appeared at the door. We went over, and I introduced the soldier, who, with tears in his eyes, expressed his gratitude for that act of Christian charity.

"Yes," said the man, when reminded of the circumstance, "we did what we could. We baked bread here night and day to give to every hungry soldier who wanted it. We sent away our own children, to make room for the wounded soldiers, and for days our house was a hospital."

Instances of this kind are not few. Let them be remembered to the honor of Gettysburg.

Of the magnitude of a battle fought so desperately during three days, by armies numbering not far from two hundred thousand men, no adequate conception can be formed. One or two facts may help to give a faint idea of it. Mr. Culp's meadow, below Cemetery Hill,—a lot of near twenty acres,— was so thickly strown with Rebel dead, that Mr. Culp declared he " could have walked across it without putting foot upon the ground." Upwards of three hundred Confederates were buried in that fair field in one hole. On Mr. Gwynn's farm, below Round Top, near five hundred sons of the South lie promiscuously heaped in one huge sepulchre. Of the quantities of iron, of the wagon-loads of arms, knapsacks, haversacks, and clothing, which strewed the country, no estimate can be made. Government set a guard over these, and for weeks officials were busy in gathering together all the more valuable spoils. The harvest of bullets was left for the citizens to glean. Many of the poorer people did a thriving business picking up these missiles of death, and selling them to dealers ; two of whom alone sent to Baltimore fifty tons of lead collected in this way from the battle-field.

3

CHAPTER III.

A REMINISCENCE OF CHAMBERSBURG.

FRIDAY afternoon, August 18th, I left Gettysburg for Chambersburg, by stage, over a rough turnpike, which had been broken to pieces by Lee's artillery and army wagons two years before, and had not since been repaired. We traversed a sleepy-looking wheat and corn country,

" Wherein it seemed always afternoon,"

so little stir was there, so few signs of life and enterprise were visible. Crossing the Blue Ridge, we passed through a more busy land later in the day, and entered the pleasant suburbs of Chambersburg at sunset.

The few scattered residences east of the railroad were soon passed, however, and we came upon scenes which quickly reminded us that we had entered a doomed and desolated place. On every side were the skeletons of houses burned by the Rebels but a little more than a year before. We looked across their roofless and broken walls, and through the sightless windows, at the red sunset sky. They stared at us with their empty eye-sockets, and yawned at us with their fanged and jagged jaws. Dead shade-trees stood solemn in the dusk beside the dead, deserted streets. In places, the work of rebuilding had been vigorously commenced; and the streets were to be traversed only by narrow paths between piles of old brick saved from the ruins, stacks of new brick, beds of mortar, and heaps of sand.

Our driver took us to a new hotel erected on the ruins of an old one. The landlord, eager to talk upon the exciting subject, told me his story while supper was preparing.

" I had jeest bought the hotel that stood where this does, and paid eight thousand dollars for it. I had laid out two thousand dollars fitting it up. All the rooms had been new papered and furnished, and there was three hundred dollars' worth of carpets in the house not put down yet, when the Rebels they jeest come in and burnt it all up."

This was spoken with a look and tone which showed what a real and terrible thing the disaster was to this man, far different from the trifle it appears on paper. I found everybody full of talk on this great and absorbing topic. On the night of July 29th, 1864, the Rebel cavalry appeared before the town. Some artillery boys went out with a field-piece to frighten them, and fired a few shots. That kept the raiders at bay till morning; for they had come, not to fight, but to destroy; and it was ticklish advancing in the dark, with the suggestive field-piece flashing at them. The next morning, however, quite early, before the alarmed inhabitants had thought of breakfast, they entered, — the field-piece keeping judiciously out of sight. They had come with General Early's orders to burn the town, in retaliation for General Hunter's spoliation of the Shenandoah Valley. That they would commit so great a crime was hardly to be credited; for what Hunter had done towards destroying that granary of the Confederacy had been done as a military necessity, and there was no such excuse for burning Chambersburg. It seemed a folly as well as a crime; for, with our armies occupying the South, and continually acquiring new districts and cities, it was in their power, had they been equally barbarous, to take up and carry on this game of retaliation until the whole South should have become as Sodom.

Chambersburg had suffered from repeated Rebel raids, but it had escaped serious damage, and the people were inclined to jeer at those neighboring towns which had been terrified into paying heavy ransoms to the marauders. But now its time had come. The Confederate leaders demanded of the authorities one hundred thousand dollars in gold, or five hundred thousand dollars in United States currency; promising that if the money was not forthcoming in fifteen minutes, the torch would be applied. I know not whether it was possible to raise so great a sum in so short a time. At all events, it was not raised.

Then suddenly from all parts of the town went up a cry of horror and dismay. The infernal work had begun. The town was fired in a hundred places at once. A house was entered, a can of kerosene emptied on a bed, and in an instant up went a burst of flame. Extensive plundering was done. Citizens were told that if they would give their money their houses would be spared. The money was in many instances promptly given, when their houses were as promptly fired.

Such a wail of women and children, fleeing for life from their flaming houses, has been seldom heard. Down the hardened cheeks of old men who could scarce remember that they had ever wept, the tears ran in streams. In the terrible confusion nothing was saved. In many houses money, which had been carefully put away, was abandoned and burned. The heat of the flames was fearful. Citizens who described those scenes to me considered it miraculous that in the midst of so great terror and excitement, with the town in flames on all sides at once, not a life was lost.

The part of the town east of the railroad is said to have been saved by the presence of mind and greatness of spirit of a heroic lady. As her house was about to be fired, she appealed to a cavalry captain, and, showing him the throngs of weeping and wailing women and children seeking refuge in the cut through which the railroad passes, said to him, with solemn emphasis, —

" In the day of judgment, sir, you will see that sight again ; then, sir, you will have this to answer for ! "

The captain was touched. " It is contrary to orders," said he, " but this thing shall be stopped." And he stationed a guard along the track to prevent further destruction of the city in that direction.

The homeless citizens crowded to a hill and watched from its summit the completion of the diabolical work. The whirl-wind of fire and smoke that went roaring up into the calm, blue heavens, soon overcanopied by one vast cloud, was indescribably appalling. Fortunately the day was still, otherwise not a house would have been left standing. As it was, three hundred and forty houses were burned, comprising about two thirds of the entire town.

The raiders were evidently afraid of being caught at the work. The smoke, which could be seen thirty or forty miles away, would doubtless prove a pillar of cloud to guide our cavalry to the spot. Having hastily accomplished their task, therefore, with equal haste they decamped.

Three of their number, however, paid the penalty of the. crime on the spot. Two, plundering a cellar, were shot by a redoubtable apothecary, — a choleric but conscientious man, who was much troubled in his mind afterwards for what he had done; for it is an awful thing to take human life even under circumstances the most justifiable. " He was down-hearted all the next day about it," said one. In the meanwhile the dead marauders were roasted and broiled, and reduced to indistinguishable ashes, in the pyre they had themselves prepared.

A major of the party, who had become intoxicated plundering the liquor-shops, lingered behind his companions. He was surrounded by the incensed populace and ordered to surrender. Refusing, and drawing his sword with maudlin threats, he was shot down. He was then buried to his breast outside of the town, and left with just his shoulders protruding from the ground, with his horrible lolling head drooping over them. Having been exhibited in this state to the multitude, many of whom, no doubt, found some comfort in the sight, he was granted a more thorough sepulture. A few weeks before my visit to the place, a gentle-faced female from the South came to claim his body; for he, too, was a human being, and no mere monster, as many supposed, and there were those that did love him.

The distress and suffering of the burnt-out inhabitants of

Chambersburg can never be told. " For six weeks they were jeest kept alive by the prowisions sent by other towns, which we dealt out here to every one that asked," said my landlord. " And I declare to fortune," he added, " there was scoundrels from the outside that had n't lost a thing, that would come in here and share with our starving people." These scoundrels, he said, were Germans, and he was very severe upon them, although he himself had a German name, and a German accent which three generations of his race in this country had not entirely eradicated.

Besides the charity of the towns, the State granted one hundred thousand dollars for the relief of the sufferers. This was but as a drop to them. Those who had property remaining got nothing. The appropriation was intended for those who had lost everything, — and there were hundreds of such ; some of whom had been stopped in the streets and robbed even of their shoes, after their houses had been fired.

" This was jeest how it worked. Some got more than they had before the fire. A boarding-house girl that had lost say eight dollars, would come and say she had lost fifty, and she 'd get fifty. But men like me, that happened to have a little property outside, never got a cent."

It will always remain a matter of astonishment that the great and prosperous State of Pennsylvania did not make a more generous appropriation. The tax necessary for the purpose would scarcely have been felt by any one, while it would have been but a just indemnification to those who had suffered in a cause which the whole loyal North was bound to uphold. Families enjoying a small competency had been at once reduced to poverty ; men doing a modest and comfortable business were unable to resume it. Those who could obtain credit before could now obtain none. Insurance was void. Householders were unable to rebuild, and at the time of my visit many were still living in shanties. Nearly all the rebuilding that was in progress was done on borrowed capital.

But there is no loss without gain. Chambersburg will in

the end be greatly benefited by the fire, inasmuch as the old two-story buildings, of which the town was originally composed, are being replaced by three-story houses, much finer and more commodious. So let it be with our country; fearful as our loss has been, we shall build better anew.

CHAPTER IV.

SOUTH MOUNTAIN.

THE next day I took the cars for Hagerstown; passed Sunday in that slow and ancient burg; and early on Monday morning set out by stage for Boonsboro'.

Our course lay down the valley of the Antietam. We crossed the stream at Funk's Town, a little over two miles from Hagerstown. "Stop at two miles and you won't be here," said the driver. The morning was fine; the air fresh and inspiring; and the fact that the country through which we passed had been fought over repeatedly during the war, added interest to the ride. A fertile valley: on each side were fields of tall and stalwart corn. Lusty milkweeds stood by the fences; the driver called them "wild cotton." And here the Jamestown-weed, with its pointed leaves, and flower resembling the bell of a morning-glory, became abundant. "That's *jimson*," said the driver; and he proceeded to extol its medicinal qualities. "Makes a good sa'v'. Rub that over a hoss, and I bet ye no fly lights on him!"

At Boonsboro' some time was consumed in finding a conveyance and a guide to take me over the battle-fields. At length I encountered Lewy Smith, light and jaunty Lewy Smith, with his light and jaunty covered carryall, — whom I would recommend to travellers. I engaged him for the afternoon of that day and for the day following; and immediately after dinner he was at the tavern-door, snapping his whip.

The traveller's most pleasant experience of Boonsboro' is leaving it. The town contains about nine hundred inhabitants; and the wonder is how so many human souls can rest content to live in such a mouldy, lonesome place. But once outside of it, you find Nature as busy in making the world beautiful, as man inside has been in making it as ugly as possible. A country village carries with it the idea of something pleasant, shady, green; therefore do not think of Boonsboro' as a country village. Leave it behind you as soon as convenient, and turn your face to the mountain.

That is the famed South Mountain, where the prologue to the Antietam fight was enacted. "I never heard it called *South Mountain* till after the battle," said Lewy Smith. "It was always the *Blue Ridge* with us." He had never heard of Turner's Gap, or Frog Gap, either. "We always called it just the gap in the mountain." The road to the gap runs southeast from Boonsboro', then turns easterly up the hills. It stretched long and pleasant before us. "The night before the battle," said Lewy Smith, "this road was lined with Rebels, I tell ye! Both sides were covered with them about as thick as they could lie. It was a great sight to see so many soldiers; and it did n't seem to us there were men enough in the Union army to fight them. . We thought the Rebels had got possession of Maryland, sure. They just went into our stores and took what they pleased, and paid in Confederate money; they had come to stay, they said, and their money would be better than ours in a little while. Some who got plenty of it did well; for when the Rebels slaughtered a drove of cattle, they would sell the hides and take their own currency for pay."

The mountain rose before us, leopard-colored, spotted with sun and cloud. A few mean log houses were scattered along the road, near the summit of which we came to the Mountain House, a place of summer resort. Here again man had done his best to defeat the aim of Nature; the house and everything about it looked dreary and forbidding, while all around lay the beautiful mountain in its wild forest-shades.

Lewy left his horse at the stable, and we entered the woods, pursuing a mountain-road which runs south along the crest. A tramp of twenty minutes brought us to the scene of General Reno's brilliant achievement and heroic death. A rude stone set up in the field, near a spreading chestnut, marks the spot where he fell. A few rods north of this, running east and west, is the mountain-road, with a stone wall on each side of it, where the Rebels fought furiously, until driven out from their defences by our boys coming up through the woods. The few wayside trees are riddled with bullets. A little higher up the crest is a log house, and a well in which fifty-seven dead Rebels are buried. " The owner of the house was offered a dollar a head for burying them. The easiest way he could do was to pitch them into the well. But he don't like to own up to having done it now."

It was a sunny, breezy field. " Up yer 's a heap of air sturrin'," said a mountaineer, whom we met coming up the road. We sat down and talked with him by the stone wall; and he told us of his tribulations and mishaps on the day of the battle, attempting to fly south over the mountain with his family; overloading his wagon, and breaking down just as the shells began to explode around him; doing everything " wrong-eend fust, he was so skeered."

We pushed along through the woods to the eastern brow of the crest, in order to obtain a general view of the field. Emerging from among the trees, a superb scene opened before us, — Catoctin Valley, like a poem in blue and gold, with its patches of hazy woods, sunlit misty fields, and the Catoctin Mountains rolling up ethereal beyond.

The bridge across Catoctin Creek, half a mile west of Middletown, where the fighting began on that memorable Sunday, September 14th, 1862, could be seen half hidden and far away below. There our troops came up with the rear-guard of the invading army. Driven back from the Creek, the Rebels massed their forces and formed their line of battle, two miles in extent, on this mountain-side, in positions of formidable strength. Standing on the brow of the commanding crest, you would say that ten thousand men, rightly posted, might here check the advance of ten times their number, hold the gap on the left there, and prevent the steep mountain-sides from being scaled.

In a barren pasture above the slope climbed by Reno's men in face of the Rebel fire, we came upon a little row of graves under some locust-trees. I took note of a few names lettered on the humble head-boards. "John Dunn;" "T. G. Dixon, Co. C, 23d Regt. O. V. I. ;" several more were of the 23d Ohio, — the impetuous regiment that had that day its famous hand-to-hand conflict with the 23d South Carolina, in which each man fought as though the honor of the nation depended upon his individual arm. Here lay the victorious fallen. A few had been removed from their rude graves. The head-boards of others had been knocked down by cows. We set them up again, and left the field to the pensive sound of the cow-bells and the teasing song of the locust.

Walking back to the road through the gap, and surveying the crests flanking and commanding it, which were held by the Rebels, but carried with irresistible impetuosity by the men of Burnside's and Hooker's corps, one is still more astonished by the successful issue of that terrible day's work. All along these heights rebel and loyal dead lie buried in graves scarcely distinguishable from each other. Long after the battle, explorers of the woods were accustomed to find, in hollows and behind logs, the remains of some poor fellow, generally a Rebel, who, wounded in the fight, or on the retreat, had dragged himself to such shelter as he could find, and died there, alone, uncared for, in the gloomy and silent wilderness.

Crampton's Gap, six miles farther south, stormed and carried that same Sabbath day by the men of Franklin's corps, I did not visit. The sun was setting as we turned our faces westward; and all the way down the mountain we had the Antietam valley before us, darkening and darkening under a sky full of the softest twilight tints and tranquillity.

CHAPTER V.

THE FIELD OF ANTIETAM.

At seven o'clock the next morning, light and jaunty Lewy Smith was snapping his whip again at the tavern-door; and I was soon riding out of the village by his side.

Our course lay along the line of the Rebel retreat and of the advance of the right wing of our army. A pleasant road, under the edge of woods still wet with recent rain, brought us to Keedysville, a little cluster of brick and log houses, all of which, Lewy told me, were turned into hospitals after the great battle. At the farther end of the town is a brick church. "That was a hospital too. Many an arm, a leg, a hand, was left there by our boys. There's a pit behind the church, five feet long, five feet deep, and two feet wide, just full of legs and arms."

We rode on until we obtained a view of the pleasant hill-sides where Porter lay with his reserves, while the other army-corps did the fighting, on the day of Antietam; then turned to the right down a little stream, and past a dam, the waters of which glided still and shadowy under fringed banks; and soon came in sight of the fields where the great fight began. There they lay, over the farther bank of the Antietam, some green, some ploughed, the latter turning up yellow as ripe grain in the morning light.

"We used to could drive all over this country where we pleased. The fences were laid down, and it was all trampled and cut up with the wagons, and soldiers, and artillery." But the fences had been replaced, and now Lewy was obliged to keep the open road.

At a turn we came to a farm-house, near which were a number of dilapidated barns and other outbuildings, and some old straw stacks. "It was a sight to behold, passing yer after the battle!" said Lewy Smith, shaking his head sadly at the reminiscence. "All in and around these yer buildings, all around the hay-stacks, and under the fences, it was just nothing but groaning, wounded men!"

Crossing the yellow-flowing Antietam, we turned up the right bank, with its wooded shores on our right, and on our left a large cornfield containing not less than forty or fifty acres. "There was right smart o' corn all through yer time of the battle. Good for the armies, but not for the farmers. Come to a cornfield like this, they just turned their horses and cattle right into it, and let 'em eat." You fortunate farmers of the North and West, so proud and so careful of your well-tilled fields never yet broken into in this ruinous fashion, have you fully realized what war is?

Leaving the course of the creek, and crossing the fields where the fighting on our extreme right began, we reached a still and shady grove, beside which, fenced in from a field, was a little oblong burying-ground of something like half an acre. In the centre was a plain wooden monument constructed of boards painted white; the pedestal bearing this inscription : —

"*Let no man desecrate this burial-place of our dead;*"

And the side of the shaft, towards the fence, these words :

"*I am the resurrection and the life. He that believeth in me, though he were dead, yet shall he live.*"

This was the hospital cemetery. The graves were close together in little rows running across the narrow field. They were all overgrown with grass and weeds. Each was marked by a small rounded head-board, painted white, and bearing the name of the soldier sleeping below. Here is one out of the number : —

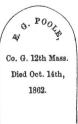

E. G. POOLE.

Co. G. 12th Mass.
Died Oct. 14th,
1862.

As I wrote down this name, the hens in the farm-yard near by were cackling jubilantly. The clouds broke also; a shaft of sunlight fell upon the glistening foliage of the grove, and slanted down through its beautiful vistas. I looked up from the sad rows of patriot graves, and saw the earth around me, all around and above the silent mouldering bodies of the slain, smiling sweetly through her misty veil. For Nature will not mourn. Nature, serene, majestic, full of faith, makes haste to cover the wounds in the Earth's fair bosom, and to smile upon them. The graves in our hearts also, which we deemed forever desolate, she clothes with the tender verdure of reviving hope before we are aware, and gilds them with the sunshine of a new love and joy. Blessed be our provident mother for this sweet law, but for which the homes in the land, bereft by these countless deaths in hospitals and on bloody fields, would lie draped in endless mourning.

Near the monument, in the midst of the level burying-place, grew a loftily nodding poke-weed, the monarch of his tribe. It was more like a tree than a weed. With its roots down among the graves, and its hundred hands stretched on high, it stood like another monument, holding up to heaven, for a sign, its berries of dark blood.

Pursuing a road along the ridge in a southwesterly direction, Lewy at length reined up his horse in another peaceful little grove. Without a word he pointed to the rotting knapsacks and haversacks on the ground, and to the scarred trees. I knew the spot; it was the boundary of the bloody " cornfield." We had approached from the side on which our boys advanced to that frightful conflict, driving the Rebels before them, and being driven back in turn, in horrible seesaw, until superior Northern pluck and endurance finally prevailed.

In a field beside the grove we saw a man ploughing, with three horses abreast, and a young lad for escort. We noticed loose head-boards, overturned by the plough, on the edge of the grove, and lying half imbedded in the furrows. This man was ploughing over graves!

Adjoining the field was the historic cornfield. I walked to the edge of it, and waited there for the man to turn his long slow furrow down that way. I sat upon the fence, near which was a trench filled with unnumbered Rebel dead.

"A power of 'em in this yer field!" said the ploughman, coming up and looking over as I questioned him. "A heap of Union soldiers too, layin' all about yer. I always skip a Union grave when I know it, but sometimes I don't see 'em, and I plough 'em up. Eight or ten thousand lays on this farm, Rebels and Union together."

Finding him honest and communicative, I wished him to go over the ground with me.

"I would willingly, stranger, but I must keep the team go'n'."

I suggested that the boy was big enough to do that.

"Wal, he kin. Plough round onct," — to the boy, — "or let 'em blow, 't ain't go'n' to hurt 'em none."

So he concluded to accompany me. We got over into the "cornfield," late a hog-pasture, and presently stopped at a heap of whitening bones.

"What 's this?" I said.

"This yer was a grave. The hogs have rooted it up. I tol' the ol' man he ought n't to turn the hogs in yer, but he said he 'd no other place to put 'em, and he had to do it."

I picked up a skull lying loose on the ground like a cobble-stone. It was that of a young man; the teeth were all splendid and sound. How hideously they grinned at me! and the eye-sockets were filled with dirt. He was a tall man too, if that long thigh-bone was his.

Torn rags strewed the ground. The old ploughman picked up a fragment.

"This yer was a Union soldier. You may know by the blue cloth. But then that ain't always a sign, for the Rebels got into our uniform when they had a chance, and got killed in it too."

I turned the skull in my hand, half regretting that I could not carry it away with me. My first shuddering aversion to the grim relic was soon past. I felt a strange curiosity to know who had been its hapless owner, carrying it safely through twenty or more years of life to lose it here. Perhaps he was even then looking over my shoulder and smiling at it ; no longer a perishable mortal, but a spirit imperishable, having no more use for such clumsy physical mechanism. The fancy came so suddenly, and was for an instant so vivid, that I looked up, half expecting that my eyes would meet the mild benignant eyes of the soldier. And these words came into my mind : "It is sown a natural body, it is raised a spiritual body."

Let him who has never thought seriously of life look at it through the vacant eye-sockets of a human skull. Then let him consider that he himself carries just such a thing around with him, useful here a little while, then to be cast aside.

> " Every face, however full,
> Padded round with flesh and fat,
> Is but modelled on a skull."

Take the lesson to heart, O Vanity ! It is but a little time, at the longest, that the immortal soul thou art will animate this bone ; but the hour comes quickly when to have been a good soldier of the truth on any field, whether resounding with arms, or silent with the calm strong struggle of love and patience, and to have given thy life to the cause, will be sweeter to thee than the fatness of the earth and length of days. No, heroic soldier ! you I do not pity, though your mortal part lies here neglected and at the mercy of swine.

The cornfield, and another field from which it was separated by a fence at the time of the battle, are now thrown together, forming a lot of about fifty acres. The upper part was dotted with little dry brown cocks of seed-clover. No hogs were on it at the time ; they had been turned out, to save the clover-seed, I presume, for that was of some consequence.

We found plenty more bones and skulls of Union soldiers rooted up and exposed, as we ascended the ridge. Beside some lay their head-boards. I noted the names of a few : " Sergt. Mahaffey, Co. C, 9th Regt. P. R. C.," for one.

" The Rebs had all the fence down 'cept a strip by the pike," said the ploughman. " That was jist like a sifter. Some of the rails have been cut up and carried away for the bullet-holes."

He showed me marks still remaining on the fence. Some of our soldiers had cut their names upon it; and on one post some pious Roman Catholic had carved the sacred initials: —

"I. H. S."

"I reckon that was a soldier's name too," said my honest ploughman. And so indeed it was,— *Jesus Hominum Salvator.*

Beyond the pike, between it and the woods, was a narrow belt of newly ploughed ground.

"You see them green spots over yon' covered with weeds? Them are graves that I skipped." In the edge of the woods beyond lay two unexploded shells which relic-hunters had not yet picked up.

Whilst I was exploring the fields with my good-natured ploughman, Lewy Smith brought his horse around by the roads. He was waiting for me on the pike. "The last time I drove by yer," he said, "there was a nigger ploughing in that field, and every time he came to a grave he would just reach over his plough, jerk up the head-board, and stick it down behind him again as he ploughed along; and all the time he never stopped whistling his tune."

We drove on to the Dunker church, sometimes called "the Schoolhouse," — a square, plain, whitewashed, one-story brick building, without steeple, situated in the edge of the woods. No one, from its appearance, would take it to be a church; and I find that soldiers who fought here still speak of it as "the Schoolhouse."

"The Dunkers are a sect of plain people," said one of the old Dutch settlers. "They don't believe in any wanities. They don't believe in war and fighting."

But their church had got pretty seriously into the fight on that occasion. "It was well smashed to pieces; all made like a riddle; you could just look in and out where you pleased," said Lewy Smith. It had been patched up with brick and whitewash, however, and the plain people, who "did not believe in wanities," once more held their quiet meetings there. I thought much of them as we rode on. A serious, unshaven

4

thrifty class of citizens, they know well how to get a living, and they bear an excellent reputation for honest industry throughout the country. Their chief fault seems to be that they persist in killing one of man's divinest faculties, — as if the sweet and refining sense of beauty would have been given us but for a beneficent purpose. At the same time they do believe sincerely in solid worldly goods, — as if they too were not, after all, quite as much one of the "wanities"! Think of it, my solemn long-bearded friend; you buy land, lay out your dollar in perishable dust, or you expend it in the cultivation of those gifts and graces which, if heaven is what I take it to be, you will find use for when you get there. Now which do you suppose will prove the better investment? All of religion does not consist in psalm-singing and sedate behavior. But I do wrong to criticise so worthy and unoffending a sect of Christians, who are no doubt nearer the kingdom than the most we call such; and I merely set out to say this: while we are in the world, all its interests, all its great struggles, concern us. We cannot sit indifferent. Non-intervention is unknown to the awakened soul. Help the good cause we must, and resist the evil; if we cannot fight, we can pray; and to think of keeping out of the conflict that is raging around us is the vainest thing of all, as yonder well-riddled plain people's church amply testifies.

As it was beginning to rain, Lewy Smith carried me on to Sharpsburg, and there left me. A more lonesome place even than Boonsboro'; the battle alone renders it in the least interesting; a tossed and broken sort of place, that looks as if the solid ground-swell of the earth had moved on and jostled it since the foundations were laid. As you go up and down the hilly streets, the pavements, composed of fragments of limestone slabs, thrust up such abrupt fangs and angles at you, that it is necessary to tread with exceeding caution. As Sharpsburg was in the thick of the fight, the battle-scars it still carries add to its dilapidated appearance. On the side of the town fronting the Federal line of battle, every house bears its marks; and indeed I do not know that any altogether escaped. Many were well peppered with bullets, shot and shell. The thousand inhabitants of the place had mostly fled to the river, where they would have been in a sad plight if McClellan had followed up the Rebels on their defeat, and done his duty by them. Imagine a bent bow, with the string drawn. The bow is the river, and the string is the Confederate line after the battle. At the angle of the string is Sharpsburg; and between the string and the bow were the fugitives. Fortunately for them, as for the enemy, McClellan did *not* do his duty.

After dinner I started to walk to the bridge, known henceforth and for all time as " Burnside's Bridge," just as the road his corps cut for itself through the forests over the mountain, on his way hither from the Sunday fight, is known to everybody as " Burnside's Road."

A shower coming up by the way, I sought shelter under the porch of a stone house, situated on a rising bank near the edge of the town. I had scarcely mounted the steps when a woman appeared, and with cordial hospitality urged me to enter the sitting-room. Although the porch was the pleasanter place, — overlooking the hills and mountains on the east, and affording a comfortable wooden bench, where I had thought to sit and enjoy the rain, — I accepted her invitation, having found by experience that every dweller on a battle-field has something interesting to tell.

She and her neighbors fled from their homes on Tuesday before the battle, and did not return until Friday. She, like nearly every person I talked with who had acted a similar part, was sorry she did not remain in the cellar of the house.

" When we came back, all I could do was jist to set right down and cry." The house had been plundered, their provisions, and the household comforts they had been slowly getting together for years, had been swept away by the all-devouring armies. " Them that stayed at home did not lose anything; but if the soldiers found a house deserted, that they robbed."

I inquired which plundered the most, our men or the Rebels.

" That I can't say, stranger.   The Rebels took; but the
Yankees took right smart.   We left the house full, and when
we got home we had n't a thing to eat.   Some wounded men
had been fetched in, and they had got all the bedding that was
left, and all our clothing had been torn up for bandages.   It
was a right hard time, stranger! " — spoken earnestly and with
tears.   " I have n't got well over it yet.   It killed my old
father ; he overworked getting the fences up again, and it
wore on him so he died within a year.   We are jist getting
things a little to rights again now, but the place a'n't what it
was, and never will be again, in my day."

She showed me, in an adjoining room, a looking-glass
hanging within an inch or two of a large patched space in the
wall.

" That glass was hanging on that nail, jist as it hangs now,
when a shell come in yer and smashed a bedstead to pieces
for me on that side of the room, and the glass was n't so much
as moved."

Suspecting that I might be keeping her from her work, I
urged her to return to it, and found she had indeed quitted some
important household task, because " it did n't seem right to leave
a stranger sitting alone."   I arose at once, on making that discovery, telling her I would rest under the porch until the rain
was over.   She appeared for a moment quite distressed, fearing
lest the subtle law of politeness should somehow suffer from her
neglect.   This woman's sense of hospitality was very strong,
her whole manner carrying with it an earnest desire to make
me comfortable and keep me entertained while in her house.
Although troubled about her kitchen affairs, she seemed far
more anxious about her duty to me, — as if the accident of
my being stopped by the rain at her gate had placed her under
sacred obligations.   At last she thought of a happy solution of
the difficulty.

" I 'll get some pears and treat ye! "   I begged her not to
take that trouble for me; but she insisted, repeating with
pleased eagerness, " Yes, I 'll get some pears and treat ye! "

She brought a dish of fruit, and afterwards sent two little

girls, her nieces, to keep me company while I ate. They were pretty, intelligent, well-dressed misses of ten and twelve; the eldest of whom opened the conversation by saying, —

"Right smart o' fruit cher." A phrase which I suspect every stranger might not have understood, notwithstanding her prettily persuasive smile. South of the Maryland and Pennsylvania line, and indeed in the southern counties of Pennsylvania, one ceases to hear of a *plenty* or a *good deal;* it is always a "*heap,*" or "*right smart.*" The word *here*, along the borders, is pronounced in various ways: *here*, rarely; *yer*, commonly; *hyer*, which is simply *yer* with an aspirate before it; *jer*, when the preceding word ends with the sound of *d*, and *cher* after a final *t*. "Rough road jer," is the southern for "Rough road here"; "out cher," means, similarly, "out here"; the final *d* and *t* blending with the *y* of *yer*, and forming *j* and *ch*, just as we hear "would jew" for "would you," and "can't chew" for "can't you," everywhere.

The little girls played their hospitable part very charmingly, and I was sorry to leave them; but the rain ceasing, I felt obliged to walk on. They took me to their aunt, whom I wished to thank for her kindness. Finding that I had not filled my pockets with the pears, as she had invited me to do, she brought some grapes and gave me. I bore the purple bunches in my hand, and ate them as I walked away from the house. They were sweet as the remembered grace of hospitality.

The bridge was a mile farther on. The road strikes the creek, and runs several rods along the right bank before crossing it. If the tourist is surprised at the strength of the positions on South Mountain, from which the Rebels were dislodged, he will be no less amazed at the contemplation of Burnside's achievement here. Above the road as it approaches the bridge, and above the creek below the bridge, rises a high steep bank, like a bluff. To approach from the opposite side, exposed to a concentrated infantry and artillery fire flashing all along this crest, — to carry the bridge, and drive back the enemy from

their vantage-ground, — one would say was a feat for the
heroes of the age of fable. But the truth is, though men are
slow to receive it, there never was any age, called "of fable,"
or another, better than this, — none that ever produced a more
heroic race of men. We have worshipped the past long enough ;
it is time now to look a little into the merits of the present.
Troy, and Greece, and Rome were admirable in their day, and
the men of Israel did some doughty deeds ; but the men of
New England, of the great Middle States, and of the vast
North-West, what have they done ? The Homeric heroes
and demigods are in no way superior, except in brag, to the
hilarious lads of Illinois, or the more serious boys of Massachusetts. Of materials such as these the poet would have
made a more resounding Iliad.

That Burnside's command could ever have crossed this
bridge, from the high banks on the other side to the steep
banks on this, in the face of superior numbers pouring their
deadly volleys upon them, that is what astonishes you ; and
what grieves you is this : that reinforcements were not sent
to enable him to hold what he gained. If Porter, who had
the reserves, had been a man of right courage and patriotism,
or anything but a pet of the commanding general, he would
have gone into the fight when needed, — for reserves were not
invented merely to be kept nice and choice, — and the results
of that day would have been very different.

I spent some hours about the bridge, the Antietam Creek
singing all the while its liquid accompaniment to my thoughts.
It sang the same song that day, but its peaceful music was
drowned by the roar and clash of the conflict. I sat down on
a rock and watched a flock of buzzards perched on the limbs of
a dead tree, looking melancholy, — resembling, to my mind,
greedy camp-followers and army speculators, who remembered
with pensive regret the spoils of the good old war-days.

The bridge is narrow, affording space for only one vehicle
at a time. It is built of stone, and rests on two solid butments
and two rounded piers. There are woods on both sides of the
stream. On the left bank they stand a little back from it ;

on the right, they cover the side of the bluff below the bridge. The trees all along here were well scarred with shot. Half a mile below the bridge the creek makes a bold turn to the right, and doubles back upon itself, forming a loop, then sweeps away to the south, between a wooded hill on the west and a magnificent growth of willows massing their delicate green and drooping foliage along the low opposite shore.

Returning to the village, I visited the spot chosen as a national cemetery for the slain. The ground had been purchased, but work upon it had not yet commenced. As Pennsylvania gave the soil for the Gettysburg Cemetery, so Maryland gives the soil for this; while each State will defray its portion of future expenses. In the Antietam cemetery it is understood that the Rebel dead are to be included. Many object to this; but I do not. Skeletons, rooted up by hogs, and blanching in the open fields, are a sight not becoming a country that calls itself Christian. Be they the bones of Patriots or Rebels, let them be carefully gathered up and decently interred without delay.

The Antietam National Burying-Ground also adjoins an old town cemetery. It is situated on the right hand, at the summit of the road, as you go up out of Sharpsburg towards Boonsboro'. Here let them rest together, they of the good cause, and they of the evil; I shall be content. For neither was the one cause altogether good, nor was the other altogether bad: the holier being clouded by much ignorance and selfishness, and the darker one brightened here and there with glorious flashes of self-devotion. It was not, rightly speaking, these brothers that were at war. The conflict was waged between two great principles, — one looking towards liberty and human advancement, the other madly drawing the world back to barbarism and the dark ages. America was the chessboard on which the stupendous game was played, and those we name Patriots and Rebels were but as the pawns.

Great was the day of Antietam. Three thousand of the enemy were buried on the field. We had two thousand killed, upwards of nine thousand four hundred wounded, and more than a thousand missing. Between the sweet dawn and the bloody dusk of that dread day there fell TWENTY-FIVE THOUSAND MEN! Can the imagination conceive of such slaughter?

And, after all, the striking fact about Antietam is this, — that it was a great opportunity lost. The premature surrender of Harper's Ferry, which set free the force besieging it, and enabled the enemy to outnumber us on the field, — for Stonewall Jackson was as anxious to get into the fight as Fitz John Porter was to keep out of it, — and the subsequent inertia of the General commanding the United States forces; these two causes combined to save the Confederate army from annihilation. No such opportunity for crushing the Rebellion at a blow had been offered, nor was any such again offered, — not even at Gettysburg, for the enemy there had no coiling river in their rear to entangle them, and we had no fresh troops to launch upon them, — nor at any period afterwards, until Grant consummated that long-desired object; God's good time having not yet come.

CHAPTER VI.

DOWN THE RIVER TO HARPER'S FERRY.

Sharpsburg is not a promising place to spend the night in, and I determined to leave it that evening. In search of a private conveyance, I entered a confectioner's shop, and asked a young lady behind the counter if she knew any person who would take me to Harper's Ferry.

"Yes; Mr. Bennerhalls," she replied; "I reckon ye can get him."

She gave me particular directions for finding his house, and I went up one of the broken pavements "fanged with murderous stones," in search of him. To my surprise I was told that Mr. Bennerhalls did not live on that street; further, that no person of that name was known in Sharpsburg. I returned to the confectioner's shop.

"You said *Mr. Bennerhalls?*"

"Yes, sir; Mr. Bennerhalls, and Mr. Cramerhalls, and Mr. Joneshalls; I should think you might get one of them."

I fancy the young lady must have seen a smile on my countenance just then. Bennerhalls, Cramerhalls, Joneshalls, — what outlandish cognomens were these? Did half the family names in Sharpsburg rejoice in the termination *halls?*

"I *know* Mr. Joneshalls," said the young lady, as I stood solving the doubt, probably with an amused expression which she mistook for sarcastic incredulity.

"Joneshalls" I had never heard of. But I had heard of Jones. Thanks to that somewhat familiar name, I had found a clue to the mystery. "Jones *hauls,*" thought I, that is to say, Jones hauls people over the road in his wagon.

And the first-mentioned individual was not *Bennerhalls* at all, but one Benner who *hauled.*

I thanked the young lady for her courtesy, — and I am sure she must have thought me a very pleasant man, — and went to find Mr. Benner without the *halls*.

No difficulty this time. He was sitting on a doorstep, where he had perhaps heard me before inquiring up and down for Mr. Bennerhalls, and scratched his head over the odd patronymic.

" Yes, I have hosses, and I haul sometimes, but I can't put one on 'em over that road to Harper's Ferry, stranger, no-how ! "

I got no more satisfaction out of Cramer, and still less out of Jones, who informed me that not only he would not go, but he did n't believe there was a man in Sharpsburg that would.

I returned to the tavern, and appealed to the landlord, a pleasant and very obliging man, although not so well versed as some in the art of keeping a hotel. To my surprise, after what Jones had told me, he said, " if I could find no one else to haul me, he would."

At five P. M. we left Sharpsburg in an open buggy under a sky that threatened rain. Black clouds and thunder-gusts were all around us. The mountains were wonderful to behold the nearer slopes lying in shadow, sombre almost to blackness, while beyond, rendered all the more glorious by that contrast, rose the loveliest sun-smitten summits, basking in the peace of paradise. Beyond these still were black-capped peaks, about which played uncertain waves of light, belts and bars of softest indescribable colors, perpetually shifting, brightening, and vanishing in mist. It was like a momentary glimpse of heaven through the stormy portals of the world. Then down came the deluging rack and enveloped all.

Through occasional spatters of rain, angrily spitting squalls, we whipped on. It was a fleet horse my friend drove. He was pleased to hear me praise him.

" That's a North-Carolina horse. I brought him home with me."

" You have been in the army then ? "

And out came the interesting fact that I was riding with Captain Speaker of the First Maryland Cavalry, a man who had seen service, and had things to tell.

Everybody remembers, in connection with the shameful surrender of Harper's Ferry just before the battle of Antietam, the brilliant episode of twenty-two hundred Federal cavalry cutting their way out, and capturing a part of one of Longstreet's trains on their escape.   Captain Speaker was the leader of that expedition.

" I was second lieutenant of the First Maryland Cavalry at the time.   I knew Colonel Davis very well ; and when I heard Harper's Ferry was to be surrendered, I remarked to him that I would not be surrendered with it alive.   He asked what I would do.   ' Cut my way out,' said I.   When he asked what I meant, I told him I believed I could not only get out myself, but that I could pilot out with safety any number of cavalry that would take the same risk and go with me.   I had lived in the country all my life, and knew every part of it.   Colonel Davis saw that I was in earnest, and knew what I was talking about.   The idea just suited him, and he applied to Colonel Miles for permission to put it into execution.   Colonel Miles was not a man to think much of such projects, and he was inclined to laugh at it.   ' Who is this Lieutenant Speaker,' said he, ' who is so courageous ? '   Colonel Davis said he knew me, and had confidence in my plan.   ' It 's all talk,' said Miles ; ' put him to the test, and he 'll back down.'

" ' Just try him,' said Davis.

" So Miles wrote on a piece of paper, —

" ' Lieutenant Speaker, will you take charge of a cavalry force and lead it through the enemy's lines ? '

" I just wrote under it, on the same piece of paper, ' Yes, with pleasure ; ' signed my name, and sent it back to him."

At ten o'clock the same night they started.   It was Sunday, the 14th of September, the day of the battle of South Mountain.   The party consisted of twenty-two hundred cavalry and a number of mounted civilians who took advantage of the expedition to escape from the town before it was surrendered.   Lieutenant Speaker and Colonel Davis rode side by side at the head of the column.   They crossed on the pontoon bridge, which formed the military connection between

Harper's Ferry and Maryland Heights, and turned up the road which runs between the canal and the Heights, riding at full charge along the left bank of the Potomac. It was a wild road; the night was dark; only the camp-fires on the mountain were visible; and there was no sound but the swift clatter of thousands of galloping hoofs, and the solitary rush of the Potomac waters.

Near a church, four miles from the Ferry, Speaker and Davis, who were riding ahead of the party, were challenged by the Rebel pickets.

" Who goes there ? "

" Friends to the guard."

" What command ? "

" Second Virginia Cavalry," said Colonel Davis, — which was true, the Second Virginia *Union* Cavalry being of the party, while the Second Virginia *Rebel* Cavalry was also in the vicinity. " Who are you ? "

" Louisiana Tigers."

" All right. We are out scouting."

" All right," said the pickets.

The leaders rode back, formed their party at a short distance, gave the word, and charged. They went through the Rebel line like an express-train. A few shots were fired at them by the astonished pickets, but they got through almost without loss. Three horses were killed and three men dismounted, but the latter escaped up the mountain side, and afterwards made their way safely into the Union lines.

They galloped on to Sharpsburg, keeping the same road all the way by which Captain Speaker was now conveying me to the Ferry. The enemy held Sharpsburg. Fortunately in every street and by-road Speaker was at home. He called up a well-known Union citizen, from whom he obtained important information. " The Rebels are in strong force on the Hagerstown Road. They have heavy batteries, too, posted on the Williamsport Pike." There was then but one thing to do. " Down with the fences and take to the fields," said the pilot of the party.

This they accordingly did ; — tramp, tramp, in the darkness, by cross-roads and through fields and woods.

" We struck the pike between Hagerstown and Williamsport about two o'clock. We came to a halt pretty quick, though, for there was a Rebel wagon-train several miles in length, passing along the pike. There were no fences ; and the woods were clear and beautiful for our purpose. Our line was formed along by the pike, extending some three-quarters of a mile. Then we charged. The first the guards and drivers knew, there were sabres at their heads ; and all they had to do was to turn their wagons right about and go with us. We captured over seventy wagons, all the rear of the train. They had to travel a little faster in the other direction than they had been going, so that some of the wagons broke down by the way; but the rest we got safely off."

It was just daylight when they arrived at Greencastle and turned the wagons over to the Federal quartermaster there. " Then you should have seen each fellow tumble himself off his horse ! Remember, we had been fighting at the Ferry, and this was the third night we had had no sleep. Each man just took a turn of the bridle around his wrist, and dropped down on the pavement in the street, anywhere, and in three minutes was fast asleep.

" Colonel Davis and I found a cellar-door, softer than stones, to lie on, and there we dropped. I was asleep as soon as my head struck the board. But it could n't have been five minutes before I was woke up by somebody pulling the bridle from my wrist.

" ' What do you want ? '

" ' Want your horse ; want you ; want to give you some breakfast.'

" I got my eyes open ; it was broad day then ; and it was a beautiful sight ! Everybody in Greencastle was crowding to see the cavalry fellows that had cut their way through the Rebel lines. The Colonel and I were surrounded with ladies bringing us breakfast. I tell you, it was beautiful ! " And the Captain's eyes glistened at the remembrance.

" We were hungry enough ! But I said, ' Just give my horse

here something to eat first; then I 'll eat.' 'Certainly.'
And they were going to take him away from me, to some
stable. 'Never mind about that,' said I. 'Just bring your
oats and empty them down here anywhere; he 's used to
eating off the ground.' The oats were not slow coming; and
Colonel Davis and I and our horses had breakfast together,
with the ladies looking on. I tell you, it was beautiful!"

It is eleven miles from Sharpsburg to Harper's Ferry. After
striking the Potomac, we continued on down its left bank, with
the canal between us and the river on one side, and Maryland
Heights, rising even more and more rugged and abrupt, on the
other; until, as we approached the bridge at the Ferry, we
looked up through the stormy dusk at mountain crags rising
precipitous several hundred feet above our heads. Crossing
the new iron bridge, near the ruins of the old one destroyed by
the Rebels, Captain Speaker landed me near the end of it on
the Virginia side.

"Where is the hotel?" I asked, looking round with some
dismay at the dismal prospect.

"That is it, the only hotel at Harper's Ferry now," —
showing me a new, unpainted, four-story wooden building,
which looked more like soldiers' barracks than a hotel. There
was not a window-blind or shutter to be seen. The main
entrance from the street was through a bar-room where merry
men were clicking glasses, and sucking dark-colored stuff
through straws. And this was a "first-class hotel kept on the
European plan." I mention it as one of the results of war,
— as an illustration of the mushroom style of building which
springs up in the track of desolation, to fill temporarily the
place of the old that has been swept away and of the better
growth to come.

One thing, however, consoled me. The hotel stood on the
banks of the Potomac, and I thought if I could get a room
overlooking the river and commanding a view of the crags
opposite, all would be well; for often the mere sight of a
mountain and a stream proves a solace for saddest things.

After supper a "room" was shown me, which turned out
to be a mere bin to stow guests in. There was no paper on

the walls, no carpet on the rough board floor, and not so much as a nail to hang a hat on. The bed was furnished with sheets which came down just below a man's knees, and a mattress which had the appearance of being stuffed with shingles. Finding it impossible, by dint of shouting and pounding, (for there was no bell,) or even by visiting the office, to bring a servant to my assistance, I went on a marauding expedition through the unoccupied rooms, and carried off a chair, a dressing-table, and another bed entire. This I placed on my mattress, hoping thereby to improve the feeling of it, — a fruitless experiment, however: it was only adding a few more shingles. Luckily I had a shawl with me. Never, — let me caution thee, O fellow-traveller, — never set out on a long journey without a good stout shawl. Such an appendage answers many purposes : a garment on a raw and gusty day, a blanket by night, a cushion for the seat, a pillow for the head, — to these and many like comfortable uses it is speedily applied by its grateful possessor. Mine helped to soften the asperities of my bed that night, and the next day served as a window-curtain.

Yet no devices availed to render the Shenandoah House a place favorable to sleep. On the river-side, close by the door, ran the track of the Baltimore and Ohio Railroad. How often during the night the trains passed I cannot now compute ; each approaching and departing with clatter and clang, and shouts of men and bell-ringing and sudden glares of light, and the voice of the steam-whistle projecting its shrill shriek into the ear of horrified night, and setting the giant mountains to tossing and retossing the echo like a ball.

The next morning I was up at dawn refreshing my eyesight with the natural beauties of the place. It was hard to believe that those beauties had been lying latent around me during all the long, wearisome night. But so it is ever; we see so little of God's great plan ! The dull life we live, close and dark and narrow as it seems, is surrounded by invisible realities, waiting only for the rays of a spiritual dawn to light them up into grandeur and glory.

CHAPTER VII.

AROUND HARPER'S FERRY.

AT Harper's Ferry the Potomac and Shenandoah unite their waters and flow through an enormous gap in the Blue Ridge. The angle of land thus formed is a sort of promontory; around the base of which, just where the rivers meet, the curious little old town is built. Higher up the promontory lie Bolivar Heights. On the north, just across the Potomac from the Ferry, rise Maryland Heights; while on the east, across the Shenandoah, are Loudon Heights, an equally precipitous and lofty crag. With sublime rocky fronts these two mountains stand gazing at each other across the river which has evidently forced its way through them here. Just where the streams are united the once happily wedded mountains are divorced. No doubt there was once a stupendous cataract here, pouring its shining sheet towards the morning sun, from a vast inland sea; for the tourist still finds, far up the steep face of the mountains, dimples which in past ages ceaselessly whirling water-eddies made. In some of these scooped places sand and smooth-worn pebbles still remain. But the mountain-wall has long since been sundered, and the inland sea drained off; the river forcing a way not only for itself but for the turnpike, railroad, and canal, fore-ordained in the beginning to appear in the ripeness of time and follow the river's course.

Thus the town, as you perceive, is situated in the midst of scenery which should make it a favorite place of summer resort. The cliffs are picturesquely tufted, and tasselled, and draped with foliage, boughs of trees, and festoons of wild vines, through which here and there upshoot the perpendicular col·

umns of some bold crag, softened into beauty by the many-colored lichens that stud its sides. I count an evening walk under Loudon Heights, with the broad, sprawling river hoarsely babbling over its rocky bed on one side, and the still precipices soaring to heaven on the other, — and the narrow stony road cut round their base lying before me, untrodden at that hour by any human foot save my own, — I count that lonely walk amid the cool, dewy scents stealing out of the undergrowth, and the colors of the evening sky gilding the cliffs, as one of the pleasantest of my life. What is there, as you look up at those soaring summits and the low clouds sailing silently over them, that fills the heart so full?

The morning after my arrival I climbed Maryland Heights by the winding military road which owes its existence to the war. I have seen nothing since the view from Mount Washington to be compared with the panorama which unrolled itself around me as I ascended. Pictures of two States were there, indescribably tinted in the early morning light, — beautiful Maryland, still more beautiful Virginia, with the green Potomac valley marking the boundary between. On the Maryland side were the little valleys of the Monocacy and the Antietam. Opposite lay the valley of the Shenandoah, dotted with trees, its green fields spotted with the darker green of groves, a vast tract stretching away into a realm of hazy light, belted with sun and mist, and bounded by faint outlines of mountains so soft they seemed built of ether but a little more condensed than the blue of the sky.

Yet it was war and not beauty which led man to these heights. The timber which once covered them was cut away when the forts were constructed, in order to afford free range for the guns; and a thick undergrowth now takes its place. There are strong works on the summit, the sight of which kindles anew one's indignation at the imbecility which surrendered them, with Harper's Ferry and a small army, at a time when such an act was sufficient to prolong the war perhaps for years.

It is a steep mile and more by the road from the Ferry to

the top of the cliffs: a mile which richly repays the travel. Yet one need not go so far nor climb so high to see the beauties of the place. Whichever way you turn, river, or rock, or wild woods charm the eye. The Potomac comes down from its verdant bowers gurgling among its innumerable rocky islets. On one side is the canal, on the other the race which feeds the government works, each tumbling its yeasty superflux over waste-weir walls into the river. With the noise of those snowy cascades sweetly blends the note of the boatman's bugle approaching the locks. The eye ranges from the river to the crags a thousand feet above, and all along the mountain side, gracefully adorned with sparse timber, feathery boughs and trees loaded down with vines, and is never weary of the picture. At evening, you sit watching the sunset colors fade, until the softened gray and dusky-brown tints of the cliffs deepen into darkness, and the moon comes out and silvers them.

But while the region presents such features of beauty and grandeur, the town is the reverse of agreeable. It is said to have been a pleasant and picturesque place formerly. The streets were well graded, and the hill-sides above were graced with terraces and trees. But war has changed all. Freshets tear down the centre of the streets, and the dreary hill-sides present only ragged growths of weeds. The town itself lies half in ruins. The government works were duly destroyed by the Rebels; of the extensive buildings which comprised the armory, rolling-mills, foundry, and machine-shops, you see but little more than the burnt-out, empty shells. Of the bridge across the Shenandoah only the ruined piers are left; still less remains of the old bridge over the Potomac. And all about the town are rubbish, and filth, and stench.

Almost alone of the government buildings, John Brown's " Engine-house " has escaped destruction. It has come out of the ordeal of war terribly bruised and battered, it is true, its windows blackened and patched like the eyes of a pugilist; but there it still stands, with its brown brick walls and little wooden belfry, like a monument which no Rebel hands were permitted to demolish. It is now used as a storehouse for arms.

The first time I visited this scene of the first blood shed in the great civil war, which, although so few dreamed of it, was even then beginning, — for John Brown's flaming deed was as a torch flung into the ready-heaped combustibles of the rebellion, — while I stood viewing the spot with an interest which must have betrayed itself, a genial old gentleman, coming out of the government repair-shop close by, accosted me. We soon fell into conversation, and he told me the story of John Brown at Harper's Ferry.

" So they took the old man and hung him; and all the time the men that did it were plotting treason and murder by the wholesale. They did it in a hurry, because if they delayed, they would n't have been able to hang him at all. A strong current of public feeling was turning in his favor. Such a sacrifice of himself set many to thinking on the subject who never thought before; many who had to acknowledge in their hearts that slavery was wrong and that old John Brown was right. I speak what I know, for I was here at the time. I have lived in Harper's Ferry fifteen years. I was born and bred in a slave State, but I never let my love of the institution blind me to everything else. Slavery has been the curse of this country, and she is now beginning to bless the day she was delivered from it."

" Are there many people here who think as you do ? "

" Enough to carry the day at the polls. The most of them are coming round to right views of negro suffrage, too. That is the only justice for the blacks, and it is the only safety for us. The idea of allowing the loyal colored population to be represented by the whites, the most of whom were traitors, — of letting a Rebel just out of the Confederate army vote, and telling a colored man just out of the Union army that he has no vote, — the idea is so perfectly absurd that the Rebels themselves must acknowledge it."

I was hardly less interested in the conversation of an intelligent colored waiter at the hotel. He had formerly been held as a slave in the vicinity of Staunton. At the close of the war he came to the Ferry to find employment.

"There was n't much chance for me up there. Besides, I came near losing my life before I got away. You see, the masters, soon as they foun l out they could n't keep their slaves, began to treat them about as bad as could be. Then, because I made use of this remark, that I did n't think we colored folks ought to be blamed for what was n't our fault, for we did n't make the war, and neitl er did we declare ourselves free, — just because I said that, not in a saucy way, but as I say it to you now, one man put a pistol to my head, and was going to shoot me. I got away from him, and left. A great many came away at the same time, for it was n't possible for us to stay there."

"Now tell me candidly," said I, "how the colored people themselves behaved."

"Well, just tolerable. They were like a bird let out of a cage. You know how a bird that has been long in a cage will act when the door is opened ; he makes a curious flutter-ing for a little while. It was just so with the colored people. They did n't know at first what to do with themselves. But they got sobered pretty soon, and they are behaving very decent now."

Harper's Ferry affords a striking illustration of the folly of secession. The governn ent works here gave subsistence to several hundred souls, aı d were the life of the place. The attempt to overturn the government failed ; but the govern-ment works, together wi h their own prosperity, the mad fa-natics of Harper's Ferry succeeded easily enough in destroying. "The place never will be anything again," said Mr. B., of the repair-shop, "unless the government decides to rebuild the armory, — and it is d ubtful if that is ever done."

Yet, with the grandeuı of its scenery, the tremendous water-power afforded by its two rushing rivers, and the natural ad-vantage it enjoys as the key to the fertile Shenandoah Valley, Harper's Ferry, redeemed from slavery, and opened to North-ern enterprise, should become a beautiful and busy town.

CHAPTER VIII.

A TRIP TO CHARLESTOWN.

ONE morning I took the train up the Valley to Charlestown, distant from Harper's Ferry eight miles.

The railroad was still in the hands of the government. There were military guards on the platforms, and about an equal mixture of Loyalists and Rebels within the cars. Furloughed soldiers, returning to their regiments at Winchester or Staunton, occupied seats with Confederate officers just out of their uniforms. The strong, dark, defiant, self-satisfied face typical of the second-rate " chivalry," and the good-natured, shrewd, inquisitive physiognomy of the Yankee speculator going to look at Southern lands, were to be seen side by side, in curious contrast. There also rode the well-dressed wealthy planter, who had been to Washington to solicit pardon for his treasonable acts, and the humble freedman returning to the home from which he had been driven by violence, when the war closed and left him free. Mothers and daughters of the first families of Virginia sat serene and uncomplaining in the atmosphere of mothers and daughters of the despised race, late their slaves or their neighbors', but now citizens like themselves, free to go and come, and as clearly entitled to places in the government train as the proudest dames of the land.

We passed through a region of country stamped all over by the devastating heel of war. For miles not a fence or cultivated field was visible.

" It is just like this all the way up the Shenandoah Valley," said a gentleman at my side, a Union man from Winchester. " The wealthiest people with us are now the poorest. With hundreds of acres they can't raise a dollar. Their slaves have

left them, and they have no money, even if they have the disposition, to hire the freed people."

I suggested that farms, under such circumstances, should be
for sale at low rates.

"They should be; but your Southern aristocrat is a mono-
maniac on the subject of owning land. He will part with his
acres about as willingly as he will part with his life. If the
Valley had not been the best part of Virginia, it would long
ago have been spoiled by the ruinous system of agriculture in
use here. Instead of tilling thoroughly a small farm, a man
fancies he is doing a wise thing by half tilling a large one.
Slave labor is always slovenly and unprofitable. But everything
is being revolutionized now. Northern men and northern
methods are coming into this Valley as sure as water runs down-
hill. It is the greatest corn, wheat, and grass country in the
world. The only objection to it is that in spots the limestone
crops out a good deal. There was scarcely anything raised
this season except grass; you could see hundreds of acres of
that waving breast-high without a fence."

At the end of a long hour's ride we arrived at Charlestown,
chiefly interesting to me as the place of John Brown's martyrdom. We alighted from the train on the edge of boundless
unfenced fields, into whose melancholy solitudes the desolate
streets emptied themselves — rivers to that ocean of weeds.
The town resembled to my eye some unprotected female sitting
sorrowful on the wayside, in tattered and faded apparel, with
unkempt tresses fallen negligently about features which might
once have been attractive.

On the steps of a boarding-house I found an acquaintance
whose countenance gleamed with pleasure "at sight," as he
said, "of a single loyal face in that nest of secession." He had
been two or three days in the place, waiting for luggage which
had been miscarried.

"They are all Rebels here, — all Rebels!" he exclaimed, as
he took his cane and walked with me. "They are a pitiably
poverty-stricken set; there is no money in the place, and
scarcely anything to eat. We have for breakfast salt-fish,

fried potatoes, and treason.   Fried potatoes, treason, and salt-fish for dinner.   At supper the fare is slightly varied, and we have treason, salt-fish, fried potatoes, and a little more treason. My landlady's daughter is Southern fire incarnate ; and she illustrates Southern politeness by abusing Northern people and the government from morning till night, for my especial edification.   Sometimes I venture to answer her, when she flies at me, figuratively speaking, like a cat.   The women are not the only out-spoken Rebels, although they are the worst.   The men don't hesitate to declare their sentiments, in season and out of season."   My friend concluded with this figure : " The war-feeling here is like a burning bush with a wet blanket wrapped around it.   Looked at from the outside, the fire seems quenched.   But just peep under the blanket, and there it is, all alive, and eating, eating in.   The wet blanket is the present government policy ; and every act of conciliation shown the Rebels is just letting in so much air to feed the fire."

A short walk up into the centre of the town took us to the scene of John Brown's trial.   It was a consolation to see that the jail had been laid in ashes, and that the court-house, where that mockery of justice was performed, was a ruin abandoned to rats and toads.   Four massy white brick pillars, still standing, supported a riddled roof, through which God's blue sky and gracious sunshine smiled.   The main portion of the building had been literally torn to pieces.   In the floorless hall of justice rank weeds were growing.   Names of Union soldiers were scrawled along the walls.   No torch had been applied to the wood-work, but the work of destruction had been performed by the hands of hilarious soldier-boys ripping up floors and pulling down laths and joists to the tune of " John Brown," — the swelling melody of the song, and the accompaniment of crashing partitions, reminding the citizens, who thought to have destroyed the old hero, that his soul was marching on.

It was also a consolation to know that the court-house and jail would probably never be rebuilt, the county-seat having been removed from Charlestown to Shepherdstown — " forever," say the resolute loyal citizens of Jefferson County, who refuse to vote it back again.

As we were taking comfort, reflecting how unexpectedly at last justice had been done in that court-house, the towns-people passed on the sidewalk, "daughters and sons of beauty," for they were mostly a fine-looking, spirited class; one of whom, at a question which I put to him, stopped quite willingly and talked with us. I have seldom seen a handsomer young face, a steadier eye, or more decided poise and aplomb; neither have I ever seen the outward garment of courtesy so plumply filled out with the spirit of arrogance. His brief replies, spoken with a pleasant countenance, yet with short, sharp, downward inflections, were like pistol-shots. Very evidently the death of John Brown, and the war that came swooping down in the old man's path to avenge him, and to accomplish the work wherein he failed, were not pleasing subjects to this young southern blood. And no wonder. His coat had an empty sleeve. The arm which should have been there had been lost fighting against his country. His almost savage answers did not move me; but all the while I looked with compassion at his fine young face, and that pendent idle sleeve. He had fought against his country; his country had won; and he was of those who had lost, not arms and legs only, but all they had been madly fighting for, and more, — prosperity, prestige, power. His beautiful South was devastated, and her soil drenched with the best blood of her young men. Whether regarded as a crime or a virtue, the folly of making war upon the mighty North was now demonstrated, and the despised Yankees had proved conquerors of the chivalry of the South. "Well may your thoughts be bitter," my heart said, as I thanked him for his information.

To my surprise he appeared mollified, his answers losing their explosive quality and sharp downward inflection. He even seemed inclined to continue the conversation; and as we passed on, we left him on the sidewalk looking after us wistfully, as if the spirit working within him had still some word to say different from any he had yet spoken. What his secret thoughts were, standing there with his dangling sleeve, it would be interesting to know.

Walking on through the town, we came to other barren and open fields on the farther side. Here we engaged a bright young colored girl to guide us to the spot where John Brown's gallows stood. She led us into the wilderness of weeds, waist-high to her as she tramped on, parting them before her with her hands. The country all around us lay utterly desolate, without enclosures, and without cultivation. We seemed to be striking out into the rolling prairies of the West, except that these fields of ripening and fading weeds had not the summer freshness of the prairie-grass. A few scattering groves skirted them ; and here and there a fenceless road drew its winding, dusty line away over the arid hills.

" This is about where it was," said the girl, after searching some time among the tall weeds. " Nobody knows now just where the gallows stood. There was a tree here, but that has been cut down and carried away, stump and roots and all, by folks that wanted something to remember John Brown by. Every soldier took a piece of it, if 't was only a little chip." So widely and deeply had the dying old hero impressed his spirit upon his countrymen ; affording the last great illustration of the power of Truth to render even the gallows venerable, and to glorify an ignominious death.

I stood long on the spot the girl pointed out to us, amid the gracefully drooping golden-rods, and looked at the same sky old John Brown looked his last upon, and the same groves, and the distant Blue Ridge, the sight of whose cerulean summits, clad in Sabbath tranquillity and softest heavenly light, must have conveyed a sweet assurance to his soul.

Then I turned and looked at the town, out of which flocked the curious crowds to witness his death. Over the heads of the spectators, over the heads of the soldiery surrounding him, his eye ranged until arrested by one strangely prominent object. There it still stands on the outskirts of the town, between it and the fields, — a church, pointing its silent finger to heaven, and recalling to the earnest heart those texts of Scripture from which John Brown drew his inspiration, and for the truth of which he willingly gave his life.

I had the curiosity to stop at this church on our way back to the town. The hand of ruin had smitten it. Only the brick walls and zinc-covered spire remained uninjured. The belfry had been broken open, the windows demolished. The doors were gone. Within, you saw a hollow thing, symbolical. Two huge naked beams extended from end to end of the empty walls, which were scribbled over with soldiers' names, and with patriotic mottoes interesting for proud Virginians to read. The floors had been torn up and consumed in cooking soldiers' rations; and the foul and trampled interior showed plainly what use it had served. The church, which overlooked John Brown's martyrdom, and under whose roof his executioners assembled afterwards to worship, not the God of the poor and the oppressed, but the God of the slaveholder and the aristocrat, had been converted into a stable.

CHAPTER IX.

A SCENE AT THE WHITE HOUSE.

LATE in the evening of the twenty-ninth of August I reached Washington.

Nearly every reader, I suppose, is familiar with descriptions of the national capital; — its superb situation on the left bank of the Potomac; the broad streets, the still more spacious avenues crossing them diagonally, and the sweeping undulations of the plain on which it is built, giving to the city its " magnificent distances " ; and those grand public buildings of which any country might be proud, — the Capitol especially, with its cloudlike whiteness and beauty, which would be as imposing as it is elegant, were it not that its windows are too many and too small.

The manner in which the streets are built up, with here and there a fine residence surrounded by buildings of an inferior character, often with mere huts adjacent, and many an open space, giving to the metropolis an accidental and heterogeneous character, — the dust in summer, the mud in winter, the fetor, the rubbish, the garbage ; and the corresponding character of the population, the most heterogeneous to be found in any American city, comprising all classes strangely mixed and fluctuating, the highest beside the lowest, the grandest and broadest human traits jostled by the meanest and foulest, — one half the people preying upon the other half, which preys upon the government ; — all this has been too often outlined by others to be dwelt upon by me.

I noticed one novel feature in the city, however. At the hotel where I stopped, at the Attorney-General's office which I had occasion to visit, and again at the White House, where

I went to call on the President's military secretary, I met, repeatedly, throngs of the same or similar strange faces.

It happened to be one of the President's reception days; and the east room, the staircases, the lower and upper halls of the White House, were crowded. The upper hall especially, and the ladies' parlor adjacent to the President's room, were densely thronged. Some were walking to and fro, singly or in pairs; some were conversing in groups; others were lounging on chairs, tables, window-seats, or whatever offered a support to limbs weary of long waiting. One was paring his nails; another was fanning himself with his hat; a third was asleep, with his head resting much cramped in a corner of the walls; a fourth was sitting in a window, spitting tobacco-juice at an urn three yards off. When he took pains, he hit the urn with remarkable precision, showing long and careful practice. But he did not always take pains, for the extreme heat and closeness of the apartments were not favorable to exertion; and, indeed, what was the use of aiming always at the urn, when nearly every man was chewing tobacco as industriously as he, and generally spitting on the floors, — which had already become the most convincing argument against the habit of tobacco-chewing of which it is possible for the nauseated imagination to conceive.

Faces of old men and young men were there, — some weary and anxious, a few persistently jocose, and nearly all betraying the unmistakable Southern type. It was, on the whole, a well-dressed crowd, for one so abominably filthy.

"Nineteen out of twenty of all these people," I was told by the President's secretary, "are pardon-seeking Rebels. The most of them are twenty-thousand-dollar men, anxious to save their estates from confiscation."

As the President's doors were expected soon to be opened, and as I wished to observe his manner of dealing with those men, I remained after finishing my business with the secretary, and mingled with the crowd. The fumes of heated bodies, in the ill-ventilated halls, were far from agreeable; and as the time dragged heavily, and the doors of the Presi-

dent's room continued closed, except when some favored individual, who had sent in his card, perhaps hours before, was
admitted, I was more than once on the point of abandoning
my object for a breath of fresh out-door air.

The conversation of my Southern friends, however, proved
sufficiently interesting to detain me. One gay and jaunty old
man was particularly diverting in his remarks. He laughed
at the melancholy ones for their long faces, pretending that
he could tell by each man s looks which clause of the exceptions, in the President's amnesty proclamation, his case came
under.

" You were a civil officer under the Confederate government. Am I right? Of course I am. Your face shows it.
My other friend here comes under No. 3, — he was an officer
in the army. That sad old gentleman yonder, with a standing collar, looks to me like one of those who left their homes
within the jurisdiction of the United States to aid the Rebellion.
He 's a number ten er. And I reckon we are all thirteen-
ers," — that is to say, persons of the thirteenth excepted class,
the value of whose taxable property exceeded twenty thousand
dollars.

" Well, which clause do you come under ? " asked one.

" I am happy to say, I come under three different clauses.
Mine 's a particularly beautiful case. I 've been here every
day for a week, waiting on the President, and I expect to
have the pleasure of standing at this door many a day to come.
Take example by me, and never despair." And the merry
old man frisked away, with his cap slightly on one side, covering gray hairs. His gay spirits, in that not very hilarious
throng, attracted a good deal of attention ; but his was not the
mirth of an inwardly happy mind.

" You are not a Southern man ? " said one, singling me out.

" No," said I ; " I am a Yankee."

" You are not after a pardon, then. Lucky for you ! "

" What have you done to be pardoned for ? " I asked.

" I am worth over twenty thousand dollars ; that 's my difficulty."

"And you aided the Rebellion?"

"Of course," — laughing. "Look here!" — his manner changed, and his bright dark eye looked at me keenly,—"what do you Northerners, you Massachusetts men particularly, expect to do now with the niggers?"

"We intend to make useful and industrious citizens of them."

"You can't!" "You never can do that!" "That's an absurdity!" exclaimed three or four voices; and immediately I found myself surrounded by a group eager to discuss that question.

"The nigger, once he's free, won't work!"

"No," said another; "he'll steal, but he won't work."

"I pity the poor niggers, after what you've done for him," said a third. "They can't take care of themselves; they'll starve before they'll work, unless driven to it; and in a little while they'll be exterminated, just like the Indians."

"I don't think so," said I. "The negro is very much like the rest of us, in many respects. He won't work unless he is obliged to. Neither will you. So don't blame him. But when he finds work a necessity, that will drive him to it more surely than any master."

"You Northerners know nothing of the negro; you should see him on our plantations!"

"I intend to do so. In the mean time you should see him in our Northern cities, where he takes care of himself very well, supports his family, and proves an average good citizen. You should look into the affairs of the Freedmen's Bureau, here in Washington. There are in this city and its vicinity upwards of thirty thousand colored people. The majority have been suddenly swept into the department from their homes by the chances of war. You would consequently expect to find a vast number of paupers among them. But, on the contrary, nearly all are industrious and self-supporting; only about three hundred of the number receiving partial support from the government. Now take my advice: give your negroes a chance, and see what they will do."

"We do give them all the chance they can have. And it's for our interest to induce them to work. We are dependent on labor; we are going to ruin as fast as possible for want of it. In the course of eight or ten years, maybe, they will begin to find out that everything in creation don't belong to them now they are free, and that they can't live by stealing. But by that time, where will we be? Where will the negro be?"

Of these men, one was from Georgia, one from North Carolina, and others from Florida and Virginia; yet they all concurred in the opinion, which no argument could shake, that the freedmen would die, but not work.

Our conversation was interrupted by the opening of the President's room. A strong tide instantly set towards it, resulting in a violent jam at the door. I was carried in by the crowd, but got out of it as soon as possible, and placed myself in a corner where I could observe the proceedings of the reception.

President Johnson was standing behind a barrier which extended the whole length of the room, separating him from the crowd. One by one they were admitted to him; each man presenting his card as he passed the barrier. Those who were without cards were refused admission, until they had provided themselves with those little conveniences at a desk in the hall.

I should scarcely have recognized the President from any of his published pictures. He appeared to me a man rather below the medium height, sufficiently stout, with a massy, well-developed head, strong features, dark, iron-gray hair, a thick, dark complexion, deep-sunk eyes, with a peculiarly wrinkled, care-worn look about them, and a weary expression generally. His voice was mild and subdued, and his manner kindly. He shook hands with none. To each applicant for pardon he put a question or two, sometimes only one, and dispatched him, with a word of promise or advice. No one was permitted to occupy more than a minute or two of his time, while some were disposed of in as many seconds. On the whole, it was an interesting but sad scene; and I still carry in my memory the President's weary look, and the disappointed faces of-the applicants, who, after long waiting, and perhaps going through with this same ceremony day after day, received no intimation that the object of their hopes was near its accomplishment.

CHAPTER X.

BULL RUN.

TAKING the train at Washington, and crossing the long railroad bridge which spans the Potomac, I entered again a portion of Virginia rendered celebrated and desolate by war.

Running down to Alexandria, and making a short stop there, we rattled on towards Manassas. All the names throughout that region are historical, stamped and re-stamped upon the memory of America by the burning brand of war. The brakeman bawls in at the door of the car words which start you with a thrill of recollection. The mind goes back through four fiery years of conflict to the campaign of '61, until it grows bewildered, in doubt whether that contest or this journey is unreal, — for surely one must be a dream! That first season of disaster and dismay, which associated the names of Fairfax Court House, Centreville, Bull Run, Manassas, with something infinitely horrible and fatal, had passed away like a cloud; the storm of the subsequent year, still more terrible, except that we had grown accustomed to such, had also passed, dissolving in thin vapor of history; and one would never have guessed that such things had been, but for the marks of the wrath of heaven, which had left the country scathed as with hailstones and coals of fire.

Yes, those skirmishes and dire contests were realities; and now this quiet journey, this commonplace mode of travel into what was then the " enemy's country," with hot-blooded Virginians (now looking cool enough) sitting upon the seats next us, and conversing tamely and even pleasantly with us when we accosted them, — no murderous masked batteries in front, no guerrillas in the woods waiting to attack the train; in short,

6

no danger threatening but the vulgar one of railroad disasters, of late become so common; this too was a reality no less wonderful, contrasted with the late rampant days of Rebel defiance.

From Alexandria to Manassas Junction it is twenty-seven miles. Through all that distance we saw no signs of human industry, save here and there a sickly, half-cultivated cornfield, which looked as if it had been put in late, and left to pine in solitude. There were a few wood-lots still left standing; but the country for the most part consisted of fenceless fields abandoned to weeds, stump-lots, and undergrowths.

"Manassas Junction!" announced the brakeman; and we alighted. A more forbidding locality can scarcely be imagined. I believe there were a number of houses and shops there before the war, but they were destroyed, and two or three rum-shanties had lately sprung up in their place. A row of black bottles, ranged on a shelf under a rudely constructed shed, were the first signs I saw of a reviving civilization. Near by a new tavern was building, of so fragile and thin a shell, it seemed as if the first high wind must blow it down. I also noticed some negroes digging a well; for such are the needs of an advancing civilization: first rum, then a little water to put into it. All around was a desolate plain, slightly relieved from its dreary monotony by two or three Rebel forts overgrown with weeds.

A tall young member of the Western press accompanied me. I went to a stable to secure a conveyance to the battle-field; and, returning, found him seated on the steps of one of the "Refreshment Saloons," engaged in lively conversation with a red-faced and excitable young stranger. The latter was speaking boastingly of "our army."

"Which army do you mean? for there were two, you know," said my friend.

"I mean the Confederate army, the best and bravest army that ever was!" said he of the red face, emphatically.

"It seems to me," remarked my friend, "the best and bravest army that ever was got pretty badly whipped."

" The Confederate army never was whipped! We were overpowered."

" I see you Southern gentlemen have a new word. With us, when a man goes into a fight and comes out second best, the condition he is in is vulgarly called *whipped*."

" We were overpowered by numbers!" ejaculated the Rebel. " Your army was three times as big as ours."

" That 's nothing, for you know one Southerner was equal to five Yankees."

" And so he is, and always will be! But you had to get the niggers to help you."

" What are a few niggers? They would always run, you know, at sight of their masters, while of course such a thing was never known as their masters running from them!"

The unhappy member of the " overpowered " party flushed and fumed a while, not knowing what answer to make, then burst forth, —

" It was the foreigners! You never would have beaten us if it had n't been for the foreigners that made up your armies!"

" What!" said my friend, " you, an American, acknowledge yourself beaten by foreigners! I am ashamed of you!"

And the wagon arriving, he jumped into it with a laugh, leaving the Southerner, not whipped of course, but decidedly " overpowered " in this little contest of wit. It was quite evident that he was not equal to five Yankees with his tongue.

" That young fellow you was talking with," said our driver, " was one of Mosby's guerrillas. There are plenty of them around here. They are terrible at talking, but that is about all."

The wagon was an ambulance which had cost the government two hundred and fifty dollars a few months before. The springs proving inferior, it was condemned, and sold at auction for twenty-four dollars. " I paid a hundred and twenty-five for it the next day," said the driver; " and it 's well worth the money." It was a strong, heavy, well-built vehicle, well suited to his business. " I was down here with my regiment when I got my discharge, and it struck me something might be made by taking visitors out to the battle-fields. But I have n't saved a cent at it yet; passengers are few, and it 's mighty hard business, the roads are so awful bad.''

Worse roads are not often seen in a civilized country. "It makes me mad to see people drive over and around these bad places, month after month, and never think of mending 'em! A little work with a shovel would save no end of lost time, and wear and tear, and broken wagons; but it 's never done.''

The original country roads had passed into disuse; and, the fences being destroyed, only the curious parallel lines of straggling bushes and trees that grew beside them remained to mark their course. Necessity and convenience had struck out new roads winding at will over the fenceless farms. We crossed thinly wooded barrens, skirted old orchards, and passed now and then a standing chimney that marked the site of some ruined homestead; up-hill and down-hill, rocking, rattling, jolting, and more than once nearly upsetting. I remember not more than three or four inhabited houses on our route. In a wild field near the shelter of some woods was a village of half-ruined huts, interesting as having served in wartime as Rebel winter-quarters. At last, eight miles north from the Junction, we reached the scene of the first battle of Bull Run.

This was the plateau, from which our almost victorious forces had driven and re-driven the enemy, when Johnston's reinforcements, arriving by the railroad, which runs obliquely towards the Junction on the west, changed what was so nearly a triumph for our arms into a frightful disaster. The ground is well described in Beauregard's official report. "It is enclosed on three sides by small watercourses which empty into Bull Run within a few rods of each other, half a mile to the south of Stone Bridge. Rising to an elevation of quite one hundred feet above Bull Run at the bridge, it falls off on three sides to the level of the enclosing streams in gentle slopes, but which are furrowed by ravines of irregular direction and length, and studded with clumps and patches of young pines and oaks." . . . . "Completely surrounding the two houses before mentioned are small open fields of irregular outline, and exceeding one hundred and fifty acres in extent. The houses, occupied at the time, the one by Widow Henry, the other by the free negro Robinson, are small wooden buildings densely embowered in trees and environed by a double row of fences on two sides. Around the eastern and southern brow of the plateau an almost unbroken fringe of second growth of pines gave excellent shelter for our marksmen, who availed them-selves of it with the most satisfactory skill. To the west, ad-joining the fields, a broad belt of oaks extends directly across the crest, on both sides of the Sudley road, in which, during the battle, regiments of both armies met and contended for the mastery. From the open ground of this plateau the view embraces a wide expanse of woods and gently undulating open country of broad grass and grain fields in all directions."

Such was the appearance of the battle-field on that memorable twenty-first of July, four years before my visit. In its external features I found it greatly changed. Many of the trees had been cut away. Every fence had disappeared. Where had waved the fields of grass and grain, extended one vast, neglected, barren tract of country. The widow's humble abode had been swept away. The widow herself was killed by a chance shot on the day of the battle. A little picket fence surrounding her grave was the only enclosure visible to us in all that region. Close by were the foundations of her house, a small square space run up to tallest weeds. Some of the poor woman's hollyhocks still survived, together with a few scattered and lonesome-looking peach-trees cut with balls. The hollyhocks were in bloom, and the peaches were ripe : a touching sight to me, who could see the haunting figure of the poor widow looking at the favorite blossoms from her door, or returning from the trees to the house with her apron full of the fruit, which appeared duly year after year to comfort her, until at last she was no longer there needing earthly comfort. We were not past that material necessity, however ; and the poor woman's peaches comforted us this year.

Within a few yards of the spot where her house was, on the

summit of the eminence, stands a pyramidal monument of rough red sand-stone, bearing this inscription : —

IN
MEMORY
OF THE
PATRIOTS
WHO FELL AT
BULL RUN
JULY 21ST, 1861.

This shaft, another inscription tells us, was erected June 10th, 1865. There it stands on the " sacred soil," recalling to the proud sons of Virginia many things. To them, and to all Americans, it has a grand and deep significance beyond anything words can convey. There it stands, a silent preacher, with its breast of stone, and its austere face of stone, preaching inaudible stern lessons. Bull Run may be called the Bunker Hill of the last revolution. It was the prologue of disaster to the far-off final triumph. Well fought at first, we had almost won the day, when, fresh troops pressing us, came the crushing defeat and horrible panic which filled the whole loyal North with dismay and the whole rebel South with exultation. Then how many a patriot heart fell sick with despair, and doubtingly murmured, " Does God still live ? and is there after all an overruling Power ? "

Look at that monument to-day. Where now is the triumph of the dark cause ? Where now is the haughty slave empire whose eternal foundations were deemed established by that victory ? Where is the banner of Freedom trailed so low, all torn and blood-stained, in the dust ? God lives ! There is an overruling Power that never sleeps ; patient, foreseeing what we cannot see, and, in sublime knowledge of the end, tolerating the wrath of the unrighteous and the arrogance of the unjust. The day of victory for freedom had not yet come ; for triumph then would have been but half triumph. Temporary success to the bad cause was necessary to draw it irretrievably into the currents of destruction.

Moreover, struggle and long agony were needful to this

nation. Frivolous, worldly, imitating other nations; nourishing in the very bosom of the Republic the serpent of a barbarous despotism ; in our heedlessness and hurry giving no ear to the cries of the oppressed ; we needed the baptism of blood and the awful lessons of loss to bring us back to sanity and soberness. The furnace of civil war was indispensable to fuse conflicting elements, and to pour the molten materials of the diverse States into the single mould of one mighty and masterful Nation. In order that it might take the lead of all the proud banners on the globe, our flag must first be humbled, and win its way through dust and battle-smoke to the eminence above all eminences of earthly power, where it is destined at last to float.

There seems to have been something fatal to our armies in the mere name of Bull Run. The visitor to the scene of the first disaster is already on the field of the second. The battles of the subsequent year, fought on a more stupendous scale, and sweeping over a vast area, included within their scope the hills on which we were standing.

To reach the scene of the principal contest in 1862, however, an advance of a mile or two had to be made. We rode on to a piece of woods, in the shade of which we halted, surrounded by marks of shot and shell in the timber, and by soldiers' graves lying lonely among the trees, with many a whitened bone scattered about or protruding. There, it being mid-day, we partook of luncheon sauced with Widow Henry's peaches.

On the west of us was a large stony field sloping up to a wood-crowned height, — a field strown thick with dead in those sanguinary days of '62. The woods in which we were, extended around the north side of it also, forming a connection with the woods beyond. Making the circuit of this shady boundary, we reached the crest, which, strengthened greatly by an unfinished railroad track cut through it, afforded the enemy their most formidable position during the second Bull Run battle.

At the summit of the open field stands another monument,

similar to that we had first seen, dedicated to the "Memory of the Patriots who fell at Groverton, August 28th, 29th, and 30th, 1862." This inscription had been mutilated by some Rebel hand, and made to read "Confederate Patriots"; but my tall friend, arming himself with a stone, stepped upon the pedestal, amid the black rows of shells surrounding it, and resolutely ground the offensive word out of the tablet.

Groverton, which has given the field its name, is a little cluster of three or four buildings lying out west of it on the turnpike.

There are two or three points of striking resemblance between the first and second battles of Bull Run. At one time almost a victory, this also proved at last a defeat; and again the North was filled with consternation at seeing the barrier of its armies broken, and the country laid open to the foe. After the first Bull Run, the Rebels might have entered Washington almost without opposition. After the second, they did invade Maryland, getting as far as Antietam. It is also a circumstance worthy of note, that in each fight the victory might have been rendered complete, but for the failure of an important command to perform the part assigned it. General Patterson remained inert at Winchester, while Johnston, whom it was his business to look after, hastened to reinforce Beauregard and turn the scale of battle. At the second Bull Run, General Porter's neglect to obey the orders of General Pope wrought incalculable mischief, and contributed similarly to change the opening successes into final discomfiture.

Lastly the lesson taught by both disasters is the same: that the triumph of a bad cause is but illusory and transient; while for the cause which moves duly in the divine currents of human progress there can be no failure, for, though tossed and buffeted, and seemingly wrecked, its keel is in the eternal waters, the winds of heaven fill its sails, and the hand of the Great Pilot is at the helm.

Returning, we stopped at the "stone house" near the first battle-field, in hopes of getting some personal information from the inhabitants. They were present during the fight, and the outer walls show enduring marks of the destructive visits of cannon-shot. The house was formerly a tavern, and the man who kept it was one of those two-faced farmers, Secessionists at heart, but always loyal to the winning side. By working well his political weathercock, he had managed to get his house through the storm, although in a somewhat dismantled condition. The bar-room was as barren as the intellect of the owner. The only thing memorable we obtained there was some most extraordinary cider. This the proprietor was too proud to sell, or else the pretence that it belonged to the " old nigger " was nearer the truth than my tall friend was willing to admit. At all events, the " old nigger " brought it in, and received pay for it besides, evidently contrary to his expectations, and to the disappointment of the landlord.

" Uncle, what sort of cider is this? how did you make it?' For neither of us had ever tasted anything resembling it before, nor did we wish ever to taste its like again.

Uncle, standing in the door, with one foot on the threshold, ducking and grinning, one hand holding his old cap, and the other his knee, after earnest urging, told us the secret.

" Dat cidah, sah, I made out o' peaches and apples mixed, 'bout half and half.   Dat's what makes it taste cur'us."

" Oh, but that's not all, uncle; you put water in it!   You meant to cheat us, I see, with your miscegenated cider and water!"

Uncle did not exactly understand the nature of this charge, but evidently thought it something serious.

" No, no, gentlemen, I did n't do it for roguishness!   I put in de peaches 'case dar was n't apples enough.   I pounded 'em up wid a pestle in a barrel.   Den I put a stake under de house corner wid rocks on to it for a press.   I put de water in to make de juice come easier, it was so dry!"

Having learned his method of manufacturing cider, we inquired his opinion of the war.

" Did n't you think, Uncle, the white folks were great fools to kill each other the way they did?" said my friend.

" 'T would n't do for me to say so; dey was old enough, and

ageable enough, to know best; but I could n't help tink'n sah!"

Returning to the Junction, I saw a very different type of the Virginia negro: an old man of seventy, who conversed intelligently, but in a strangely quiet and subdued tone, which bespoke long suffering and great patience. He had been a free man seven years, he told me; but he had a brother who still served the man he belonged to.

"But he, too, is free now," I said. "Don't he receive wages?"

The old man shook his head sadly. "There's nothing said about wages to any of our people in this part of the country. They don't dare to ask for them, and their owners will hold them as they used to as long as they can. They are very sharp with us now. If a man of my color dared to say what he thought, it would be all his life was worth!"

CHAPTER XI.

A VISIT TO MOUNT VERNON.

On a day of exceeding sultriness (it was the fourth of September) I left the dusty, stifled streets of Washington, and went on board the excursion steamer Wawaset, bound for Mount Vernon.

Ten o'clock, the hour of starting, had nearly arrived. No breath of air was stirring. The sun beat down with torrid fervor upon the boat's awnings, which seemed scarce a protection against it, and upon the glassy water, which reflected it with equal intensity from below. Then suddenly the bell rang, the boat swung out in the river, the strong paddles rushed, and almost instantly a magical change took place. A delightful breeze appeared to have sprung up, increasing as the steamer's speed increased. I sat upon a stool by the wheelhouse, drinking in all the deliciousness of that cooling motion through the air, and watching compassionately the schooners with heavy and languid sails lying becalmed in the channel,— indolent fellows, drifting with the tide, and dependent on influences from without to push them, — while our steamer, with flashing wake, flag gayly flying, and decks swept by wholesome, animating winds, resembled one of your energetic, original men, cutting the sluggish current, and overcoming the sultriness and stagnation of life by a refreshing activity.

On we sped, leaving far behind the Virginia long-boats, with their pointed sails on great poles swung aslant across the masts, — sails dingy in color and irregular in shape, looking, a little way off, like huge sweet potatoes. Our course was southward, leaving far on our right the Arlington estate embowered in foliage on the Virginia shore ; and on our left the Navy Yard and Arsenal, and the Insane Asylum standing like a stern castle, half hidden by trees, on the high banks back from the river. As we departed from the wharves, a view of the city opened behind us, with its two prominent objects, — the unfinished Washington Monument, resembling in the distance a tall, square, pallid sail; and the many-pillared, beautiful Capitol, rising amid masses of foliage, with that marvellous bubble, its white and airy dome, soaring superbly in the sun.

Before us, straight in our course, was Alexandria, quaint old city, with its scanty fringe of straight and slender spars, and its few anchored ships suspended in a glassy atmosphere, as it seemed, where the river reflected the sky. We ran in to the wharves, and took on board a number of passengers; then steamed on again, down the wide Potomac, until, around a bend, high on a wooded shore, a dim red roof and a portico of slender white pillars appeared visible through the trees.

It was Mount Vernon, the home of Washington. The shores here, on both the Maryland and Virginia sides, are picturesquely hilly and green with groves. The river between flows considerably more than a mile wide: a handsome sheet, reflecting the woods and the shining summer clouds sailing in the azure over them, although broad belts of river-grass, growing between the channel and the banks like strips of inundated prairie, detract from its beauty.

As we drew near, the helmsman tolled the boat's bell slowly. "Before the war," said he, "no boat ever passed Mount Vernon without tolling its bell, if it had one. The war kind of broke into that custom, as it did into most everything else; but it is coming up again now."

We did not make directly for the landing, but kept due on down the channel until we had left Mount Vernon half a mile away on our right. Then suddenly the steamer changed her course, steering into the tract of river-grass, which waved and tossed heavily as the ripple from the bows shook it from its drowsy languor. The tide rises here some four feet. It was low tide then, and the circuit we had made was necessary to avoid grounding on the bar. We were entering shallow water.

We touched and drew hard for a few minutes over the yielding sand. The dense grass seemed almost as serious an impediment as the bar itself. Down among its dark heaving
masses we had occasional glimpses of the bottom, and saw
hundreds of fishes darting away, and sometimes leaping sheer
from the surface, in terror of the great, gliding, paddling
monster, invading, in that strange fashion, their peaceful do-
main.

Drawing a well-defined line half a mile long through that
submerged prairie, we reached the old wooden pier, built out
into it from the Mount Vernon shore. I did not land immediately, but remained on deck, watching the long line of pilgrims going up from the boat along the climbing path and
disappearing in the woods. There were, perhaps, a hundred
and fifty in the procession, men and women and children,
some carrying baskets, with intent to enjoy a nice little picnic
under the old Washington trees. It was a pleasing sight,
rendered interesting by the historical associations of the place,
but slightly dashed with the ludicrous, it must be owned, by
a solemn tipsy wight bringing up the rear, singing, or rather
bawling, the good old tune of Greenville, with maudlin nasal
twang, and beating time with profound gravity and a big
stick.

As the singer, as well as his tune, was tediously slow, I
passed him on the way, ascended the long slope through the
grove, and found my procession halted under the trees on the
edge of it. Facing them, with an old decayed orchard behind it, was a broad, low brick structure, with an arched entrance and an iron-grated gate. Two marble shafts flanked
the approach to it on the right and left. Passing these, I
paused, and read on a marble slab over the Gothic gateway
the words, —

"WITHIN THIS ENCLOSURE REST THE REMAINS OF GEN
ERAL GEORGE WASHINGTON."

The throng of pilgrims, awed into silence, were beginning
to draw back a little from the tomb. I approached, and leaning against the iron bars, looked through into the still, damp

chamber. Within, a little to the right of the centre of the
vault, stands a massive and richly sculptured marble sarcoph-
agus, bearing the name of "Washington." By its side, of
equal dimensions, but of simpler style, is another, bearing the
inscription, "Martha, the consort of Washington."

It is a sequestered spot, half enclosed by the trees of the
grove on the south side, — cedars, sycamores, and black-walnuts, heavily hung with vines, sheltering the entrance from the
mid-day sun. Woodpeckers flitted and screamed from trunk
to trunk of the ancient orchard beyond. Eager chickens were
catching grasshoppers under the honey-locusts, along by the
old wooden fence. And, humming harmlessly in and out
over the heads of the pilgrims, I noticed a colony of wasps,
whose mud-built nests stuccoed profusely the yellowish ceiling
of the vault.

There rest the ashes of the great chieftain, and of Martha
his wife. I did not like the word "consort." It is too fine
a term for a tombstone. There is something lofty and romantic about it; but "wife" is simple, tender, near to the
heart, steeped in the divine atmosphere of home, —

> " A something not too bright and good
> For human nature's daily food."

She was the *wife* of Washington: a true, deep-hearted
woman, the blessing and comfort, not of the Commander-in-
chief, not of the first President, but of the MAN. And Washington, the MAN, was not the cold, majestic, sculptured figure
which has been placed on the pedestal of history. There was
nothing marble about him but the artistic and spotless finish
of his public career. Majestic he truly was, as simple greatness must be ; and cold he seemed to many ; — nor was it fitting
that the sacred chambers of that august personality should be
thrown open to the vulgar feet and gaze of the multitude. It
is littleness and vanity that are loose of tongue and unseason-
ably familiar.

> " Yet shine forever virgin minds,
> Beloved by stars and purest winds,

Which, o'er passion throned sedate,
Have not hazarded their state ;
Disconcert the searching spy,
Rendering, to the curious eye,
The durance of a granite ledge
To those who gaze from the sea's edge."

Of these virgin minds was Washington. The world saw
him through a veil of reserve, as habitual to him as the sceptre
of self-control. Yet beneath that veil throbbed a fiery nature,
which on a few rare occasions is known to have flamed forth
into terrible wrath. Anecdotes, recording those instances of
volcanic eruption from the core of this serene and lofty character, are refreshing and precious to us, as showing that the
ice and snow were only on the summit, while beneath burned
those fountains of glowing life which are reservoirs of power
to the virtue and will that know how to control them. A
man of pure, strong, constant affections, his love of tranquil
domestic enjoyments was as remarkable as his self-sacrificing
patriotism. I know not Washington's " consort " ; but to me
a very sweet, beautiful, and touching name is that of " Martha,
Washington's wife."

Quitting the tomb, I walked along by the old board fence
which bounds the corner of the orchard, and turned up the
locust-shaded avenue leading to the mansion. On one side
was a wooden shed, on the other an old-fashioned brick barn.
Passing these, you seem to be entering a little village. The
out-houses are numerous; I noticed the wash-house, the meat-
house, and the kitchen, the butler's house, and the gardener's
house, — neat white buildings, ranged around the end of the
lawn, among which the mansion stands the principal figure.

Looking in at the wash-house, I saw a pretty-looking colored girl industriously scrubbing over a tub. She told me
that she was twenty years old, that her husband worked
on the place, and that a bright little fellow, four years old,
running around the door, handsome as polished bronze, was
her son. She formerly belonged to John A. Washington,
who made haste to carry her off to Richmond, with the money

the Ladies' Mount Vernon Association had paid him, on the
breaking out of the war. She was born on the place, but
had never worked for John A. Washington. "He kept me
hired out; for I s'pose he could make more by me that way."
She laughed pleasantly as she spoke, and rubbed away at the
wet clothes in the tub.

I looked at her, so intelligent and cheerful, a woman and a
mother, though so young; and wondered at the man who
could pretend to own such a creature, hire her out to other
masters, and live upon her wages! I have heard people scoff
at John A. Washington for selling the inherited bones of
the great, — for surely the two hundred thousand dollars,
paid by the Ladies' Association for the Mount Vernon estate,
was not the price merely of that old mansion, these out-houses,
since repaired, and two hundred acres of land, — but I do not
scoff at him for that. Why should not one, who dealt in living
human flesh and blood, also traffic a little in the ashes of the
dead?

"After the war was over, the Ladies' Association sent for
me from Richmond, and I work for them now," said the girl,
merrily scrubbing.

"What wages do you get?"

"I gits seven dollars a month, and that's a heap better 'n
no wages at all!" laughing again with pleasure. "The
sweat I drap into this yer tub is my own; but befo'e, it belonged to John A., Washington." As I did not understand
her at first, she added, "You know, the Bible says every one
must live by the sweat of his own eyebrow. But John A.
Washington, he lived by the sweat of my eyebrow. I alluz
had a will'n mind to work, and I have now; but I don't work
as I used to; for then it was work to-day and work to-mor-
row, and no stop."

Beside the kitchen was a well-house, where I stopped
and drank a delicious draught out of an "old oaken bucket,"
or rather a new one, which came up brimming from its cold
depths. This well was dug in General Washington's time, the
cook told me; and as I drank, and looked down, down into the

dark shaft at the faintly glimmering water, — for the well was deep, — I thought how often the old General had probably come up thither from the field, taken off his hat in the shade, and solaced his thirst with a drink from the dripping bucket.

Passing between the kitchen and the butler's house, you come upon a small plateau, a level green lawn, nearly surrounded by a circle of large shade-trees. The shape of this pleasant esplanade is oblong : at the farther end, away on the left, is the ancient entrance to the grounds ; close by on the right, at the end nearest the river, is the mansion.

Among the shade-trees, of which there are a great variety, I noticed a fine sugar-maple, said to be the only individual of the species in all that region. It was planted by General Washington, " who wished to see what trees would grow in that climate," the gardener told me. It has for neighbors, among many others, a tulip-tree, a Kentucky coffee-tree, and a magnolia set out by Washington's own hand. I looked at the last with peculiar interest, thinking it a type of our country, the perennial roots of which were about the same time laid carefully in the bosom of the eternal mother, covered and nursed and watered by the same illustrious hand,—a little tree then, feeble, and by no means sure to live ; but now I looked up, thrilling with pride at the glory of its spreading branches, its storm-defying tops, and its mighty trunk which not even the axe of treason could sever.

I approached the mansion. It was needless to lift the great brass knocker, for the door was open. The house was full of guests thronging the rooms and examining the relics; among which were conspicuous these : hanging in a little brass-framed glass case in the hall, the key of the Bastile, presented to Washington by Lafayette ; in the dining-hall, a very old-fashioned harpsichord that had entirely lost its voice, but which is still cherished as a wedding-gift from Washington to his adopted daughter ; in the same room, holsters and a part of the Commander-in-chief's camp-equipage, very dilapidated ; and, in a square bedroom up-stairs, the bedstead on which Washington slept, and on which he died. There is no sight

7

more touching than this bedstead, surrounded by its holy associations, to be seen at Mount Vernon.

From the house I went out on the side opposite that on which I had entered, and found myself standing under the portico we had seen when coming down the river. A noble portico, lofty as the eaves of the house, and extending the whole length of the mansion,— fifteen feet in width and ninety-six in length, says the Guide-Book. The square pillars supporting it are not so slender, either; but it was their height which made them appear so when we first saw them miles off up the Potomac.

What a portico for a statesman to walk under, — so lofty, so spacious, and affording such views of the river and its shores, and the sky over all! Once more I saw the venerable figure of him, the first in war and the first in peace, pacing to and fro on those pavements of flat stone, solitary, rapt in thought, glancing ever and anon up the Potomac towards the site of the now great capital bearing his name, contemplating the revolution accomplished, and dreaming of his country's future. There was one great danger he feared : the separation of the States. But well for him, O, well for the great-hearted and wise chieftain, that the appalling blackness of the storm, destined so soon to deluge the land with blood for rain-drops, was hidden from his eyes, or appeared far in the dim horizon no bigger than a man's hand!

Saved from the sordid hands of a degenerate posterity, saved from the desolation of unsparing civil war, Mount Vernon still remains to us with its antique mansion and its delightful shades. I took all the more pleasure in the place, remembering how dear it was to its illustrious owner. There is no trait in Washington's character with which I sympathize so strongly as with his love for his home. True, that home was surrounded with all the comforts and elegancies which fortune and taste could command. But had Mount Vernon been as humble as it was beautiful, Washington would have loved it scarcely less. It was dear to him, not as a fine estate, but as the home of his heart. A simply great and truly wise man, free from foolish vanity and ambition, he served his country with a willing spirit; yet he knew well that happiness does not subsist upon worldly honors nor dwell in high places, but that her favorite haunt is by the pure waters of domestic tranquillity.

There came up a sudden thunder-shower while we were at the house. The dreadful peals rolled and rattled from wing to wing of the black cloud that overshadowed the river, and the rain fell in torrents. Umbrellas were scarce, and I am sorry to say the portico leaked badly. But the storm passed as suddenly as it came; the rifted clouds floated away with sun-lit edges glittering like silver fire, and all the wet leafage of the trees twinkled and laughed in the fresh golden light. I did not return to the boat with the crowd by the way we came, but descended the steep banks through the drenched woods in front of the mansion, to the low sandy shore of the Potomac, then walked along the water's edge, under the dripping boughs, to the steamer, and so took my leave of Mount Vernon.

CHAPTER XII.

" STATE PRIDE."

LEAVING Washington by steamer again, early on the morning of the twelfth of September, a breezy sail of three hours down the Potomac brought us to Acquia Creek.

The creek was still there, debouching broad and placid into the river, for, luckily, destroying armies cannot consume the everlasting streams. The forests, which densely covered all that region before the war, had been cut away. Not a building of any kind was to be seen ; and only the blackened ruins of half-burnt wharves, extending out into the river, remained to indicate that here had been an important depot of supplies.

Taking the cars near an extemporized landing, we traversed a country of shaggy hills, completely clad in thick undergrowths which had sprung up where the ancient forests stood. At the end of two hours' slow travel, through a tract almost exclusively of this character, we arrived at a hiatus in the railroad. The bridge over the Rappahannock not having been rebuilt since the war, it was necessary to cross to Fredericksburg by another conveyance than the cars. A long line of coaches was in waiting for the train. I climbed the topmost seat of the foremost coach, which was soon leading the rumbling, dusty procession over the hills toward the city.

From a barren summit we obtained a view of Fredericksburg, pleasantly situated on the farther bank of the river, with the high ridge behind it which Burnside endeavored in vain to take. We crossed the brick-colored Rappahannock (not a lovely stream to look upon) by a pontoon bridge, and ascending the opposite shore, rode through the half-ruined city.

Fredericksburg had not yet begun to recover from the effects of Burnside's shells. Scarcely a house in the burnt portions had been rebuilt. Many houses were entirely destroyed, and only the solitary chimney-stacks remained. Of others, you saw no vestige but broken brick walls, and foundations overgrown with Jamestown-weeds, sumachs, and thistles. Farther up from the river the town had been less badly used; but we passed even there many a dwelling with a broken chimney, and with great awkward holes in walls and roofs. Some were windowless and deserted; but others had been patched up and rendered inhabitable again. High over the city soar the church-spires, which, standing between two artillery fires on the day of the battle, received the ironical compliments of both. The zinc sheathing of one of these steeples is well riddled and ripped, and the tipsy vane leans at an angle of forty-five degrees from its original perpendicular.

Sitting next me on the stage-top was a vivacious young expressman, who was in the battle, and who volunteered to give me some account of it. No doubt his description was beautifully clear, but as he spoke only of " our army," without calling it by name, it was long before I could decide which army was meant. Sometimes it seemed to be one, then it was more likely the other; so that, before his account of its movements was ended, my mind was in a delightful state of confusion. A certain delicacy on my part, which was quite superfluous, had prevented me from asking him plainly at first on which side he was fighting. At last, by inference and indirection, I got at the fact; — " our army " was the Rebel army.

" I am a son of Virginia ! " he told me afterwards, his whole manner expressing a proud satisfaction. " I was opposed to secession at first, but afterwards I went into it with my whole heart and soul. Do you want to know what carried me in? State pride, sir! nothing else in the world. I 'd give more for Virginia than for all the rest of the Union put together ; and I was bound to go with my State."

This was spoken with emphasis, and a certain rapture, as a lover might speak of his mistress. I think I never before realized so fully what " State pride " was. In New England and the West, you find very little of it. However deep it may

lie in the hearts of the people, it is not thei. habit to rant
about it.   You never hear a Vermonter or an Indianian ex
claim, "I believe my State is worth all the rest of the Union!"
with excited countenance, lip curved, and eye in fine frenzy
rolling.   Their patriotism is too large and inclusive to be
stopped by narrow State boundaries.   Besides, in communities where equality prevails there is little of that peculiar pride
which the existence of caste engenders.   Accustomed to look
down upon slaves and poor whites, the aristocratic classes soon
learn to believe that they are the people, and that wisdom will
die with them.

In the case of Virginians, I think that the mere name of
the State has also something to do with their pride in her.
To hear one of them enunciate the euphonious syllables when
asked to what portion of the Union he belongs, is wonderfully
edifying; it is as good as eating a peach. "*V-i-r—g-i-n—i-a*," he
tells you, dwelling with rich intonations on the luscious vowels
and consonants, — in his mind doubtless the choicest in the
alphabet; and he seems proudly conscious, as he utters
them, of having spoken a charm which enwraps him in an
atmosphere of romance.   Thenceforth he is unapproachable
on that verdurous ground, the envy and despair of all who
are so unfortunate as to have been born elsewhere.   Thus a
rich word surrounds itself with rich associations.   But suppose
a different name: instead of Virginia, Stubland, for example.
It might indeed be the best State of all, yet, believe me, *Stubland* would have in all its borders no soil fertile enough to
grow the fine plant of State pride.

"I believe," said I, "there is but one State as proud as
Virginia, and that is the fiery little State of South Carolina."

"I have less respect for South Carolina," said he, "than
for any other State in the Union.   South Carolina troops
were the worst troops in the Confederate army.   It was South
Carolina's self-conceit and bluster that caused the war."

(So, State pride in another State than Virginia was only
"self-conceit.")

"Yes," said I, "South Carolina began the war; but Vir-

TAKING THE OATH OF ALLEGIANCE.

ginia carried it on. If Virginia had thrown the weight of her very great power in the Union against secession, resort to arms would never have been necessary. She held a position which she has forfeited forever, because she was not true to it. By seceding she lost wealth, influence, slavery, and the blood of her bravest sons; and what has she gained? I wonder, sir, how your State pride can hold out so well."

"Virginia," he replied, with another gleam, his eyes doing the fine frenzy again, "Virginia made the gallantest fight that ever was; and I am prouder of her to-day than I ever was in my life!"

"But you are glad she is back in the Union again?"

"To tell the truth, I am. I think more of the Union, too, than I ever did before. It was a square, stand-up fight; we got beaten, and I suppose it is all for the best. The very hottest Secessionists are now the first to come back and offer support to the government." He tapped a little tin trunk he carried. "I have fifty pardons here, which I am carrying from Washington to Richmond, for men who, a year ago, you would have said would drown themselves sooner than take the oath of allegiance to the United States. It was a rich sight to see these very men crowding to take the oath. It was a bitter pill to some, and they made wry faces at it; but the rest were glad enough to get back into the old Union. It was like going home."

"What astonishes me," said I, "after all the Southern people's violent talk about the last ditch, — about carrying on an endless guerrilla warfare after their armies were broken up, and fighting in swamps and mountains till the last man was exterminated, — what astonishes me is, that they take so sensible a view of their situation, and accept it so frankly; and that you, a Rebel, and I, a Yankee, are sitting on this stage talking over the bloody business so good-naturedly!"

"Well, it is astonishing, when you think of it! Southern men and Northern men ride together in the trains, and stop at the same hotels, as if we were all one people, — as indeed we are: one nation now," he added, "as we never were before, and never could have been without the war."

I got down at the hotel, washed and brushed away the dust of travel, and went out to the dining-room. There the first thing that met my eye was a pair of large wooden fans, covered with damask cloth which afforded an ample flap to each, suspended over the table, and set in motion by means of a rope dropped from a pulley by the door. At the end of the rope was a shining negro-boy about ten years old, pulling as if it were the rope of a fire-bell, and the whole town were in flames. The fans swayed to and fro, a fine breeze blew all up and down the table, and not a fly was to be seen. I noticed before long, however, that the little darkey's industry was of an intermittent sort; for at times he would cease pulling altogether, until the landlady passed that way, when he would seem to hear the cries of fire again, and once more fall to ringing his silent alarm-bell in the most violent manner.

The landlady was the manager of the house; and I naturally took her to be a widow until her husband was pointed out to me, — a mere tavern lounger, of no account any way. It is quite common to find Virginia hotels kept in this manner. The wife does the work; the husband takes his ease in his inn. The business goes in her name; — he is the sleeping partner.

After dinner I went out to view the town. As I stood looking at the empty walls of the gutted court-house, a sturdy old man approached. He stopped to answer my questions, and pointing at the havoc made by shells, exclaimed, —

" You see the result of the vanity of Virginia ! "

" Are you a Virginian ! "

" I am ; but that is no reason why I should be blind to the faults of my State. It was the vanity of Virginia, and nothing else, that caused all our trouble."

(Here was another name for " State pride.")

" You were not very much in favor of secession, I take it ? "

" In favor of it ! " he exclaimed, kindling. " Did n't they have me in jail here nine weeks because I would not vote for it ? If I had n't been an old man, they would have hung me. Ah, I told them how it would be, from the first; but they would n't believe me. Now they see ! Look at this

ruined city! Look at the farms and plantations laid waste!
Look at the complete paralysis of business; the rich reduced
to poverty; the men and boys with one arm, one leg, or one
hand; the tens of thousands of graves; the broken families;
— it is all the result of vanity! vanity!"

He showed me the road to the Heights, and we parted on
the corner.

CHAPTER XIII.

THE FIELD OF FREDERICKSBURG.

FREDERICKSBURG stands upon a ridge on the right bank of the river. Behind the town is a plain, with a still more elevated ridge beyond. From the summit of the last you obtain an excellent view of the battle-field; the plain below the town where Hooker fought; the heights on the opposite side of the river manned by our batteries; the fields on the left; and the plain between the ridge and the town, where the frightfullest slaughter was.

Along by the foot of the crest, just where it slopes off to the plain, runs a road with a wall of heavy quarried stones on each side. In this road the Rebels lay concealed when the first attempt was made to storm the Heights. The wall on the lower side, towards the town, is the "stone wall" of history. It was a perfect breastwork, of great strength, and in the very best position that could have been chosen. The earth from the fields is more or less banked up against it; and this, together with the weeds and bushes which grew there, served to conceal it from our men. The sudden cruel volley of flame and lead which poured over it into their very faces, scarce a dozen paces distant, as they charged, was the first intimation they received of any enemy below the crest. No troops could stand that near and deadly fire. They broke, and leaving the ground strown with the fallen, retreated to the "ravine," — a deep ditch with a little stream flowing through it, in the midst of the plain.

"Just when they turned to run, that was the worst time for them!" said a young Rebel I met on the Heights. "Then our men had nothing to fear; but they just rose right up and let 'em have it! Every charge your troops made afterwards, it was the same. The infantry in the road, and the artillery on these Heights, just mowed them down in swaths! You never saw anything look as that plain did after the battle. Saturday morning, before the fight, it was brown; Sunday it was all blue; Monday it was white, and Tuesday it was red."

I asked him to explain this seeming riddle.

" Don't you see? Before the fight there was just the field. Next it was covered all over with your fellows in blue clothes. Saturday night the blue clothes were stripped off, and only their white under-clothes left. Monday night these were stripped off, and Tuesday they lay all in their naked skins."

" Who stripped the dead in that way? "

" It was mostly done by the North Carolinians. They are the triflin'est set of men! "

" What do you mean by *triflin'est?* "

" They ha'n't got no sense. They 'll stoop to anything. They 're more like savages than civilized men. They say ' *we 'uns* ' and ' *you 'uns,* ' and all such outlandish phrases. They 've got a great long tone to their voice, like something wild."

" Were you in the battle? "

" Yes, I was in all of Saturday's fight. My regiment was stationed on the hill down on the right there. We could see everything. Your men piled up their dead for breastworks. It was an awful sight when the shells struck them, and exploded! The air, for a minute, would be just full of legs and arms and pieces of trunks. Down by the road there we dug out a wagon-load of muskets. They had been piled up by your fellows, and dirt thrown over them, for a breastwork. But the worst sight I saw was three days afterwards. I did n't mind the heaps of dead, nor nothing. But just a starving dog sitting by a corpse, which he would n't let anybody come near, and which he never left night nor day; — by George, that just made me cry! We finally had to shoot the dog to get at the man to bury him."

The young Rebel thought our army might have been easily destroyed after Saturday's battle, — at least that portion of it which occupied Fredericksburg. "We had guns on that point that could have cut your pontoon bridge in two; and then our artillery could have blown Burnside all to pieces, or have compelled his surrender."

" Why did n't you do it ? "

" Because General Lee was too humane. He did n't want to kill so many men."

A foolish reason, but it was the best the young man could offer. The truth is, however, Burnside's army was in a position of extreme danger, after its failure to carry the Heights, and had not Lee been diligently expecting another attack, instead of a retreat, he might have subjected it to infinite discomfiture. It was to do us more injury, and not less, that he delayed to destroy the pontoon bridge and shell the town while our troops were in it.

The young man gloried in that great victory.

" But," said I, " what did you gain ? It was all the worse for you that you succeeded then. That victory only prolonged the war, and involved greater loss. We do not look at those transient triumphs ; we look at the grand result. The Confederacy was finally swept out, and we are perfectly satisfied."

" Well, so am I," he replied, looking me frankly in the face. " I tell you, if we had succeeded in establishing a separate government, this would have been the worst country, for a poor man, under the sun."

" How so ? "

" There would have been no chance for white labor. Every rich man would have owned his nigger mason, his nigger carpenter, his nigger blacksmith ; and the white mechanic, as well as the white farm-laborer, would have been crushed out."

" You think, then, the South will be better off without slavery ? "

" Certainly, I do. So does every white man that has to work for a living, if he is n't a fool."

" Then why did you fight for it ? "

" We was n't fighting for slavery ; we was fighting for our independence. That 's the way the most of us understood it ; though we soon found out it was the rich man's war, and not the pore man's. We was fighting against our own interests, that 's shore ! "

There is a private cemetery on the crest, surrounded by a brick wall. Burnside's artillery had not spared it. I looked over the wall, which was badly smashed in places, and saw the overthrown monuments and broken tombstones lying on the ground. The heights all around were covered with weeds, and scarred by Rebel intrenchments ; here and there was an old apple-tree ; and I marked the ruins of two or three small brick houses.

On the brow of the hill, overlooking the town, is the Marye estate, one of the finest about Fredericksburg before the blast of battle struck it. The house was large and elegant, occupying a beautiful site, and surrounded by terraces and shady lawns. Now if you would witness the results of artillery and infantry firing, visit that house. The pillars of the porch, built of brick, and covered with a cement of lime and white sand, were speckled with the marks of bullets. Shells and solid shot had made sad havoc with the walls and the woodwork inside. The windows were shivered, the partitions torn to pieces, and the doors perforated.

I found a gigantic negro at work at a carpenter's bench in one of the lower rooms. He seemed glad to receive company, and took me from the basement to the zinc-covered roof, showing me all the more remarkable shot-holes.

" De Rebel sharpshooters was in de house ; dat 's what made de Yankees shell it so."

" Where were the people who lived here ? "

" Dey all lef' but me. I stopped to see de fight. I tell ye, I would n't stop to see anoder one !   I thought I was go'n' to have fine fun, and tell all about it. I *heerd* de fight, but I did n't *see* it ! "

" Were you frightened ? "

"Hoo!" flinging up his hands with a ludicrous expression. "Don't talk about skeered! I never was so skeered since I was bo'n! I stood hyer by dis sher winder; I 'spected to see de whole of it; I know I was green! I was look'n' to see de fir'n' down below dar, when a bullet come by me, *h't!* quick as dat. 'Time fo' me to be away f'om hyer!' and I started; but I'd no sooner turned about, when de bullets begun to strike de house jes' like dat!" drumming with his fingers. "I went down-stars, and out dis sher house, quicker 'n any man o' my size ever went out a house befo'e! Come, and I'll show you whar I was hid."

It was in the cellar of a little dairy-house, of which nothing was left but the walls.

"I got in thar wid anoder cullud man. I thought I was as skeered as anybody could be; but whew! he was twicet as skeered as I was. B-r-r-r-r! b-r-r-r-r! de fir'n' kep' up a reg'lar noise like dat, all day long. Every time a shell struck anywhar near, I knowed de next would kill me. 'Jim,' says I, 'now de next shot will be our own!' Dem's de on'y wu'ds I spoke; but he was so skeered he never spoke at all."

"Were you here at the fight the year after?"

"Dat was when Shedwick [Sedgwick] come. I thought if dar was go'n' to be any fight'n', I'd leave dat time, shore. I hitched up my oxen, think'n' I'd put out, but waited fo' de mo'nin' to see. Dat was Sunday mo'nin'. I hadn't slep' none, so I jest thought I'd put my head on my hand a minute till it growed light. I hadn't mo'e 'n drapped asleep; I'd nodded oncet or twicet: so;" illustrating; "no longer 'n dat; when — c-r-r-r-r, — I looked up, — all de wu'ld was fir'n'! Shedwick's men dey run up de road, got behind de batteries on dis sher hill, captured every one; and I never knowed how dey done it so quick. Dat was enough fo' me. If dar's go'n' to be any mo'e fight'n', I go whar da' an't no wa'!'"

"A big fellow like you tell about being skeered!" said the young Rebel.

"I knowed de bigger a man was, de bigger de mark fo' de balls. I weighs two hundred and fifty-two pounds."

" Where is your master ? " I asked.

" I ha'n't got no master now ; Mr. Marye was my master. He 's over de mountain. I was sold at auction in Fredericks-burg oncet, and he bought me fo' twelve hundred dolla's. Now he pays me wages, — thirty dolla's a month. I wo'ked in de mill while de wa' lasted. Men brought me co'n to grind. Some brought a gallon ; some brought two qua'ts ; it was a big load if anybody brought half a bushel. Dat's de way folks lived. Now he 's got anoder man in de mill, and he pays me fo' tak'n' keer o' dis sher place and fitt'n' it up a little."

" Are you a carpenter ? "

" Somethin' of a carpenter ; I kin do whatever I turns my hand to."

The young Rebel afterwards corroborated this statement. Although he did not like niggers generally, and wished they were all out of the country, he said Charles (for that was the giant's name) was an exception ; and he gave him high praise for the fidelity and sagacity he had shown in saving his master's property from destruction.

While we were sitting under the portico, a woman came up the hill, and began to talk and jest in a familiar manner with Charles. I noticed that my Rebel acquaintance looked ex-ceedingly disgusted.

" That woman," said he to me, " has got a nigger husband. That 's what makes her talk that way. White folks won't associate with her, and she goes with the darkies. We used to have lynch law for them cases. Such things wa'n't allowed. A nigger had better have been dead than be caught living with a white woman. The house would get torn down over their heads some night, and nobody would know who did it."

" Are you sure such things were not allowed ? Five out of six of your colored population have white blood in their veins. How do you account for it ? "

" O, that comes from white fathers ! "

" And slave mothers," said I. " That I suppose was all right ; but to a stranger it does n't look very consistent. You would lynch a poor black man for living in wedlock with a white woman, and receive into the best society white men who were raising up illegitimate slave children by their colored mistresses."

" Yes, that 's just what was done ; there 's no use denying it. I 've seen children sold at auction in Fredericksburg by their own fathers. But nobody ever thought it was just right. It always happened when the masters was in debt, and their property had to be taken."

The field below the stone wall belonged to this young man's mother. It was now a cornfield ; a sturdy crop was growing where the dead had lain in heaps.

"Soon as Richmond fell I came home ; and 'Lijah and I went to work and put in that piece of corn. I didn't wait for Lee's surrender. Thousands did the same. We knew that if Richmond fell, the war would be removed from Virginia, and we had no notion of going to fight in other States. The Confederate army melted away just like frost in the sun, so that only a small part of it remained to be surrendered."

He invited me to go through the cornfield and see where the dead were buried. Near the middle of the piece a strip some fifteen yards long and four wide had been left uncultivated. " There 's a thousand of your men buried in this hole ; that 's the reason we didn't plant here." Some distance below the cornfield was the cellar of an ice-house, in which five hundred Union soldiers were buried. And yet these were but a portion of the slain ; all the surrounding fields were scarred with graves.

Returning to Fredericksburg, I visited the plain northwest of the town, also memorable for much hard fighting on that red day of December. I found a pack of government wagons there, an encampment of teamsters, and a few Yankee soldiers, who told me they were tired of doing nothing, and " three times as fast for going home " as they were before the war closed.

In the midst of this plain, shaded by a pleasant grove, stands a brown brick mansion said to have been built by

George Washington for his mother's family. Not far off is a monument erected to Mary, the mother of Washington, whose mortal remains rest here. It is of marble, measuring some nine feet square and fifteen in height, unfinished, capped with a mat of weeds, and bearing no inscription but the names of visitors who should have blushed to desecrate the tomb of the venerated dead. The monument has in other ways been sadly misused ; in the first place, by balls which nicked and chipped it during the battle ; and afterwards by relic-hunters, who, in their rage for carrying away some fragment of it, have left scarce a corner of cornice or pilaster unbroken.

I had afterwards many walks about Fredericksburg, the most noteworthy of which was a morning-visit to the Lacy House, where Burnside had his headquarters. Crossing the Rappahannock on the pontoon bridge, I climbed the stone steps leading from terrace to terrace, and reached the long-neglected grounds and the old-fashioned Virginia mansion. It was entirely deserted. The doors were wide open, or broken from their hinges, the windows smashed, the floors covered with rubbish, and the walls with the names of soldiers and regiments, or pictures cut from the illustrated newspapers.

The windows command a view of Fredericksburg and the battle-field ; and there I stood, and saw in imagination the fight reënacted, — the pontoniers at their work in the misty morning, the sharpshooters' in rifle-pits and houses opposite driving them from it with their murderous fire, the shelling of the town, the troops crossing, the terrible roaring battle, the spouting flames, the smoke, the charging parties, and the horrible slaughter ; — I saw and heard it all again, and fancied for a time that I was the commanding general, whose eyes beheld, and whose wrung heart felt, what he would gladly have given his own life to prevent or retrieve.

8

CHAPTER XIV.

TO CHANCELLORSVILLE.

In conversation with my Rebel acquaintance at the Marye House, I had learned that his friend "'Lijah" sometimes conveyed travellers over the more distant battle-fields. Him, therefore, I sent to engage with his horse and buggy for the following day.

Breakfast was scarcely over the next morning, when, as I chanced to look from my hotel-window, I saw a thin-faced countryman drive up to the door in an old one-horse wagon with two seats, and a box half filled with corn-stalks. I was admiring the anatomy of the horse, every prominent bone of which could be counted through his skin, when I heard the man inquiring for me. It was "'Lijah," with his "horse and buggy."

I was inclined to criticise the establishment, which was not altogether what I had been led to expect.

"I allow he a'n't a fust-class hoss," said Elijah. "Only give three dollars for him. Feed is skurce and high. But let him rest this winter, and git some meal in him, and he'll make a plough crack next spring."

"What are you going to do with those corn-stalks?"

"Fodder for the hoss. They're all the fodder he'll git till night; for we're go'n' into a country whar thar's noth'n' mo'e for an animal to eat than thar is on the palm of my hand."

I took a seat beside him, and made use of the stalks by placing a couple of bundles between my back and the sharp board which travellers were expected to lean against. Elijah cracked his whip, the horse frisked his tail, and struck into a cow-trot which pleased him.

"You see, he'll snake us over the ground right peart!"

He proceeded to tantalize me by telling what a mule he had, and what a little mare he had, at home.

"She certainly goes over the ground! I believe she can run ekal to anything in this country for about a mile. But she's got a set of legs under her jest like a sheep's legs."

He could not say enough in praise of the mule.

"Paid eight hundred dollars for him in Confederate money. He earned a living for the whole family last winter. I used to go reg'lar up to Chancellorsville and the Wilderness, buy up a box of clothing, and go down in Essex and trade it off for corn."

"What sort of clothing?"

"Soldiers' clothes from the battle-fields. Some was flung away, and some, I suppose, was stripped off the dead. Any number of families jest lived on what they got from the Union armies in that way. They'd pick up what garments they could lay hands on, wash 'em up and sell 'em. I'd take a blanket, and git half a bushel of meal for it down in Essex. Then I'd bring the meal back, and git maybe two blankets, or a blanket and a coat, for it. All with that little mule. He'll haul a load for ye! He'll stick to the ground go'n' up hill jest like a dry-land tarrapin! But I take the mare when I'm in a hurry; she makes them feet rattle ag'in the ground!"

We took the plank-road to Chancellorsville, passing through a waste country of weeds or undergrowth, like every other part of Virginia which I had yet seen.

"All this region through yer," said Elijah, "used to be grow'd up to corn and as beautiful clover as ever you see. But since the wa', it's all turned out to bushes and briers and hog-weeds. It's gitt'n' a start ag'in now. I'll show 'em how to do it. If we git in a crap o' wheat this fall, which I don't know if we sha'n't, we kin start three big teams, and whirl up twenty acres of land directly. That mule," etc.

Elijah praised the small farmers.

"People in ordinary sarcumstances along yer are a mighty industrious people. It's the rich that keep this country down.

The way it generally is, a few own too much, and the rest own noth'n'. I know hundreds of thousands of acres of land put to no uset, which, if it was cut up into little farms, would make the country look thrifty. This is mighty good land; clay bottom; holds manure jest like a chany bowl does water. But the rich ones jest scratched over a little on 't with their slave labor, and let the rest go. They would n't sell; let a young man go to 'em to buy, and they 'd say they did n't want no poo' whites around 'em; they would n't have one, if they could keep shet of 'em. And what was the result? Young men would go off to the West, if they was enterpris'n', and leave them that wa'n't enterpris'n' hyer to home. Then as the old heads died off, the farms would run down. The young women would marry the lazy young men, and raise up families of lazy children."

The country all about Fredericksburg was very unhealthy. Elijah, on making inquiries, could hear of scarcely a family on the road exempt from sickness.

" It was never so till sence the wa'. Now we have chills and fever, jest like they do in a new country. It 's owin' to the land all comin' up to weeds; the dew settles in 'em and they rot, and that fills the air with the ager. I 've had the ager myself till about a fortnight ago; then soon as I got shet of that, the colic took me. Eat too much on a big appetite, I suppose. I like to live well; like to see plenty of everything on the table, and then I like to see every man eat a heap."

I commended Elijah's practical sense; upon which he replied, —

" The old man is right ignorant; can't read the fust letter; never went to school a day; but the old man is right sharp!"

He was fond of speaking of himself in this way. He thought education a good thing, but allowed that all the education in the world could not give a man sense. He was fifty years old, and had got along thus far in life very well.

" I reckon thar 's go'n' to be a better chance for the poo' man after this. The Union bein' held together was the greatest thing that could have happened for us."

" And yet you fought against it."

" I was in the Confederate army two year and a half. I was opposed to secession; but I got my head a little turned after the State went out, and I enlisted. Then, when I had time to reconsider it all over, I diskivered we was wrong. I told the boys so.

" ' Boys,' says I, ' when my time's up, I'm go'n' out of the army, and you won't see me in ag'in.'

" ' You can't help that, old man,' says they; ' fo' by that time the conscript law 'll be changed so 's to go over the heads of older men than you.'

" ' Then,' says I, ' the fust chance presents itself, I fling down my musket and go spang No'th.'

" They had me put under arrest for that, and kep' me in the guard-house seven months. I liked that well enough. I was saved a deal of hard march'n' and lay'n' out in the cold, that winter.

" ' Why don't ye come in boys,' says I, ' and have a warm ? '

" I knowed what I was about! The old man was right ignorant, but the old man was right sharp ! "

We passed the line of Sedgwick's retreat a few miles from Fredericksburg.

" Shedrick's men was in line acrost the road hyer, extendin' into the woods on both sides ; they had jest butchered their meat, and was ishyin' rations and beginnin' to cook their suppers, when Magruder struck 'em on the left flank." (Elijah was wrong; it was not Magruder, but McLaws. These local guides make many such mistakes, and it is necessary to be on one's guard against them.) " They jest got right up and skedaddled! The whole line jest faced to the right, and put for Banks's Ford. Thar's the road they went. They left it piled so full of wagons, Magruder could n't follah, but his artillery jest run around by another road I 'll show ye, hard as ever they could lay their feet to the ground, wheeled their guns in position on the bluffs by the time Shedrick got cleverly to crossin', and played away. The way they heaped up Shedrick's men was awful ! "

Every mile or two we came to a small farm-house, commonly of logs, near which there was usually a small crop of corn growing.

"Every man after he got home, after the fall of Richmond, put in to raise a little somethin' to eat. Some o' the corn looks poo'ly, but it beats no corn at all, all to pieces."

We came to one field which Elijah pronounced a "monstrous fine crap." But he added, —

"I 've got thirty acres to home not a bit sorrier 'n that. Ye see, that mule of mine," etc.

I noticed — what I never saw in the latitude of New England — that the fodder had been pulled below the ears and tied in little bundles on the stalks to cure. Ingenious shifts for fences had been resorted to by the farmers. In some places the planks of the worn-out plank-road had been staked and lashed together to form a temporary enclosure. But the most common fence was what Elijah called " bresh wattlin'." Stakes were first driven into the ground, then pine or cedar brush bent in between them and beaten down with a maul.

"Ye kin build a wattlin' fence that way so tight a rabbit can't git through."

On making inquiries, I found that farms of fine land could be had all through this region for ten dollars an acre.

Elijah hoped that men from the North would come in and settle.

"But," said he, " 't would be dangerous for any one to take possession of a confiscated farm. He would n't live a month."

The larger land-owners are now more willing to sell.

"Right smart o' their property was in niggers; they 're pore now, and have to raise money.

"The emancipation of slavery," added Elijah, "is wo'kin' right for the country mo'e ways 'an one. The' a'n't two men in twenty, in middlin' sarcumstances, but that 's beginnin' to see it. I 'm no friend to the niggers, though. They ought all to be druv out of the country. They won't wo'k as long as they can steal. I have my little crap o' corn, and wheat, and po'k. When night comes, I must sleep ; then the niggers come and steal all I 've got."

I pressed him to give an instance of the negroes' stealing his property. He could not say that they had taken anything from him lately, but they " used to" rob his cornfields and hen-roosts, and "they would again." Had he ever caught them at it? No, he could not say that he ever had. Then how did he know that the thieves were negroes? He knew it, because " niggers would steal."

" Won't white folks steal too, sometimes ? "

" Yes," said Elijah, " some o' the poo' whites are a durned sight wus 'n the niggers ! "

" Then why not drive them out of the country too? You see," said I, "your charges against the negroes are vague, and amount to nothing."

" I own," he replied, " thar 's now and then one that 's ekal to any white man. Thar 's one a-comin' thar."

A load of wood was approaching, drawn by two horses abreast and a mule for leader. A white-haired old negro was riding the mule.

" He is the greatest man ! " said Elijah, after we had passed. " He 's been the support of his master's family for twenty year and over. He kin manage a heap better 'n his master kin. The' a'n't a farmer in the country kin beat him. He keeps right on jest the same now he 's free ; though I suppose he gits wages."

" You acknowledge, then, that some of the negroes are superior men ? "

" Yes, thar 's about ten in a hundred, honest and smart as anybody."

" That," said I, " is a good many. Do you suppose you could say more of the white race, if it had just come out of slavery ? "

" I don't believe," said Elijah, " that ye could say as much ! "

We passed the remains of the house " whar Harrow was shot." It had been burned to the ground.

" You 've heerd about Harrow ; he was Confederate commissary ; he stole mo'e hosses f'om the people, and po'ed the
money down his own throat, than would have paid fo' fo'ty
men like him, if he was black."

A mile or two farther on, we came to another house.

" Hyer's whar the man lives that killed Harrow.   He was
in the army, and because he objected to some of Harrow's
doin's, Harrow had him arrested, and treated him very much
amiss.   That ground into his conscience and feelin's, and he
deserted fo' no other puppose than to shoot him.   He 's a
mighty smart fellah !   He 'll strike a man side the head, and
soon 's his fist leaves it, his foot 's thar.   He shot Harrow in
that house you see burnt to the ground, and then went spang
to Washington.   O, he was sharp ! "

On our return we met the slayer of Harrow riding home
from Fredericksburg on a mule, — a fine-looking young fellow, of blonde complexion, a pleasant countenance, finely chiselled nose and lips, and an eye full of sunshine.   " Jest the
best-hearted, nicest young fellah in the wo'ld, till ye git him
mad ; then look out ! "   I think it is often the most attractive
persons, of fine temperaments, who are capable of the most
terrible wrath when roused.

The plank-road was in such a ruined condition that nobody
thought of driving on it, although the dirt road beside it was
in places scarcely better.   The back of the seat was cruel,
notwithstanding the corn-stalks.   But by means of much
persuasion, enforced by a good whip, Elijah kept the old horse
jogging on.   Oak-trees, loaded with acorns, grew beside the
road.   Black-walnuts, already beginning to lose their leaves,
hung their delicate balls in the clear light over our heads.
Poke-weeds, dark with ripening berries, wild grapes festoon-
ing bush and tree, sumachs thrusting up through the foliage
their sanguinary spears, persimmon-trees, gum-trees, red cedars,
with their bluish-green clusters, chestnut-oaks, and chincapins,
adorned the wild wayside.

So we approached Chancellorsville, twelve miles from Fredericksburg.   Elijah was raised in that region, and knew everybody.

" Many a frolic have I had runnin' the deer through these woods ! Soon as the dogs started one, he 'd put fo' the river, cross, take a turn on t' other side, and it would n't be an hour 'fo'e he 'd be back ag'in. Man I lived with used to have a mare that was trained to hunt; if she was in the field and heard the dogs, she 'd whirl her tail up on her back, lope the fences, and go spang to the United States Ford, git thar 'fo'e the dogs would, and hunt as well without a rider as with one."

But since then a far different kind of hunting, a richer blood than the deer's, and other sounds than the exciting yelp of the dogs, had rendered that region famous.

" Hyer we come to the Chancellorsville farm. Many a poo' soldïer's knapsack was emptied of his clothes, after the battle, along this road ! " said Elijah, remembering last winter's business with his mule.

The road runs through a large open field bounded by woods. The marks of hard fighting were visible from afar off. A growth of saplings edging the woods on the south had been killed by volleys of musketry: they looked like thickets of bean-poles. The ground everywhere, in the field and in the woods, was strewed with mementos of the battle, — rotting knapsacks and haversacks, battered canteens and tin cups, and fragments of clothing which Elijah's customers had not deemed it worth the while to pick up. On each side of the road were breastworks and rifle-pits extending into the woods. The clearing, once a well-fenced farm of grain-fields and clover-lots, was now a dreary and deserted common. Of the Chancellorsville House, formerly a large brick tavern, only the half-fallen walls and chimney-stacks remained. Here General Hooker had his headquarters until the wave of battle on Sunday morning rolled so hot and so near that he was compelled to withdraw. The house was soon after fired by a Rebel shell, when full of wounded men, and burned.

" Every place ye see these big bunches of weeds, that 's whar tha' was hosses or men buried," said Elijah. " These holes are whar the bones have been dug up for the bone-factory at Fredericksburg."

It was easy for the bone-seekers to determine where to dig. The common was comparatively barren, except where grew those gigantic clumps of weeds. I asked Elijah if he thought many human bones went to the factory.

" Not unless by mistake. But people a'n't always very partic'lar about mistakes thar 's money to be made by."

Seeing a small enclosure midway between the road and the woods on the south, we walked to it, and found it a burying-ground ridged with unknown graves. Not a head-board, not an inscription, indicated who were the tenants of that little lonely field. And Elijah knew nothing of its history ; it had been set apart, and the scattered dead had been gathered together and buried there, since he passed that way.

We found breastworks thrown up all along by the plank-road west of the farm, — the old worn planks having been put to good service in their construction. The tree-trunks pierced by balls, the boughs lopped off by shells, the strips of timber cut to pieces by artillery and musketry fire, showed how desperate the struggle on that side had been. The endeavors of the Confederates to follow up with an overwhelming victory Jackson's swift and telling blows on our right, and the equally determined efforts of our men to retrieve that disaster, rendered this the scene of a furious encounter.

Elijah thought that if Jackson had not been killed by his own men after delivering that thunderstroke, Hooker would have been annihilated. " Stonewall " was undoubtedly the enemy's best fighting General. His death was to them equal to the loss of many brigades. With regard to the manner of his death there can be no longer any doubt. I have conversed with Confederate officers who were in the battle, all of whom agree as to the main fact. General Jackson, after shattering our right wing, posted his pickets at night with directions to fire upon any man or body of men that might approach. He afterwards rode forward to reconnoitre, returned inadvertently by the same road, and was shot by his own orders.

CHAPTER XV.

THE WILDERNESS.

THE Battle of Bull Run in 1861, Pope's campaign, and Burnside's defeat at Fredericksburg in 1862, and, lastly, Hooker's unsuccessful attempt at Chancellorsville in the spring of 1863, had shown how hard a road to Richmond this was to travel. Repeatedly, as we tried it and failed, the hopes of the Confederacy rose exultant; the heart of the North sank as often, heavy with despair. McClellan's Peninsular route had resulted still more fatally. We all remember the anguish and anxiety of those days. But the heart of the North shook off its despair, listened to no timid counsels; it was growing fierce and obdurate. We no longer received the news of defeat with cries of dismay, but with teeth close-set, a smile upon the quivering lips, and a burning fire within. Had the Rebels triumphed again ? Then so much the worse for them! Had we been once more repulsed with slaughter from their strong line of defences ? Was the precious blood poured out before them all in vain ? At last it should not be in vain ! Though it should cost a new thirty years' war and a generation of lives, the red work we had begun must be completed ; ultimate failure was impossible, ultimate triumph certain.

This inflexible spirit found its embodiment in the leader of the final campaigns against the Rebel capital. It was the deep spirit of humanity itself, ready to make the richest sacrifices, calm, determined, inexorable, moving steadily towards the great object to be achieved. It has been said that General Grant did not consider the lives of his men. Then the people did not consider them. But the truth lies here : precious as were those lives, something lay beyond far more precious, and they were the needful price paid for it. We had learned the dread price, we had duly weighed the worth of the object to be purchased; what then was the use of hesitating and higgling?

We were approaching the scene of Grant's first great blow aimed at the gates of the Rebel capital. On the field of Chancellorsville you already tread the borders of the field of the Wilderness, — if that can be called a field which is a mere interminable forest, slashed here and there with roads.

Passing straight along the plank-road, we came to a large farm-house, which had been gutted by soldiers, and but recently reoccupied. It was still in a scarcely habitable condition. However, we managed to obtain, what we stood greatly in need of, a cup of cold water. I observed that it tasted strongly of iron.

"The reason of that is, we took twelve camp-kettles out of the well," said the man of the house, "and nobody knows how many more there are down there."

The place is known as Locust Grove. In the edge of the forest, but a little farther on, is the Wilderness Church, — a square-framed building, which showed marks of such usage as every uninhabited house receives at the hands of a wild soldiery. Red Mars has little respect for the temples of the Prince of Peace.

"Many a time have I been to meet'n' in that shell, and sot on hard benches, and heard long sermons!" said Elijah. "But I reckon it 'll be a long while befo'e them doo's are darkened by a congregation ag'in. Thar a'n't the population through hyer thar used to be. Oncet we 'd have met a hundred wagons on this road go'n' to market; but I count we ha'n't met mo'e 'n a dozen to-day."

Not far beyond the church we approached two tall guide-posts erected where the road forks. The one on the right pointed the way to the "Wilderness National Cemetery, No. 1, 4 miles," by the Orange Court-House turnpike. The other indicated the "Wilderness National Cemetery, No. 2," by the plank-road.

"All this has been done sence I was this way," said Elijah.

We kept the plank-road, — or rather the clay road beside it, which stretched before us dim in the hollows, and red as brick on the hillsides. We passed some old fields, and entered the great Wilderness, — a high and dry country, thickly overgrown with dwarfish timber, chiefly scrub oaks, pines, and cedars. Poles lashed to trees for tent-supports indicated where our regiments had encamped; and soon we came upon abundant evidences of a great battle. Heavy breastworks thrown up on Brock's cross-road, planks from the plank-road piled up and lashed against trees in the woods, to form a shelter for our pickets, knapsacks, haversacks, pieces of clothing, fragments of harness, tin plates, canteens, some pierced with balls, fragments of shells, with here and there a round-shot, or a shell unexploded, straps, buckles, cartridge-boxes, socks, old shoes, rotting letters, desolate tracts of perforated and broken trees, — all these signs, and others sadder still, remained to tell their silent story of the great fight of the Wilderness.

A cloud passed over the sun: all the scene became sombre, and hushed with a strange brooding stillness, broken only by the noise of twigs crackling under my feet, and distant growls of thunder. A shadow fell upon my heart also, as from the wing of the Death-Angel, as I wandered through the woods, meditating upon what I saw. Where were the feet that wore those empty shoes? Where was he whose proud waist was buckled in that belt? Some soldier's heart was made happy by that poor, soiled, tattered, illegible letter, which rain and mildew have not spared; some mother's, sister's, wife's, or sweetheart's hand, doubtless, penned it; it is the broken end of a thread which unwinds a whole life-history, could we but follow it rightly. Where is that soldier now? Did he fall in the fight, and does his home know him no more? Has the poor wife or stricken mother waited long for the answer to that letter, which never came, and will never come? And this cap, cut in two by a shot, and stiff with a strange incrustation, — a small cap, a mere boy's, it seems, — where now the fair head and wavy hair that wore it? Oh, mother and sisters at home, do you still mourn for your drummer-boy? Has the story reached you, — how he went into the fight to carry off his wounded comrades, and so lost his life for their sakes ? — for so I imagine the tale which will never be told.

And what more appalling spectacle is this ? In the cover of thick woods, the unburied remains of two soldiers, — two skeletons side by side, two skulls almost touching each other, like the cheeks of sleepers ! I came upon them unawares as I picked my way among the scrub oaks. I knew that scores of such sights could be seen here a few weeks before; but the United States Government had sent to have its unburied dead collected together in the two national cemeteries of the Wilderness ; and I had hoped the work was faithfully done.

" They was No'th-Carolinians ; that 's why they did n't bury 'em," said Elijah, after a careful examination of the buttons fallen from the rotted clothing.

The ground where they lay had been fought over repeatedly, and the dead of both sides had fallen there. The buttons may, therefore, have told a true story : North-Carolinians they may have been ; yet I could not believe that the true reason why they had not been decently interred. It must have been that these bodies, and others we found afterwards, were overlooked by the party sent to construct the cemeteries. It was shameful negligence, to say the least.

The cemetery was near by, — a little clearing in the woods by the roadside, thirty yards square, surrounded by a picket fence, and comprising seventy trenches, each containing the remains of I know not how many dead. Each trench was marked with a headboard inscribed with the invariable words :

" Unknown United States soldiers, killed Ma,, 1864."

Elijah, to whom I read the inscription, said, pertinently, that the words *United States soldiers* indicated plainly that it had not been the intention to bury Rebels there. No doubt : but these might at least have been buried in the woods where they fell.

As a grim sarcasm on this neglect, somebody had flung three human skulls, picked up in the woods, over the paling into the cemetery, where they lay blanching among the graves.

Close by the southeast corner of the fence were three or four Rebel graves with old headboards. Elijah called my attention to them, and wished me to read what the headboards said. The main fact indicated was, that those buried there were North-Carolinians. Elijah considered this somehow corroborative of his theory derived from the buttons. The graves were shallow, and the settling of the earth over the bodies had left the feet of one of the poor fellows sticking out.

The shadows which darkened the woods, and the ominous thunder-growls, culminated in a shower. Elijah crawled under his wagon; I sought the shelter of a tree; the horse champed his fodder, and we ate our luncheon. How quietly upon the leaves, how softly upon the graves of the cemetery, fell the perpendicular rain! The clouds parted, and a burst of sunlight smote the Wilderness; the rain still poured, but every drop was illumined, and I seemed standing in a shower of silver meteors.

The rain over, and luncheon finished, I looked about for some solace to my palate after the dry sandwiches moistened only by the drippings from the tree, — seeking a dessert in the Wilderness. Summer grapes hung their just ripened clusters from the vine-laden saplings, and the chincapin bushes were starred with opening burrs. I followed a woodland path embowered with the glistening boughs, and plucked, and ate, and mused. The ground was level, and singularly free from the accumulations of twigs, branches, and old leaves with which forests usually abound. I noticed, however, many charred sticks and half-burnt roots and logs. Then the terrible recollection overtook me: these were the woods that were on fire during the battle. I called Elijah.

"Yes, all this was a flame of fire while the fight was go'n' on. It was full of dead and wounded men. Cook and Stevens, farmers over hyer, men I know, heard the screams of the poor fellahs burnin' up, and come and dragged many a one out of the fire, and laid 'em in the road."

The woods were full of Rebel graves, with here and there a heap of half-covered bones, where several of the dead had been hurriedly buried together.

I had seen enough.   We returned to the cemetery.   Elijah hitched up his horse, and we drove back along the plank-road, cheered by a rainbow which spanned the Wilderness and moved its bright arch onward over Chancellorsville towards Fredericksburg, brightening and fading, and brightening still again, like the hope which gladdened the nation's eye after Grant's victory.

CHAPTER XVI.

SPOTTSYLVANIA COURT-HOUSE.

ELIJAH wished to drive me the next day to Spottsylvania Court-House, and, as an inducement for me to employ him, promised to tackle up his mare. He also proposed various devices for softening the seats of his wagon. No ingenuity of plan, however, sufficed to cajole me. There was a livery-stable in Fredericksburg, and I had conceived a strong prejudice in its favor.

The next morning, accordingly, there might have been seen wheeling up to the tavern-door a shining vehicle, — a bran-new buggy with the virgin gloss upon it, — drawn by a prancing iron-gray in a splendid new harness. The sarcastic stable-man had witnessed my yesterday's departure and return, and had evidently exhausted the resources of his establishment to furnish forth a dazzling contrast to Elijah's sorry outfit. The driver was a youth who wore his cap rakishly over his left eyebrow. I took a seat by his side on a cushion of the softest, and presently might have been seen riding out of Fredericksburg in that brilliant style, — nay, *was* seen, by one certainly, who was cut to the heart. We drove by the "stone-wall" road under the Heights, and passed a house by the corner of which a thin-visaged "old man" of fifty was watering a sad little beast at a well. The beast was "that mare"; and the old man was Elijah. I shall never forget the look he gave me. I bade him a cheerful good-morning; but his voice stuck in his throat; he could not say "good-morning." Our twinkling wheels almost grazed the hubs of the old wagon standing in the road as we passed.

That I might have nothing to regret, the stable-keeper had given me a driver who was in the Spottsylvania battle.

9

" You cannot have seen much service, at your age," I said, examining his boyish features.

" I was four year in de army, anyhow," he replied, spitting tobacco-juice with an air of old experience. " I enlisted when I was thirteen. I was under de quartermaster at fust; but de last two year I was in de artillery."

I observed that he used *de* for *the* almost invariably, with many other peculiarities of expression which betrayed early association with negroes.

" What is your name ? "

" Richard H. Hicks."

" What is your middle name ? "

" I ha'n't got no middle name."

" What does the *H* stand for ? "

" *H* stands for Hicks: Richard H. Hicks; dat 's what dey tell me."

" Can't you read ? "

" No, I can't read. I never went to school, and never had no chance to learn."

Somehow this confession touched me with a sadness I had not felt even at the sight of the dead men in the woods.   He, young, active, naturally intelligent, was dead to a world without which this world would seem to us a blank, — the world of literature. To him the page of a book, the column of a newspaper, was meaningless. Had he been an old man, or black, or stupid, I should not have been so much surprised. I thought of Shakspeare, David, the prophets, the poets, the romancers ; and as my mind glanced from name to name on the glittering entablatures, I seemed to be standing in a glorious temple, with a blind youth at my side.

" Did you ever hear of Sir Walter Scott ? "

" No, I never heerd of that Scott.   But I know a William Scott."

" Did you ever hear of Longfellow ? "

" No, I never heerd of him ? "

" Did you never hear of a great English poet called Lord Byron ? "

" No, sir, I never knowed dar was such a man."

What a gulf betwixt his mind and mine! Sitting side by side there, we were yet as far apart as the great globe's poles.

" Do you mean to go through life in such ignorance ? "

" I don't know; I 'd learn to read if I had de chance."

" Find a chance! make a chance! Even the little negro boys are getting the start of you."

" I reckon I 'll go to school some dis winter," said he. " Dar 's go'n' to be a better chance fo' schools now ; dat 's what dey say."

" Why now ? " I asked.

" I don't know ; on'y dey say so."

" You think, then, it was a good thing that the Confederacy got used up and slavery abolished ? "

" It mought be a good thing. All I know is, it 's so, and it can't be ho'ped " (helped). " It suits me well enough. I 've been gitt'n' thirty dollars a month dis summer, and that 's twicet mo'e 'n I ever got befo'e."

I could not discover that this youth of seventeen had ever given the great questions involving the welfare of his country a serious thought. However, the vague belief he had imbibed regarding better times coming in consequence of emancipation, interested me as a still further evidence of the convictions entertained by the poorer classes on this subject.

As we rode over the hills behind Fredericksburg, a young fellow came galloping after us on a mule.

" Whar ye go'n', Dick ? "

" I 'm go'n' to de battle-field wi' dis gentleman."

" He 's from the No'th, then," said the young fellow.

" How do you know that ? " I asked.

" Because no South'n man ever goes to the battle-fields : we 've seen enough of 'em." He became very sociable as we rode along. " Ye see that apple-tree ? I got a right good pair o' pants off one o' your soldier's under that tree once."

" Was he dead ? "

" Yes. He was one of Sedgwick's men ; he was killed when Sedgwick took the Heights. Shot through the head. The pants wa'n't hurt none." And putting spurs to his mule, he galloped ahead.

I noticed that he and Richard, like many of the young men, white and black, I had seen about Fredericksburg, wore United States army trousers.

" Dey was all we could git one while," said Richard. " I reckon half our boys 'u'd have had to go widout pants if it had n't been for de Union army. Dar was right smart o' trad'n' done in Yankee clothes, last years o' de wa'."

" Did you rob a dead soldier of those you have on ? "

" No ; I bought dese in Fredericksburg. I never robbed a dead man."

" But how did you know they were not taken from a corpse ? "

" Mought be ; but it could n't be ho'ped. A poo' man can't be choice."

Richard expressed great contempt — inspired by envy, I thought — of the young chap riding the mule.

" United States gov'ment give away a hundred and fifty old wore-out mules in Fredericksburg, not long ago ; so now every lazy fellow ye see can straddle his mule ! He a'n't nobody, though he thinks he 's a heavy coon-dog ! "

" What do you mean by a *heavy coon-dog ?* "

" Why, ye see, when a man owns a big plantation, and a heap o' darkeys, and carries a heavy pocket, or if he 's do'n' a big thing, den we call him a heavy coon-dog. Jeff Davis was a heavy coon-dog ; but he 's a light coon-dog now ! "

Our route lay through a rough, hilly country, never more than very thinly inhabited, and now scarcely that. About every two miles we passed a poor log house in the woods, or on the edge of overgrown fields, — sometimes tenantless, but oftener occupied by a pale, poverty-smitten family afflicted with the chills. I do not remember more than two or three framed houses on the road, and they looked scarcely less disconsolate than their log neighbors.

It is twelve miles from Fredericksburg to Spottsylvania Court-House. At the end of nine or ten miles we began to meet with signs of military operations, — skirmish-lines, rifle-pits, and graves by the roadside.

Rising a gentle ascent, we had a view of the Court-House, and of the surrounding country, — barren, hilly fields, with here and there a scattered tree, or clump of trees, commonly pines, and boundaries of heavier timber beyond. There were breastworks running in various directions, — along by the road, across the road, and diagonally over the crests. The country was all cut up with them ; and I found the Rebel works strangely mixed up with our own. As our army advanced, it had possessed itself of the enemy's rifle-pits, skirmish-line, and still more important intrenchments, and converted them to its own use.

Grant's main line of breastworks, very heavy, constructed of rails and stakes and earth, crosses the road at nearly right angles, and stretches away out of sight on either side over the hills and into the woods. I was reminded of what Elijah had told me the day before at Brock's Road, in the Wilderness. " Grant's breastworks run thirty miles through the country, from near Ely's Ford on the Rapidan, spang past Spottsyl-vany Court-House and the Mattapony River."

The road to the Court-House runs south. On the left was Beverly's house, and a shattered empty house on the right Richard pointed out the hill on which his battery was stationed early in the battle. " We had to git away f'om dar, though. Your batteries drove us."

We rode on to the Court-House : a goodly brick building, with heavy pillars in front, one of which had been broken off by a shell, leaving a corner of the portico hanging in the air. There were but six other buildings of any importance in the place, — one jail, one tavern, (no school-house,) one private dwelling, and three churches ; all of brick, and all more or less battered by artillery.

Entering the Court-House amid heaps of rubbish which littered the yard about the doors, I had the good fortune to find the county clerk at his desk. He received me politely, and offered to show me about the building. It had been well riddled by shot and shell; but masons and carpenters were at work repairing damages; so that there was a prospect of the county, in a few months, having a court-house again.

" What is most to be regretted," the clerk said, " is the destruction of documents which can't be restored. All the records and papers of the court were destroyed by the Union soldiers after they got possession." And he showed me a room heaped with the fragments. It looked like a room in a rag-man's warehouse.

Returning to his office, he invited me to sit down, and commenced talking freely of the condition and prospects of the country. The area of corn-land planted was small; but the soil had been resting two or three years, the season had been favorable, and the result was an excellent crop. " We shall probably have a surplus to dispose of for other necessaries." The county had not one third the number of horses, nor one tenth the amount of stock, it had before the war. Many families were utterly destitute. They had nothing whatever to live upon until the corn-harvest; and many would have nothing then. The government had been feeding as many as fifteen hundred persons at one time.

" How many of these were blacks? "

" Perhaps one fifth."

" How large a proportion of the population of the county are blacks? "

" Not quite one half."

" The colored population require proportionately less assistance, then, than the white? " He admitted the fact. " How happens it? " I inquired; for he had previously told me the old hackneyed tale, that the negroes would not work, and that in consequence they were destined to perish like the Indians.

" They 'll steal," said he; and he made use of this expression, which he said was proverbial: " An honest nigger is as rare as a lock of har on the palm of my hand."

" But," I objected, " it seems hardly possible for one class of people to live by stealing in a country you describe as so destitute."

" A nigger will live on almost nothing," he replied. " It is n't to be denied, however, but that some of them work."

He criticised severely the government's system of feeding the destitute. " Hundreds are obtaining assistance who are not entitled to any. They have only to go to the overseers of the poor appointed by government, put up a poor mug, and ask for a certificate in a weak voice ; they get it, and come and draw their rations. Some draw rations both here and at Fredericksburg, thus obtaining a double support, while they are well able to work and earn their living, if left to themselves. The system encourages idleness, and does more harm than good. All these evils could be remedied, and more than half the expense saved the government, if it would intrust the entire management of the matter in the hands of citizens."

" Is it the whites, or the blacks, who abuse the government's bounty ? "

" The whites."

" It appears, then, that they have the same faults you ascribe to the blacks : they are not over-honest, and they will not work unless obliged to."

" Yes, there are shiftless whites to be sure. There 's a place eight miles west from here, known as Texas, inhabited by a class of poor whites steeped in vice, ignorance, and crime of every description. They have no comforts, and no energy to work and obtain them. They have no books, no morality, no religion ; they go clothed like savages, half sheltered, and half fed, — except that government is now supporting them."

" Do the whites we are feeding come mostly from that region ? "

" O, no ; they come from all over the county. Some walk as far as twenty miles to draw their fortnight's or three weeks' rations. Some were in good circumstances before the war ; and some are tolerably well off now. A general impression prevails that this support comes from a tax on the county ; so every man, whether he needs it or not, rushes in for a share. It is impossible to convince the country people that it is the United States government that is feeding them. Why, sir, there are men in the back districts who will not yet believe that the war is over, and slavery at an end! "

" It appears," said I, " that ignorance is not confined to the region you call Texas; and that, considering all things, the whites are even more degraded than the blacks. Why does n't some prophet of evil arise and predict that the white race, too, will die out because it is vicious and will not work ? "

" The whites are a different race, sir, — a different race," was the emphatic, but not very satisfactory reply. " The negro cannot live without the care and protection of a master."

" You think, then, the abolition of slavery a great misfortune ? "

" A great misfortune to the negroes, certainly; but not to the whites: we shall be better off without them."

" It is singular that the negroes have no fear of the fate you predict for them. They say, on the contrary, ' We have been supporting our masters and their families all our lives, and now it is a pity if we cannot earn a living for ourselves.' "

" Well, I hope they will succeed! "

This is the reply the emancipated slave-owners almost invariably make to the above argument; sometimes sarcastically, sometimes gravely, sometimes commiseratingly, but always incredulously. " The negro is fated; " this is the real or pretended belief; and this they repeat, often with an ill-concealed spirit of vindictiveness, an " I-told-you-so ! " air of triumph, until one is forced to the conclusion that their prophecy is their desire.

CHAPTER XVII.

THE FIELD OF SPOTTSYLVANIA.

I WALKED on to the tavern where Richard H. Hicks was baiting his horse. The landlord took me to a lumber-room where he kept, carefully locked up, a very remarkable curiosity. It was the stump of a tree, eleven inches in diameter, which had been cut off by bullets — not by cannon-shot, but by leaden bullets — in the Spottsylvania fight. It looked like a colossal scrub-broom. " I had a stump twice as big as this, cut off by bullets in the same way, only much smoother ; but some Federal officers took it from me and sent it to the War Department at Washington."

He had many battle-scars about his house to show; one of which I remember : " A shell come in through the wall thar, wrapped itself up in a bed that stood hyer, and busted in five pieces."

In one of the rooms I found a Union officer lying on a lounge, sick with the prevailing fever. He seemed glad to see a Northern face, and urged me to be seated.

" It is fearfully lonesome here ; and just now I have no companion but the ague."

Learning that he had been some time in command of the post, I inquired the reason why the citizens appeared so eager to save the government expense in feeding their poor.

" It is very simple : they wish to get control of the business in order to cut off the negroes. They had rather have the assistance· the government affords withdrawn altogether, than that the freedmen should come in for a share. It is their policy to keep the blacks entirely dependent upon their former masters, and consequently as much slaves as before."

" You of course hear many complaints that the blacks will not work ? "

" Yes, and they are true in certain cases : they will not work for such wages as their late owners are willing to give ; in other words, they will not work for less than nothing. But when they have encouragement they work very well, in their fashion, — which is not the Yankee fashion, certainly, but the fashion which slavery has bred them up to. They have not yet learned to appreciate, however, the binding character of a contract. It is a new thing to them. Besides, the master too often sets them bad examples by failing to keep his own engagements. He has been in the habit of breaking his promises to them at his convenience ; and now he finds fault that they do not keep theirs any better. The masters have not yet learned how to treat their old servants under the new conditions. They cannot learn that they are no longer slaves. That is one great source of trouble. On the other hand, where the freedman receives rational, just, and kind treatment, he behaves well and works well, almost without exception. I expect a good deal of difficulty soon. The negroes have in many places made contracts to work for a part of the crop ; now when the corn comes to be divided, their ideas and their master's, with regard to what ' a part ' of the crop is, will be found to differ considerably. I was not an anti-slavery man at home," he added ; " and I give you simply the results of my observation since I have been in the South."

" What do you think would be the effect if our troops were withdrawn ? "

" I hardly know ; but I should expect one of two things : either that the freedmen would be reduced to a worse condition than they were ever in before, or that they would rise in insurrection."

The landlord wished me to go and look at his corn. It was certainly a noble crop. The tops of the monstrous ears towered six or eight feet from the ground ; the tops of the stalks at least twelve or fourteen feet. He maintained that it would average fifty bushels (of shelled corn) to the acre. I thought the estimate too high.

" Good corn," said he, " measures finely ; sorry corn porely.
And consider, not a spoonful of manure has been put on this
ground fo' fou' years."

" But the ground has been resting ; and that is as good as
manure."

" Yes ; but it 's mighty good soil that will do as well as this.
Now tell your people, if they want to buy good land cheap,
hyer 's their chance. I 've got a thousand acres ; and I 'll
sell off seven hundred acres, claired or timber land, to suit purchasers. It 's well wo'th twenty dollars an acre ; I 'll sell for
ten. It a'n't fur from market ; and thar 's noth'n' ye can't
raise on this yer land."

Of all his thousand acres he had only about fifteen under
cultivation. His cornfield was not as large as it appeared ;
for, running through the centre of it, like a titanic furrow,
were Lee's tremendous intrenchments. These few acres were
all the old man had been able to enclose. There was not
another fence on his farm. " I had over ten thousand panels
of fence burnt up for me during the wa' ; over eighty thousand
rails."

" By which army ? "

" Both : fust one, and then the other. Our own troops were
as bad as the Yankees."

Afterwards, as we rode away from the tavern, Richard H.
Hicks gave me the following succinct account of the landlord :

" He used to be a heavy coon-dog. He had fifty head o'
darkeys. He would n't hire 'em, and dey lef'. Now he has
nobody to wo'k de land, he 's got a light pocket, and so he 's a
mind to sell."

Riding west from the Court-House, and striking across the
fields on the right, we passed McCool's house, in a pleasant
shady place, and reached the scene where the eight days' fighting culminated. Of the woods, thinned and despoiled by the
storm of iron and lead, only a ghostly grove of dead trunks
and dreary dry limbs remained. Keeping around the western
edge of these, we came to a strange medley of intrenchments,
which it would have required an engineer to unravel and

understand.   Here Grant's works had been pushed up against Lee's, swallowing them as one wave swallows another.   Nowhere else have I seen evidences of such close and desperate fighting.   For eight days Grant had been thundering at the gates of the Confederacy ; slowly, with fearful loss, he had been pressing back the enemy and breaking through the obstructions ; until here at last he concentrated all his strength.   Each army fought as if the gods had decreed that the issue of the war depended upon that struggle.   And so indeed they had : the way to Richmond by this route, so long attempted in vain, was here opened.   The grand result proclaimed that the eight days' battles were victories ; that the enemy, for the first time on his own chosen ground, had met with ominous defeat.   Inconceivable was the slaughter.   Here two red rivers met and spilled themselves into the ground.   Swift currents from the great West, tributaries from the Atlantic States and from the Lake States, priceless rills, precious drops, from almost every community and family in the Union, swelled the northern stream which burst its living banks and perished here.   Every state, every community, every family mourned.

But behind this curtain of woe was the chiselled awful form, the terrible front and sublime eyes, of the statue of Fate, the nation's unalterable Will.   Contemplating that, we were silenced, if not consoled.   Every breast — that of the father going to search for the body of his dead son, that of the mother reading the brief despatch that pierced her as the bullet pierced her dear boy, that of the pale wife hastening to the cot-side of her dying husband, nay, the bleeding breasts of the wounded and dying, while yet they felt a throb of life — thrilled responsive to Grant's simple, significant announcement —

" I propose to fight it out on this line, if it takes all summer."

It took all summer, indeed, and all winter too ; but the result had been decided at Spottsylvania.

The Rebel armies had invaded the North and been driven ingloriously back.   Many times we had started for Richmond and been repulsed.   But at length we were not repulsed : the overwhelming wave poured over the embankments.

Such thoughts — or rather deep emotions, of which such thoughts are but the feeble expression — possess the serious tourist, who stands upon that field furrowed and ridged with earthworks and with graves, — beside that grove of shattered and shrivelled trees. A conscious solemnity seems brooding in the air. If the intrenchments could speak, what a history could they disclose! But those sphinx-like lips of the earth are rigid and still. Even the winds seem to hush their whispers about that scene of desolation. All is silence ; and the heart of the visitor is constrained to silence also.

Upon a hacked and barkless trunk at the angle of the woods, in the midst of the graves, was nailed aloft a board bearing these lines :

> " On Fame's eternal camping-ground
> Their silent tents are spread,
> And glory guards with solemn round
> The bivouac of the dead."

A thick undergrowth had sprung up in the woods. I noticed, stooping among the bushes along by the breastworks, an old woman and two young girls.

" Dey 're chincapinnin'," said Richard.

But I observed that they gathered the nuts, not from the bushes, but from the ground. Curiosity impelled me to follow them. The woman had a haversack slung at her side ; one of the girls carried an open pail. They passed along the intrench-ments, searching intently, and occasionally picking something out of the dirt. Pressing into the bushes, I accosted them. They scarcely deigned to look at me, but continued their strange occupation. I questioned them about the battle ; but their answers were as vague and stupid as if they then heard of it for the first time. Meanwhile I obtained a glance at the open mouth of the heavily freighted haversack and the half-filled pail, and saw not chincapins, but several quarts of old bullets.

Wandering along by the intrenchments, I observed the half-rotted fragments of a book on the ground. They were leaves from a German pocket Testament, which doubtless some soldier had carried into the fight. I picked them up, and glanced my eye over the mildewed pages. By whom were they last perused? What poor immigrant's heart, fighting here the battles of his adopted country, had drawn consolation from those words of life, which lose not their vitality in any language? What was the fate of that soldier? Was he now telling the story of his campaigns to his bearded comrades, wife and children; or was that tongue forever silent in the dust of the graves that surrounded me? While I pondered, these words caught my eye: —

"Die du mir gegeben hast, die habe ich bewahret, und ist keiner von ihnen verloren." — "Those that thou gavest me I have kept, and none of them is lost."

I looked round upon the graves; I thought of the patriot hosts that had fallen on these fearful battle-fields, — of the households bereft, of the husbands, fathers, brothers, and sons, who went down to the Wilderness and were never heard of more; and peace and solace, sweet as the winds of Paradise, came to me in these words, as I repeated them, —

"None of them is lost, none of them is lost!"

CHAPTER XVIII.

"ON TO RICHMOND."

AT mid-day, on the fifteenth of September, I took the train at Fredericksburg for Richmond, expecting to make in three hours the journey which our armies were more than as many years in accomplishing.

" On to Richmond! On to Richmond! " clattered the cars; while my mind recalled the horrors and anxieties of those years, so strangely in contrast with the swiftness and safety of our present speed. Where now were the opposing Rebel hosts? Where the long lines of bristling musketry, the swarms of cavalry, and the terrible artillery? Where the great Slave Empire, the defiant Confederacy itself?

> " The earth hath bubbles as the water has,
>   And these were of them."

We passed amid the same desolate scenes which I had everywhere observed since I set foot upon the soil of Virginia, — old fields and undergrowths, with signs of human life so feeble and so few, that one began to wonder where the country population of the Old Dominion was to be found. All the region between Fredericksburg and Richmond seems not only almost uninhabited now, but always to have been so, — at least to the eye familiar with New-England farms and villages. But one must forget the thriving and energetic North when he enters a country stamped with the dark seal of slavery. Large and fertile Virginia, with eight times the area of Massachusetts, scarcely equals in population that barren little State. The result is, that, where Southern State pride sees prosperous settlements, the travelling Yankee discovers little more than uncultivated wastes.

Ashton, sixteen miles from Richmond, was the first really civilized-looking place we passed. Farther on I looked for the suburbs of the capital. But Richmond has no suburbs. The pleasant villages and market-gardens that spread smilingly for miles around our large Northern towns, are altogether wanting here. Suddenly the melancholy waste of the country disappears, and you enter the outskirts of the city.

And is this indeed Richmond into which the train glides so smoothly along its polished rails? Is this the fort-encircled capital whose gates refused so long to open to our loudly knocking armies? — and have we entered with so little ado? Is the " Rome of the Confederacy " sitting proudly on her seven hills, aware that here are detestable Yankees within her walls? Will she cast us into Libby? or starve us on Belle Island? or forward us to Wirtz at Andersonville? — for such we know was the fate of Northern men who *did* get into Richmond during the past four years! You think of what *they* suffered, as you walk unmolested the pavements of the conquered capital; and something swells within you, which is not exultation, nor rage, nor grief, but a strange mingling of all these.

> " Time the Avenger! unto thee I lift
> My hands and eyes and heart! "

for what a change has been wrought since those days of horror and crime! Now no Rebel guard is at hand to march you quickly and silently through the streets ; but friendly faces throng to welcome you, to offer you seats in carriages, and to invite you to the hospitalities of hotels. And these people, meeting or passing you, or seated before their doors in the warm September afternoon, are no longer enemies, but tamed complacent citizens of the United States like yourself.

I was surprised to find that the storm of war had left Richmond so beautiful a city ; although she appeared to be mourning for her sins at the time in dust and ashes, — dust which every wind whirled up from the unwatered streets, and the ashes of the Burnt District.

Here are no such palatial residences as dazzle the eye in New York, Chicago, and other Northern cities ; but in their place you see handsome rows of houses, mostly of brick, shaded by trees, and with a certain air of comfort and elegance about them which is very inviting. The streets are sufficiently spacious, and regularly laid out, many of them being thrown up into long, sweeping lines of beauty by the hills on which they are built. The hills indeed are the charm of Richmond, overlooking the falls of the James, on the left bank of which it stands; giving you shining glimpses of the winding river up and down, — commanding views of the verdant valley and of the hilly country around, — and here, at the end of some pleasant street, falling off abruptly into the wild slopes of some romantic ravine.

In size, Richmond strikes one as very insignificant, after all the noise it has made in the world. Although the largest city of Virginia, and ranking among Southern cities of the second magnitude, either of our great Northern towns could swallow it, as one pickerel swallows a lesser, and scarcely feel the morsel in its belly. In 1860 it had a population of not quite thirty-eight thousand, — less than that of Troy or New Haven, and but a little larger than that of Lowell.

I had already secured a not very satisfactory room at a crowded hotel, when, going out for an afternoon ramble, I came by chance to Capitol Square. Although a small park, containing only about eight acres, I found in its shady walks and by its twinkling fountains a delightful retirement after the heat and dust of the streets. It is situated on the side of a hill sloping down to the burnt district which lies between it and the river. On the brow of the slope, at an imposing elevation, its pillared front looking towards the western sun, stands the State Capitol, which was also the capitol of the Confederacy. Near by is Crawford's equestrian statue of Washington, which first astonishes the beholder by its vast proportions, and does not soon cease to be a wonder to his eyes.

Coming out of the Park, at the corner nearest the monu-

10

ment, I noticed, on the street-corner opposite, a hotel, whose range of front rooms overlooking the square, made me think ruefully of the lodgings I had engaged elsewhere. To exchange a view of back yards and kitchen-roofs from an upper story for a sight from those commanding windows, entered my brain as an exciting possibility. I went in. The clerk had two or three back rooms to show, but no front room, until he saw that nothing else would suffice, when he obligingly sent me to the very room I wished. Throwing open the shutters, I looked out upon the Park, the Capitol, the colossal Washington soaring above the trees, and the far-off shining James. I caught glimpses, through the foliage, of the spray of one of the fountains, and could hear its ceaseless murmur mingle with the noise of the streets.

I took possession at once, sent for my luggage, slept that night in my new lodgings, and was awakened at dawn the next morning by a sound as of a dish of beans dashed into a ringing brass kettle. This was repeated at irregular intervals, and with increasing frequency, as the day advanced, breaking in upon the plashy monotone of the fountain, and the rising hum of the city, with its resounding rattle. Stung with curiosity, I arose and looked from my open window. Few white citizens were astir, but I saw a thin, ceaseless stream of negroes, who " would not work," going cheerfully to their daily tasks. The most of them took their way towards the burnt district; some crossed Capitol Square to shorten their route; and the sounds I had heard were occasioned by the slamming of the iron gates of the Park.

CHAPTER XIX.

THE BURNT DISTRICT.

AGAIN that morning I visited the burnt district, of which I had taken but a cursory view the evening before.

All up and down, as far as the eye could reach, the business portion of the city bordering on the river lay in ruins. Beds of cinders, cellars half filled with bricks and rubbish, broken and blackened walls, impassable streets deluged with *débris*, here a granite front still standing, and there the iron fragments of crushed machinery, — such was the scene which extended over thirty entire squares and parts of other squares.

I was reminded of Chambersburg; but here was ruin on a more tremendous scale. Instead of small one- and two-story buildings, like those of the modest Pennsylvania town, tall blocks, great factories, flour-mills, rolling-mills, foundries, machine-shops, warehouses, banks, railroad, freight, and engine houses, two railroad bridges, and one other bridge spanning on high piers the broad river, were destroyed by the desperate Rebel leaders on the morning of the evacuation.

" They meant to burn us all out of our homes," said a citizen whom I met on the butment of the Petersburg railroad bridge. " It was the wickedest thing that ever was done in this world! You are a stranger; you don't know; but the people of Richmond know, if they will only speak their minds."

" But," said I, " what was their object in burning their own city, the city of their friends? "

" The devil only knows, for he set 'em on to do it! It was spite, I reckon. If they could n't hold the city, they determined nobody else should. They kept us here four years under the worst tyranny under the sun; then when they found they could n't keep us any longer, they just meant to burn us up. That 's the principle they went on from the beginning."

I had already conversed with other citizens on the subject of the fire, some of whom maintained that it was never the design of the Confederate leaders to burn anything but the railroad bridges and public stores. But this man laughed at the idea.

" That 's what they pretend ; but I know better. What was the water stopped from the reservoirs for ? So that we should have none to put out the fire with ! "

" But they say the water was shut off in order to make repairs."

" It 's all a lie ! I tell ye, stranger, it was the intention to burn Richmond, and it 's a miracle that any part of it was saved. As luck would have it, there was no wind to spread the fire ; then the Federals came in, let on the water, and went to work with the engines, and put it out."

" Why did n't the citizens do that ? "

" I don't know. Everybody was paralyzed. It was a perfect panic. The Yankees coming ! the city burning ! our army on a retreat ! — you 've no idea of what it was. Nobody seemed to know what to do. God save us from another such time ! It was bad enough Sunday. If the world had been coming to an end, there could n't have been more fright and confusion. I was watchman on this railroad bridge, — when there was a bridge here. I was off duty at midnight, and I went home and went to bed. But along towards morning my daughter woke me. ' Father,' says she, ' the city 's afire ! ' I knew right away what was the matter. The night was all lit up, and I could hear the roar of something besides the river. I run out and started for the bridge, but I 'd got quite near enough, when the ammunition in the tobacco-warehouses begun to go off. Crack ! — crack ! — crack, crack, crack ! One piece of shell whirred past my head like a pa'tridge. I did n't want to hear another. I put home and went to getting my truck together, such as I could tote, ready to leave if my house went."

Subsequently I conversed with citizens of every grade upon this exciting topic, and found opinions regarding it as various as the political views of their authors. Those aristocrats who went in for the war but kept out of the fight, and who favored the Davis government because it favored them, had no word of censure for the incendiaries.

"The burning of the city was purely accidental," one blandly informed me.

"No considerable portion of it would have been destroyed if it had n't been for private marauding parties," said another. "The city was full of such desperate characters. They set fires for the purpose of plundering. It was they, and nobody else, who shut off the water from the reservoirs."

The laboring class, on the other hand, generally denounced the Confederate leaders as the sole authors of the calamity. It was true that desperadoes aided in the work, but it was after the fugitive government had set them the example.

Here is the opinion of a Confederate officer, Colonel D——, whom I saw daily at the table of the hotel, and with whom I had many interesting conversations.

"It is not fair to lay the whole blame on the Confederate government, although, Heaven knows, it was bad enough to do anything! The plan of burning the city had been discussed beforehand: Lee and the more humane of his officers opposed it; Early and others favored it; and Breckinridge took the responsibility of putting it into execution."

Amid all these conflicting opinions there was one thing certain — the fact of the fire; although, had it not been written out there before our eyes in black characters and lines of desolation, I should have expected to hear some unblushing apologist of the Davis despotism deny even that.

And, whoever may have been personally responsible for the crime, there is also a truth concerning it which I hold to be undeniable. Like the assassination of Lincoln, like the systematic murder of Union prisoners at Andersonville and elsewhere, — like these and countless other barbarous acts which have branded the Rebel cause with infamy, — this too was inspired by the spirit of slavery, and performed in the interest of slavery. That spirit, destructive of liberty and law, and self-destructive at last, was the father of the rebellion and of all the worst crimes of its adherents. As I walked among the ruins, pondering these thoughts, I must own that my heart swelled with pride when I remembered how the fire was extinguished. It was by no mere chance that the panic-stricken inhabitants were found powerless to save their own city. That task was reserved for the Union army, that a great truth might be symbolized. The war, on the part of the North, was waged neither for ambition nor revenge; its design was not destructive, but conservative. Through all our cloudy mistakes and misdeeds shone the spirit of Liberty; and the work she gave us to do was to quench the national flames which anarchy had kindled, and to save a rebellious people from the consequences of their own folly.

Richmond had already one terrible reminiscence of a fire. On the night of the 26th of December, 1811, its theatre was burned, with an appalling catastrophe: upward of seventy spectators, including the Governor of the State, perishing in the flames. The fire of the 3d of April, 1865, will be as long remembered.

The work of rebuilding the burnt district had commenced, and was progressing in places quite vigorously. Here I had the satisfaction of seeing the negroes, who " would not work," actually at their tasks. Here, as everywhere else in Richmond, and indeed in every part of Virginia I visited, colored laborers were largely in the majority. They drove the teams, made the mortar, carried the hods, excavated the old cellars or dug new ones, and, sitting down amid the ruins, broke the mortar from the old bricks and put them up in neat piles ready for use. There were also colored masons and carpenters employed on the new buildings. I could not see but that these people worked just as industriously as the white laborers. And yet, with this scene before our very eyes, I was once more informed by a cynical citizen that the negro, now that he was free, would rob, steal, or starve, before he would work.

I conversed with one of the laborers going home to his dinner. He was a stalwart young black, twenty-one years old, married, and the father of two children. He was earning a dollar and a half a day.

"Can you manage to live on that, and support your family?"

"It's right hard, these times, — everything costs so high. I have to pay fifteen dollars a month rent, and only two little rooms. But my wife takes in washing and goes out to work; and so we get along."

"But," said I, "were not your people better off in slavery?"

"Oh no, sir!" he replied, with a bright smile. "We're a heap better off now. We haven't got our rights yet, but I expect we're go'n' to have 'em soon."

"What rights?"

"I don't know, sir. But I reckon government will do something for us. My master has had me ever since I was seven years old, and never give me nothing. I worked for him twelve years, and I think something is due me."

He was waiting to see what the government would do for his people. He rather expected the lands of their Rebel masters would be given them, insisting that they ought to have some reward for all their years of unrequited toil. Of course I endeavored to dissuade him from cherishing any such hope.

"What you ask for may be nothing but justice; but we must not expect justice even in this world. We must be thankful for what we can get. You have your freedom, and you ought to consider yourself lucky."

His features shone with satisfaction as he replied, —

"That ought to be enough, if we don't get no mo'e. We're men now, but when our masters had us we was only change in their pockets."

Unlike what I saw in Chambersburg, the new blocks springing up in the burnt district did not promise to be an improvement on the old ones. Everywhere were visible the **results**

of want of capital and of the hurry of rebuilding. The thin
ness of the walls was alarming; and I was not surprised to
learn that some of them had recently been blown down on a
windy night. Heaven save our country, thought I, from such
hasty and imperfect reconstruction !

CHAPTER XX.

LIBBY, CASTLE THUNDER, AND BELLE ISLE.

STROLLING along a street near the river, below the burnt district, I looked up from the dirty pavements, and from the little ink-colored stream creeping along the gutter, (for Richmond abounds in these villanous rills,) and saw before me a sign nailed to the corner of a large, gloomy brick building, and bearing in great black letters the inscription, —

LIBBY PRISON.

Passing the sentinel at the door, I entered. The ground-floor was partitioned off into offices and store-rooms, and presented few objects of interest. A large cellar room below, paved with cobble-stones, was used as a cook-house by our soldiers then occupying the building. Adjoining this, but separated from it by a wall, was the cellar which is said to have been mined for the purpose of blowing up Libby with its inmates, in case the city had at one time been taken.

Ascending a flight of stairs from the ground-floor, I found myself in a single, large, oblong, whitewashed, barren room. Two rows of stout wooden posts supported the ceiling. The windows were iron-grated, those of the front looking out upon the street, and those of the rear commanding a view of the canal close by, the river just beyond it, and the opposite shore.

There was an immense garret above, likewise embracing the entire area of the floor. These were the prison-rooms of the infamous Libby. I found them occupied by a regiment of colored troops, some sitting in Turkish fashion on the floor, (for there was not a stool or bench,) some resting their backs against the posts or whitewashed walls, and others lying at length on the hard planks, with their heads pillowed on their knapsacks.

But the comfortable colored regiment faded from sight as I ascended and descended the stairs, and walked from end to end of the dreary chambers. A far different picture rose before me, — the diseased and haggard men crowded together there, dragging out their weary days, deeming themselves oftentimes forgotten by their country and their friends, — men who mounted those dungeon-stairs, not as I mounted them, but to enter a den of misery, starvation, and death.

On the opposite side of the same street, a little farther up, was Castle Thunder, — a very commonplace brick block, considering its formidable name. It was still used as a prison; but it had passed into the hands of the United States military authorities. At the iron-barred windows of the lower story, and behind the wooden-barred windows above, could be seen the faces of soldiers and citizens imprisoned for various offences.

Belle Island I had already seen from the heights of Richmond, — a pleasant hill rising out of the river above the town, near the farther shore. The river itself is very beautiful there, with its many green islets, its tumbling rapids sweeping down among rocks and foaming over ledges, and its side-dams thrown out like arms to draw the waters into their tranquil embrace. My eye, ranging over this scene, rested on that fair hill; and I thought that, surely, no pleasanter or more healthful spot could have been selected for an encampment of prisoners. But it is unsafe to trust the enchantment of distance; and after seeing Libby and Castle Thunder, I set out to visit Belle Island.

I crossed over to Manchester by a bridge which had been constructed since the fire. As both the Richmond and Danville, and the Richmond and Petersburg railroad bridges were destroyed, an extraordinary amount of business and travel was thrown upon this bridge. It was shaken with omnibuses and freight-wagons, and enveloped in clouds of dust. Loads of cotton and tobacco, the former in bales, the latter in hogsheads, were coming into the city, and throngs of pedestrians were passing to and fro. Among these I noticed a number of negroes with little bundles on their backs. One of them, a very old man, was leaning against the railing to rest.

" Well, uncle, how are you getting along ? "

" Tolerable, mahster ; only tolerable."   And he lifted his tattered cap from his white old head with a grace of politeness which a courtier might have envied.

" Where are you going ? "

" I 's go'n' to Richmond, mahster."

" What do you expect to do in Richmond ? "

" I don't know right well.   I thought I could n't be no wus off than whar I was ; and I had n't no place to go."

" How so, uncle ? "

" You see, mahster, thar a'n't no chance fo' people o' my color in the country I come from."

" Where is that ? "

" Dinwiddie County."

" You have walked all the way from Dinwiddie County ? "

" Yes, mahster ; I 'se walked over fo'ty mile.   But I don't mind that."

" You 're very old, uncle."

" Yes, I 've a right good age, mahster.   It 's hard fo' a man o' my years to be turned out of his home.   I don't know what I shall do ; but I reckon the Lord will take keer of me."

The tone of patience and cheerfulness in which he spoke was very touching.   I leaned on the bridge beside him, and drew out from him by degrees his story.   His late master refused to give wages to the freedmen on his lands, and the result was that all the able-bodied men and women left him. Enraged at this, he had sworn that the rest should go too, and had accordingly driven off the aged and the sick, this old man among them.

" He said he 'd no use fo' old wore-out niggers.   I knowed I was old and wore-out, but I growed so in his service.   I served him and his father befo'e nigh on to sixty year ; and he never give me a dollar.   He 's had my life, and now I 'm old and wore-out I must leave.   It 's right hard, mahster ! "

" Not all the planters in your county are like him, I hope ? "

" Some of 'em is very good to their people, I believe. But none of 'em is will'n' to pay wages a man can live by. Them that pays at all, offers only five dollars a month, and we must pay fo' ou' own clothes and doctor's bills, and suppo't ou' families.'

" It seems you were better off when in slavery," I suggested.

" I don't say that, mahster. I 'd sooner be as I is to-day." And cheerfully shouldering his bundle, the old African tramped on towards Richmond. What was to become of him there ?

I kept on to Manchester, passed the great humming mills by the river-side, and turning to the right, up the Danville railroad, reached Belle Island bridge after a brisk fifteen minutes' walk. Crossing over, I entered the yard of a nail-factory, where some men were breaking up heavy old iron, cannons, mortars, and car-wheels, by means of a four-hundred pound shot dropped from a derrick forty feet high. Beyond the factory rose the pleasant hill I had viewed from the city. I climbed its southern side, and found myself in the midst of a scene not less fair than I had anticipated. Behind me was a cornfield, covering the summit; below rushed the river among its green and rocky islands ; while Richmond rose beyond, picturesquely beautiful on its hills, and rosy in the flush of sunset.

But where had been the prisoners' camp ? I saw no trace of it on that slope. Alas, that slope was never trodden by their feet, and its air they never breathed. At the foot of it is a flat, spreading out into the stream, and almost level with it at high water. Already the night-fog was beginning to creep over it. This flat, which was described to me as a marsh in the rainy season, and covered with snow and slush and ice in winter, was the " Belle Isle " of our prisoners. Yet they were not allowed the range even of that. A trench and embankment enclosing an oblong space of less than six acres formed the dead-line which it was fatal to pass. Within this as many as twelve thousand men were at times crowded, with no shelter but a few tattered tents.

As I was examining the spot, a throng of begrimed laborers

crossed the flat, carrying oars, and embarking in boats on the low shore looking towards the city.   They were workmen from the nail-factory returning to their homes.   One of them, passing alone after his companions, stopped to talk with me at the dead-line, and afterwards offered me a place in his boat. It was a leaky little skiff: I perched myself upon a seat in the bow ; and he, standing in the stern, propelled it across with a pole.

" Where were the dead buried ? " I asked.

" The dead Yankees ?   They buried a good many thar in the sand-bar.   But they might about as well have flung 'em into the river.   A freshet washed out a hundred and twenty bodies at one time."

" Did you see the prisoners when they were here ? "

" I was n't on the Island.   But from Richmond anybody could see their tents hyer, and see them walking around.   I was away most of the time."

" In the army ? "

" Yes, sir ; I was in the army.   I enlisted fo' three months, and they kept me in fou' years," he said, as men speak of deep and unforgiven wrongs.   " The wa' was the cruelest thing, and the wust thing fo' the South that could have been.   What do you think they 'll do with Jeff Davis ? "

" I don't know," I replied ; " what do you think ? "

" I know what I 'd like to do with him: I 'd hang him as quick as I would a mad dog !   Him and about fo'ty others : old Buchanan along with 'em."

" Why, what has Buchanan done ? "

" He was in cohoot with 'em, and as bad as the baddest. If we had had an honest President in his place, thar never 'd have been wa'."

From the day I entered Virginia it was a matter of continual astonishment to me to hear the common people express views similar to those, and denounce the Davis despotism. They were all the more bitter against it because it had deceived them with lies and false promises so long.   Throughout the loyal North, the feeling against the secession leaders was naturally strong; but it was mild as candle-light compared with the fierce furnace-heat of hatred which I found kindled in many a Southern breast.

The passage of the river was delightful, in the fading sunset light. On a bluff opposite Belle Island was Hollywood, the fashionable cemetery of Richmond, green-wooded, and beautiful at that hour in its cool and tranquil tints. As we glided down the river, and I took my last view of the Island, I thought how often our sick and weary soldiers there must have cast longing eyes across at that lovely hill, and wished themselves quietly laid away in its still shades. Nor could I help thinking of the good people of Richmond, the Christian citizens of Richmond, taking their pleasant walks and drives to that verdant height, and looking down on the camp of prisoners dying from exposure and starvation under their very eyes. How did these good people, these Christian citizens, feel about it, I wonder?

Avoiding the currents sweeping towards the Falls, my man pushed into the smooth waters of a dam that fed a race, and landed me close under the walls of his own house.

" This yer is Brown's Island," he told me. " You 've heerd of the laboratory, whar they made ammunition fo' the army?" He showed me the deserted buildings, and described an explosion which took place there, blowing up the works, and killing, scalding, and maiming many of the operatives.

Passing over a bridge to the main land, and crossing the canal which winds along the river-bank, I was hastening towards the city, when I met, emerging from the sombre ruins of the burnt district, a man who resembled more a wild creature than a human being. His hands, arms, and face were blackened with cinders, his clothes hung upon him in tatters, and the expression of his countenance was fierce and haggard. He looked so much like a brigand that I was not a little startled when, with a sweeping gesture of his long lean arm and claw-like fingers, he clutched my shoulder.

" Come back with me," said he, " and I 'll tell ye all about it; I 'll tell ye all about it, stranger."

" About what ? "

" The explosion, — the explosion of the laboratory thar ! "

Dragging me towards Brown's Island with one hand, and gesticulating violently with the other, he proceeded to jabber incoherently about that dire event.

" Wait, wait," said he, " till I tell you ! " — like the Ancient Mariner with skinny hand holding his unwilling auditor. " My daughter was work'n' thar at the time ; and she was blowed all to pieces ! all to pieces ! My God, my God, it was horrible ! Come to my house, and you shall see her ; if you don't believe me, you shall see her ! Blowed all to pieces, all to pieces, my God ! "

His house was close by, and the daughter, who was " blowed all to pieces," was to be seen standing miraculously at the door, in a remarkable state of preservation, considering the circumstances. She seemed to be looking anxiously at the old man and the stranger he was bringing home with him. She came to the wicket to meet us ; and then I saw that her hands and face were covered with cruel scars.

" Look ! " said he, clutching her with one hand, while he still held me with the other. " All to pieces, as I told you ! "

" Don't, don't, pa ! " said the girl, coaxingly. " You must n't mind him," she whispered to me. " He is a little out of his head. Oh, pa ! don't act so ! "

" He has been telling me how you were blown up in the laboratory. You must have suffered fearfully from those wounds ! "

" Oh, yes ; there was five weeks nobody thought I would live. But I did n't mind it," she added with a smile, " for it was in a good cause."

" A good cause ! " almost shrieked the old man ; and he burst forth with a stream of execrations against the Confederate government which made my blood chill.

But the daughter smilingly repeated, " It was a good cause, and I don't regret it. You must n't mind what he says."

I helped her get him inside the wicket, and made my escape, wondering, as I left them, which was the more insane of the two.

But she was not insane; she was a woman. A man may be reasoned and beaten out of a false opinion, but a woman never. She will not yield to logic, not even to the logic of events. Thus it happens that, while the male secessionists at the South have frankly given up their cause, the female secessionists still cling to it with provoking tenacity. To appeal to their intelligence is idle; but they are vulnerable on the side of the sentiments; and many a one has been authentically converted from the heresy of state rights by some handsome Federal officer, who judiciously mingled love with loyalty in his speech, and pleaded for the union of hands as well as the union of States.

DISTRIBUTING RATIONS.

CHAPTER XXI.

FEEDING THE DESTITUTE.

As I was passing Castle Thunder, I observed, besieging the doors of the United States Commissary, on the opposite side of the street, a hungry-looking, haggard crowd, — sickly-faced women, jaundiced old men, and children in rags; with here and there a seedy gentleman who had seen better days, or a stately female in faded apparel, which, like her refined manners, betrayed the aristocratic lady whom the war had reduced to want.

These were the destitute of the city, thronging to receive alms from the government. The regular rations, issued at a counter to which each was admitted in his or her turn, consisted of salt-fish and hard-tack ; but I noticed that to some tea and sugar were dealt out. All were provided with tickets previously issued to them by the Relief Commission. One tall, sallow woman requested me to read her ticket, and tell her if it was a " No. 2."

" They told me it was, whar I got it, but I like to be shore."

I assured her that it was truly a " No. 2," and asked why it was preferable to another.

" This is the kind they ishy to sick folks ; it allows tea and sugar," she replied, wrapping it around her skinny finger.

Colored people were not permitted to draw " destitute rations " for themselves at the same place with the whites. There were a good many colored servants in the crowd, however, drawing for their mistresses, who remained at home, too ill or too proud to come in person and present their tickets.

11

At the place where " destitute rations " were issued to the blacks, business appeared very dull. I inquired the reason of it, and learned this astonishing fact.

The colored population crowded into Richmond at that time equalled the white population; being estimated by some as high as twenty-five thousand. Of the whites, over TWO THOUSAND were at that time receiving support from the government. The number of blacks receiving such support was less than two hundred.

How is this discrepancy to be accounted for?

Of the freedmen's willingness to work under right conditions there can be no question. It is true, they do not show a disposition to continue to serve their former masters for nothing, or at starvation prices. And many of them had a notion that lands were to be given them ; for lands had been promised them. At the same time, where they have a show of a chance for themselves, they generally go to work, and manifest a commendable pride in supporting themselves and their families. Until he does that, the negro does not consider that he is fully free. He has no prejudice against labor, as so many of the whites have. We must give slavery the credit of having done thus much for him : it has bred him up to habits of temperance and industry. Notwithstanding the example of the superior race, which he naturally emulates, he has not yet taken to drink ; and his industry, instead of being checked, has received an impulse by emancipation. Now that he has inducements to exert himself, he proceeds to his task with an alacrity which he never showed when driven to it by the whip.

Another thing must be taken into account. His feeling for those who have liberated him is that of unbounded gratitude. He is ashamed to ask alms of the government which has already done so much for him. No case was known in Richmond of his obtaining destitute rations under false pretences ; but in many instances, as I learned, he had preferred to suffer want rather than apply for aid.

The reverse of all this may be said of a large class of whites.

Many, despising labor, would not work if they could. Others, reared amid the influences of wealth, which had now been stripped from them, could not work if they would. Towards the United States Government they entertained no such feeling of gratitude as animated the freedmen. On the contrary, they seemed to think that they were entitled to support from it during the remainder of their lives.

" You ought to do something for us, for you 've took away our niggers," whined a well-dressed woman one day in my hearing. To the force of the objection, that the South owed the loss of its slaves to its own folly, she appeared singularly insensible ; and she showed marked resentment because nothing was done for her, although obliged to confess that she owned the house she lived in, and another for which two colored families were paying rent.

I was sitting in one of the tents of the Relief Commission one morning, when a woman came to complain that a ticket issued to her there had drawn but fifteen rations, instead of twenty-one, as she had expected.

" I did n't think it was you all's fault," she said, with an apologetic grimace ; " but I knowed I 'd been powerfully cheated."

This was the spirit manifested by very many, both of the rich and the poor. They felt that they had a sacred right to prey upon the government, and any curtailment of that privilege they regarded as a wrong and a fraud. So notorious was their rapacity, that they were satirically represented as saying to the government, —

" We have done our best to break you up, and now we are doing our best to eat you up."

Where such a spirit existed, it was not possible to prevent hundreds from obtaining government aid who were not entitled to it. It was the design of the Relief Commission to feed only indigent women and children. No rations were issued by the Commissary except to those presenting tickets ; and tickets were issued for the benefit only of those whose destitute condition was attested by certificates signed by a clergyman or phy-

sician.[1] To secure these certificates, however, was not difficult, even for those who stood in no need of government
charity. Clergymen and physicians were not all honest.
Many of them believed with the people that the government
was a fit object for good secessionists to prey upon. Some
were faithful in the performance of their duty; but if one
physician refused to sign a false statement, it was easy to dismiss him, and call in another less scrupulous.

"I have just exposed two spurious cases of destitution,"
said an officer of the Relief Commission, one day as I entered his tent. "Mrs. A——, on Fourth Street, has been
doing a thriving business all summer, by selling the rations
she has drawn for a fictitious family. Mrs. B—— has been
getting support for herself, and two sick daughters, that turn
out to be two great lazy sons, who take her hard-tack and salt-
fish, and exchange them for whiskey, get drunk every night,
and lie abed till noon every day."

"What do you do with such cases?"

"Cut them off: that is all we can do. This whole business
of feeding the poor of Richmond," he added, "is a humbug.
Richmond is a wealthy city still; it is very well able to take
care of its own poor, and should be taxed for the purpose."
I found this to be the opinion of many intelligent unbiased
observers.

Besides the Relief Commission, and the Freedmen's Commission, both maintained by the government, I found an
agency of the American Union Commission established in
Richmond. This Commission, supported by private benevolence, was organized for the purpose of aiding the people of

---

[1] Form of certificate: —

RICHMOND, VA.,..............., 1865.

I CERTIFY, on honor, that I am well acquainted with Mrs. Jane Smith, and that she
is the owner of no real estate or personal property, or effects of any kind; and that she
has no male member of her family who is the owner of real estate or personal property
or effects of any kind, upon which there can be realized sufficient money for the maintenance of her family; and that she has no means of support, and is a proper object
of charity; and that her family consists of four females and five children.

Given under my hand, this 17th day of September, 1865.

JEFFERSON JONES, M. D.

the South, " in the restoration of their civil and social condition, upon the basis of industry, education, freedom, and Christian morality." In Richmond, it was doing a useful work. To the small farmers about the city it issued ploughs, spades, shovels, and other much needed implements, — for the war had beaten pitchforks into bayonets, and cast ploughshares into cannon. Earlier in the season it had distributed many thousand papers of garden-seeds to applicants from all parts of the State, — a still greater benefit to the impoverished people, with whom it was a common saying, that " good seed ran out under the Confederacy." It had established a free school for poor whites. I also found Mr. C. the Commission's Richmond agent, indefatigable in assisting other associations in the establishment of schools for the Freedmen.

The Union Commission performed likewise an indispensable part in feeding the poor. Those clergymen and physicians who were so prompt to grant certificates to secessionists not entitled to them, were equally prompt to refuse them to persons known as entertaining Union sentiments. To the few genuine Union people of Richmond, therefore, the Commission came, and was welcomed as an angel of mercy. But it did not confine its favors to them ; having divided the city into twelve districts, and appointed inspectors for each, it extended its aid to such of the needy as the Relief Commission had been unable to reach.

CHAPTER XXII.

THE UNION MEN OF RICHMOND.

AT the tent of the Union Commission, pitched near a fountain on Capitol Square, I met a quiet little man in laborer's clothes, whom the agent introduced to me as "Mr. H——," adding, "There were two votes cast against the ordinance of secession in this city: one of those votes was cast by Mr. H——. He is one of the twenty-one Union men of Richmond."

He looked to be near fifty years of age; but he told me he was only thirty-two. "I've been through such things as make a man look old!" He showed me his gray hair, which he said was raven black, without a silver streak, before the war.

"I was four times taken to the conscript camp, but never sent off to fight. I worked in a foundery, and my employer got out exemption papers for me. The Confederates, when they wanted more men, would declare any time that all the exemption papers then out were void, and go to picking us up in the street and sending us off to camp before we knew it. Some would buy themselves off, and a few would get off as I did, — because they could do work nobody else could do."

He was a man of intuitive ideas and originality of character. Although bred up under the influence of the peculiar institution, poor, and uneducated, he had early formed clear and strong convictions on the subject of slavery. "I was an Abolitionist before I ever heard the word abolitionist." He believed in true religion, but not in the religion of traitors.

"I never hesitated to tell 'em what I thought. 'God has no more to do with you all,' says I, 'than he has with last year's rain. I'd as lieves go to a gambling-house, as to go and hear a minister pray that God would drive back the armies of the North. You are on your knees mocking at God, and He laughs at you!' Events proved that what I said was true. After every Fast, the Rebels lost some important point. There was a Fast-day just before Fort Donelson; another before New Orleans was taken; another before Gettysburg and Vicksburg; another before Atlanta fell; and another before the evacuation of Richmond. That was the way God answered their prayers."

He corroborated the worst accounts I had heard concerning the state of society in Richmond during the war.

"It seemed as though there was nothing but thieving and robbery going on. The worst robbers were Hood's men, set to guard the city. They'd halt a man, and shoot him right down if he would n't stop. They'd ask a man the time, and snatch his watch. They went to steal some chickens of a man I knew, and as he tried to prevent them, they killed him. At last the women got to stealing. We had an insurrection of women here, you know. I never saw such a sight. They looked like flocks of old buzzards, picked geese, and cranes; dressed in all sorts of odd rigs; armed with hatchets, knives, axes, — anything they could lay their hands on. They collected together on the Square, and Governor Letcher made 'em a speech from the Monument. They hooted at him. Then Jeff Davis made a speech; they hooted at him too; they did n't want speeches, they said; they wanted bread. Then they begun to plunder the stores. They'd just go in and carry off what they pleased. I saw three women put a bag of potatoes, and a barrel of flour, and a firkin of butter in a dray; then they ordered the darkey to drive off, with two women for a guard."

Another of the faithful twenty-one was Mr. L———, whom I found at a restaurant kept by him near the old market. It was he who carried off Col. Dahlgren's body, after it had been buried by the Rebels at Oak Wood.

"I found a negro who knew the spot, and hired him to go with me one dark night, and dig up the body. We carried it to Mr. Rowlett's house [Mr. Rowlett was another of the faithful], and afterwards took it through the Confederate lines, in broad daylight, hid under a load of peach-trees, and buried it in a metallic case. It lay there until after the evacuation, when it was dug up and sent home to Admiral Dahlgren's family."

Mr. L—— devoted much of his time and means during the war to feeding Union prisoners, and helping Union men through the lines. "I was usually at work that way all night; so the next day I'd be looking sick and sleepy; and that way, — with a little money to bribe the doctors, — I kept out of the Rebel army." In January, 1865, he was arrested for sending information through the lines to General Butler, and lay in prison until the evacuation.

One of the most interesting evenings in my Richmond experience I passed at the house of Mr. W——, on Twenty-fifth Street. A Northern man by birth and education, he had remained true to his nativity at a time when so many from the Free States living at the South had proved renegades and apostates. Arrested early in the war for "disloyalty," he had suffered six months in Salisbury Prison because he would not take the oath of allegiance to the Confederate Government.

"I could have got my liberty any day by taking that oath. But I never would, and never did. As good and true men as ever trod the earth died there because they would not take it. Mr. Buck, of Kentucky, was one. Almost his last words were, 'Tell my wife I would be glad to go home, but I'd rather die here than take an oath that will perjure my soul.' He was happy; he died. Dying was not the worst part of it, by any means; our sufferings every day were worse than death."

Liberated at last, through the intercession of his wife, Mr. W—— came home, and devoted himself to feeding and rescuing Union prisoners, and to serving his country in other perilous ways.

He corroborated what had been told me with regard to the number of Union men in Richmond.

" You will find men enough now, who claim to have been Union men from the first. But of those whose loyalty stood the test of persecution in every shape, there are just twenty-one, — no more, and no less. I 've watched them all through, and if there 's a Union man I don't know, I should like to see him. Those men of influence, who opposed secession in the beginning, and afterwards voted for it, but who pretend now to have been in favor of the Union all the while, were the most mischievous traitors of all, for they carried the lukewarm with them."

There were Union women, however, who worked and suffered as heroically for the cause as the men. " One lady was nine months in prison here for sending information through the lines to our armies. She was very ill at one time, and wished to see a minister. They sent her Jeff Davis's minister. ' Miserable wretch ! ' said he, ' I suppose I must pray with you, but I don't see how I can ! ' "

" When my husband was in prison," said Mrs. W——, " we suffered greatly for the necessaries of life. We had a little money in the savings-bank ; and he sent us an order for it : ' Please pay to my little son,' and so forth. Payment was refused, because he had not taken the oath of allegiance, and the money was confiscated."

Of the labors, perils, sacrifices, and anxieties which the Union men of Richmond underwent, in giving secret aid to the good cause, no adequate account has ever been published, nor ever will be published. " I did no other business at the time. I gave my whole life to it, and all my means. I nearly went crazy. Besides Libby and Castle Thunder, there were several smaller prisons in Richmond. There was one next door to us here. There was another on the opposite side, a little farther up the street. We had the prisoners under our very eyes, and could n't help doing something for them. We could see their haggard faces and imploring eyes looking out at us from the windows, — or from behind the windows, — for it was n't safe for them to come too near. One day I saw one approach a little nearer than usual, — his head was perhaps a foot from the window, — when the guard deliberately put up his gun and blew out his brains. He was immediately carried away in a cart; and as a little red stream trickled along the ground, a boy ran after it, shouting, ' Thar 's some Yankee blood; bring a cup and ketch it ! ' The papers next day boasted that in an hour the dead man was under the sod."

A fund was secretly collected for the benefit of the prisoners. One of the first contributors towards it was an illiterate poor man named White. He put in five dollars. Mr. W—— told him that was too much for a man in his circumstances. " No," said White, " I 's got two fives, and I reckon the least I can do is to go halves." From that small beginning the fund grew to the handsome sum of thirteen thousand dollars.

White, concealing his Union sentiments from the authorities, got permission to sell milk and other things to the prisoners, which they paid for often with money he smuggled in to them. With small bribes he managed to secure the goodwill of the guard. He played his part admirably, higgling with his customers, and complaining of hard times and small profits, while he gave them milk and money, and carried letters for them. One day a prisoner was observed to slip something into his can. To divert suspicion, White pretended great surprise, and, appearing to fish out a dime, held it up to the light as if to assure himself that it was real. " I 's durned if there a'n't one honest Yankee ! " said he, with a grin of satisfaction.

Mrs. W—— obtained permission to send some books to the prisoners ; very few reached them, however, — the greater part being appropriated by the Rebels. Donations of clothing and other necessaries met with a similar fate. In this state of things, White's ancient mule-cart and honest face proved invaluable. He carried a pass-book, in which exchanged prisoners were credited with sums subscribed for the benefit of their late companions. Many of these subscriptions were purely fictitious, — the money coming from the Union-men's fund. On the strength of one fabulous contribution, set down at fifty dollars, he had given the prisoners over a hundred dollars' worth of provisions, when a Rebel surgeon stopped him.

" Have n't you paid up that everlasting fifty dollars yet ? "

" Doctor," said White, producing his pass-book, " I 's an honest man, I is ; and if you say I can't put in no more on this yer score, you jest write your name hyer."

The surgeon declining to assume the responsibility, White managed to take in to the prisoners, on the same imaginary account, milk and eggs to the amount of fifty dollars more.

" I told you there were only twenty-one Union men in Richmond," said Mr. W——. " I meant *white* Union men. Some of the colored people were as ready to give their means and risk their lives for the cause as anybody. One poor negro woman, who did washing for Confederate officers, spent her earnings to buy flour and bake bread, which she got in to the prisoners through a hole under the jail-yard fence ; knowing all the while she 'd be shot, if caught at it."

Mr. W—— assisted over twenty Union prisoners to escape. Among other adventures, he related to me the following : —

" From our windows we could look right over into the prison-yard adjoining us here. Every day we could see the dead carried out. In the evening they carried out those who had died since morning, and every morning they carried out those that had died over night. Once we counted seventeen dead men lying together in the yard, all stripped of their clothes, ready for burial ; so terrible was the mortality in these prisons. The dead-house was in a corner of the yard. A negro woman occupied another house outside of the guard-line, and close to my garden fence."

He took me to visit the premises. We entered by a heavy wooden gate from the street, and stood within the silent enclosure. It was a clear, beautiful evening, and the moon light lay white and peaceful upon the gable of the ware house that had served as a prison, upon the old buildings and fences, and upon the ground the weary feet of the sick prisoners had trodden, and where the outstretched corpses had lain.

"Every day some of the prisoners would be marched down to the medical department, a few blocks below, to be examined. A colored girl who lived with us, used to go out with bread hid under her apron, and slip it into their hands, if she had a chance, as she met them coming back. One morning she brought home a note, which one of them, Capt. ——, had given her. It was a letter of thanks ' to his unknown bene-factors.' Miss H——, who was visiting us at the time, pro-posed to answer it. It was much less dangerous for her to do so, than it would have been for me, for I was a suspected man ; I had already been six months in a Rebel prison. But if she was discovered writing to a Yankee, her family would be prepared to express great surprise and indignation at the circumstance, and denounce it as a ' love affair.' " (The H——s are one of the Union families of Richmond ; and Miss H—— was a young girl of nerve and spirit.)

" In this way we got into communication with the Captain. It was n't long, of course, before he made proposals to Miss H—— ; not of the usual sort, however, but of a kind we expected. He and another of the prisoners, a surgeon, had resolved to attempt an escape, and they wanted our assist-ance. After several notes on the subject had passed, — some through the hands of the colored girl, some through a crack in the fence, — everything was arranged for a certain evening.

" Citizens' clothes were all ready for them ; and I obtained a promise from G——, a good Union man, to conceal them in his house until they could be got away. To avoid the very thing that happened, he was not to tell his wife ; but she sus-pected mischief, — for it 's hard for a man to hide what he feels, when he knows his life is at stake, — and she gave him no peace until he let her into the secret. She declared that the men should never be brought into their house.

" ' We 've just got shet of one boarder,' says she, meaning a prisoner they had harbored, ' and I never 'll have another.'

" I could n't blame her much ; for we were trifling with our lives. But G—— felt terribly about it. He came down to let me know. It was the very evening the men were to come out, and too late to get word to them. If their plans succeeded, they would be sure to come out; and what was to be done with them? They would not be safe with me an hour. My house would be the first one searched. G—— went off, for he could do nothing. Then, as it grew dark, we were expecting them every moment. There was nobody here but Miss H——, my wife, and myself. The colored girl was in the kitchen. It was dangerous to make any unusual movements, for the Rebel guard in the street was marching past every three minutes, and looking in. We sat quietly talking on indifferent subjects, with such sensations inside as nobody knows anything about who has n't been through such a scene. My clothes were wet through with perspiration. Every time after the guard had passed, we held our breath, until — tramp, tramp ! — he came round again.

"At last in came the colored girl, rushing from the kitchen, in great fright, and gasped out in a hoarse whisper, — 'Lord Jesus, master ! two Yankees done come right into our backyard ! '

" ' We have nothing to do with the Yankees,' I said; 'go about your work, and let 'em alone.' And still we sat there, and talked, or pretended to read, while once more — tramp, tramp, tramp — the guard marched by the windows."

"But there was a guard inside the prison-yard; how then had the Yankees managed to get out? "

"I 'm coming to that now. I told you the dead were borne out every morning and evening. That evening there was an extra body. It was the Yankee Doctor. He had bribed the prisoners, who carried out the dead, to carry him out. The dead-house was outside of the guard. They laid him with the corpses, and returned to the prison. Poor fellows ! there were four of them ; they were sent to Andersonville for their share in the transaction, and there every one of them died.

" A little while after, as some prisoners were going in from the yard, they got into a fight near the door. The guard ran to interfere ; and the Captain, who was waiting for this very chance, — for the scuffle was got up by his friends ex pressly for his benefit, — darted into the negro woman's house, and ran up-stairs. From a window he jumped down into my garden. In the mean time the Doctor came to life, crawled out from among the dead men, pushed a board from the back side of the dead-house, climbed the fence, and joined his friend the Captain, under our kitchen windows.

" Not a move was made by any of us. We kept on chatting, yawning, or pretending to read the newspaper ; and all the while the guard in the street was going his rounds and peeping in. Everything — the freedom of these men, and my life — was hanging by a cobweb. One mistake, a single false step, would ruin us. But everything had been prearranged. They found the clothes ready for them, and we were waiting only to give them time to disguise themselves. So far, it could not be proved that I had anything to do with the business, but the time was coming for me to take it into my own hands.

" I showed you the alley running from the street to my back-yard, and now you 'll see why I took you around there. The Captain and the Doctor after getting on their disguise, were to keep watch by the corner of the house at the end of the alley, and wait for the signal, — a gentleman going out of the house with a lady on his arm and a white handkerchief in his hand. They were to come out of the alley immediately, and follow at a respectful distance.

" Having given them plenty of time, — not very many minutes, however, though they seemed hours to us, — Miss H—— put on her bonnet, and I took my hat ; I watched my opportunity, and just as the guard had passed, gave her my arm, and set out to escort her home. As we went out, I had occasion to use my handkerchief, which I flirted, and put back into my pocket. We did n't look behind us once, but walked on, never knowing whether our men were following or not, until, after we had passed several corners, Miss H—— ventured to peep over her shoulder. Sure enough, there were two men coming along after us.

" We walked past Jeff Davis's house, and stopped at her father's door. There I took leave of her, and walked on alone. I had made up my mind what to do. G—— having failed us, I must try R——; an odd old man, but true as steel. It was a long walk to his house, and it was late when I got there. I hid my men in a barn, and knocked at the door.

" ' Anything the matter ? ' says Mrs. R——, from the window.

" ' I want to speak with Mr. R—— a moment,' I said. I saw she was frightened, when she found out who I was; but she made haste to let me in. Serious as my business was, I could n't help laughing when I found R——. He sleeps on a mattress, his wife sleeps on feathers; and both occupy the same bed. They compromise their difference of taste in this way: they double up the feather-bed for Mrs. R——; that gives her a double portion, and makes room for R—— on the mattress. She sleeps on a mountain in the foreground; he, in the valley behind her.

" ' W——,' says he, looking up over the mountain, ' there 's mischief ahead ! You would n't be coming here at this hour if there was n't. Is it a Castle Thunder case ? '

" ' No,' I said, quietly as I could, for he was very much agitated.

" ' I 'm afraid of Castle Thunder ! ' says he. ' I 'm afraid of you ! If it is n't a Castle Thunder case, I demand to know what it is.'

" ' It 's a halter case,' I said. And then I told him. He got up and pulled on his clothes. I took out fifty dollars in Rebel money, and offered him, for the feeding of the men till they could be got away.

" ' You can't get any of that stuff on to me ! ' says he. ' I 'm afraid of it. We shall all lose our lives, this time, I 'm sure. Why did you bring 'em here ? '

" But though fully convinced he was to die for it, he finally consented to take in the fugitives. So I delivered them into his hands; but my work did n't end there. They were nine days at his house. Meantime, through secret sources, by means of bribes, I got passes to take them through the lines. These cost me a hundred dollars in greenbacks; then, when everything was ready, all passes were revoked, and they were good for nothing. Finally Dennis Shane took the job of running them through the lines for five hundred dollars in Rebel money.

"He got them safely through; and just a month from that time one of those men came back for me. General Butler sent him: he wanted to talk with me about affairs in Richmond. I went out with a party of seven; and when near Williamsburg we were all captured by a band of Confederate soldiers.

"I determined not to be taken back to Richmond and identified, if I could help it. I got down at a spring to drink, crawled along under the bank a little way, as fast as I could, then jumped up, and ran for my life. I was shot at, and chased; they put dogs on my track; I was four days and nights without food; but I escaped, while all the rest were carried back. After that I ran the lines to Butler whenever he wanted to see me, until it was n't safe for me to go back to Richmond, where my operations had become known.

"After the war was over, and our troops had possession," added Mr. W——, "then I came back, and saw what I had never expected to see in this world. I saw the very men who had robbed, persecuted, and imprisoned me, rewarded by our government. I came back to find that under the administration of our own generals, Ord and Patrick, it was in a man's favor to be known as a secessionist, and against him to be known as a Union man. The Union men were insulted and bullied by them, the colored people were treated worse under their rule than they had ever been by the Rebels themselves, and the secessionists were coaxed and petted. A Rebel could obtain from government whatever he asked for; but a Union man could obtain nothing. When we were feeding and flattering them at a rate that made every loyal man sick at heart, I sent a request in writing for a little hay for my horse. I got a refusal in writing: I could n't have any hay. At the same time the government was feeding in its stables thirty horses for General Lee and his staff."

A hundred similar instances of partiality shown to the Rebels by the Ord and Patrick administration were related to me by eye-witnesses; coupled with accounts of insults and outrages heaped upon loyal men and Freedmen. Happily Ord and Patrick and their pro-slavery rule had passed away; but there were still complaints that it was not the true Union men who had the ear of the government, but those whose unionism had been put on as a matter of policy and convenience. This was no fault of General Terry, although he was blamed for it. When I told him what I had heard, he said warmly, —

" Why don't these men come to me? They are the very men I wish to see."

" The truth is, General, they were snubbed so often by your predecessors that they have not the heart to come."

" But I have not snubbed them. I have not shown partiality to traitors. Everybody that knows me knows that I have no love for slavery or treason, and that every pulse of my heart throbs with sympathy for these men and the cause in which they have suffered."

One evening I met by appointment, at the tent of the Union Commission, a number of the dauntless twenty-one, and accompanied them to a meeting of the Union League. It was a beautiful night, and as we walked by the rainy fountain, under the still trees, one remarked, —

" Many an evening, when there was as pretty a moon as this, I have wished that I might die and be out of my misery. That was when I was in prison for being loyal to my country."

At the rooms of the League I was surrounded by these men, nearly every one of whom had been exiled or imprisoned for that cause. I witnessed the initiation of new-comers; but in the midst of the impressive solemnities I could not but reflect, " How faint a symbol is this of the *real League* to which the twenty-one were sworn in their hearts! To belong to this is now safe and easy enough; but to have been a true member of that, under the reign of terror, — how very different!"

12

CHAPTER XXIII.

MARKETS AND FARMING.

THE negro population of Richmond gives to its streets a peculiarly picturesque and animated appearance. Colored faces predominate; but of these not more than one in five or six shows unmixed African blood; and you are reminded less of an American city than of some town of Southern Europe. More than once I could have fancied myself in Naples, but that I looked in vain for the crowds of importunate beggars, and the dark-skinned lazzaroni lying all day in the sunshine on the street corners. I saw no cases of mendicancy among the colored people of Richmond, and very little idleness. The people found at work everywhere belonged to the despised race; while the frequenters of bar-rooms, and loungers on tavern-steps, were white of skin. To get drunk, especially, appeared to be a prerogative of the chivalry.

The mules and curious vehicles one sees add to the picturesqueness of the streets. The market-carts are characteristically droll. A little way off you might fancy them dogcarts. Under their little ribbed canvas covers are carried little jags of such produce as the proprietor may have to sell, — a few cabbages, a few pecks of sweet potatoes, a pair of live chickens, tied together by the legs; a goose or a duck in a box, its head sticking out; with perhaps a few eggs and eggplants. These little carts, drawn by a mule or the poorest of ponies, have been driven perhaps a dozen or fifteen miles, bringing to market loads, a dozen of which would scarcely equal what a New-York farmer, or a New-England market-gardener often heaps upon a single wagon.

In the markets, business is transacted on the same petty scale. You see a great number of dealers, and extraordinary throngs of purchasers, considering the little that appears to be sold. Not every producer has so much even as an antiquated mule-cart. Many come to market with what they can carry on their backs or in their hands. Yonder is an old negro with a turkey, which he has walked five miles to dispose of here. That woman with a basket of eggs, whose rags and sallow complexion show her to be one of the poor whites whom respectable colored people look down upon, has travelled, it may be, quite as far. Here comes a mulatto boy, with a string of rock-fish caught in the James. This old man has hard peaches in his bag; and that other woman contributes a box of wild grapes.

People of all colors and all classes surround the sheds or press in throngs through the passages between the stalls. The fine lady, followed by her servant bearing a basket, has but little money; and although she endeavors to make it go as far as possible, it must be a small family that can subsist until Monday upon what she carries away. There is little money to be seen anywhere; in which respect these scenes are very different from those witnessed during the last years of Confederate rule, when it was said that people went to market with baskets to carry their money, and wallets to bring home what it would buy. The markets are not kept open during the evening, and as the hour for closing them arrives, the bargaining and loud talking grow more and more vivacious, while prices decline. I remember one fellow who jumped upon his table, and made a speech, designed to attract the patronage of the freedmen.

"Walk up hyer, and buy cheap!" he shouted. "I don't say niggers; I say ladies and gentlemen. Niggers is played out; they 're colored people now, and as good as anybody."

The markets indicate the agricultural enterprise of a community. Yet, even after seeing those of Richmond, I was amazed at the petty and shiftless system of farming I witnessed around the city. I was told that it was not much better before the war. The thrifty vegetable gardens of the North, producing two or three crops a year; the long rows of hot-beds by the fences, starting cucumbers and supplying the market with greens sometimes before the snow is gone, — such things are scarcely known in the capital of Virginia. " We have lettuce but a month or two in the year," said a lady, who was surprised to learn how Northern gardeners managed to produce it in and out of season.

In one of my rides I passed the place of a Jersey farmer, about three miles from the city. It looked like an oasis in the desert. I took pains to make the proprietor's acquaintance, and learn his experience.

" I came here and bought in '59 one hundred and twenty-seven acres for four thousand dollars. The first thing I did was to build that barn. Everybody laughed at me. The most of the farms have no barns at all; and such a large one was a wonder, — it must have been built by a fool or a crazy man. This year I have that barn full to the rafters.

" I found the land worn out, like nearly all the land in the country. The way Virginia folks have spoilt their farms looks a good deal more like fools or crazy men than my barn. First, if there was timber, they burnt it off and put a good coat of ashes on the soil. Then they raised tobacco three or four years. Then corn, till the soil got run out and they could n't raise anything. Then they went to putting on guano, which was like giving rum to an exhausted man ; it just stimulated the soil till all the strength there was left was burnt out. That was the condition of my farm when I came here.

" The first thing I did, I went to hauling out manure from Richmond. I was laughed at for that too. The way people do here, they throw away their manure. They like to have their farm-yards high and dry ; so they place them on the side of a hill, where every rain washes them, and carries off into the streams the juices that ought to be saved for the land. They left their straws-tacks any number of years, then drew the straw out on the farms dry. I made my barn-yard in a hollow, and rotted the straw in it. Now I go to market every day with a big Jersey farm-wagon loaded down with stuff."

He had been getting rich, notwithstanding the war. I asked what labor he employed.

"Negro labor mostly. It was hard to get any other here. I did n't own slaves, but hired them of their masters. Only the poorest hands were usually hired out in that way; I could seldom get first-class hands; yet I always found that by kind treatment and encouragement I could make very good laborers of those I had. I get along still better with them now they are free."

"Do you use horses?"

"No; mules altogether. Two mules are equal to three horses. Mules are not subject to half the diseases horses are. They eat less, and wear twice as long."

I found farms of every description for sale, around Richmond. The best land on the James River Bottom could be bought at prices varying from forty to one hundred dollars an acre. I remember one very desirable estate, of eight hundred acres, lying on the river, three miles from the city, which was offered for sixty dollars. There were good buildings on it; and the owner was making fences of old telegraph wire, to replace those destroyed during the war.

CHAPTER XXIV.

IN AND AROUND RICHMOND.

IF temples are a token of godliness, Richmond should be a holy city. It has great pride in its churches; two of which are noteworthy.

The first is St. John's Church, on Church Hill, — a large, square-looking wooden meeting-house, whose ancient walls and rafters once witnessed a famous scene, and reëchoed words that have become historical. Here was delivered Patrick Henry's celebrated speech, since spouted by every schoolboy, — " Give me liberty or give me death ! " Those shining sentences still hang like a necklace on the breast of American Liberty. The old meeting-house stands where it stood, overlooking the same earth and the same beautiful stream. But the men of that age lie buried in the dust of these old crowded church-yards; and of late one might almost have said that the wisdom of Virginia lay buried with them.

On the corner of Grace Street, opposite my hotel, I looked out every morning upon the composite columns and pilasters, and spire clean as a stiletto, of St. Paul's Church, with which are connected very different associations. This is the church, and (if you enter) yonder is the pew, in which Jeff Davis sat on Sundays, and heard the gospel of Christ interpreted from the slave-owners' point of view. Here he sat on that memorable Sabbath when Lee's dispatch was handed in to him, saying that Richmond was lost. The same preacher who preached on that day, still propounds his doctrines from the desk. The same sexton who handed in the dispatch glances at you, and, if you are well dressed, offers you a seat in a good place. The same white congregation that arose then in confusion and dismay, on seeing the President go out, sit quietly once more in their seats; and the same colored congregation looks down from the nigger gallery. The seats are still bare, — the cushions that were carried to the Rebel hospitals, to serve as mattresses, having not yet been returned.

Within an arrow's shot from St. Paul's, in the State Capitol, on Capitol Square, were the halls of the late Confederate Congress. I visited them only once, and found them a scene of dust and confusion, — emblematical. The desks and seats had been ripped up, and workmen were engaged in sweeping out the last vestiges of Confederate rule. The furniture, as I learned, was already at an auction-room on Main Street, selling under the hammer. I reported the fact to Mr. C——, of the Union Commission, who was looking for furniture to be used in the freedmen's schools; and he made haste to bid for the relics. I hope he got them; for I can fancy no finer stroke of poetical justice than the conversion of the seats on which sat the legislators of the great slave empire, and the desks on which they wrote, into seats and desks for little negro children learning to read.

It was interesting, by the light of recent events, and in company with one who knew Richmond of yore, to make the tour of the old negro auction-rooms. Davis & Co.'s Negro Bazaar was fitting up for a concert hall. We entered a grocery store, — a broad basement room, with a low, dark ceiling, supported by two stout wooden pillars. "I 've seen many a black Samson sold, standing between those posts; and many a woman too, as white as you or I." Now sugar and rice were sold there, but no more human flesh and blood. The store was kept by a Northern man, who did not even know what use the room had served in former years.

A short ride from the city are two cemeteries worth visiting. On one side, Hollywood, where lie buried President Monroe and his doctrine. On the other side, Oak Wood, a wild, uncultivated hill, half covered with timber and brush, shading numerous Confederate soldiers' graves. Here, set apart from the rest by a rude fence, is the "Yankee Cemetery," crowded with the graves of patriot soldiers, who fell in battle, or died of slow starvation and disease in Richmond prisons ; a melancholy field, which I remember as I saw it one gusty September day, when wild winds swept it, and shook down over it whirling leaves from the reeling and roaring trees.

Lieut. M——, of the Freedmen's Commission, having invited me to visit Camp Lee, about two miles from the city, came for me one afternoon in a fine large carryall, comfortably covered, cushioned, and carpeted.

" Perhaps you will not feel honored," he remarked, as we rattled up Broad Street, " but you will be interested to know that this is General Robert E. Lee's head-quarters' wagon. You are riding on the seat he rode on through the campaigns of the last two years. Your feet are on a piece of carpet which one of the devoted secessionists of Richmond took up from his hall-floor expressly to line the General's wagon-bottom, — little thinking Yankee boot-soles would ever desecrate it ! After Lee's surrender, this wagon was turned over to the quartermaster's department, and the quartermaster turned it over to us." I was interested, indeed ; I was carried back to those sanguinary campaigns ; and I fancied I could see the face of him sitting there where I sat, and read the thoughts of his mind, and the emotions of his heart, in those momentous nights and days. I imagined the plans he revolved in his brain, shut in by those dark curtains ; what he felt after victory, and what after defeat ; the weariness of body and soul ; the misgivings, the remorse, when he remembered his treason and the folly of Virginia, — for he certainly remembered them in the latter gloomy periods, when he saw the black cloud of doom settling down upon a bad and failing cause.

Camp Lee, formerly a fair ground, was the conscript camp of the Confederacy. I had been told many sad stories of young men, and men of middle age, some of them loyal, seized by the conscript officers and sent thither, as it were to a reservoir of the people's blood, whose stream was necessary to keep the machinery of despotism in motion. I paced the grounds where, with despairing hearts, they took their first lessons in the art by which they were to slay and be slain. I stood by the tree under which deserters were shot. Then I turned to a very different scene.

The old barrack buildings were now the happy homes of a village of freedmen. Groups of barefooted and woolly-headed negro children were at play before the doors, filling the air with their laughter, and showing all their ivory with grins of delight as I passed among them. The old men took off their caps to me, the wise old aunties welcomed me with dignified smiles, and the younger women looked up brightly from their ironing or cooking as I went by. The young men were all away at their work. It was, with few exceptions, a self-supporting community, only about a dozen old or infirm persons, out of three hundred, receiving aid from the government.

A little removed from the negro village was a cottage formerly occupied by Confederate officers.

"In that house," said the Lieutenant, "is living a very remarkable character. You know him by reputation, ——, formerly one of the ablest writers on 'De Bow's Review,' and considered the great champion of slavery in the South."

"What! the author of —— ?" a somewhat celebrated book in its day, and in the latitude for which it was written; designed to set forth the corrupt and perishable nature of free societies and progressive ideas, and to show that slavery was the one divine and enduring institution.

"The very man. He is now a pauper, living on the bounty of the government. The rent of that cottage is given him, and he draws rations of the Relief Commission. He will be glad to see you; and he has two accomplished daughters you will be glad to see."

Accordingly we called upon him; but, declining to enter the house, we sat under the stoop, where we could look across the desolate country at the sunset sky.

Mr. ——, an emaciated, sallow, feeble old man, received us affably, and talked with us freely on his favorite topics. He had lived to see the one divine and enduring institution die ; but civilization still survived ; and the race that found its welfare and happiness only in bondage seemed pretty well off, and tolerably happy, — witness the negro village close by ; and the world of progressive ideas still moved on. Yet this great champion of slavery did not appear to have learned the first lesson of the times. All his arguments were the old arguments; he knew nothing but the past, which was gone forever ; and the future to him was chaos.

His two daughters, young and accomplished, came and sat with us in the twilight, together with a vivacious young lady from Richmond. On our return to the city, Miss —— accomaccompanied us, with their visitor. The latter proved to be an audacious and incorrigible little Rebel, and regaled us with secesh songs. I remember a few lines.

> " You can never win us back,
>   Never, never,
> Though we perish in the track
>   Of your endeavor ! "

> " You have no such noble blood
>   For the shedding :
> In the veins of Cavaliers
>   Was its heading !
> You have no such noble men
> In your abolition den,
> To march through fire and fen,
>   Nothing dreading ! "

CHAPTER XXV.

PEOPLE AND POLITICS.

One day I dined at the house of a Union man of a different stamp from the twenty-one I have mentioned. He was one of the wealthy citizens of Richmond, — a man of timid disposition and conservative views, who had managed admirably to conceal his Union sentiments during the war. He had been on excellent terms with Jeff Davis and members of his cabinet; and he was now on excellent terms with the United States authorities. A prudent citizen, not wanting in kindness of heart; yet he could say of the Emancipation Act, —

"It will prove a good thing for the slave-owners; for it will be quite as cheap to hire our labor as to own it, *and we shall now be rid of supporting the old and decrepit servants, such as were formerly left to die on our hands.*"

On being asked if he considered that he owed nothing to those aged servants, he smoothed his chin, and looked thoughtful, but made no reply.

An anecdote will show of what stuff the Unionism of this class is composed. His name happened to be the same as that of one of our generals. During the war, a Confederate officer, visiting his house, said to him, — " I am told you are a near relative of General ——, of the Federal army."

"It's a slander!" was the indignant reply. "He is no kin of mine, and I would disown him if he was."

After the occupation by our troops, Union officers were welcomed at his house; one of whom said to him, —

" Are you related to our famous General —— ? "

" Very likely, very likely," was the complacent answer; " the ——'s are all connected."

Next to the uncompromising Union men, the most sincerely loyal Virginians I saw in Richmond, or elsewhere, were those who had been lately fighting against us. Only now and then a Confederate soldier had much of the spirit of the Rebellion left in him.

"The truth is," said Colonel D——, "we have had the devil whipped out of us. It is only those who kept out of the fight that are in favor of continuing it. I fought you with all my might until we got whipped; then I gave it up as a bad job; and now there's not a more loyal man in the United States than I am." He had become thoroughly converted from the heresy of secession. "No nation can live that tolerates such a doctrine; and, if we had succeeded, the first thing we should have done would have been to repudiate it."

I became acquainted with several officers of this class, who inspired me with confidence and sympathy. Yet when one of them told me he had been awarded a government place, with four thousand a year, I could not help saying, —

"What right have you to such a place? How many capable and worthy men, who have been all the while fighting *for* the government you have been fighting *against*, would be thankful for a situation with one half or one quarter the salary!"

The animus of the secessionists who kept out of the war, and especially of the women, still manifested itself spitefully on occasions.

"It is amusing," said Mrs. W——, "to see the pains some of them take to avoid walking under the flag we keep flying over our door."

Two female teachers of the freed people had, after much trouble, obtained board and lodgings in a private family, where the treatment they received was such as no sensitive person could endure. They were obliged to leave, and accept quarters in a Confederate government building not much better than a barn. Many Richmond families were glad enough to board army officers for their money; but few were prepared to receive and treat decently "nigger teachers," at any price.

INDUSTRY OF LADIES IN CLOTHING THE SOLDIERS, AND ZEAL IN URGING THEIR BEAUX TO GO TO THE WAR.

" Yet the people of Richmond are not what they were five years ago," said General S——, who knew them well, being himself a Virginian. " Their faces have changed. They have a dazed look, like owls in a sudden light. To any one who used to see them in the old days of their pride and spirit, this is very striking. There never was such a downfall, and they have not yet recovered from the shock. They seem to be groping about, as if they had lost something, or were waiting for something. Whatever may be said of them, or whatever they may say of themselves, they feel that they are a conquered people."

" They *were* a conquered people," said the radical Union men. " There never was a rebellious class more thoroughly subdued. They expected no mercy from the government, for they deserved none. They were prepared to submit to everything, even to negro suffrage; for they supposed nothing less would be required of them. But the more lenient the government, the more arrogant they become."

Of Confederate patriotism I did not hear very favorable accounts. It burst forth in a beautiful tall flame at the beginning of the war. There were soldiers' aid societies, patronized by ladies whose hands were never before soiled by labor. Stockings were knit, shirts cut and sewed, and carpets converted into blankets, by these lovely hands. If a fine fellow appeared among them, more inclined to gallantry in the parlor than to gallantry in the field, these same lovely hands thrust him out, and he was told that " only 'the brave deserve the fair.' " But Southern heat is flashy and intense; it does not hold out like the slow, deep fire of the north. The soldiers' aid societies soon grew to be an old story, and the lovely ones contented themselves with cheering and waving their handkerchiefs when the " noble defenders of the south " marched through the streets.

The " noble defenders of the south " did not, I regret to say, appreciate the cheers and the handkerchiefs as they did the shirts and the blankets.

" Many a time," said Mrs. H——, " I have heard them

yell back at the ladies who cheered them, ' Go to ——! If you care for us, come out of your fine clothes and help us!' After the people stopped giving, the soldiers began to help themselves. I 've seen them rush into stores as they passed, snatch whatever they wanted, and march on again, hooting, with loaves of bread and pieces of meat stuck on the points of their bayonets."

The sons and brothers of influential families were kept out of the war by an ingenious system of details. Every man was conscripted; but, while the poor and friendless were hurried away to fight the battles of slavery, the favored aristocrat would get " detailed " to fill some " bomb-proof" situation, as it was called.

" These ' bomb-proofs' finally got to be a very great nuisance. Men were ' detailed' to fill every comfortable berth the government, directly or indirectly, had anything to do with; and as the government usurped, in one way or another, nearly all kinds of business, it soon became difficult for an old or infirm person to get any sort of light employment. A friend of mine, whom the war had ruined, came down from the country, thinking he could get something to do here. He saw able-bodied young men oiling the wheels of the cars. He was old and lame, but he felt himself well able to do that kind of work. So he applied for a situation, and found that the young men he saw were ' detailed' from the army. Others were ' detailed' to carry lanterns for them when they had occasion to oil the car-wheels at night. It was so with every situation the poor man could have filled."

This was the testimony of a candid old gentleman, himself an aristocrat, at whose house I passed an evening.

I took an early opportunity to make the acquaintance of Governor Pierpoint, whom I found to be a plain, somewhat burly, exceedingly good-humored and sociable person. The executive mansion occupies pleasant grounds, enclosed from a corner of Capitol Square; and as it was not more than three minutes' walk from my hotel, I found it often very agreeable to go over and spend a leisure hour or two in his library.

Once I remarked to him : " What Virginia needs is an in-
flux of Northern ideas, Northern energy, Northern capital;
what other way of salvation is open to her ? "

" None ; and she knows it. It is a mistake to suppose that
Northern men and Northern capital are not welcome here.
They are most heartily welcome ; they are invited. Look at
this."

He showed me a beautiful piece of white clay, and a handsome pitcher made from it.

" Within eighty miles of Richmond, by railroad, there are
beds of this clay from which might be manufactured pottery
and porcelain sufficient to supply the entire South. Yet they
have never been worked ; and Virginia has imported all her
fine crockery-ware. Now Northern energy will come in and
coin fortunes out of that clay. Under the old labor system,
Virginia never had any enterprise ; and now she has no
money. The advantages she offers to active business men
were never surpassed. Richmond is surrounded with iron
mines and coal-fields, wood-lands and farm-lands of excellent
quality ; and is destined from its very position, under the new
order of things, to run up a population of two or three hundred
thousand, within not many years."

I inquired about the state finances.

" The Rebel State debt will, of course, never be paid. The
old State debt, amounting to forty millions, will eventually be
paid, although the present is a dark day for it. There is no
live stock to eat the grass ; the mills are destroyed ; business
is at a stand-still ; there is no bank-stock to tax, — nothing to
tax, I might almost say, but the bare land. We shall pay no
interest on the debt this year ; and it will probably be three
years before the back interest is paid. We have twenty-two
millions invested in railroads, and these will all be put in a living
condition in a short time. Then I count upon the development
of our natural resources. In mineral wealth and agricultural
advantages Virginia is inconceivably rich, as a few years will
amply testify."

As an illustration of native enterprise, he told me that there was but one village containing fifty inhabitants on the canal between Richmond and Lynchburg, a distance of one hundred and fifty miles; and land lying upon it was worth no more to-day than it was before the canal was constructed. "Neither is there a village of any size on the James River, between Richmond and Norfolk. How long would it be before brick villages and manufacturing towns would spring up on such a canal and river in one of the free States? Was n't it about time," he added, "for the old machine to break to pieces?"

At the hotel I used to meet a prosperous looking, liberal faced, wide-awake person, whom I at once set down as a Yankee. On making his acquaintance, I learned that he was at the head of a company of Northern men who had recently purchased extensive coal-fields near the James River, twelve miles above Richmond.

"The mines," he said, "had been exhausted once, and abandoned, so we bought them cheap. These Virginians would dig a little pit and take out coal until water came in and interfered with their work; then they would go somewhere else and dig another little pit. So they worked over the surface of the fields, but left the great body of the coal undisturbed. They baled with a mule. Now we have come in with a few steam-pumps which will keep the shafts free from water as fast as we sink them; and we are taking out cargoes of as good anthracite as ever you saw. Here is some of it now," pointing to a line of loaded carts coming up from the wharf, where the coal was landed.

I asked what labor he employed.

"Negro labor. There is none better. I have worked negroes all my life, and prefer them in my business to any other class of laborers. Treat a negro like a man, and you make a man of him."

I also made the acquaintance of a New Yorker, who was working a gold mine in Orange County, Va., and whose testimony was the same with regard to native methods and negro labor. In short, wherever I went, I became, every day, more strongly convinced that the vast, beautiful, rich, torpid state of Virginia was to owe her regeneration to Northern ideas and free institutions.

Hearing loud laughter in the court-house one evening, I looked in, and saw a round, ruddy, white-haired, hale old man making a humorous speech to a mixed crowd of respectable citizens and rowdies. It was the Honorable Mr. P——, bidding for their votes. A played-out politician, he had disappeared from public view a quarter of a century before, but had now come up again, thinking there was once more a chance for himself in the paucity of able men, whom the barrier of the test-oath left eligible to Congress.

"As for that oath," said he, with a solemn countenance, "I confess it is a bitter cup ; and I have prayed that it might pass from me."

Here he paused, and took a sip of brandy from a glass on the desk before him. Evidently that cup was n't so bitter, for he smacked his lips, and looked up with a decidedly refreshed expression.

"Fellow-citizens," said he, "I am going to tell you a little story," — clapping his cane under his arm, and peering under his gray eyebrows. "It will show you my position with regard to that abominable oath. In the good old Revolutionary times, there lived somewhere on the borders a pious Scotchman, whose farm was run over one day by the red-coats, and the next by the Continentals; so that it required the most delicate manoeuvering on his part to keep so much as a pig or a sheep (to say nothing of his own valuable neck) safe from the two armies. Now what did this pious Scotchman do ? In my opinion he did very wisely. When the red-coats caught him, he took the oath of allegiance to the Crown. The next day, when the Continentals picked him up, he took the same oath to the Continental Congress. Now, being a deacon of the Presbyterian Church, in good and regular standing, certain narrow-minded brethren saw fit to remonstrate with him, asking how he could reconcile his conscience to such a course.

" 'My friends,' said he, 'I have thought over the matter, and I have prayed over it; and I have concluded that it is

13

safer to trust my soul in the hands of a merciful God, than my property in the hands of those thieving rascals.'

"Fellow-citizens," resumed the candidate, after a storm of laughter on the part of the crowd, and another a sip of the cup not bitter, on his part, " I have thought over it, and prayed over it, and I have concluded that I can conscientiously take that abominable test-oath ; in other words, that it is safer to trust my soul in the hands of a merciful God, than my country in the hands of the Black Republicans."

He then proceeded to malign the people of the North, and to misrepresent their motives, in a spirit of buffoonery and shameless mendacity, which amazed me. The more out-rageous the lies he told, the louder the screams of applause from his delighted audience. I could not have helped laugh-ing at the ludicrousness of his caricatures, had I not seen that they passed for true pictures with a majority of his hearers ; or had I not remembered that it was such reckless political lying as this, which had so lately misled to their ruin the ignorant masses of the South.

Having finished his speech and his brandy, he sat down ; and a rival candidate mounted the platform.

" B—— ! B—— ! " shrieked the ungrateful crowd, clap-ping and stamping as frantically for the new speaker as for him who had labored so long for their amusement. There-upon, the Honorable Mr. P——, pitching his hat over his eyes, and brandishing his cane, advanced upon his rival.

B——, a much younger and more slender man, quietly stripped up his coat-sleeves, exposing his linen to the elbows, and showing himself prepared for emergencies ; whereat the yells became deafening. A few words passed between the rival candidates ; after which B—— folded his arms and per-mitted P—— to make an explanation. It appeared from this that P—— had written to B——, inviting him to become a candidate for Congress. B—— had declined. Then P—— came forward as a candidate ; and then B——, changing his mind, said he would be a candidate too. Hence their quarrel.

Calmly, with his sleeves still up, or ready to come up,

for P—— was continually advancing upon him with cane lifted and hat set fiercely on his head, — B—— replied, giving his version of the misunderstanding. He admitted that P—— had written him such a letter. "But .his suggestion with regard to my becoming a candidate was very feeble, while the intimation which accompanied it, that he meant to run if I did n't, was very strong; reminding me of the boarder at the hotel-table, who coveted a certain dish of cakes. 'Here, waiter,' said he, 'see if any of the gentlemen will have these cakes, for if they won't, I will.' Of course I declined the cakes. But they have been passed to me by others in a very different spirit, and now I mean to have them if I can get them, — with all deference to the appetite of my venerable friend."

The crowd hooted, shrieked, roared. "Venerable friend" grasped his glass savagely, but, finding it empty, dashed it down again, and sprang to his feet. Desperately puffed, red in the face, once more whirling his cane aloft and knocking his hat over his brows, I thought, if he did not first get a stroke of apoplexy, B—— would this time surely get a stroke of the stick. But B—— grimly stood his ground; and, after glaring at him a moment as if about to burst, P—— muttered, "Go to the devil, then!" buttoned his coat, gave his hat another knock, and stalked out of the house amid a tumult of merriment and derision.

Nearly always, on such occasions, the disputant who loses his temper, loses his cause. B—— now had everything his own way; and a very good speech he made. He was one of those original Union men who had at first opposed secession, but afterwards yielded to the storm that swept over the State. Sent to the Convention to oppose it there, he had ended by voting for it, under instructions from his constituency. He had kept aloof from war and politics during the Rebellion, and could take the test oath; that was no such bitter cup to him. He spoke very feelingly of the return of Virginia to her place in the Union; praised the government for its clemency and moderation, and advocated a forbearing policy towards the freedmen, whom the previous speaker wished to see driven out of the State; seasoning his speech for the vulgar with timely panegyrics on the heroism of the Confederate soldiers.

The election took place a few days later; and I thought it creditable to the good sense of the district that the younger candidate was chosen.

Of the political views of the people, or of the real sentiments of the speakers themselves, not much was to be learned at such a meeting. The heart of the South was boiling with thoughts and emotions which did not come openly to the surface. On the subject of the national debt, for example. Public speakers and public prints were ominously silent about it; and seldom could a discreet citizen be induced to speak of it with any degree of frankness. I was plainly told, however, by a gentleman of Richmond, that the question was often privately discussed, and that the secessionists would never, if they could help it, submit to be taxed to pay the expenses of their own subjugation.

" But how is it proposed to help it ? "

" The first step is to resume their place in the Union. Until that is accomplished, they will remain silent on this and some other delicate subjects. They hope gradually to regain their old power in the nation, when they will unite with the Democratic party of the North, and repudiate the debt."

If I could have been seriously alarmed by such a prospect, what I witnessed at political meetings and elsewhere, would have done much to dispel my apprehensions. I was strongly impressed by this important fact. The old trained politicians, — whom a common interest, slavery, banded together, and whom no consideration of reason or justice could turn from their purpose, — that formidable phalanx had been broken : nearly every man of them had taken an active part in the Rebellion, and could not therefore, without shameful recreancy and voluntary humiliation on the part of the North, be readmitted to the councils of the nation they had attempted to destroy. In their place we may for some years hope to see a very different class of men, whose youth, or modesty, or good fortune, or good sense, before kept them aloof from political life ; men new to the Congressional arena, and therefore more susceptible to the regenerating influence of national ideas and institutions.

CHAPTER XXVI.

FORTIFICATIONS. — DUTCH GAP. — FAIR OAKS.

At nine o'clock one fine morning, Major K——, the young Judge-Advocate of the Department of Virginia, called for me by appointment, accompanied by an orderly bringing a tall war-horse General Terry was so kind as to furnish for my use.

I was soon mounted, and riding out of the city by the Major's side, — down the long, hilly street, past the Rocketts, by the left bank of the river, taking the New-Market Road. First we came to a circle of detached forts surrounding the city; a few minutes' ride farther on brought us to a heavy continuous line of earthworks surrounding the first line. These were the original fortifications of Richmond. Crossing a desolate undulating country of weeds and undergrowth, we reached the works below Laurel Hill, of more recent construction, and of a more formidable character. The embankments were eighteen feet high from the bottom of the ditch. This was some six feet deep and twelve broad. There were two lines of bristling abatis. These, together with the wooden revetments of the works, had been levied upon by the inhabitants in search of firewood.

Three quarters of a mile beyond we came to the heavy intrenchments of the Army of the James. Between the two lines were the picket-lines of the opposing forces, in places no more than three hundred yards apart. Here the two armies lay and watched each other through the last weary Autumn and Winter of the war. The earth was blotched with "gopher holes," — hasty excavations in which the veteran videttes proceeded at once to intrench themselves, on being sent out to a new post. "It was astonishing," said the Major, "to see

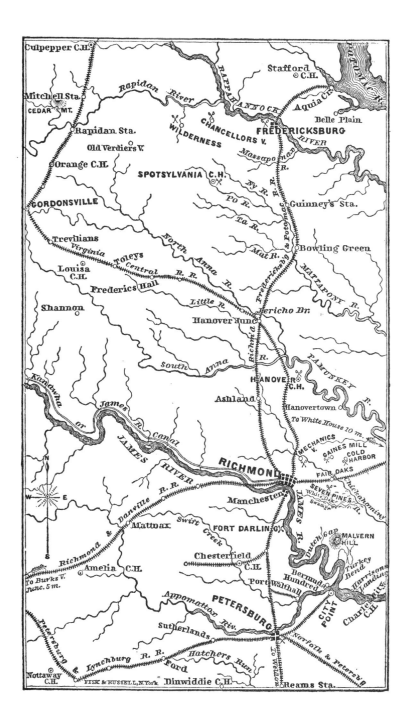

what a breastwork they would throw up in a few minutes, with no other tools than a bayonet and a tin-plate. The moment they were at their station, down they went, scratching and digging."

We had previously stopped at Laurel Hill, to look across the broken country on the south, at Fort Gilmer, which the troops of General Foster's division charged with such unfortunate results. The Major, then serving on Foster's staff, participated in that affair. " I never can look upon this field," said he, " without emotion. I lost some of my dearest friends in that assault."

So it is in every battle : *somebody* loses his dearest friends.

We rode on past the Federal works into the winter-quarters of the army, — a city of huts, with streets regularly laid out, now deserted and in ruins. Here and there I noted an old-fashioned New-England well-sweep still standing. The line of works was semicircular, both ends resting on the river. Within that ox-bow was the encampment of the Army of the James.

We next visited New-Market Heights, where Butler's colored regiments formed unflinchingly under fire, and made their gallant charge, wiping out with their own blood the insults that had been heaped upon them by the white troops. " The army saw that charge, and it never insulted a colored soldier after that," said the Major.

We then galloped across the country, intending to strike Dutch Gap Canal. Not a habitation was in sight. Vast fields spread before us, and we rode through forests of weeds that overtopped our horses' heads. We became entangled in earth-works, and had to retrace our course. More than once we were compelled to dismount and tear our way through abatis and *chevaux-de-frize*. The result was, we lost our bearings, and, after riding several miles quite blindly, struck the James at Deep Bottom. Then up the river we galloped, traversing pine woods and weedy plains, avoiding marsh and gully, and leaping ditches, past Aiken's Landing, to a yellow elevation of earth across a narrow peninsula, which proved to be Dutch Gap.

The canal was there, — a short, deep channel connecting the river with the river again. The James here describes a long loop, seven miles in extent, doubling back upon itself, so that you may stand on this high bank, and throw a stone either into the southward-flowing or the northward-returning stream.

The canal, which cuts off these seven miles, is four hundred and eighty-six feet in length and fifty in depth from the summit of the bank. It is one hundred and twenty-two feet broad at the top, forty at the bottom, and sixty-five at the high-water level. On the lower side the channel is deep enough for ships. Not so at the upper end, — the head that was blown out having fallen back and filled up the canal. At high water, however, small vessels sometimes get through. The tide had just turned, and we found a considerable body of water pouring through the Gap.

Different accounts are given of the origin of the name of Dutch Gap. It is said that a Dutch company was once formed for digging a ship-canal at that place. But a better story is told of a Dutchman who made a bet with a Virginian, that he could beat him in a skiff-race between Richmond and City Point. The Virginian was ahead when they reached the Gap; what then was his astonishment, on arriving at City Point, to find the Dutchman there before him. The latter had saved the roundabout seven miles by dragging his canoe across the peninsula and launching it on the other side.

Riding up the Richmond road, we stopped at the first human habitation we had seen since leaving Laurel Hill. We had been several hours in the saddle, and stood greatly in need of refreshments. The sight of a calf and a churn gave us a promise of milk, and we tied our horses at the door. The house had been a goodly mansion in its day, but now everything about it showed the ruin and dilapidation of war. The windows were broken, and the garden, out-houses, and fences destroyed. This proved to be Cox's house, and belonged to a plantation of twenty-three hundred acres which included Dutch Gap. Looking at the desolation which surrounded it, I could hardly believe that this had formerly been one of the finest farms in Virginia, worked by a hundred negroes, and furnished with reapers, threshers, a grist-mill, and saw-mill, — all of which had been swept away as if they had never been.

We found lying on a bed in a dilapidated room a poor man sick with the prevailing chills. He had some bread and milk brought for us, and gave us some useful hints about avoiding the torpedoes when we should reach Fort Harrison. He described to us the depredations committed on the place by " Old Butler " ; and related how he himself was once taken prisoner by the Yankee marines on the river. " They gave me my choice, — to be carried before the admiral, or robbed of my horse and all the money I had about me. I preferred the robbing ; so they cleared me out and set me free."

I said, " If you had been taken before the admiral, you would have got your liberty and saved your property."

His voice became deep and tremulous as he replied: " But I did n't consider horse nor money ; I considered my wife. I 'd sooner anything than that she should be distressed. She knew I was a prisoner, and all I thought of was to hurry home to her with the news that I was safe." Thus in every human breast, even though wrapped in rags, and guilty of crimes against country and kindred, abides the eternal spark of tenderness which atones in the sight of God for all.

Taking leave of the sick man, we paid a brief visit to the casemates of Fort Harrison, then spurred back to Richmond, which we reached at sunset, having been nine hours in the saddle and ridden upwards of forty miles.

Another morning, with two gentlemen of General Terry's staff, and an orderly to take care of our horses, I rode out of the city on the Nine Mile Road, which crosses the Chickahominy at New Bridge ; purposing to visit some of the scenes of McClellan's Richmond campaign.

Passing the fortifications, and traversing a level, scarcely inhabited country, shorn of its forests by the sickle of war, we reached, by a cross-road, the line of the Richmond and York River Railroad. But no railroad was there ; the iron of the track having been taken up to be used elsewhere.

Near by was Fair Oaks Station, surrounded by old fields, woods, and tracts of underbrush. Here was formerly a yard, in which stood a group of oaks, the lower trunks of which had been rendered conspicuous, if not beautiful, by whitewash: hence, "*fair* oaks."

It was a wild, windy, dusty day. A tempest was roaring through the pines over our heads as we rode on to the scene of General Casey's disaster. I asked an inhabitant why the place was called " Seven Pines." " I don't know, unless it 's because there 's about seven hundred."

He was living in a little wooden house, close by a negro hut. " The Yankees took me up, and carried me away, and destroyed all I had. My place don't look like it did before, and never will, I reckon. They come again last October; Old Butler's devils; all colors; heap of black troops; they did n't leave me anything."

He spoke with no more respect of the Confederates. " We had in our own army some of the durn'dest scapegalluses! The difference 'twixt them and the Yankees was, the Yankees would steal before our eyes, and laugh at us; but the Rebels would steal behind our backs."

On the south, we found the woods on fire, with a furious north wind fanning the flames. The only human being we saw was a man digging sweet potatoes. We rode eastward, along the lines of intrenchments thrown up by our troops after the battle; passed through a low, level tract of woods, on the borders of the Chickahominy swamps; and, pressing northward, struck the Williamsburg Road.

Colonel G——, of our party, was in the Fair Oaks' fight. He came up with the victorious columns that turned back the tide of defeat.

" I never saw a handsomer sight than Sickles's brigade advancing up that road, Sunday morning, the second day of the battle. The enemy fired upon them from these woods, but never a man flinched. They came up in column, magnificently, to that house yonder; then formed in line of battle across these fields, and went in with flags flying and bayonets shining, and drove the Rebels. After that we might have walked straight into Richmond, but McClellan had to stop and go to digging."

We dismounted in a sheltered spot, to examine our maps, then passed through the woods by a cross-road to Savage's Station, coming out upon a large undulating field. Of Savage's house only the foundations were left, surrounded by a grove of locust-trees. My companions described to me the scene of McClellan's retreat from this place, — the hurry, the confusion, the flames of government property abandoned and destroyed. Sutlers forsook their goods. Even the officers' baggage was devoted to the torch. A single pile of hard tack, measuring forty cubic feet, was set on fire, and burned. Then came the battle of Savage's Station, in which the corps of Franklin and Sumner, by determined fighting, saved our army from being overwhelmed by the entire Rebel force. This was Sunday again, the twenty-ninth of June : so great had been the change wrought by four short weeks ! On that other Sunday the Rebels were routed, and the campaign, as some aver, might have been gloriously ended by the capture of Richmond. Now nothing was left for us but ignominious retreat and failure, which proved all the more humiliating, falling so suddenly upon the hopes with which real or fancied successes had inspired the nation.

CHAPTER XXVII.

IN AND ABOUT PETERSBURG.

On Wednesday, September 27th, I left Richmond for Petersburg. The railroad bridge having been burned, I crossed the river in a coach, and took the cars at Manchester. A ride of twenty miles through tracts of weeds and undergrowth, pine barrens and oaken woods, passing occasionally a dreary-looking house and field of " sorry " corn, brought us within sight of the " Cockade City." [1]

It was evening when I arrived. Having a letter from Governor Pierpoint to a prominent citizen, I sallied out by moonlight from my hotel, and picked my way, along the streets sloping up from the river bank, to his house.

Judge —— received me in his library, and kept me until a late hour listening to him. His conversation was of the war, and the condition in which it had left the country. He portrayed the ruin of the once proud and prosperous State, and the sufferings of the people. " Yet, when all is told," said he, " you cannot realize their sufferings, more than if you had never heard of them." His remarks touching the freedmen were refreshing, after the abundance of cant on the subject to which I had been treated. He thought they were destined to be crowded out of Virginia, which was adapted to white labor, but that they would occupy the more southern States, and become a useful class of citizens. Many were leaving their homes, with the idea that they must do so in order fully to assert their freedom; but the majority of them were still at work for their old masters. He was already convinced that the new system would prove more profitable to employers

---

[1] The title given to it by President Madison, in speaking of the gallantry of the Petersburg Volunteers, in the war of 1812.

than the old one. Formerly he kept eight family servants;
now he had but three, who, stimulated by wages, did the
work of all.

One of his former servants, to whom he had granted many
privileges, came to him, after the war closed, and said, " You
a'n't going to turn me away, I hope, master."

" No, William," said the Judge. " As long as I have a
home, you have one. But I have no money to hire you."

William replied that he would like to stay, and work right
along just as he had done hitherto. " And as for money,
master, I reckon we can manage that."

" How so, William ? "

" You see, master, you 've been so kind to me these past
years I 've done a good deal outside, and if you have no money
now, I reckon I must lend you some."

The faithful fellow brought out his little treasure, and offered
it to his old master, who, however, had not the heart to accept it.

The Judge also told a story of a free negro to whom he had
often loaned money without security before the war. Recently
this negro had come to him again, and asked the old question,
" Have you plenty of money, master ? "

" Ah, James," said the Judge, " I used to have plenty, and
I always gave you what you wanted, but you must go to somebody else now, for I have n't a dollar."

" That 's what I was thinking," said James. " I have n't
come to borrow this time, but to lend." And, taking out a
fifty - dollar note, with tears in his eyes he entreated the
Judge to take it.

I noticed that the library had a new door, and that the walls
around it were spotted with marks of repairs. " These are
the effects of a shell that paid us a flying visit one morning,
during the bombardment. Fortunately, no one was hurt."

He accepted the results of the war in such a candid and
loyal spirit as I had rarely seen manifested by the late govern-
ing class in Virginia. If such men could be placed in power,
the sooner the State were fully restored to its place in the
Union, the better ; but, alas ! —

Returning to the hotel, I missed my way, and seeing a light in a little grocery store, went in to make inquiries. I found two negroes talking over the bombardment. Finding me a stranger, and interested, they invited me to stop, and rehearsed the story for my benefit.

The shelling began on the first of July, 1864. It was most rapid on the third. Roofs and chimneys and walls were knocked to pieces. All the lower part of the town was deserted. Many of the inhabitants fled to the country; some remained there in camps, others got over their fright and returned. "We went up on Market Street, and got into a bomb-proof we made of cotton bales." The bombardment was kept up until the first of October, and afterwards resumed at intervals. "Finally people got so they did n't care anything about it. I saw two men killed by picking up shells and looking at them; they exploded in their hands."

At the time of the evacuation the negroes "had to keep right dark" to avoid being carried away by their masters. Some went across the Appomattox, and had to swim back, the bridges being burned.

They described to me the beauty of the scene when the mortars were playing in the night, and the heavens were spanned with arches of fire.

"It was a right glad day for us when the Rebels went out and the Federals came in; and I don't believe any of the people could say with conscientiousness they were sorry, — they had all suffered so much. The Rebels set all the tobacco-warehouses afire, and burned up the foundery and commissary stores. That was Sunday. Monday morning they went out, and the Federals came in, track after track, without an hour between them."

These two negroes were brothers, and men of decided character and intelligence, although they had been slaves all their lives. They learned to read in a spelling-book when children by the firelight of their hut. "I noticed how white children called their letters; and afterwards I learned to write without any showing, by copying the writing-letters in the spelling-book. I learned to read in such a silent manner, it was a long time before I could make any head reading loud. I learned arithmetic by myself in the same way."

If any person of white skin, who has risen to eminence, is known to have acquired the rudiments of education under such difficulties, much is made of the circumstance. But in the case of a poor black man, a slave, I suppose it is different.

The two addressed each other with great respect and affection. Their feeling of kinship and of family worth was very strong. " There were four brothers of us," said the elder; " and I am the only one of them that ever went to the prison-house. After my old, kind master died, I had a difficulty with my mistress; she was very exasperating in her language to me, till I lost my temper, and said I could live in torment, but I could n't live with her, and wished she would sell me. She sent for an officer; and I said, ' I am as willing to go to jail as I am to take a drink of water.' When the sheriff saw me, he was very much surprised, and he said, ' Why, John, why are you here?' I told him I had parted with my temper, and said what no man ought to have said to a woman. He said, ' What a pity ! such a name as your master gave you, John !' He interceded with my mistress, and the fourth day she had me taken out. I told her I had acknowledged my fault to my Maker, and I was willing to acknowledge it to her. She said she was wrong too; and we agreed very well after that. I was a very valuable servant to her. I could whitewash, mend a fence, put in glass, use tools, serve up a dinner, and then wait on it as gracefully as any man that ever walked around a table. Then I would hitch up the carriage, and drive her out. And I have never seen the day yet when she has given me five dollars."

He had always thought deeply on the subject of his condition. " But I never felt at liberty to speak my mind until they passed an act to put colored men into the army. That wrought upon my feelings so I could n't but cry;" and the tears were in his eyes again at the recollection. " They asked me if I would fight for my country. I said, ' I have no country.'

They said I should fight for my freedom. I said, ' To gain my freedom, I must fight to keep my wife and children slaves.' Then, after the war was over, they told us they had no more use for niggers. I said I thought it hard, after they'd lived by the sweat of our faces all our days, that now we must be banished from the country, because we were free."

He spoke hopefully of his race. " If we can induce them to be united, and to feel the responsibility that rests upon them, they will get along very well. Many have bought themselves, and paid every dollar to their masters, and then been sold again, and been treated in this way till they have no longer any confidence in the promises a white man makes them. They won't stay with their old masters on any terms. Then there are some that expect to live without work. There are some colored men, just as there are white men, that won't work to save their lives. Others won't stay, for this reason : The master takes their old daddy, and old mammy, and little children, and casts them out on the forks of the road, and tells them to go to the Court House, where the Yankees are, for he don't want 'em ; then of course the young men and young women go too."

Early next morning, I went out to view the town. In size and importance Petersburg ranks as the second city in the State. In 1860 it had 18,275 inhabitants. It had fifty manufacturing establishments in operation, employing three thousand operatives, and consuming annually $2,000,000 worth of raw material. Twenty factories manufactured yearly 12,000,000 pounds of tobacco. The falls of the Appomattox afford an extensive water-power, and the river is navigable to this place.

I found the city changed greatly from its old prosperous condition. Its business was shattered. Its well-built, pleasant streets, rising upon the south bank of the Appomattox, were dirty and dilapidated. All the lower part of the town showed the ruinous effect of the shelling it had received. Tenantless and uninhabitable houses, with broken walls, roofless, or with roofs smashed and torn by missiles, bear silent witness to the

14

havoc of war. In the ends of some buildings I counted more than twenty shot-holes. Many battered houses had been repaired, — bright spots of new bricks in the old walls showing where projectiles had entered.

The city was thronged by a superfluous black population crowding in from the country. I talked with some, and tried to persuade them to go back and remain at their old homes. But they assured me that they could not remain : their very lives had been in danger ; and they told me of several murders perpetrated upon freedmen by the whites, in their neighborhoods, besides other atrocities. Yet it was evident many had come to town in the vague hope of finding happy adventures and bettering their condition.

I remember a gang of men, employed by the government, waiting for orders, with their teams, on the sunny side of a ruined street. Several, sitting on the ground, had spelling-books : one was teaching another his letters ; a third was reading aloud to a wondering little audience ; an old man, in spectacles, with gray hair, was slowly and painfully spelling words of two letters, which he followed closely with his heavy dark finger along the sunlit page, — altogether a singular and affecting sight.

Having letters to General Gibbon commanding the military district, I called on him at his head-quarters in a fine modern Virginia mansion, and through his courtesy obtained a valuable guide to the fortifications, in the person of Colonel E ——, of his staff.

We drove out on the Jerusalem plank-road, leaving on our right the reservoir, which Kautz's cavalry in their dash at the city mistook for a fort, and retired from with commendable discretion.

Leaving the plank-road, and striking across the open country, we found, in the midst of weedy fields, the famous " crater," — scene of one of the most fearful tragedies of the war. It was a huge irregular oblong pit, perhaps a hundred feet in length and twenty in depth. From this spot, spouted like a vast black fountain, from the earth, rose the garrison,

and guns, and breastworks, of one of the strongest Rebel
forts, mined by our troops, and blown into the air on the
morning of July 30th, 1864.

There was a deep ravine in front, up in the side of which
the mine had been worked.   The mouth was still visible, half
hidden by rank weeds.   In spots the surface earth had caved,
leaving chasms opening into the mine along its course.   The
mouth of the Rebel counter-mine was also visible, — a deep,
dark, narrow cavern, supported by framework, in the lower
side of the crater.   Lying around were relics of the battle, —
bent and rusted bayonets, canteens, and fragments of shells.
In front were the remains of wooden *chevaux-de-frise*, which
had been literally shot to pieces.   And all around were
graves.

In the earthworks near by I saw a negro man and woman
digging out bullets.   They told me they got four cents a pound
for them in Petersburg.   It was hard work, but they made a
living at it.

Riding southward along the Confederate line of works, we
came to Fort Damnation, where the Rebels used to set up a
flag-staff for our boys to fire at with a six-pound Parrott gun,
making a wild sport of warfare.   Opposite was Fort Hell,
built by our troops, and named in compliment to its profane
neighbor.   The intrenched picket-lines between the two were
not more than seventy-five yards apart ; each connected with
its fort by a covered way.   These works were in an excellent
state of preservation.   Fort Hell especially, constructed with
bomb-proofs and galleries which afforded the most ample protection to its garrison, was in as perfect a condition as when
first completed.   With a lighted torch I explored its magazine,
a Tartarean cave, with deep dark chambers, and walls covered
with a cold sweat.

All along in front of the Rebel defences extended the
Federal breastworks, and it was interesting to trace the zigzag lines by which our troops had, slowly and persistently, by
scientific steps, pushed their position ever nearer and nearer
to the enemy's.   Running round all, covered by an embankment, was Grant's army railroad.

Having driven southward along the Rebel lines to Fort Damnation, and there crossed over to Fort Hell, we now returned northward, riding along the Federal lines. A very good corduroy road, built by our army, took us through deserted villages of huts, where had been its recent winter-quarters; past abandoned plantations and ruined dwellings; over a plain which had been covered with forests before the war, but where not a tree was now standing; and across the line of the Norfolk Railroad, of which not a sleeper or rail remained. We passed Fort Morton, confronting the " crater "; and halted on a hill, in a pleasant little grove of broken and dismantled oaks. Here were the earthworks and bomb-proofs of Fort Stedman, the possession of which had cost more lives than any other point along the lines, not excepting the " crater." Captured originally from the Rebels, retaken by them, and recaptured by us, it was the subject of incessant warfare.

At the Friend House, farther on, stationed on an eminence overlooking Petersburg, was the celebrated " Petersburg Express," — the great gun which used to send its iron messengers regularly into the city.

On the Friend Estate I saw, for the first time, evidences of reviving agriculture in this war-blasted region. A good crop of corn had been raised, and some five and thirty negro men and women were beginning the harvest. There was no white man about the place ; but they told me they were working on their own account for a portion of the crop.

Returning to town by the City-Point Road, we set out again, in the afternoon, to visit the more distant fortifications beyond Forts Hell and Damnation.

Driving out on the Boydton Plank Road to the Lead Works, we there left it on our right, and proceeded along a sandy track beside the Weldon Railroad where wagon-loads of North Carolina cotton, laboring through the sand, attested that the damage done to this railroad, in December of the previous year, by Warren's Corps, — which destroyed with conscientious thoroughness fifteen miles of the track, — had not yet been repaired.[1]

Passing the Rebel forts, I was struck with the peculiar construction of the Federal works. As we pushed farther and farther our advanced lines around the city, they became so extended that, to prevent raids on our rear, it was necessary to construct rear lines of defence. Our intrenchments accordingly took the form of a hook, doubled backward, and terminating in something like a barbed point.

Cities of deserted huts, built in the midst of a vast level plain, despoiled of its forests, showed where the winter-quarters of our more advanced corps had been, during this last great campaign.

Passing the winter-quarters of the Sixth Corps, we approached one of the most beautiful villages that ever were seen. It was sheltered by a grove of murmuring pines. An arched gateway admitted us to its silent streets. It was constructed entirely of pine saplings and logs. Even the neat sidewalks were composed of the same material. The huts — if those little dwellings, built in a unique and perfect style of architecture, may be called by that humble name — were furnished with bedrooms and mantel-pieces within, and plain columns and fluted pilasters without, all of rough pine. The plain columns were formed of single trunks, the fluted ones of clusters of saplings, — all with the bark on, of course. The walls were similarly constructed. The village was deserted, with the exception of a safeguard, consisting of half a dozen United States soldiers, stationed there to protect it from vandalism.

The gem of the place was the church. Its walls, pillars, pointed arches, and spire, one hundred feet high, were composed entirely of pines selected and arranged with surprising taste and skill. The pulpit was in keeping with the rest. Above it was the following inscription : —

" Presented to the members of the Poplar Spring Church,

---

[1] Four months later I returned northward from the Carolinas by this road, and found that the bent rails had been straightened and replaced, in an exceedingly scaly condition.

by the 50th N. Y. V. Engineers. Capt. M. H. McGrath, architect."

The Poplar. Spring Church, which formerly stood some-where in that vicinity, had been destroyed during the war; and this church had been left as a fitting legacy to its congregation by the soldiers who built it. The village had been the winter-quarters of the engineer corps.

Driving westward along the track of the army railroad, and past its termination, we struck across the open fields to the Federal signal-tower, lifting skyward its lofty open framework and dizzy platforms, in the midst of an extensive plain. To ascend a few stages of this breezy observatory, and see the sun go down behind the distant dim line of forests, while the evening shadows thickened upon the landscape, was a fit termination to the day's experience; and we returned with rapid wheels to the city.

CHAPTER XXVIII.

JAMES RIVER AND FORTRESS MONROE.

THE next day I proceeded to City Point by railroad, — riding in an old patched-up car marked outside "*U. S. Military R. R.*," and furnished inside with pine benches for seats and boards nailed up in place of windows.   There was nothing of interest on the road, which passed through a region of stumps and undergrowth, with scarce an inhabitant, save the few negro families that had taken up their abode in abandoned army huts.   City Point itself was no less dull.   Built on high and rolling ground, at the confluence of the Appomattox and the James, — a fine site for a village, — it had nothing to show but an ugly cluster of rough wooden buildings, such as spring up like fungus in the track of an army, and a long line of government warehouses by the river.

I took the first steamer for Richmond; returning thence, in a few days, down the James to Norfolk and Fortress Monroe. This voyage possesses an interest which can merely be hinted at in a description.   You are gliding between shores rich with historical associations old and new.   The mind goes back to the time when Captain John Smith, with the expedition of 1607, sailed up this stream, which they named in honor of their king.   But you are diverted from those recollections by the landmarks of recent famous events : — the ruins of iron-clads below Richmond ; the wrecks of gunboats ; obstructions in the channel ; Fort Darling, on a high bluff ; every commanding eminence crowned by a redoubt ; Dutch Gap Canal ; Deep Bottom ; Butler's tower of observation ; Malvern Hill, where the last battle of McClellan's retreat was fought, — a gentle elevation on the north bank, marked by a small house and clumps of trees ; Harrison's Landing, — a long pier extending out into the river; Jamestown, the first settlement in Virginia, — now an island with a few huts only, and two or three chimney-stacks of burnt houses, — looking as desolate as when first destroyed, at the time of Bacon's rebellion, near two hundred years ago; Newport News below, a place with a few shanties, and a row of grinning batteries; Hampton Roads, bristling and animated with shipping, — the scene of the fight between the "Merrimac" and the "Monitor," initiating a new era in naval warfare; Hampton away on the north, with its conspicuous square white hospital; Norfolk on the south, up the Elizabeth River; the Rip-Raps, and Sewall's Point; and, most astonishing object of all, that huge finger of the military power, placed here to hold these shores, — Fortress Monroe.

It was a wild, windy day; the anchored ships were tossing on the white-capped waves; but the Fortress presented a beautiful calm picture, as we approached it, with its proud flag careering in the breeze, its white light-house on the beach, and the afternoon sunshine on its broad walls and grassy ramparts.

Before the war, there was a large hotel between the Fortress and the wharves, capable of accommodating a thousand persons. This was torn down, because it obstructed the range of the guns; and a miserable one-and-a-half story dining-saloon had been erected in its place. Here, after much persuasion, I managed to secure a lodging under the low, unfinished roof. The proprietor told me that the government, which owns the land on which his house stands, exacted no payment for it, under General Dix's administration; but that General Butler, on coming into power, immediately clapped on a smart rent of five hundred dollars a month, which the landlord could pay, or take his house elsewhere. I thought the circumstance characteristic.

The next morning, having a letter to General Miles, in command at the Fortress, I obtained admission within the massy walls. I crossed the moat on the drawbridge, and entered the gate opening under the heavy bastions. I found myself in the midst of a village, on a level plain, shaded by trees. A guard was given me, with orders to show me whatever I wished to see, with one exception, — the interior of Mr. Jefferson Davis's private residence. This retired Rebel chief had been removed from the casemate in which he was originally confined, and was occupying Carrol Hall, a plain, three-story, yellow-painted building, built for officers' quarters. I walked past the doors, and looked up at the modest window-curtains, wondering what his thoughts were, sitting there, meditating his fallen fortunes, with the flag of the nation he had attempted to overthrow floating above his head, and its cannon frowning on the ramparts around him. Did he enjoy his cigar, and read the morning newspaper with interest?

The strength and vastness of Fortress Monroe astonishes one. It is the most expensive fortress in the United States, having cost nearly two and a half million dollars. It is a mile around the ramparts. The walls are fifty feet thick. The stone masonry which forms their outward face rises twenty feet above high-water mark in the moat; and the grassy parapets are built ten feet higher. There were only seven hundred men in the fort, — a small garrison.

I was shown the great magazine which Arnold, one of the Booth conspirators, proposed to blow up. His plan was to get a clerkship in the ordnance office, which would afford him facilities for carrying out his scheme. Had this succeeded, the terrible explosion that would have ensued would not only have destroyed the Fortress, but not a building on the Point would have been left standing.

I made the circuit of the ramparts, overlooking Hampton Roads on one side, and the broad bay on the other. The sun was shining; the waves were breaking on the shore; the band was playing proud martial airs; the nation's flag rolled voluptuously in the wind; steamers and white-sailed ships were going and coming; the sky above was of deep blue, full of peace. It was hard to realize that the immense structure on which I walked, amid such a scene, was merely an engine of war.

While I was at General Miles's head-quarters an interesting case of pardoned rebellion was developed. Mr. Y——, a noted secessionist of Warwick County, was one of those who had early pledged his life, his fortune, and his sacred honor to the Confederate cause. He had commenced his patriotic service by seizing at his wharf on the Warwick River a private vessel which happened to be loading with lumber at the time when the State seceded, and sending her as a prize up to Richmond; and he had crowned his career by assisting Wirz in his official work at Andersonville. During the war the government against which he was fighting had taken the liberty of cutting a little lumber on this gentleman's abandoned lands. He had since become professedly loyal, paid a visit to the good President at Washington, and returned to his estates with his pardon in his pocket. The first thing he did was to drive off the government contractor's employees with threats of violence. He would not even allow them to take away the government property he found on his place, but threatened to shoot every man who approached for that purpose. An officer came to head-quarters, when I was there, requesting a guard of soldiers to protect the lives of the laborers during the removal of this property.

CHAPTER XXIX.

ABOUT HAMPTON.

As it was my intention to visit some of the freedmen's settlements in the vicinity, the General kindly placed a horse at my disposal, and I took leave of him. A short gallop brought me to the village of Hampton, distant from the Fortress something over two miles.

"The village of Hampton," says a copy of the "Richmond Examiner" for 1861, "is beautifully situated on an arm of the sea setting in from the adjacent roadstead which bears its name. The late census showed that the aggregate white and black population was nearly two thousand." Some of the residences were of brick, erected at a heavy cost, and having large gardens, out-houses, and other valuable improvements. The oldest building, and the second oldest church in the State, was the Episcopal Church, made of imported brick, and surrounded by a cemetery of ancient graves. "Here repose the remains of many a cavalier and gentleman, whose names are borne by numerous families all over the Southern States."

On the night of August 7th, 1861, the Rebels, under General Magruder, initiated what has been termed the "warfare against women and children and private property," which has marked the war of the Rebellion, by laying this old aristocratic town in ashes. It had been mostly abandoned by the secessionist inhabitants on its occupation by our troops, and only a few white families, with between one and two hundred negroes, remained. Many of the former residents came back with the Rebel troops and set fire to their own and their neighbors' houses. Less than a dozen buildings remained standing; the place being reduced to a wilderness of naked chimneys, burnt-out shells, and heaps of ashes.

I found it a thrifty village, occupied chiefly by freedmen.
The former aristocratic residences had been replaced by negro
huts.   These were very generally built of split boards, called
pales, overlapping each other like clapboards or shingles.
There was an air of neatness and comfort about them which
surprised me, no less than the rapidity with which they were
constructed.   One man had just completed his house.   He
told me that it took him a week to make the pales for it and
bring them from the woods, and four days more to build it.

A sash-factory and blacksmith's shop, shoemakers' shops
and stores, enlivened the streets.   The business of the place
was carried on chiefly by freedmen, many of whom were
becoming wealthy, and paying heavy taxes to the government.

Every house had its wood-pile, poultry and pigs, and little
garden devoted to corn and vegetables.   Many a one had its
stable and cow, and horse and cart.   The village was sur
rounded by freedmen's farms, occupying the abandoned plantations of recent Rebels.   The crops looked well, though the
soil was said to be poor.   Indeed, this was by far the thriftiest
portion of Virginia I had seen.

In company with a gentleman who was in search of laborers,
I made an extensive tour of these farms, anxious to see with
my own eyes what the emancipated blacks were doing for
themselves.   I found no idleness anywhere.   Happiness and
industry were the universal rule.   I conversed with many of
the people, and heard their simple stories.   They had but one
trouble : the owners of the lands they occupied were coming
back with their pardons and demanding the restoration of
their estates.   Here they had settled on abandoned Rebel
lands, under the direction of the government, and with the
government's pledge, given through its officers, and secured
by act of Congress, that they should be protected in the use and
enjoyment of those lands for a term of three years, each freedman occupying no more than forty acres, and paying an annual
rent to government not exceeding six per cent. of their value.
Here, under the shelter of that promise, they had built their

little houses and established their humble homes. What was to become of them? On one estate of six hundred acres there was a thriving community of eight hundred freedmen. The owner had been pardoned unconditionally by the President, who, in his mercy to one class, seemed to forget what justice was due to another.

The terms which some of these returning Rebels proposed to the freedmen they found in possession of their lands, interested me. One man, whose estate was worth sixteen dollars an acre, offered to rent it to the families living on it for eight dollars an acre, provided that the houses, which they had themselves built, should revert to him at the end of the year.

My friend broke a bolt in his buggy, and we stopped at a blacksmith-shop to get another. While the smith, a negro, was making a new bolt, and fitting it neatly to its place, I questioned him. He had a little lot of half an acre; upon which he had built his own house and shop and shed. He had a family, which he was supporting without any aid from the government. He was doing very well until the owner of the soil appeared, with the President's pardon, and orders to have his property restored to him. The land was worth twenty dollars an acre. He told the blacksmith that he could remain where he was, by paying twenty-four dollars a year rent for his half acre. " I am going to leave," said the poor man, quietly, and without uttering a complaint.

Except on the government farm, where old and infirm persons and orphan children were placed, I did not find anybody who was receiving aid from the government. Said one, " I have a family of seven children. Four are my own, and three are my brother's. I have twenty acres. I get no help from government, and do not want any as long as I can have land." I stopped at another little farm-house, beside which was a large pile of wood, and a still larger heap of unhusked corn, two farm wagons, a market wagon, and a pair of mules. The occupant of this place also had but twenty acres, and he was " getting rich."

" Has government helped you any this year ? " I asked a young fellow we met on the road.

" *Government* helped *me ?* " he retorted proudly.   " No ; I am helping government."

We stopped at a little cobbler's shop, the proprietor of which was supporting not only his own wife and children, but his aged mother and widowed sister.   " Has government helped you any ? " we inquired.   " Nary lick in the world ! " he replied, hammering away at his shoe.

Driving across a farm, we saw an old negro without legs hitching along on his stumps in a cornfield, pulling out grass between the rows, and making it up into bundles to sell.   He hailed us, and wished to know if we wanted to buy any hay. He seemed delighted when my companion told him he would take all he had, at his own price.   He said he froze his legs one winter when he was a slave, and had to have them taken off in consequence.   Formerly he had received rations from the government, but now he was earning his own support, except what little he received from his friends.

It was very common to hear of families that were helping not only their own relatives, but others who had no such claim of kindred upon them.   And here I may add that the account which these people gave of themselves was fully corroborated by officers of the government and others who knew them.

My friend did not succeed very well in obtaining laborers for his mills.   The height of the freedmen's ambition was to have little homes of their own and to work for themselves. And who could blame this simple, strong instinct, since it was not only pointing them the way of their own prosperity, but serving also the needs of the country ? [1]

Notwithstanding the pending difficulty with the land-owners, those who had had their lots assigned them were going on to put up new houses, from which they might be

---

[1] For example: the freedmen on the Jones Place, with one hundred and twenty acres under cultivation, where they had commenced work with nothing for which they did not have to run in debt, were now the owners of both stock and farming implements; and, besides supporting their families, they were paying to the United States a large annual rent.

driven at any day, — so great was their faith in the honor of the government which had already done so much for them.

Revisiting Virginia some months later, I learned that the Freedmen's Bureau had interposed to protect these people in their rights, showing that their faith had not been in vain.

CHAPTER XXX.

A GENERAL VIEW OF VIRGINIA.

CALLED home from Fortress Monroe by an affair of business requiring my attention, I resumed my Southern tour later in the fall, passing through Central and Southwestern Virginia, and returning from the Carolinas through Eastern Virginia in the following February. I am warned by a want of space to omit the details of these transient journeys, and to compress my remaining notes on the State into as narrow a compass as possible.[1]

Virginia was long a synonym for beauty and fertility. In the richness of her resources, she stood unrivalled among the earlier States. In wealth and population, she led them all. She was foremost also in political power; and the names she gave to our Revolutionary history still sparkle as stars of the first magnitude.

This halo about her name has been slow to fade; although, like a proud and indolent school-girl, once at the head of her class, she has been making steady progress towards the foot. Five of the original States have gone above her, and one by one new-comers are fast overtaking her. Little Massachusetts excels her in wealth, and Ohio in both wealth and population.

The causes of this gradual falling back are other than physical causes. Her natural advantages have not been overrated. The Giver of good gifts has been munificent in his bounties to her. She is rich in rivers, forests, mines, soils. That broad avenue to the sea, the Chesapeake, and its affluents, solicit commerce. Her supply of water-power is limitless and

---

[1] West Virginia, which seceded from the State after the State seceded from the Union, and which now forms a separate sovereignty under the National Government, I can scarcely say that I visited. I saw but the edges of it; it is touched upon, therefore, only in the general remarks which follow.

well distributed. She possesses a variety of climate, which is, with few exceptions, healthful and delightful.

The fertility of the State is perhaps hardly equal to its fine reputation, which, like that of some old authors, was acquired in the freshness of her youth, and before her powerful young competitors appeared to challenge the world's attention. Such reputations acquire a sanctity from age, which the spirit of conservatism permits not to be questioned.

The State has many rich valleys, river bottoms, and alluvial tracts bordering on lesser streams, which go far towards sustaining this venerable reputation. But between these valleys occur intervals of quite ordinary fertility, if not absolute sterility, and these compose the larger portion of the State. Add the fact that the best lands of Eastern and Southeastern Virginia have been very generally worn out by improper cultivation, and what is the conclusion?

A striking feature of the country is its " old fields." The more recent of these are usually found covered with briers, weeds, and broom-sedge, — often with a thick growth of infant pines coming up like grass. Much of the land devastated by the war lies in this condition. In two or three years, these young pines shoot up their green plumes five or six feet high. In ten years there is a young forest. In some of the oldest of the old fields, now heavily timbered, the ridges of the ancient tobacco lands are traceable among the trees.

Tobacco has been the devouring enemy of the country. In travelling through it one is amazed at the thought of the regions which have been burned and chewed up by the smokers and spitters of the world.

East Virginia is hilly. The southeast portion of the State is undulating, with occasional plains, and swamps of formidable extent. The soil of the tide-water districts is generally a light sandy loam. A belt of mountain ranges, a hundred miles in breadth, runs in a northeast and southwest direction across the State, enclosing some of its richest and loveliest portions. The Valley of Virginia, — as that fertile stripe is called lying west of the Blue Ridge, drained by the Shenandoah and the head-

15

waters of the James, — is fitly called the granary of the State. It is a limestone region, admirably adapted for grains and grazing. The virginity of its soil has not been polluted by tobacco.

In 1860 there were in the State less than eleven and a half million acres of improved land, out of an area of near forty millions. Over thirteen million bushels of wheat were produced; one million of rye, Indian corn, and oats; one hundred and twenty-four million pounds of tobacco; twelve thousand seven hundred and twenty-seven bales of cotton; and two and a half million pounds of wool (in round numbers). There were four thousand nine hundred manufacturing establishments, the value of whose manufactures was fifty-one million three hundred thousand dollars. There were thirteen cotton factories, running twenty-eight thousand seven hundred spindles. The most important article of export before the war was negroes. There were sold out of the State annually twenty thousand.[1]

With the exception of the last-named staple, these annual productions are destined to be multiplied indefinitely by a vigorous system of free labor and the introduction of Northern capital. The worn-out lands can be easily restored by the application of marl and gypsum, with which the State abounds, and of other natural fertilizers. The average value of land, in 1850, was eight dollars an acre; while that of New Jersey, which never bragged of its fertility, was forty-four dollars. The former price will now buy lands in almost any section of Virginia except the Shenandoah Valley; while there is no question but that they can be raised to the latter price, and beyond, in a very few years, by judicious cultivation, united with such internal improvements as are indispensable to make the wealth of any region available.

Still greater inducements are presented to manufacturers than

[1] In 1850, the number of slave-owners in the State was 55,063. Of these 11,385 owned one slave each; 15,550, more than one and less than 5; 13,030, more than 5 and less than 10; 9,456, more than 10 and less than 20; 4,880, more than 20 and less than 50; 646, more than 50 and less than 100; 107, over 100 and less than 200; 8 over 200 and less than 300; and 1, over 300.

to farmers. To large capitalists, looking to establish extensive cotton-mills, I do not feel myself competent to offer any suggestions. But of small manufactures I can speak with confidence. Take the Shenandoah Valley for example. The wool that is raised there is sent North to be manufactured, and brought back in the shape of clothing, having incurred the expense of transportation both ways, and paid the usual tariff to traders through whose hands it has passed. The Valley abounds in iron ore of the best quality; and it imports its kettles and stoves. The same may be said of nearly all agricultural implements. The freight on many of these imports is equal to their original cost. It was said before the war that scarce a wagon, clock, broom, boot, shoe, coat, rake or spade, or piece of earthen ware, was used in the South, that was not manufactured at the North; and the same is substantially true to-day, notwithstanding the change in this particular which the war was supposed to have effected. Let any enterprising man, or company of men, with sufficient experience for the work and capital to invest, go into Virginia, make use of the natural water-power which is so copious that no special price is put upon it, and manufacture, of the materials that abound on the spot, articles that are in demand there, establishing a judicious system of exchange, and who can doubt the result, now that the great obstacle in the way of such undertakings, slavery, has been removed?

In speaking of the products of Virginia, we should not forget its oysters; of which near fourteen and a half million bushels, valued at four million eight hundred thousand dollars, were sent from Chesapeake Bay in one year, previous to the war.

Virginia never had any common-school system. One third of her adult population can neither read nor write. There was a literary fund, established to promote the interests of education, which amounted, in 1861, to something over two millions of dollars; but it was swallowed by the war. At the present time the prospect for white common schools in the State is discouraging. The only one I heard of in anything like a flourishing condition was a school for poor whites, established by the Union Commission in the buildings of the Confederate naval laboratory, at Richmond. It numbers five hundred pupils, and is taught by experienced teachers from the North. The prospect is better for the education of the freedmen. There were in the State last winter ninety freedmen's schools, with an aggregate of eleven thousand five hundred pupils. There were two hundred teachers; twenty-five of whom were colored men and women at the head of self-supporting schools of their own race. The remaining schools, taught by experienced individuals from the North, were supported mainly by the following benevolent associations: The New-York National Freedmen's Relief; American Missionary; Pennsylvania Freedmen's Relief; Baptist Home Mission; New-England Freedmen's Aid; and Philadelphia Friends' Freedmen's Relief.

The opposition manifested by a large class of whites to the establishment of these schools was at first intense and bitter. It had nearly ceased, — together with the outrages on freedmen, which had been frequent, — when, on the removal of the troops from certain localities,[1] it recommenced, and was, at my last visit, fearfully on the increase. Teachers were threatened and insulted, and school-houses broken into or burned. The better class of citizens, — many of whom see the necessity of educating the negro now that he is free, — while they have nothing to do with these acts of barbarism, are powerless to prevent them. The negro-haters are so strong an element in every society that they completely shield the wrong-doers from the reach of civil law.

The great subject of discussion among the people everywhere was the "niggers." Only a minority of the more enlightened class, out of their large hearts and clear heads, spoke of them kindly and dispassionately. The mass of the people, including alike the well-educated and the illiterate, generally detested the negroes, and wished every one of them driven out of the State. The black man was well enough as a slave;

---

[1] In February, 1866, there were but 2500 troops left in the State.

but even those who rejoiced that slavery was no more, desired to get rid of him along with it. When he was a chattel, like a horse or dog, he was commonly cherished, and sometimes even loved like a favorite horse or dog, and there was not a particle of prejudice against him on account of color ; but the master-race could not forgive him for being free ; and that he should assume to be a man, self-owning and self-directing, was intolerable. I simply state the fact ; I do not condemn anybody. That such a feeling should exist is, I know, the most natural thing in the world ; and I make all allowances for habit and education.

It is this feeling which makes some protection on the part of the government necessary to the negro in his new condition. The Freedmen's Bureau stands as a mediator between him and the race from whose absolute control he has been too recently emancipated to expect from it absolute justice. The belief inheres in the minds of the late masters, that they have still a right to appropriate his labor. Although we may acquit them of intentional wrong, it is impossible not to see how far their conduct is from right.

Before the war, it was customary to pay for ordinary able-bodied plantation slaves, hired of their masters, at rates varying from one hundred and ten to one hundred and forty dollars a year for each man, together with food, clothing, and medical attendance. After the war, the farmers in many counties of Virginia entered into combinations, pledging themselves to pay the freed slave only sixty dollars a year, exclusive of clothing and medical attendance, with which he was to furnish himself out of such meagre wages. They also engaged not to hire any freedman who had left a former employer without his consent. These were private leagues instituting measures similar to those which South Carolina and some other States afterwards enacted as laws, and having in view the same end, namely, — to hold the negro in the condition of abject dependence from which he was thought to have been emancipated.

That the freedman's supposed unwillingness to work, and the employer's poverty occasioned by the war, were not the reasons why he was to be paid less than half the wages he earned when hired out as a slave, I had abundant evidence. One illustration will suffice. Visiting the tobacco factories of Richmond, I found them worked entirely by freedmen under white superintendents. I never saw more rapid labor performed with hands than the doing up of the tobacco in rolls for the presses; nor harder labor with the muscles of the whole body than the working of the presses. The superintendents told me they had difficulty in procuring operatives. I inquired if the freedmen were well paid; and was informed that good workmen earned a dollar and a half a day.

"If the negroes will not engage in the business, why not employ white labor?"

"We tried that years ago, and it would n't answer. White men can't stand it; they can't do the work. This press-work is a dead strain; only the strongest niggers are up to it."

Those putting up the tobacco in rolls, — three ounces in each, though they rarely stopped to place one on the scales, — showed a skill which could have resulted only from years of practice. I learned, from conversing with them, that they were dissatisfied with their pay; and the superintendents admitted that, while the negroes worked as well as ever, labor was much cheaper than formerly. On further investigation I ascertained that a combination between the manufacturers kept the wages down; that each workman had to employ a "stemmer," who made the tobacco ready for his hands; and that his earnings were thus reduced to less than five dollars a week, out of which he had himself and his family to support.[1]

[1] After my visit to the tobacco factories, the following statement, drawn up for the colored workmen by one of their number, was placed in my hands by a gentleman who vouched for its truthfulness. I print it verbatim: —

Richmond September 18, 1865 Dear Sirs We the Tobacco mechanicks of this city and Manchester is worked to great disadvantage In 1858 and 1859 our masters hiered us to the Tobacconist at a prices ranging from $150 to 180. The Tobacconist furnished us lodging food & clothing. They gave us tasks to performe. all we made over this task they payed us for. We worked faithful and they paid us faithful. They Then gave us $2 to 2.50 cts, and we made double the amount we now make. The Tobacconist held a meeting, and resolved not give more than $1.50 cts per hundred, which is about one days work — in a week we may make 600 lbs apece with a stemer. The weeks work then at $1.50 amounts to $9 — the stemers wages is from $4 to $4.50

The Bureau labored to break up these combinations, and to secure for the freedmen all the rights of freemen. Colonel Brown, the Assistant-Commissioner for Virginia, divided the State into districts, and assigned a superintendent to each. The districts were subdivided into sub-districts, for which assistant superintendents were appointed. Thus the Bureau's influence was felt more or less throughout the State. It assisted the freedmen in obtaining employment, regulated contracts, and secured to them fair wages. It had a general superintendence of freedmen's schools. It used such powers as it possessed to scatter the negroes, whom the exigencies of the war had collected together in great numbers at places where but few could hope for employment. It fed the destitute, the aged, the orphan, the infirm, and such as were unable to find work, — who, in that period of transition, must have perished in masses without such aid. It likewise established courts for the trial of minor cases of litigation or crime in which persons of color were concerned. Each court was originally presided over by an officer of the Bureau; but in order to secure impartial justice to all, there were associated with him two agents, one chosen by the citizens of the sub-district in which it was located, and the other by the freedmen.

There is in every community a certain percentage of its members that look to get a living without honest toil. I am not aware that the negro has any more love for work than another man. Coming into the enjoyment of freedom before they knew what freedom meant, no wonder that many should have regarded life henceforth as a Christmas frolic. The system

cts which leaves from $5 to 4-50 cts per week about one half what we made when slaves. Now to Rent two small rooms we have to pay from $18 to 20. We see $4.50 cts or $5 will not more then pay Rent say nothing about food Clothing medicin Doctor Bills. Tax and Co. They say we will starve through lazines that is not so. But it is true we will starve at our present wages. They say we will steal we can say for ourselves we had rather work for our living. give us a Chance. We are Compeled to work for them at low wages and pay high Rents and make $5 per week and sometimes les. And paying $18 or 20 per month Rent. It is impossible to feed ourselves and family — starvation is Cirten unles a change is brought about

Tobacco Factory Mechanicks of Richmond and Manchester.

which had held them in bondage had kept them ignorant
Having always been provided for by their masters, they were
as improvident as children. They believed that the government which had been their Liberator would likewise be their
Provider: the lands of their Rebel masters were to be given
them, and their future was to be licensed and joyous. They
had the vices of a degraded and enslaved race. They would
lie and steal and shirk their tasks. Their pleasures were of
a sensuous character; even their religion was sensuous; the
sanctity of the marriage-tie, so long subject to the caprices
of the master-race, was lightly esteemed. Under these circumstances the proportion of those who have shown a persistent determination to lead lives of vice and vagrancy,
appears to me surprisingly small. Their number still de-
creases as their enlightenment increases. The efforts of the
Freedmen's Bureau, and Northern missionary and educational labors among them, have contributed greatly towards
this desirable result. Still more might be done if additional
discretionary powers were granted the Assistant-Commissioner. Vagrants, whether white or black, should be treated
as vagrants; and I thought it would have been a wholesome
measure for the Bureau to make contracts for those freedmen
who refused to make contracts for themselves, and were without any visible means of support.

There are in Virginia half a million negroes. Those appear
most thriving and happy who are at work for themselves. I
have described the freedmen's farms about Hampton. In
other portions of Southeast Virginia, where the Federal influence has been longest felt, they are equally industrious and
prosperous. Captain Flagg, the superintendent at Norfolk,
whose district comprises seven counties, told me that he was
not issuing rations to a hundred persons, besides orphan children. In Northampton and Accomack counties every negro
owns his boat, and earns with it three dollars a day at oystering, in the oyster season. There are perhaps eighteen thousand freedmen in those counties, all engaged in oystering,
fishing, and the cultivation of lands which they own or hire.

In Norfolk, Princess Anne, and other counties adjacent, planters were very generally renting or selling lands to the freedmen, who were rapidly becoming a respectable, solid, tax-paying class of people. Many colored soldiers were coming back and buying small farms with money earned in the service of the government. Captain Flagg, a man of sense and discretion, said to me deliberately, and gave me leave to publish the statement: —

" I believe the negro population of the seven counties of my district will compare favorably, in respect to industry and thrift, with any laboring white population of similar resources at the North." Adding, " I believe most thoroughly in the ability of these people to get a living even where a white man would starve."

The freedmen in other parts of the State were not doing as well, being obliged generally to enter into contracts with the land-owners. Many of these, impoverished by the war, could not afford to pay them more than seven or eight dollars a month for their labor ; while some were not able to pay even that. Their fences destroyed, buildings burned, farming implements worn out, horses, mules, and other stock consumed by both armies, investments in Confederate bonds worthless, bank-stock gone, without money, or anything to exchange for money, they had often only their bare lands on which to commence life anew ; and could not therefore give much encouragement to the freedman, whatever may have been their disposition towards him.

The legislative and local affairs of the State had very generally fallen under the influence, or into the hands, of those who had given aid and sympathy to the Rebellion. Indeed, Governor Pierpoint told me that there were not unquestionably loyal men enough in Virginia to form a government. " In many counties," said he, " you will not find one."

Yet Virginia sent to the convention of February 13th, 1861, a majority of Union delegates. It was only after the fall of Fort Sumter, and President Lincoln's call for troops, that a vote could be had taking the State out of the Union. Eighty-eight delegates voted for the ordinance of secession, fifty-five against it. It was afterwards — in the tempest of excitement which swept over the State — adopted by the people by a majority of ninety-four thousand. It was an act of passion and madness. Travelling through the State, I found a majority of the people professing to have been at heart Union men all the while. They could never forgive South Carolina for the evil course in which she had led them ; and it was very common to hear the wish expressed, " that South Carolina and Massachusetts were kicked out into the Atlantic together." Having, however, against her better reason, seceded, Virginia became the most devoted and self-sacrificing of all the States in the cause in which she had embarked.

The railroads of the State [1] were, both financially and physically, in a bad condition. They had been used excessively during the war, and stood in need of repairs. The iron taken from the Richmond and York River Road had not been replaced. The time made by trains was necessarily slow. The

---

[1] In 1860, there were in Virginia $66,000,000 of capital invested in 1675 miles of railroad, distributed over sixteen lines. This estimate includes 287 miles of the Baltimore and Ohio Road. In all the important roads except this, the State is a principal shareholder. The management of some of them has always been loose and uneconomical.

Governor Pierpoint wisely recommends a consolidation of certain lines: — " On the south side of James River we have the Norfolk and Petersburg, South-Side, Virginia and Tennessee, and the Richmond and Danville railroads. These roads are under the management of four different corps of officers, employed at remunerative salaries. Three of these roads form a continuous line of about four hundred miles, and all three of them afford business for the fourth. By working these roads separately a car is loaded at Norfolk with freight for Danville or Abingdon; it is brought to Petersburg to the South-Side Road, and there transferred from the Norfolk to a South-Side car; thence it is taken to Burkeville, where it is again transferred to a Danville car, — if its destination is to that town, — or taken to Lynchburg and reshipped on the Virginia and Tennessee Road, if it goes to Abingdon. In these transactions the cars are delayed, thereby causing a much larger investment in rolling-stock to accommodate the business of these roads, in addition to the labor required to load and unload the freight, besides exposing the merchandise to loss and delaying its transportation. The Baltimore and Ohio Railroad, with the Northwestern Virginia and Washington branches, is nearly as long as the four roads above named, and the gross earnings of that railroad is about three times as great, the charges for passengers and freight being thirty-three per cent. less than on the Virginia roads referred to; yet the whole business of the Baltimore and Ohio road is done by one corps of officers with moderate salaries. There is the same reason for consolidating the Orange and Alexandria and Virginia Central Roads."

The rolling-stock was limited, and generally in a worse condition than the roads. But few lines were paying anything more than the expenses of running them.

The old State banks went down with the Confederacy. The circulation of the new National Banks in the State did not, in January 1866, exceed $1,300,000.

There was necessarily a great scarcity of money. It was difficult to raise funds even on the mortgage of real estate. The existence of usury laws, limiting the rate of interest at six per cent., operated to shut out Northern capital, which could find investments nearer home at more remunerative rates. When I was last in Richmond there was pending in the legislature a bill for the repeal of those laws, which, however, did not pass.

The immediate prospects of Virginia are dismal enough. But beyond this morning darkness I see the new sun rising. The great barrier, slavery, removed, all the lesser barriers to her prosperity must give way. The current of emigration, of education, of progressive ideas, is surely setting in ; and in a few years we shall see this beautiful torpid body rise up, renewed with health and strength, a glory to herself and to the Union.

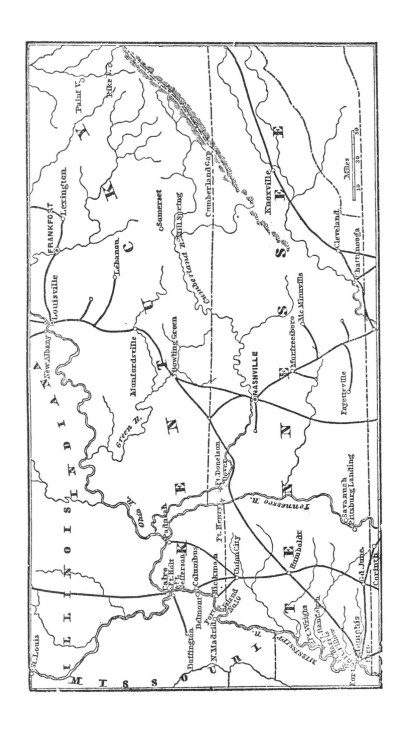

CHAPTER XXXI.

THE "SWITZERLAND OF AMERICA."

FROM the grassy hills and vales of Southwest Virginia, I passed over by railroad into East Tennessee.

At first sight, the "Switzerland of America" is apt, I think, to disappoint one. It is a country of pleasant hills, bounded and broken into by mountains which do not remind you of the Alps. The cottages of the inhabitants lack the picturesque element. A few first-class farmers have comfortable-looking painted or brick houses ; while scattered everywhere over the country are poverty-stricken, weather-blackened little framed dwellings and log-huts. Many of these are without windows ; the inmates living by the daylight let in through doors, and the firelight from open chimneys. Good barns are rare. The common class of villages are without sidewalks or paved streets. In the rainy season they are wretched. They look like Northern villages that have set out to travel and got stuck in the mud. One or two are noteworthy.

Greenville, the county seat of Greene County, is chiefly interesting as being the home of the President. It stands on broken ground, and is surrounded by a fine hilly country shaded by oaken groves. The town, as I saw it one wet morning, was eminently disagreeable. The mud came up to the very doors of its old, dilapidated, unpainted wooden houses. Its more pretentious, white-painted and brick dwellings were not quite so deep in the mire. A hundred chimney smokes draped the brown irregular roofs. President Johnson's house is on Main Street; a commonplace, respectable brick dwelling. The Rebels smashed the windows for him in wartimes, but they have been replaced, and the house is now occupied by the county sheriff. Every man knows "Andy Johnson." He has a good reputation for honesty, but I was told he was "hard on money matters." A prominent citizen who knew him intimately, said to me, "Johnson is a man of much greater ability than he has ever had credit for. When he was a tailor, he did his work well, — always a good honest job. He has many good traits, and a few bad ones. He is surly and vindictive, and a man of strong prejudices, but thoroughly a patriot."

There is in Greenville a spring which bursts out of a hill-side in sufficient volume to carry a mill. The country abounds in springs, some of a curious character. In Johnson County, in the mountainous northeast corner of the State, there is a subterranean reservoir of water, out of which issue in the night-time, during the spring months, numbers of small black perch, of a blind species, which are caught in traps at the mouth of the spring.

Knoxville, (named in honor of Revolutionary General Knox,) the most considerable town of East Tennessee, is situated on abrupt hills, on the north bank of the Holston River, which is navigable by steamers to this point. Here is the junction of the East Tennessee and Virginia, and East Tennessee and Georgia railroads. The city has something more than eight thousand inhabitants. It was formerly the capital of the State. It is surrounded by fortified hills.

The place received rough treatment during the war. The Bell House, at which I stopped, was a miserable shell, carpetless and dilapidated, full of broken windows. The landlord apologized for not putting it into repair. "I don't know how long I shall stop here. Hotel-keeping a'n't my business. Nigger-dealing is my business. But that's played out. I've bought and sold in my day over six hundred niggers," — spoken with mournful satisfaction, mingled pride and regret. "Now I don't know what I shall turn my hand to. I'm a Georgian; I came up here from Atlanta time it was burned."

At the table of the Bell House, a Southern gentleman who

sat next me called out to one of the waiters, a good-looking colored man, perhaps thirty years of age, — " Here, boy ! "

" My name is Dick," said the " boy," respectfully.

" You 'll answer to the name I call you, or I 'll blow a hole through you ! " swore the Southern gentleman.

Dick made no reply, but went about his business. The Southern gentleman proceeded, addressing the company : —

" Last week, in Chattanooga, I said to a nigger I found at the railroad, ' Here, Buck ! show me the baggage-room.' He said, ' My name a'n't Buck.' I just put my six-shooter to his head, and, by ——! he did n't stop to think what his name was, but showed me what I wanted."

This gentlemanly way of dealing with the " d——d impudent niggers " was warmly applauded by all the guests at the table, except one, who did not see the impudence ; showing that they were gentlemen of a similar spirit.

There were a great many freedmen crowded into Knoxville from Georgia and the Carolinas, whence they had escaped during the war. The police were arresting and sending them back. East Tennesseeans, though opposed to slavery and secession, do not like niggers. There is at this day more prejudice against color among the middle and poorer classes — the " Union " men, of the South, who owned few or no slaves — than among the planters who owned them by scores and hundreds. There was a freedmen's school-house burned in Knoxville, while I was in that part of the State ; and on reaching Nashville, I learned that the negro testimony bill had been defeated in the legislature by the members from East Tennessee.

East Tennessee, owning but a handful of slaves, and having little interest in slavery, opposed secession by overwhelming majorities. She opposed the holding of a convention, at the election of February, 1861, by a vote of 30,903 against 5,577 ; and, at the election in June following, opposed the ordinance of separation submitted to the people by the legislature, by 32,923 votes against 14,780. The secession element proved a bitter and violent minority. Neighborhood feuds ensued, of a fierce political and personal character. When the Confederate army came in, the secessionists pointed out their Union neighbors, and caused them to be robbed and maltreated. They exposed the retreats of hunted conscripts lying out in forests and caves, and assisted in the pursuit of loyal refugees. When the National forces possessed the country, the Union men retaliated. It was then the persecutor's turn to be stripped of his property and driven from his home.

I was sorry to find the fires of these old feuds still burning. The State Government was in the hands of Union men, and Rebels and refugees from the Union army were disfranchised. Secessionists, who assisted at the hanging and robbing of Union men, and burned their houses, were receiving just punishment for their crimes in the civil courts and at the hands of the sheriff. This was well; and it should have been enough. But those who had suffered so long and so cruelly at the hands of their enemies did not think so. Returning Rebels were mobbed; and if one had stolen back unawares to his home, it was not safe for him to remain there. I saw in Virginia one of these exiles, who told me how homesickly he pined for the hills and meadows of East Tennessee, which he thought the most delightful region in the world. But there was a rope hanging from a tree for him there, and he dared not go back. "The bottom rails are on top," said he : "that is the trouble." The Union element, and the worst part of the Union element, was uppermost. There was some truth in this statement. It was not the respectable farming class, but the roughs, who kept the old fires blazing. Many secessionists and Union men, who had been neighbors before the war, were living side by side again, in as friendly relations as ever.

At Strawberry Plain, on the Holston River, I saw a manifestation of this partisan spirit. A laboring man, whom I met on the butment of the burned railroad bridge, was telling me about the Rebel operations at that place, when a fine fellow came dashing into the village on horseback.

"There's a dog-goned Rebel now!" said my man, eyeing him with baleful glances. "He's a rebel colonel, just come back.   He 'll get warned; and then if he don't leave, he must look out ! '

I think if the " dog-goned Rebel " had seen what I saw, in the deadly determination of the man, he would have needed no further warning.

I listened to many tales of persecution and suffering endured by loyal East Tennesseeans during the war.   Here is the outline of one, related to me by a farmer in Greene County.

" After the Rebel Conscript Act passed, I started with my son and a hundred other refugees to go over the mountains into Kentucky.   The Rebels pursued us, put on the track by some of our secesh neighbors.   Some escaped, my son with them; but I was taken, and brought back with irons on my wrists.   That was the twenty-fifth of July, 1863.   I was carried to Richmond, and kept in Castle Thunder till the twentieth of October.   They then put me on a train to take me to Salisbury prison, in North Carolina.   I was in a box car, and I found that a board at one corner of it was so loose that I could pull it off with my hands.   Just at night, when we were about eighteen miles from Salisbury, and the train was running about ten miles an hour, I pulled away the board, and jumped off.   I took to the fields, and tramped till I came to the Yadkin River, where a nigger took me over in his canoe. I tramped all night, and lay by the next day in the woods, and tramped again the next night, and lay by again the next day, and so on for fourteen nights and days ; in which time I travelled three hundred miles.   They were moonlight nights, and I got along very well, only I near-about starved.   I lived on raw corn and pumpkins.   I kept the line of the Western Railroad ; I flanked the depots and pickets, but I was several times nigh being caught.   I never entered a house, or passed near one, if I could help it.   It was a hard, long, lonesome tramp. I did not speak to a human being, except the nigger that took me across the Yadkin, and another I almost run over on the road as I was coming to Asheville.   He said to me, ' Good evening.'   I muttered back something, and went on.   I had n't gone far before I changed my mind.   Something said to me,

16

'Ask help of that nigger.' I was sick and worn out, and almost perishing for want of food. Besides, I did not know the country ; I saw I was coming to a town, and there was danger I might be taken. I went back, and said to the nigger, 'Can you give me something to eat ? ' He was sitting on the ground; but he jumped up, and looked at me by the moonlight, and said, ' Where do you want to go ? ' I told him. Then he knew I was a Union man running away from the Rebels. He told me to wait for him there, and came back in a little while with a heap of bread and beef. Never anything tasted so good. After I had eaten, he gave me directions how to avoid the guard, and strike the road beyond Asheville. I came over the mountains, and reached here the fourteenth night."

East Tennessee contributed a liberal quota to the national army. Twenty-five thousand loyal refugees escaped into Kentucky, and fought their way back again with Burnside's forces in 1863.

CHAPTER XXXII.

EAST TENNESSEE FARMERS.

I FOUND the East Tennesseeans a plain, honest, industrious, old-fashioned people. Only about four out of five can read and write. Men of the North and West would consider them slow. They are dressed, almost without exception, in coarse, strong "domestic," as the home-manufactured cloth of the country is called. It is woven on hand-looms, which are to be found in nearly every farm-house. Domestic is, in fact, an institution, not of Tennessee alone, but of the entire Southern country. In the absence of manufacturing establishments, the interest in this primitive private industry has not been suffered to decline. It stood the South in good stead during the war. After the importation of goods was cut off, it clothed the people. All classes wore it. Even at the time of my visit, I found many proprietors of large estates, the aristocrats of the country, wearing garments which had been spun, colored, and woven by their own slaves.

Tennessee has no system of free schools. There was a common-school fund, derived mainly from public lands given for the purpose by the United States. The State was the trustee of this fund, which the Constitution declared " permanent, never to be diminished by legislative appropriation," nor " devoted to any other use than the support and encouragement of common schools." The proceeds of this fund distributed among the schools in 1859, amounted to $230,430, or seventy-five cents for each scholar in the State. Treason, which betrayed so many sacred trusts, betrayed this. According to Governor Brownlow " a more perfidious act than the appropriation of this fund to treasonable purposes was not committed during the late perfidious rebellion."

The people of East Tennessee took more interest, perhaps, in common-school education, than the inhabitants of other parts of the State; but that was not much. The school-fund went but a little way toward the support of schools. There were scattered throughout the country log school-houses capable of accommodating fifty pupils each. The tuition varied from two dollars and a half to three dollars a scholar. The teachers were supported by neighborhood subscriptions. But education was regarded by the poor as a luxury which they could not afford; and even the middling class was apt to consider their money and their children's labor of more importance than book-learning. The war, and the waste of the school-fund, had for four years put an end to schools, and I found the new generation growing up in ignorance.

The school-houses serve as meeting-houses. There are few churches beside. Outside of the larger towns, scarce a spire points its finger towards heaven. This is true not only of Tennessee, but of the whole South. It is one of the peculiarities of the country which strike the Northern traveller unpleasantly. The village green, with the neat white-steepled edifice standing upon it, distinguishable from all other buildings, is no feature of the Southern landscape. You may travel thousands of miles and not meet with it.

Yet the East Tennesseeans are a church-going people. No especial form of meeting-house, any more than form of worship, is necessary to the exercise of that divine faculty by which man communes with his Maker. The Holy Spirit enters as readily the log-hut, where two or three are gathered together, as the great temples where multitudes assemble.

The Methodist Church predominates in East Tennessee. The United Brethren, who admit to their communion no rum-seller, rum-drinker, nor slaveholder, have a powerful influence. They were much persecuted in the South before the war, as was natural in a country where the prejudice in favor of rum and slavery was so strong; but of late, in East Tennessee, they have grown in strength and popularity.

Farming is behind the age. Mowers and reapers, which

might be employed to fine advantage on the beautiful smooth meadows and grain-fields of East Tennessee, have scarcely come into use at all. In Greene County I heard of but three. Manures are wasted. It is customary to rotate crops, until even rotation must cease, giving place to a usurpation of weeds and broom-sedge. A favorite method of improving land is to "clover" it; that is, to plough in crops of clover and grass. Farming utensils are nearly all brought from the North; and there is a great need for home manufactures here also. The farmers generally work mules and mares. The mares are kept chiefly for breeding mules. For which purpose likewise every neighborhood, if not every farm, has its "jack."

The further my observations extended, the more strongly I was convinced that mules were an indispensable substitute for horses in the South. Animals there do not receive the cherishing care they get at the North; and the rough, careless treatment which I saw almost universally shown to beasts of burden, not only by the negroes, but also by the whites, can be endured by nothing less hardy than the mule. This valuable creature, besides possessing the advantages I have elsewhere alluded to, is recommended for his brave appetite, which slights no part of the product of a hill of corn, but sturdily masters stalk, cob, and shucks.

Animals are driven, both at ploughing and teaming, by one rein, which is attached to the middle of the bridle-rein on the neck of the "lead" horse or mule, as the "near" or left-hand beast is called. The driver gives two little jerks for *gee*, and a steady pull for *haw*. This is the custom throughout the South.

I found horses cheap in Tennessee. A farmer said to me, "A hundred and a half will buy our best animal. This is not because horses are plenty, but because money is scarce. Formerly we used to take large droves of our stock to Georgia and the Carolinas; but that market is closed now, there is no money there." Several weeks afterwards, in one of the middle counties of South Carolina, I met this very man, who told me he had come into the State with eleven horses, and sold them all at good prices. There had been more money hoarded, and more cotton reserved to be exchanged for money, in parts of the South than was at first supposed.

Tennessee and Kentucky are the two great mule-breeding States. East Tennessee takes first rank among the grazing sections of the South and West. Wild grass abounds in the uncultivated districts. Interminable forests on the mountain sides are carpeted with it. The woods are kept open and free from undergrowth by fires ; and this native grass springs up and covers the ground. The mountains are full of deer which feed upon it. Many a beautiful range of thousands of acres is also afforded the farmers' stock, which is sent in vast numbers to occupy this wild, free, unfenced pasturage. Neighbors club together to make up a herd of four or five hundred head of cattle, enough to render profitable the employment of a herds-man. Farmers have but little hay to provide for the winter season. The climate is such that there is no month in the year during which cattle cannot gain at least a partial subsist-ence by grazing. This I account one of the great advantages of the country.

One of the great disadvantages is the want of a market. I saw a farmer in Jefferson County who had five thousand bushels of corn, for which he could find no sale near home ; and the cost of transportation was too great to think of taking it out of the State. Said he, " We find it for our interest to feed our farm-produce into stock, and drive it."

I was told there was " a heap of thin, poor soil in East Tennessee." The ordinary land produces fifteen bushels of wheat, and thirty-five of corn to the acre. The lands on the river bottoms are incomparably better. Prices range from eight and ten to eighty and a hundred dollars per acre, accord-ing to the situation and quality. There are farms to be had in every section ; it can scarcely be said that they are for sale, there being no sale for them. Such is the distress for money among holders of real estate, that land can be had in some of the most desirable locations almost at the buyer's own price. It is claimed that before the war the wheat of East Tennessee commanded the highest market-prices in Richmond and New York, as having that fine, enduring quality wheat derives only from good limestone soils. Fruits abound, — apples, peaches, pears, plums; and both climate and soil are admirably adapted to the grape. The country is well watered, and its climate is mild and salubrious. Manufacturing facilities are abundant. There are forests and coal-mines, lead, zinc, iron, copper, marble, and unimproved water-power to any extent.

Farmers told me they were paying the freedmen from eight to fifteen dollars a month, and boarding them. They said, "We can afford to pay more than Virginians can, because we farm it better." They laughed at the Virginians' shiftless methods. Yet a few were beginning to learn that even they were not perfect in the business. One who had visited Iowa, where he saw men plough out two rows of corn at a time, and mow and reap with machinery, one hand doing the work of four or five men, said he had concluded that they in Tennessee did n't know anything.

CHAPTER XXXIII.

IN AND ABOUT CHATTANOOGA.

Two hundred and fifty miles from Knoxville, lying within a coil of the serpentine Tennessee, on its south bank, surrounded by mountains, is the town of Chattanooga. Here the East Tennessee and Virginia Railroad connects with the Nashville and Chattanooga, and with the Western and Atlantic, making the place an important centre of railroad communications. The river is navigable for steamboats during eight months of the year. Here are shipped the principal exports of East Tennessee and of Southern Middle Tennessee. Hence the military importance of the place, and its historical interest.

Although embosomed amid strikingly bold and grand scenery, Chattanooga is anything but a lovely town. On the east, but a few miles distant, is Missionary Ridge,[1] a range of forest-covered mountains rising from the river and sweeping away southward into Georgia. On the southwest is Lookout Mountain, with rugged, precipitous front overlooking the river and the town. Between this mountain and Missionary Ridge lies Chattanooga Valley. Rising steeply from the edge of the town, within the curve of the river which encloses it on the north and west, is Cameron Hill, a sort of miniature copy of Lookout. A miniature only by comparison; for it is a little mountain by itself: a peaked bluff, its summit flanked by forts, and crowned by a battery of a single huge gun.

If you visit Chattanooga, climb, as I did, this hill the first fair morning after your arrival. Away on the south are the mountains of Georgia; on the north, those of Tennessee.

[1] Or Mission Ridge; named from an Indian mission formerly located in this vicinity.

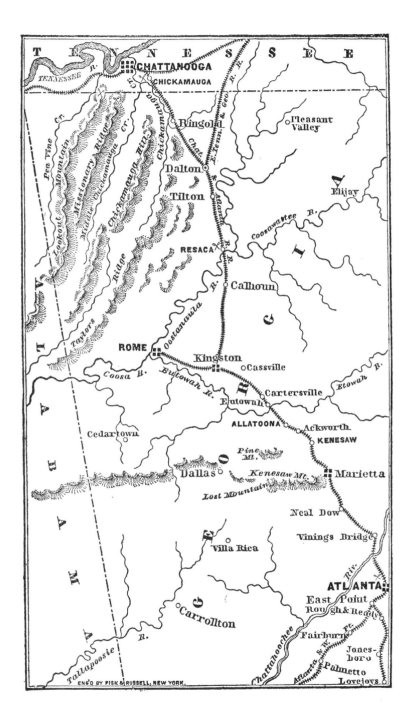

ENG'D BY FISK & RUSSELL, NEW YORK.

Dividing these peaks and ranges with its shining cimetar, curves the river, overhung by precipitous crags. Far beneath you, as you look from the northern brow of the hill, ply the steamboats, breaking the surface into streaks of foam, and puffing white wreaths up into the clear, still air. Opposite, across the river, are clusters of high, wooded hills, with signal-stations on their peaks.

In the valley at the foot of Cameron, is Chattanooga, with its multitude of long, low, whitewashed wooden buildings, government store-houses, barracks, shops, rows of huts, and corrals, such as make haste always to spring up around an army's base of supplies. Surrounding the town are red earthworks, and hills of red earth with devious roads and paths winding over them.

I found a strangely mixed population in Chattanooga, — traders, adventurers, soldiers, poor whites, refugees, and negroes. There were many Union men from the Cotton States, who had escaped into our lines during the war, and either could not or dared not return. Here is a sample of them, — a lank, sallow, ragged individual with long black hair and wild beard, whose acquaintance I made in the streets. He was a shoemaker from Georgia. His Rebel neighbors had burned his house and shop, destroyed his tools, and forced him to flee for his life. He enlisted in our army, and had been fighting his daddy and two brothers.

"My daddy," said he, "is as good a Rebel as you 'll find. He has grieved himself nigh-about to death because he did n't gain his independence."

I asked him how his father would receive him if he should go back.

"I allow we should n't git along together no hack! The first question I 'd ask him would be if he 'd tuck the oath of allegiance. That would devil him to death. Then I 'd ask him if he knowed whar his President Jeff was. Then he 'd jest let in to cussin' me. But I can't go back. The men that robbed me are jest as bad Rebels as ever, and they 'd burn my house again, or give me a bullet from behind some bush."

There was in Chattanooga a post-school for the children of poor whites and refugees. It numbered one hundred and fifty pupils of various ages, — young children, girls of fifteen and sixteen, one married woman, and boys that were almost men, all wofully ignorant. Scarcely any of them knew their letters when they entered the school. The big boys chewed tobacco, and the big girls "dipped." The mothers, when they came to talk with the teacher about their children, appeared with their nasty, snuffy sticks in their mouths: some chewed and spat like men. One complained that she was too poor to send her children to school; at the same time she was chewing up and spitting away more than the means needful for the purpose. Tobacco was a necessity of life; education wasn't. The tax upon pupils was very small, the school being mainly supported by what is called the " post-fund," accruing from taxes on sutlers, rents of buildings, and military fines. The post-school is usually designed for the children of soldiers; but Chattanooga being garrisoned by colored troops, their chil dren attended the freedmen's schools.

The freedmen's schools were not in session at the time of my visit, owing to the small-pox then raging among the negro population; but I heard an excellent account of them. They numbered six hundred pupils. The teachers were furnished by the Western Freedmen's Aid Society and paid by the freedmen themselves. One dollar a month was charged for each scholar. " The colored people," said the school-superintendent, " are far more zealous in the cause of education than the whites. They will starve themselves, and go without clothes, in order to send their children to school."

Notwithstanding there were three thousand negroes in and around Chattanooga, Captain Lucas, of the Freedmen's Bu reau, informed me that he was issuing no rations to them. All were finding some work to do, and supporting themselves. To those who applied for aid he gave certificates, requesting the Commissary to sell them rations at Government rates. He was helping them to make contracts, and sending them away to plantations at the rate of fifty or one hundred a

week. "These people," said he, "have been terribly slandered and abused. They are willing to go anywhere, if they
are sure of work and kind treatment. Northern men have
no difficulty in hiring them, but they have no confidence in
their old masters." It was mostly to Northern men, leasing
plantations in the Mississippi Valley, that the freedmen were
hiring themselves. The usual rate of wages was not less
than twelve nor more than sixteen dollars a month, for full
hands.

The principal negro settlement was at Contraband, a village
of huts on the north side of the river. Its affairs were administered by a colored president and council chosen from among
the citizens. These were generally persons of dignity and
shrewd sense. They constituted a court for the trial of minor
offences, under the supervision of the Bureau. Their decis-
ions, Captain Lucas informed me, were nearly always wise
and just. "I have to interfere, sometimes, however, to miti-
gate the severity of the sentences." These men showed no
prejudice in favor of their own color, but meted out a rugged
and austere justice to all.

One afternoon I crossed the river to pay a visit to this little
village. The huts, built by the negroes themselves, were of a
similar character to those I had seen at Hampton, but they
lacked the big wood-piles and stacks of corn, and the general
air of thrift. Excepting the ravages of the small-pox, the
community was in a good state of health. I found but one
case of sickness, — that of an old negro suffering from a cold
on his lungs, who told me there was nothing in the world he
would n't give to "git shet of dis sher misery."

I entered several of these houses ; in one of which I surprised
a young couple courting by the fire, and withdrew precipitately,
quite as much embarrassed as they were. In another I found
a middle-aged woman patching clothes for her little boy, who
was at play before the open door. Although it was a summer-
like December day, there was a good fire in the fireplace.
The hut was built of rails and mud ; the chimney of sticks and
sun-dried bricks, surmounted by a barrel. The roof was of

split slabs. There was a slab mantel-piece crowded with bottles and cans ; a shelf in one corner loaded with buckets and pans ; and another in the opposite corner devoted to plates, cups, and mugs. I noticed also in the room a table, a bed, a bunk, a cupboard, a broom without a handle, two stools, and a number of pegs on which clothing was hung. All this within a space not much more than a dozen feet square.

I asked the woman how her people were getting along.

"Some are makin' it right shacklin'," she replied, "there's so many of us here. A heap is workin', and a heap is lazin' around." Her husband was employed whenever he could get a job. "Sometimes he talks like he 'd hire out, then like he 'd sooner take land, — any way to git into work. All have to support themselves somehow."

She knew me for a Northern man. "I 'm proud of Northern men ! They 've caused me to see a heap mo'e pleasuré 'n I ever see befo'e." Her husband was a good man, but she was not at all enthusiastic about him. "I had one husband ; I loved him ! He belonged to a man that owned a power o' darkeys. He sold him away. It just broke my heart. But I could n't live without some man, no how ; so I thought I might as well marry again." She regretted the closing of the schools. "My chap went a little, but not much."

"Are these your chickens ? "

"No, I can't raise chickens." It was the fault of her neighbors. "They just pick 'em up and steal 'em in a minute ! Heap of our people will pick up, but they 're sly. That comes from the way they was raised. I never stole in my life but from them that owned me. They 'd work me all day, and never give me enough to eat, and I 'd take what I could from 'em, and believe it was right."

Hearing martial music as I returned across the river, I went up on a hill east of the town and witnessed the dress-parade of the sixteenth colored regiment (Tennessee). I never saw a finer military display on a small scale. The drill was perfect. At the order, a thousand muskets came to a thousand shoulders with a single movement, or the butts struck the ground with one sound along the whole line. The contrast of colors was superb, — the black faces, the white gloves, the blue uniforms, the bright steel. The music by the colored band was mellow and inspiring; and as a background to the picture we had a golden sunset behind the mountains.

CHAPTER XXXIV.

LOOKOUT MOUNTAIN.

THE next morning General Gillem, in command at Chatta-nooga, supplied me with a horse, and gave me his orderly for an attendant, and I set out to make the ascent of Lookout Mountain.

Riding out southward on one of the valley roads, we had hardly crossed Chattanooga Creek before we missed our way. Fortunately we overtook a farmer and his son, who set us right. They were laboring over the base of the mountain with a wagon drawn by a pair of animals that appeared to have been mated by some whimsical caprice. A tall, bony horse was harnessed in with the smallest mule I ever saw. Imagine a lank starved dog beside a rat, and you have an idea of the ludicrous incongruity of the match.

The man had in his wagon a single bag of grist, which he had to help over the rough mountain-roads by lifting at the wheels. He had been twelve miles to mill: "away beyant Missionary Ridge." I asked him if there was no mill nearer home. "Thar 's a mill on Wahatchie Crick, but it 's mighty hard to pull thar. Wahatchie Hill is a powerful bad hill to pull up." He did not seem to think twelve miles to mill anything, and we left him lifting cheerfully at the wheels, while his son shouted and licked the team. I trust his wife appreciated that bag of grist.

Riding southward along the eastern side of the mountain, we commenced the ascent of it by a steep, rough road, wind-ing among forest-trees, and huge limestone rocks colored with exquisite tints of brown and gray and green, by the moss and lichens that covered them. A range of precipitous crags rose before us, and soon hung toppling over us as we continued to climb. A heavy cloud was on the mountain, combed by the pine-tops a thousand feet above our heads.

As we proceeded, I conversed with the General's orderly. He was a good-looking young fellow with short curly hair and a sallow complexion. I inquired to what regiment he belonged.

"The Sixth Ohio, colored." I looked at him with surprise. "You did n't take me for a colored man, I reckon," he said laughingly.

I thought he must be jesting, but he assured me that he was not.

"I was born in bondage," he said, "near Memphis. My master was my father, and my mother's owner. He made a will that she was to be free, and that I was to learn a trade, and have my freedom when I was twenty-one. He died when I was seven years old, and the estate was divided between his mother and two sisters. I don't know what became of the will. I was run off into Middle Tennessee and sold for three hundred dollars. I was sold again when I was fourteen for sixteen hundred dollars. I was a carpenter; and carpenters was high. When I saw other men no whiter than me working for themselves and enjoying their freedom, I got discontented, and made up my mind to put out. The year Buchanan run for President I run for freedom. I got safe over into Ohio, and there I worked at my trade till the war broke out. I went out as an officer's servant."

He met with various adventures, and at length became General Grant's body-servant. He described the General as "a short, chunked man, like a Dutchman;" quiet, kind, a great smoker, a heavy drinker, very silent, and seldom excited. "There was only one time when he appeared troubled in his mind. That was on the road to Corinth, after the battle of Shiloh. He used to walk his room all night."

After the government began to make use of colored troops he went back to Ohio and enlisted. Since the war closed, he had obtained a furlough, returned to his native place, and found his mother, who in the mean time had been held as a slave.

The clouds lifted as we reached the summit of the mountain, fifteen hundred feet above the river. We passed through Summer Town, a deserted village, formerly a place of resort for families from Tennessee, Georgia, and Alabama, during the hot season. A rough road over the rocks and through the woods took us to Point Lookout, a mile farther north.

A *lookout* indeed! What cloud shadows were sweeping the mountains and valleys! We left our horses tied to some trees, and clambered down over the ledges to the brink of the precipice. Away on the northeast was Chattanooga, with its clusters of roofs resembling saw-teeth. Below us was the crooked Tennessee, sweeping up to the base of the mountain, in a coil enclosing on the opposite side a foot-shaped peninsula, to which the Indians gave the appropriate name of Moccasin Point.

Immediately beneath us, on a shelf of the mountain, between its river-washed base and the precipice on which we stood, was the scene of Hooker's famous " battle in the clouds." The Rebels occupied a cleared space on that tremendous elevation. Behind them rose the crags; before them gloomed the woods, covering the lower part of the mountain. Along the cleared space, between the woods and the crags, ran their line of stone breastworks, which still remained, looking like a common farm-wall. The enemy had heavy guns on the summit of the mountain, but they could not be got into position, or sufficiently depressed, to be of service. Beside, the summit, on the morning of the attack, was immersed in mist, which concealed everything. The mist did not envelop the scene of the fight, however, but hung over it; so that the " battle in the clouds " was in reality a battle under the clouds.

The Nashville and Chattanooga Railroad runs around the curve of the river, under the mountain. As we sat looking down from the Point, a coal-train appeared, crawling along the track like a black snake.

Returning over the crest to the summit of the road, we paid a visit to Mr. Foster, known as the " Old Man of the Mountain." He was living in a plain country-house on the eastern

17

brow, with the immense panorama of hills and vales and forests daily before his eyes. He was one of the valiant, unflinching Union men of the South. In its wild nest on that crag his liberty-loving soul had lived, untamed as an eagle, through the perils and persecutions of the war. He was sixty-nine years old; which fact he expressed in characteristically quaint style: "Tennessee came into the Union the sixth day of June, 1796; and on the twenty-second day of June I came into the world to see about it."

His father was a Revolutionary soldier. "He was shot to pieces, in a manner. It took a heap of his blood to nourish Uncle Sam when he was a little feller. I recollect his saying to me, 'There's going to be wars; and when they come, I want you to remember what the Stars and Stripes cost your old father.' I did not forget the lesson when this cursed secession war begun."

He was by trade a carpenter. He came up on the mountain to live twenty years before, on account of his health, which was so poor in the valley that people said he was going to die, but which had been robust ever since. Twice during the war he was condemned by the Vigilance Committee to be hung for his Union sentiments and uncompromising freedom of speech. Twice the assassins came to his house to take him.

"The first time they came, it was Sunday. My wife had gone over the mountain to preaching, and I was alone. I loaded up my horse-pistol for 'em, — sixteen buck-shot: I put in a buck load, I tell ye. There was only two of 'em; and I thought I was good for three or four. They'd hardly got inside the gate when I went out to 'em, and asked what they wanted. One said, 'We've come for Old Foster!' I just took the rascal by the arm, and gave him a monstrous clamp, — I thought I felt the bone, — and shoved him head-over-heels out of that gate. I was going to shoot t'other feller, but they rode off so fast down the mountain I had no chance."

The next attempt on his life resulted similarly. After that, the Committee did not persist in getting him executed. "I was so old, I suppose they thought I was of no account." He told of several other Union men, however, whom they had caused to be hung. " After the Rebels got brushed out, Sherman and Hooker came to pay me a visit, and denominated me the ' Old Man of the Mountain.' "

CHAPTER XXXV.

THE SOLDIERS' CEMETERY.

A MILE and a quarter southeast from the town is the National Cemetery of Chattanooga. An area of seventy-five acres has there been set apart by the military authorities for the burial of the soldiers who died in hospitals or fell on battle-fields in that region renowned for sanguinary conflicts. It occupies a hill which seems to have been shaped by Providence for this purpose: its general form is circular, and it rises with undulations, showing a beautiful variety of curves and slopes, to a superb summit, which swells like a green dome over all.

General Thomas, commanding the Division of the Tennessee, was nominally the director of the cemetery works. But he appears to have left all in the hands of Mr. Van Horne, chaplain of the post, who, in addition to his other duties, assumed the responsible task of laying out the grounds and supervising the interments. His plan has certainly the merit of originality, and will prove, in the end, I have no doubt, as beautiful as it is unique. Copying nothing from the designs of other cemeteries, he has taken Nature for his guide. The outline of each separate section is determined by its location. Here, for example, is a shield, — the rise of the ground and the natural lines of depression suggesting that form. In the centre of each section is a monument; immediately surrounding which are the graves of officers, in positions according to their numbers and rank; while around the latter are grouped the graves of private soldiers, in lines adapted to the general shape of the section. The paths and avenues follow the hollows and curves which sweep from the base in every direction towards the summit. This is surrounded by a single circular avenue; and is to be crowned, according to the chaplain's plan, with a grand central monument, an historic temple overlooking the whole.

The place will abound in groups of trees, verdant lawns and slopes, magnificent vistas, and concealed views designed to surprise the visitor at every step. Outcropping ledges and bold, romantic rocks afford a delightful contrast to the green of the trees and grass, and to the smoothness of the slopes.

Beside the avenue which girds the base of the hill is a cave with galleries and chambers sculptured in a variety of forms by the action of water on the limestone rock. The chaplain, who accompanied me on my visit to the cemetery, sent for a guide and a light, and we explored this natural grotto a hundred feet or more, until we came to passages too narrow to admit us into the unknown chambers beyond. Besides the entrance from the avenue, there is an opening which affords a glimpse of the blue sky by day, or of the stars by night, through the roof of the cave.

The hill rises from the Valley midway between Lookout Mountain and Missionary Ridge, commanding a view of all that historic region. The Tennessee is visible, distant a mile or more. The chaplain told me that when the river was very high, water came in and filled the galleries of the cave; thus showing that they were of great extent, and mysteriously connected with the stream.

The work on the cemetery had thus far been performed by details from the army. The post-fund, which amounted to twenty-seven thousand dollars, had defrayed all expenses. But this cannot continue. The time is coming when the people of the States will be called upon to pay the debt they owe to the heroic dead, in liberal contributions towards the completion and adornment of this spot, where probably will be gathered together a more numerous host of the slain than in any other national cemetery. From Chickamauga and Mission Ridge, from Lookout Mountain and Wahatchie, from the scenes of many lesser fights, from the hospitals, and possibly also from the fields of Sherman's Atlanta campaign, thousands upon thousands they will come, a silent host, to this goal of future pilgrimages, this "Mecca of American memories."

Nine thousand had already been interred there at the time of my visit. No attempt was made to bury the dead by States. "I am tired of State Rights," said General Thomas; "let's have a *national* cemetery." Out of six thousand interred before the removal of the dead of Chickamauga was begun, only four hundred were unknown. A military record is kept, in which are inscribed all ascertainable facts respecting each, — his name, rank, company, arm of service, native State, age; time, place, and cause of death; address of nearest friends, and so forth; accompanied by a full regimental index, and an individual index; so that persons in search of the graves of friends can learn by a brief examination all that is known about them, and be guided at once to the section and number where their remains are deposited. The chaplain told me that many who had come with a determination to remove the bodies of their dead, immediately on seeing the cemetery had changed that determination, convinced that they could have no more fitting resting-place.

The dead of Chickamauga were being interred while I was there; and the chaplain kindly offered to accompany me to the battle-field, where a regiment of colored soldiers were at work exhuming the buried, and gathering together the remains of the unburied dead.

CHAPTER XXXVI.

MISSION RIDGE AND CHICKAMAUGA.

ACCORDINGLY, one cloudy December morning the chaplain, accompanied by two ladies of his household, took me up at my hotel, and drove us out of Chattanooga on the Rossville Road.

Leaving the open valley behind us we crossed a bushy plain, and passed through a clump of oaken woods. Before us, on the east, rose Missionary Ridge, forest-covered, its steep sides all russet-hued with fallen leaves, visible through the naked brown trees.

The chaplain who witnessed the scene, described to us the storming of those heights by the Army of the Cumberland, on the twenty-fifth of November, a little more than two years before. It was the finishing stroke to which the affair at Lookout Mountain was the brilliant prelude. It was the revenge for Chickamauga. There was a Rebel line of works along the base of the ridge; and the crests were defended by infantry and heavy artillery. The charge was ordered; and forward across the plain and up the slope swept a single glittering line of steel six miles in length. The Rebels were driven from their lower works by the bayonet. The army rushed forward without firing a shot, and pausing only to take breath for a moment in the depressions of the hill; then onward again, storming the heights, from which burst upon them a whistling and howling storm of iron and lead. General Thomas says the Ridge was carried simultaneously at six different points. The attack commenced at three o'clock in the afternoon; at four the crests were taken, and Bragg's army in flight. The first captured gun was turned upon the enemy by Corporal Kramer of the Forty-first Ohio regiment, belonging to Hazen's brigade of Wood's division. He discharged it by firing his musket over the vent. It took six men to carry the colors of the First Ohio to the summit, five falling by the way in the attempt. Corporal Angelbeck, finding a Rebel caisson on fire, cut it loose from the horses and run it off down the hill before it exploded. These instances of personal intrepidity (which I give on the authority of Major-General Hazen, whom I saw afterwards at Murfreesboro') are but illustrations of the gallantry shown by our troops along the whole line.

The plain we were crossing was the same which General Hooker's forces swept over in their pursuit of the enemy. We passed the Georgia State-line ; and, amid hilly woods filled with a bushy undergrowth, entered the mountain solitudes ; crossing Missionary Ridge by the Rossville Gap. Rossville, which consisted of a blacksmith-shop and dwelling in the Gap, had been burned to the ground. Beyond this point the road forked ; the left-hand track leading to Ringold, the right to Lafayette.

Driving southward along the Lafayette Road we soon reached the site of Cloud Spring Hospital, in the rear of the battle-field. A desolate, dreary scene : the day was cold and wet ; dead leaves strewed the ground ; the wind whistled in the trees. There were indications that here the work of disinterment was about to begin. Shovels and picks were ready on the ground ; and beside the long, low trenches of the dead waited piles of yellow pine coffins spattered with rain.

A little further on we came to traces of the conflict, — boughs broken and trees cut off by shells. We rode southward along the line of battle, over an undulating plain, with sparse timber on one side, and on the other a field of girdled trees, which had been a cotton-field at the time of the battle. These ghostly groves, called " deadenings," sometimes seen in other parts of the country, are an especial feature of the Southern landscape. . When timbered land is to be put under cultivation, the trees, instead of being cut away, are often merely deadened with the axe, which encircles them with a line severing the bark, and there left to stand and decay slowly through a series of years. First the sapless bark flakes and falls piecemeal, and the wind breaks off the brittle twigs and small boughs. Next the larger branches come down; and the naked trunk, covered in the course of time by a dry-rot, and perforated by worms and the bills of woodpeckers, stands with the stumps of two or three of its largest topmost limbs upstretched in stern and sullen gloom to heaven. There is something awful and sublime in the aspect of a whole forest of such. The tempest roars among them, but not a limb sways. Spring comes, and all around the woods are green and glad, but not a leaf or tender bud puts forth upon the spectral trunks. The sun rises, and the field is ruled by the shadows of these pillars, which sweep slowly around, shortening as noon approaches, and lengthening again at the approach of night. Corn and cotton flourish well; the powdery rot and half-decayed fragments which fall serving as a continual nourishment to the soil. It takes from ten to twenty years for these corpses standing over their graves to crumble and disappear beneath them. Sometimes they rot to the roots; or, when all is ready, a hurricane hurls his crashing balls, and the whole grove goes down in a night-time, like ten-pins.

Dismal enough looked the " deadening," in the cold and drizzling rain that morning on the battle-field. Scarcely less so seemed the woods beyond, all shattered and torn by shot and shell, as if a tornado had swept them. On the northern side of these was Kelly's house. The Dyer Farm was beyond; upon which we found two hundred colored soldiers encamped, in a muddy village of winter huts near the ruins of the burned farm-house. The Dyer family were said to be excellent Rebels. Dyer served as a guerilla; and it was his wife who burned her feather-bed in order that it might not be used by our wounded soldiers. After that patriotic act she wandered off in the woods and died. Her husband had since returned, and was now living in a new log-hut within sight of the camp.

The camp was a strange spectacle. The men were cooking their dinners or drying their clothes around out-door fires of logs which filled the air with smoke. Near by were piles of coffins, — some empty, some containing the remains of soldiers that had just been disinterred. The camp was surrounded by fields of stumps and piny undergrowth. Here and there were scattered trees, hitched at some of which were mules munching their dinners of wet hay.

There were two hundred and seventeen soldiers in camp. At first they had a horror of the work for which they were detailed. All the superstition of the African was roused within them at sight of the mouldering dead. They declared that the skulls moved, and started back with shrieks. An officer, to encourage them, unconcernedly took out the bones from a grave and placed them carefully in a coffin. They were induced to imitate his example. In a few hours they chatted or whistled and sang at their work ; and in a few days it was common to see them perform their labor and eat their luncheons at the same time, — lay bones into the coffin with one hand, and hold with the other the hard-tack they were nibbling.

More than nine tenths of the bodies taken from Chickamauga were unknown. Some had been buried in trenches; some singly ; some laid side by side, and covered with a little earth, perhaps not more than six inches deep, leaving feet and skull exposed ; and many had not been buried at all. Throughout the woods were scattered these lonely graves. The method of finding them was simple. A hundred men were deployed in a line, a yard apart, each examining half a yard of ground on both sides of him, as they proceeded. Thus was swept a space five hundred yards in breadth. Trees were blazed or stakes set along the edge of this space, to guide the company on its return. In this manner the entire battle-field had been or was to be searched. When a grave was found, the entire line was halted until the teams came up and the body was removed. Many graves were marked with stakes, but some were to be discovered only by the raised or disturbed appearance of the ground. Those bodies which had been buried in trenches were but little decomposed ; while of those buried singly in boxes not much was left but the bones and a handful of dust.

We had diverged from the Lafayette Road in order to ride along the line of battle east of it, — passing the positions occupied on Sunday, the second day, by Baird, Johnson, and Palmer's divisions, respectively. Next to Palmer was Reynolds ; then came Brannan, then Wood, then Davis, then Sheridan, on the extreme right. The line, which on Saturday ran due north and south, east of the road, — the left resting at Kelly's house and the right at Gordon's Mills, — was on Sunday curved, the right being drawn in and lying diagonally across and behind the road. In front (on the east) was Chickamauga Creek. Missionary Ridge was in the rear ; on a spur of which the right rested. I recapitulate these positions, because newspaper accounts of the battle, and historical accounts based upon them, are on two or three points confused and contradictory ; and because an understanding of them is important to what I am about to say.

Quitting the camp, we approached the scene of the great blunder which lost us the battle of Chickamauga. At half-past nine in the morning the attack commenced, the Rebels hurling masses of troops with their accustomed vigor against Rosecrans's left and centre. Not a division gave way : the whole line stood firm and unmoved : all was going well ; when Rosecrans sent the following imperative order to General Wood : —

" *Close up as fast as possible on General Reynolds, and support him.*"

General Brannan's division, as you have noticed, was between Wood and Reynolds. How then could Wood close up on Reynolds without taking out his division and marching by the left flank in Brannan's rear ? In military parlance, to *close up* may mean two quite different things. It may mean to move by the flank in order to close a gap which occurs between one body of troops and another body. Or it may mean to make a similar movement to that by which a rank of sol·diers is said to *close up* on the rank in front of it. To *close to the right or left*, is one thing ; to *close up on*, another. To General Wood, situated as he was, the order could have no other meaning than the latter. He could not *close up* on General Reynolds and support him without taking a position in his rear. Yet the order seemed to him very extraordinary. To General McCook, who was present when it was received, he remarked, —

" This is very singular ! What am I to do ? " For to take out his division was to make a gap in the army which might prove fatal to it.

" The order is so positive," replied McCook, " that you must obey it at once. Move your division out, and I will move Davis's in to fill the gap. Move quick, or you won't be out of the way before I bring in his division."

General Wood saw no alternative but to obey the order. He would have been justified in disobeying it, only on the supposition that the commanding general was ignorant of the position of his forces. Had Rosecrans been absent from the field, such a supposition would have been reasonable, and such disobedience duty. But Rosecrans was on the field ; and he was supposed to know infinitely more than could be known to any division commander concerning the exigencies of the battle. Had Wood kept his place, and Reynolds been over- whelmed and the field lost in consequence of that act of insubordination, he would have deserved to be court-mar- tialled and shot. On the contrary, he moved his division out, and in consequence of his strict *obedience* to orders the field was lost. He had scarcely opened the gap between Brannan and Davis, when the Rebels rushed in and cut the army to pieces.

General Rosecrans, in his official report, sought to shift the responsibility of this fatal movement from his own shoulders to those of General Wood. This was manifestly unjust. It appears to me that the true explanation of it lies in the fact that Rosecrans, although a man of brilliant parts, had not the steady balance of mind necessary to a great general. He could organize an army, or plan a campaign in his tent ; but he had no self-possession on the field of battle. In great emergencies he became confused and forgetful. It was probably this nervousness and paralysis of memory which caused the disaster at Chickamauga. He had forgotten the position of his forces. He intended to order General Wood to close to the left on Brannan; or on Reynolds, forgetting that Brannan was between them. But the order was to close up on and *support* Reynolds; whereas Reynolds, like Brannan, was doing very well, and did not particularly need support.

The routed divisions of the army fled to Chattanooga, — the commanding general among the foremost; where he hastened to telegraph to the War Department and the dismayed nation that all was lost; while General Garfield, his chief of staff, extricating himself from the rabble, rode back to the part of the field where firing was still heard, — running the gauntlet of the enemy's lines, — and joined General Thomas, who, rallying fragments of corps on a spur of Missionary Ridge, was stemming the tide of the foe, and saving the army from destruction.

Through woods dotted all over with the graves of soldiers buried where they fell, we drove to the scene of that final fight.

Bones of dead horses strewed the ground. At the foot of the wooded hill were trenches full of Longstreet's slaughtered men. That was to them a most tragical termination to what had seemed a victory. Inspired by their recent success, they charged again and again up those fatal slopes, only to be cut down like ripe grain by the deadly volleys which poured from a crescent of flame and smoke, where the heroic remnant of the army had taken up its position, and was not to be dislodged.

CHAPTER XXXVII.

FROM CHATTANOOGA TO MURFREESBORO'.

The military operations, of which Chattanooga was so long the centre, have left their mark upon all the surrounding country. Travel which way you will, you are sure to follow in their track. There are fortifications at every commanding point. Every railroad bridge is defended by redoubts and block-houses; and many important bridges have been burned. The entire route to Atlanta is a scene of conflict and desolation: earthworks, like the foot-prints of a Titan on the march; rifle-pits extending for miles along the railroad track; hills all dug up into forts and entrenchments; the town of Marietta in ruins; farms swept clean of their fences and buildings; everywhere, along the blackened war-path, solitary standing chimneys left, "like exclamation points," to emphasize the silent story of destruction.

I saw a few "Union men" at Chattanooga. But their loyalty was generally of a qualified sort. One, who was well known for his daring opposition to the secession leaders, and for his many narrow escapes from death, told me how he lived during the war. Once when the Rebels came to kill him, they took his brother instead. His residence was on a hill, and three times subsequently he saved his life by taking a canoe and crossing the river in it when he saw his assassins coming. Yet this man hated the free negro worse than he hated the Rebels; and he said to me, "If the government attempts now to force negro-suffrage upon the South, it will have to wade through a sea of blood to which all that has been shed was only a drop!" Another, who claimed also to be a Union man, said, "Before the South will ever consent to help pay the National debt, there will be another rebellion bigger than the last. You would make her repudiate her own war-debt, and then pay the expenses of her own whipping. I tell you, this can't be done." The threats of another rebellion, and of an extraordinarily large sea of blood, were not, I suppose, to be understood literally. This is the fiery Southron's metaphorical manner of expressing himself. Yet these men were perfectly sincere in their profession of sentiments which one would have expected to hear only from the lips of Rebels.

On the morning of Thursday, December 14th, I bid a joyful farewell to Chattanooga, which is by no means a delightful place to sojourn in, and took the train for Murfreesboro'. The weather was cold, and growing colder. Winter had come suddenly, and very much in earnest. Huge icicles hung from the water-tanks by the railroad. The frost, pushing its crystal shoots up out of the porous ground, looked like thick growths of fungus stalks. The rain and mist of the previous night were congealed upon the trees; and the Cumberland Mountains, as we passed them, appeared covered with forests of silver.

The country was uninteresting. Well-built farm-houses were not common; but log-huts, many of them without windows, predominated. These were inhabited by negroes and poor whites. I remember one family living in a box-car that had been run off the track. Another occupied a grotesque cabin having for a door the door of a car, set up endwise, marked conspicuously in letters reading from the zenith to the nadir, " U. S. MILITARY R. R." We passed occasionally cotton-fields, resembling at that season and in that climate fields of low black weeds, with here and there a bunch of cotton sticking to the dry leafy stalks.

Next me sat a gentleman from Iowa, whose history was a striking illustration of the difference between a slave State and a free State. He had just been to visit a brother living in Georgia. They were natives of North Carolina, from which State they emigrated in early manhood. He chose the North-west; his brother chose the South; and they had now met for the first time since their separation.

" To me," said he, " it was a very sad meeting. Georgia is a hundred years behind Iowa. My brother has always been poor, and always will be poor. If I had to live as he does, I should think I had not the bare necessaries of life, not to speak of comforts. His children are growing up in ignorance. When I looked at them, and thought of my own children, — intelligent, cultivated, with their schools, their books, and magazines, and piano, — I was so much affected I could n't speak, and for a minute I 'd have given anything if I had n't seen how he was situated. It is n't my merit, nor his fault, that there is so great a difference now, between us, who were so much alike when boys. If he had gone to Iowa, he would have done as well as I have. If I had gone to Georgia, I should have done as poorly as he has."

He was the only Northern man in the car besides myself, — as was to be seen not only by the countenances of the other passengers, but also by the spirit of their conversation. Behind us sat an ignorant brute, with his shirt bosom streaked with tobacco drizzle, who was saying in a loud, fierce tone, that " we 'd better kill off the balance of the niggers," for he had " no use for 'em now they were free." Others were talking about Congress and the President. One little boy four years old amused us all. He enjoyed the range of the car, and had made several acquaintances, some of whom, to plague him, called him Billy Yank. Great was the little fellow's indignation at this insult. " I a'n't Billy Yank! I 'm Johnny Reb!" he insisted. As the teasing continued, he flew to his mother, who received him in her arms. " Yes, he *is* Johnny Reb! *so he is!*" And his little heart was comforted.

At half-past three we reached Murfreesboro', having been nine hours travelling one hundred and nine miles. This I found about the average rate of speed on Southern roads. The trains run slow, and a great deal of time is lost at stopping-places. Once, when we were wooding up, I went out to learn what was keeping us so long, and saw two of the hands engaged in a scuffle, which the rest were watching with human interest. On another occasion the men had to bring wood out of the forest, none having been provided for the engine near the track.

Murfreesboro' is situated very near the centre of the State. It had in 1860 three thousand inhabitants. It has six churches, and not a decent hotel. Before the war it enjoyed the blessing of a University, a military institute, two female colleges, and two high-schools; all of which had been discontinued. It was also described to me as "a pretty, shady village, before the war." But the trees had been cut away, leaving ugly stump-lots; and the country all around was laid desolate.

Knowing how wretched must be my accommodations at the only tavern then open to the public, General Hazen hospitably insisted on my removal to his head-quarters on the evening of my arrival. I found him occupying a first-class Tennessee mansion on a hill just outside the town. The house was cruciform, with a spacious hall and staircase in the centre, opening into lofty wainscoted rooms above and below. The richness of the dark panels, and the structural elegance of the apartments, were unexceptionable. But the occupants of these could never have known comfort in wintry weather. The house was built, like all southern houses, for a climate reputed mild, but liable to surprises of cruel and treacherous cold, against which the inhabitants make no provision. The General and I sat that evening talking over war times, with a huge fire roaring before us in the chimney, and roasting our faces, while the freezing blast blew upon our backs from irremediable crevices in the ill-jointed wainscots and casements. I slept that night in a particularly airy chamber, with a good fire striving faithfully to master the enemy, and found in the morning the contents of the water-pitcher, that stood in the room, fast frozen.

I was amused by the grimaces of the negro servant who came in to replenish the fire before I was up. He inquired if we had any colder weather than that in the North, and when I told him how I had seen iron pump-handles stick to a wet hand on a fine wintry morning, involving sometimes the sacri-

18

fice of epidermis before the teeth of the frost could be made to let go, he remarked excitedly, —

" I would n't let de iron git holt o' my hand ! I hain't no skin to spar', mornin' like dis sher ! "

As I sat at breakfast with the General, he told me of his official intercourse with the inhabitants, since he had been in command of the post. " The most I have to do," said he, " is to adjust difficulties between Union men and Rebels. There are many men living in this country who acted as scouts for our army, and who, when they wanted a horse to use in the service of the government, took it without much ceremony where they could find it. For acts of this kind the law-loving Rebels are now suing them for damages before the civil courts, and persecuting them in various ways, so that the military power has to interfere to protect them."

CHAPTER XXXVIII.

STONE RIVER.

AFTER breakfast in a large dining-room which no fuel could heat, we went and stood by the hearth, turning ourselves on our heels, as the earth turns on its axis, warming a hemisphere at a time, until the wintry condition of our bodies gave place to a feeling of spring, half sunshine and half chill; then we clapped on our overcoats and mufflers; then two powerful war-horses of the General's came prancing to the door, ready bridled and saddled; and we mounted. A vigorous gallop across the outskirts of the town and out on the Nashville Pike set the sympathetic blood also on a gallop, and did for us what fire in a Tennessee mansion could not do. In ten minutes we were thoroughly warm, with the exception of one thumb in a glove which I wore, and an ear on the windward side of the General's rosy face.

Riding amid stump-fields, where beautiful forests had cast their broad shades before the war, we entered the area of the vast fortress constructed by the army of Rosecrans, lying at Murfreesboro' after the battle. This is the largest work of the kind in the United States. A parapet of earth three miles in circumference encloses a number of detached redoubts on commanding eminences. The encircled space is a mile in diameter. It contained all Rosecrans's store-houses, and was large enough to take in his entire army. It would require at least ten thousand troops to man its breast-works. The converging lines of the railroad and turnpike running to Nashville pass through it; and across the north front sweeps a bend of Stone River. We found the stream partly frozen, chafing between abrupt rocky shores sheathed in ice.

A mile beyond, the converging lines above mentioned cut each other at a sharp angle ; the railroad, which goes out of Murfreesboro' on the left, shifting over to the right of the turnpike. Crossing them at nearly right angles, a short distance on the Murfreesboro' side of their point of intersection, was the Rebel line of battle, on the morning of the thirty-first of December. Half a mile beyond this point, on the Nashville side, was the Union line.

The railroad here runs through a cut, with a considerable embankment, — a circumstance of vital importance to our army, saving it, probably, from utter rout and destruction, on that first day of disaster. The right wing, thrown out two miles and more to the west of the railroad, rested on nothing. It was left hanging in the air, as the French say. An attack was expected, yet no precautions were taken to provide against an attack. General Wood, who had posted scouts in trees to observe the movements of the Rebels, reported to the commanding general that they were rapidly moving troops over and massing them on their left. Rosecrans says he sent the information to McCook ; McCook says he never received it. When the attack came, it was a perfect surprise. It was made with the suddenness and impetuosity for which the enemy was distinguished, and everything gave way before it. Division after division was pushed back, until the line, which was projected nearly perpendicular to the railroad in the morning, lay parallel to it, — that providential cut affording an opportune cover for the rallying and re-forming of the troops.

Another feature of the field is eminently noticeable. The bold river banks, curving in and out, along by the east side of the railroad, made a strong position for the Union left to rest upon. Here, in a little grove called by the Rebels the " Round Forest," between the river and the railroad, was General Wood's division, planted like a post. On his right, like a bolt of iron in that post, was Hazen's brigade, serving as a pivot on which the whole army line swung round like a gate. The pivot itself was immovable. In vain the enemy concentrated his utmost efforts against it.   Terribly smitten and battered, but seemingly insensible as iron itself, there it stuck.[1]

It was extremely interesting to visit this portion of the field in company with one who played so important a part in the events enacted there.   We rode through a cotton-field of black leafy stalks, with little white bunches clinging to them like feathers or snow.   It was across that field, between Round Forest and the railroad, that Hazen's line was formed.   On the edge of it, by the forest, still lay the bones of a horse shot under him during the battle.

Near by was a little cemetery, within which the dead of Hazen's brigade were buried.   A well-built stone wall encloses an oblong space one hundred feet in length by forty in breadth. Within are thirty-one limestone tablets marking the graves of the common soldiers.   In the midst of these stands a monument, on which are inscribed the names of officers whose remains are deposited beneath it.   This is also of limestone, massy, well formed, ten feet square on the ground and eleven feet in height.   It is interesting as being the only monument of importance and durability erected by soldiers during the war.

On the south side, facing the railroad and turnpike, is the following legend : —

"HAZEN'S BRIGADE

TO

THE MEMORY OF ITS SOLDIERS

WHO FELL AT

STONE RIVER, DEC. 31, 1862.

' *Their faces toward heaven, their feet to the foe.*' "

---

[1] The right brigade of Palmer's division had been the last to yield.   The left brigade, in command of Hazen, was thus exposed to fire in flank and rear, and to the attempts of the enemy to charge in front.   It required terrible fighting to beat back the enemy's double lines: it cost a third of the brave brigade; but every moment the enemy was held back was worth a thousand men to the main line.   General Rosecrans improved the time so well, in hurrying troops to the new position, that, when the enemy assailed that line, the fresh divisions of Van Cleve, Wood, and Rousseau, and the artillery massed on a commanding point, not only repulsed them, but they were charged while retiring by one of Crittenden's brigades. . . . The enemy had miscalculated the temper of Hazen's brigade; and Bragg was obliged to report, as he did in his first despatch, that he " had driven the whole Federal line, except his left, which stubbornly resisted." — *Annals of the Army of the Cumberland.*

On the east side is the following : —

" THE VETERANS OF SHILOH HAVE LEFT A DEATHLESS HERITAGE OF FAME UPON THE FIELD OF STONE RIVER."

On the north side : —

" Erected 1863, upon the ground where they fell, by their comrades of the Nineteenth Brigade, Buell's Army of the Ohio, Col. W. B. Hazen 41st Infantry O. Vols. commanding."

On the west side : —

" The blood of one third its soldiers twice spilled in Tennessee crimsons the battle-flag of the brigade and inspires to great deeds."

From the soldiers' cemetery at Round Forest we rode on to the new National Cemetery of Stone River, then in process of construction. It lies between the railroad and the turnpike, in full view from both. A massy square-cornered stone wall encloses a space of modest size, sufficiently elevated, and covered with neatly heaped mounds, side by side, and row behind row, in such precise order, that one might imagine the dead who sleep beneath them to have formed their ghostly ranks there after the battle, and carefully laid themselves down to rest beneath those small green tents. The tents were not green when I visited the spot, but I trust they are green to-day, and that the birds are singing over them.

CHAPTER XXXIX.

THE HEART OF TENNESSEE.

HAVING spent the remainder of the forenoon in riding over other portions of the field, we returned to Murfreesboro'; and at half-past three o'clock I took the train for Nashville.

At Nashville I remained four days, — four eminently disagreeable days of snow, and rain, and fog, and slush, and mud. Yet I formed a not unfavorable impression of the city. I could feel the influence of Northern ideas and enterprise pulsating through it. Its population, which was less than twenty-four thousand at the last census, nearly doubled during the war. Its position gives it activity and importance. It is a nostril through which the State has long breathed the Northern air of free institutions. It is a port of entry on the Cumberland, which affords it steamboat communication with the great rivers. It is a node from which radiate five important railroads connecting it with the South and North. The turnpikes leading out of it in every direction are the best system of roads I met with anywhere in the South.

Middle Tennessee is the largest of the three natural divisions of the State. It is separated from the West division by the Tennessee River, and from East Tennessee by the Cumberland Mountains. It is a fine stock-raising country ; and the valley of the Cumberland River affords an extensive tract of excellent cotton and tobacco lands.

Nashville is the great commercial emporium of this division. The largest annual shipment of cotton from this port was fifty thousand bales ; the average, before the war, was about half as many: during 1865, it was fully up to this average, consisting mostly of old cotton going to market. Six thousand hogsheads of tobacco, two million bushels of corn, and twenty-five thousand hogs, — besides ten thousand casks of bacon and twenty-five hundred tierces of lard, — were yearly shipped from this port. The manufacturing interest of the place is insignificant.

The prospects of the country for the present year seemed to me favorable. The freedmen were making contracts, and going to work. Returned Rebels were generally settling down to a quiet life, and turning their attention to business. The people were much disposed to plant cotton, and every effort was making to put their desolated farms into a tillable condition.

Yet Middle Tennessee is but an indifferent cotton-growing region. It is inferior to West Tennessee, and can scarcely be called a cotton country, when compared with the rich valleys of the more Southern States. Eight hundred pounds of seed cotton[1] to the acre are considered a good crop on the best lands. The quality of Middle Tennessee cotton never rates above "low middling," but generally below it, (the different qualities of cotton being classed as follows: inferior, ordinary, good ordinary, low middling, middling, good middling, middling fair, good fair, and fine.)

I found considerable business doing with an article which never before had any money-value. Cotton seed, which used to be cast out from the gin-houses and left to rot in heaps, the planter reserving but a small portion for the ensuing crop, was now in great demand, prices varying from one to three dollars a bushel. In some portions of the Rebel States it had nearly run out during the war, and those sections which, like Tennessee, had continued the culture of the plant, were supplying the deficiency. The seed, I may here mention, resembles, after the fibre is removed by the gin, a small-sized pea covered with fine white wool. It is very oily, and is considered the best known fertilizer for cotton lands.

Nashville is built on the slopes of a hill rising from the

---

[1] That is, of cotton and seed: the gin takes out fifty or sixty per cent. of the gross weight.

south bank of the Cumberland. Near the summit, one hundred and seventy-five feet above the river, stands the capitol, said to be the finest State capitol in the United States. The view it commands of the surrounding country is superb; and seen from afar off, it seems, with its cupola and Ionic porticoes, to rest upon the city like a crown. It is constructed of fine fossiliferous limestone, three stories in height; with a central tower lifting the cupola two hundred feet from the ground. This tower is the one bad feature about the building. It is not imposing. The site is a lofty crest of rock, which was fortified during the war, converting the capitol into a citadel. The parapets thrown up around the edifice still remain.

My visit happened on the first anniversary of the battle of Nashville, which took place on the fifteenth and sixteenth days of December, 1864; — a battle which, occurring after many great and sanguinary conflicts, did not rise to highest fame; and which has not yet had ample justice done it. It is to be distinguished as the only immediately decisive battle of the war, — the only one in which an army was destroyed. By it the army of Hood was annihilated, and a period put to Rebel power in the States which Sherman had left behind him on his great march.

The scene of the battle, the sweeping undulations of the plain, the fields, the clumps of woods, and the range of hills beyond, are distinctly visible in fair weather from the house-tops of the city, and especially from the capitol. The fight took place under the eyes of the citizens. Every " coigne of vantage " was black with spectators. Patriots and Rebel sympathizers were commingled: the friends and relatives of both armies crowding together to witness the deadly struggle; a drama of fearfully intense reality! The wife of a noted general officer who was in the thickest of the fight, told me something of her experience, watching from the capitol with a glass the movements of his troops, the swift gallop of couriers, the charge, the repulse, the successful assault, the ground dotted with the slain, and the awful battle cloud, rolling over all, enfolding, as she at one time believed, his dead form with the rest. But he lived ; he was present when she told me the story ; — and shall I ever forget the emotion with which he listened to the recital? The battle was no such terrible thing to the soldier in the midst of it, as to the loved one look- ing on.

The State legislature adjourned for the Christmas holidays on the morning of my visit to the capitol ; but I was in time to meet and converse with members from various parts of the State. They were generally a plain, candid, earnest class of men. They were the loyal salt of the State. Some of them were from districts in which there were no Union men to elect them ; to meet which contingency the names of the candidates for both houses had been placed on a general ticket. Thus members from West and Middle Tennessee, where the Rebel element was paramount, were elected by votes in East Tennessee, which was loyal.

With Mr. Frierson, Speaker of the Senate, I had a long conversation. He was from Maury County, and a liberal- minded, progressive man, for that intensely pro-slavery and Rebel district. We talked on the exciting topic of the hour, — negro suffrage, and the admission of negro testimony in the courts. " My freedmen," he said, " are far more intelligent and better prepared to vote, than the white population around us." Yet as a class he did not think the negroes prepared to exercise the right of suffrage, and he was in favor of granting it only to such as had served in the Union army. To the ne- groes' loyalty and good behavior he gave the highest praise. " It is said they would have fought for the Confederacy, if the opportunity had been given them in season. But I know the negro, and I know that his heart was true to the Union from the first, and throughout ; and I do not believe he would have fought for the Rebellion, even on the promise of his liberty." He thought the blacks competent to give testimony in the courts ; but for this step society in Tennessee was not pre- pared. Both the right of voting and of testifying must be given them before long, however.

There were two classes of Union men in Tennessee. One class had manifested their loyalty by their uncompromising acts and sacrifices. The other class were merely *legal* Union men, professing loyalty to the government and friendliness to the negro. " These are not to be trusted," said Mr. Frierson. " Their animosity against the government and the freedmen, and more particularly against *heart* Union men, is all the more dangerous because it is secret." And it was necessary in his opinion to retain the Freedmen's Bureau in the State, and to keep both Rebels and rebel sympathizers excluded from power, for some years.

I have given so much of this conversation to illustrate the views entertained by the average, moderate, common-sense Union men of Tennessee. Far behind them, on the question of human rights, were some of the negro-haters and Rebel-persecutors of East Tennessee; while there was a handful of leading men as far in advance of them. A good sample of these was the honorable John Trimble, of Nashville, also a member of the legislature, whom I had the satisfaction of meeting on two or three occasions: a man of liberal and culti-vated mind, singularly emancipated from cant and prejudice. He had just introduced into the General Assembly a bill ex-tending the elective franchise to the freedmen, with certain restrictions; for the passage of which there was of course little chance.

I was just in time to catch Governor Brownlow as he was about going home for the holidays. I should have been sorry to miss seeing this remarkable type of native Southern-West-ern wit. As an outspoken convert from the pro-slavery doc-trines he used to advocate, to the radical ideas which the agita-tions of the times had shaken to the surface of society, he was also interesting to me. I found him a tall, quiet individual, of a nervous temperament, intellectual forehead, and a gift of language, — with nothing of the blackguard in his manners, as readers of his writings might sometimes be led to expect. His conversation was characteristic. He believed a Rebel had no rights except to be hung in this world, and damned after death. But this and other similar expressions did not proceed so much from a vindictive nature, as from that tendency to a strong, extravagant style of statement, for which Western and Southern people, and especially the people of Tennessee, are noted.

Of his compatriots, the Union-loving East Tennesseeans, he said, " It is hard to tell which they hate most, the Rebels, or the negroes." He did not sympathize with them in the ill-feeling they bestowed upon the latter. He was in favor of the Negro Testimony Bill, which had just been defeated in the legislature by East Tennessee members; and as for negro suffrage, he thought it was sure to come in a few years.

" The Rebels," said he, " are as rebellious now as ever. If Thomas and his bayonets were withdrawn, in ten days a Rebel mob would drive this legislature out. Congress," he added, " will have to legislate for all the Rebel States, Tennessee with the rest."

From the Governor's I went over to the division head-quarters to call on Major-General Thomas, — a very different type of native Southern men. Born and bred a Virginian, his patriotism was national, knowing no State boundaries. In appearance, he is the most lion-like of all the Union generals I have seen. An imperturbable, strong soul, never betrayed into weakness or excess by any excitement, his opinions possessed for me great value.

We spoke of the national soldiers' cemeteries in his division; and he informed me that besides those I had visited at Chattanooga and Murfreesboro', others proposed by him had been sanctioned by the War Department. " We shall have one here at Nashville; and I have already selected the site' for t," — a fortified hill in the suburbs. " There will be one at Franklin; also one at Memphis; another at Shiloh; and another large one at Atlànta; " for he did not favor the plan of burying the dead of the Atlanta campaign at Chattanooga.

The military division, called the " Division of the Tennessee," which General Thomas commands, comprises the States of Kentucky, Tennessee, Georgia, Alabama, and Mississippi.

He did not think that in either of those States there was any love for the Union, except in the hearts of a small minority. Tennessee was perhaps an exception. It was the only one of the Southern States that had reorganized on a strictly Union basis. It had disfranchised the Rebels. The governor, the legislature, and the recently elected members of Congress, were unquestionably loyal men. The Rebel State debt had been repudiated, and the Constitutional Amendment abolishing slavery adopted. East Tennessee could take care of itself; but in Middle and West Tennessee, where the Rebel sentiment predominated, personal and partisan animosities were so strong that Union men must for some time to come have the protection of the government. There were then in Tennessee about six thousand troops, stationed chiefly at Chattanooga, Memphis, and Nashville, with smaller garrisons scattered throughout the State, sufficient to remind the people that the government still lived.

As for the freedman, General Thomas thought the respectable classes, and especially the intelligent large planters, were inclined to treat him with justice; but habit and prejudice were so strong even with them, that the kind of justice he might expect would be largely mixed with wrong and outrage, if the Bureau was withdrawn.

The General was in the receipt of information, from entirely distinct and reliable sources, concerning secret organizations in the Southern States, the design of which was to embarrass the Federal Government and destroy its credit, to keep alive the fires of Rebel animosity, and to revive the cause of the Confederacy whenever there should occur a favorable opportunity, such as a political division of the North, or a war with some foreign power. As his testimony on this subject has been made public, I shall say nothing further of it here, except to express my sense of the weight to be attached to the conclusions of so calm and unprejudiced a man.

He had great faith in the negro. "I may be supposed to know something about him, for I was raised in a slave State; and I have certainly seen enough of him during and since the war. There is no doubt about his disposition to work and take care of himself, now he is free." When I spoke of the great difference existing between different African races, he replied, " There is more ability and fidelity in these apish-looking negroes than you suppose " ; and he proceeded to relate the following story : —

" I had a servant of the kind you speak of during the war. I saw him first at a hotel in Danville, Kentucky; he waited on me a good deal, and attracted my attention because he looked so much like a baboon. He took a liking to me, from some cause, and in order to be near me, engaged in the service of one of my staff-officers. I saw him occasionally afterwards, but gave him little attention, and had no suspicion of the romantic attachment with which I had inspired him. At length I had the misfortune to lose a very valuable servant, and did not know how I should replace him : servants were plenty enough, but I wanted one who could understand what I wished to have done without even being told my wishes, and who would have it done almost before I was aware of the necessity. I happened to name these qualities of a perfect valet in the presence of one of my aides, who said to me, ' I have just the man you want ; and though I would n't part with him for any other cause, you shall have him.' I accepted his offer ; and what was my surprise when he introduced to me the baboon. I at first thought it a jest ; but soon learned that he had conferred upon me a great favor. I never had such a servant. In a week's time he understood perfectly all my habits and requirements, and it was very rare I ever had to give him a verbal order. We had difficulty in getting our washing and ironing properly done, in the army ; but one day I noticed my linen was looking better than usual. The fellow had anticipated my want in that respect, and learned to wash and iron expressly to please me. He soon became one of the best washers and ironers I ever saw ; I don't think a woman in America could beat him. As soon as his newly acquired art became known, it was in demand ; and he asked permission to do the linen of some of my officers, which I granted.

He was industrious and provident ; he supported a family, and, during the three years he was with me, laid by two thousand dollars."

Among other prominent men I saw was General Fiske, of the Freedmen's Bureau, Assistant-Commissioner for the States of Tennessee and Kentucky. There were in his district six hundred thousand freedmen. He was issuing eight hundred rations daily to colored women and children, and three times as many to white refugees. " During the past four years," said he, " between Louisville and Atlanta, we have fed with government charity rations sixty-four white to one colored person." The local poor he refused to feed. " I told the Mayor of Nashville the other day that if he did not take care of his poor, I would assess the whiskey shops for their benefit. There are four hundred and eighteen shops of that kind in this city ; and eighteen thousand dollars a day are poured down the throats of the people."

The colored people of Nashville had organized a provident association managed exclusively by themselves, the object of which was the systematic relief of the poor, irrespective of color.

Speaking of the differences arising between the freedmen and the whites, General Fiske said, " In thirteen cases out of fifteen, the violation of contracts originates with the whites." Since the defeat of the Negro Testimony Bill in the legislature, he had taken all cases, in which freedmen were concerned, out of the civil courts, and turned them over to freedmen's courts, where alone justice could be done them.

" In my work of elevating the colored race," said he, " I get more hearty coöperation from intelligent and influential Rebel slave-holders, than from the rabid Unionists of East Tennessee."

Speaking of the laziness with which the negroes were charged, he said, " They are more industrious than the whites. You see young men standing on street corners with cigars in their mouths and hands in their pockets, swearing the negroes won't work ; while they themselves are supported by their own mothers, who keep boarding-houses. The idle colored families complained of are usually the wives and children of soldiers serving in the Federal army ; and they have as good a right to be idle as the wives and children of any other men who are able and willing to support their families. In this city, it is the negroes who do the hard work. They handle goods on the levee and at the railroad ; drive drays and hacks ; lay gas-pipes ; and work on new buildings. In the country they are leasing farms ; some are buying farms ; others are at work for wages. Able-bodied plantation hands earn fifteen and twenty dollars a month ; women, ten and twelve dollars ; the oldest boy and girl in a family, five and nine dollars. Hundreds of colored families are earning forty dollars a month, besides their rations, quarters, medical attendance, and the support of the younger children."

The schools of General Fiske's district, under the superintendence of Professor Ogden, were in a promising condition. There were near fifteen thousand pupils, and two hundred and sixty-four teachers. Many summer schools, which for want of school-houses were kept under trees, had been discontinued at the coming on of winter. Rebels returning home with their pardons were also turning the freedmen out of buildings used as school-houses. The consequence was a falling off of nearly one third in the number of pupils since September.

In Nashville there was a school supported by the United Presbyterian Mission, numbering eight hundred pupils ; and another by the Pennsylvania Freedmen's Relief Association, numbering three hundred and fifty. The American Missionary Association and Western Freedmen's Aid had united in purchasing, for sixteen thousand dollars, land on which had been erected twenty-three government hospital buildings, worth fifty thousand dollars, which, " by the superior management of General Fiske," said Professor Ogden, " have been secured for our schools." It was proposed to establish in them a school, having all grades, from the primary up to the normal. There was a great need of properly qualified colored teachers to send into by-places; which this school was designed to supply.

General Fiske had introduced a system of plantation schools, which was working well. Benevolent societies furnished the teachers, and planters were required to furnish the school-houses. A plantation of one hundred and fifty hands and forty or fifty children would have its own school-house. Smaller plantations would unite and build a school-house in some central location. These conditions were generally put into the contracts with the planters, who were beginning to learn that there was nothing so encouraging and harmonizing to the freedmen as the establishment of schools for their children.

19

CHAPTER XL.

BY RAILROAD TO CORINTH.

I LEFT Nashville for Decatur on a morning of dismal rain The cars were crowded and uncomfortable, with many passengers standing. The railroad was sadly short of rolling-stock, having (like most Southern roads) only such as happened to be on it when it was turned over to the directors by the government. It owned but three first-class cars, only one of which we had with us. The rest of the passenger train was composed of box-cars supplied with rude seats.

We passed the forts of the city ; passed the battle-ground of Franklin, with its fine rolling fields, marked by entrenchments ; and speeding on through a well-wooded handsome section of country, entered Northern Alabama. As my observations of that portion of the State will be of a general character, I postpone them until I shall come to speak of the State at large.

It was raining again when I left Decatur, ferried across the Tennessee in a barge manned by negroes. Of the railroad bridge burned by General Mitchell, only the high stone piers remained ; and freight and passengers had to be conveyed over the river in that way. I remember a black ferryman whose stalwart form and honest speech interested me, and whose testimony with regard to his condition I thought worth noting down.

" I works for my old master. He raised me. He 's a right kind master. I gits twenty dollars a month, and he finds me. Some of the masters about hyere is right tight on our people. Then thar 's a heap of us that won't work, and that steal from the rest. They 're my own color, but I can't help saying what 's true. They just set right down, thinking they 're free, and waiting for luck to come to 'em." But he assured me that the most of his people were at work, and doing well.

From the miserable little ferry-boat we were landed on the other side in the midst of a drenching rain. To reach the cars there was a steep muddy bank to climb. The baggage was brought up in wagons and pitched down into mud several inches deep, where passengers had to stand in the pouring shower and see to getting their checks.

On the road to Tuscumbia I made the acquaintance of a young South Carolinian, whose character enlisted my sympathy, and whose candid conversation offers some points worth heeding.

" I think it was in the decrees of God Almighty that slavery was to be abolished in this way ; and I don't murmur. We have lost our property, and we have been subjugated, but we brought it all on ourselves. Nobody that has n't experienced it knows anything about our suffering. We are discouraged : we have nothing left to begin new with. I never did a day's work in my life, and don't know how to begin. You see me in these coarse old clothes ; well, I never wore coarse clothes in my life before the war."

Speaking of the negroes : " We can't feel towards them as you do ; I suppose we ought to, but 't is n't possible for us. They 've always been our owned servants, and we 've been used to having them mind us without a word of objection, and we can't bear anything else from them now. If that 's wrong, we 're to be pitied sooner than blamed, for it 's something we can't help. I was always kind to my slaves. I never whipped but two boys in my life, and one of them I whipped three weeks ago."

" When he was a free man ? "

" Yes ; for I tell you that makes no difference in our feeling towards them. I sent a boy across the country for some goods. He came back with half the goods he ought to have got for the money. I may as well be frank, — it was a gallon of whiskey. There were five gentlemen at the house, and I wanted the whiskey for them. I told Bob he stole it.

Afterwards he came into the room and stood by the door, — a big, strong fellow, twenty-three years old. I said, 'Bob, what do you want?' He said, 'I want satisfaction about the whiskey.' He told me afterwards, he meant that he was n't satisfied I should think he had stolen it, and wanted to come to a good understanding about it. But I thought he wanted satisfaction gentlemen's fashion. I rushed for my gun. I'd have shot him dead on the spot if my friends had n't held me. They said I'd best not kill him, but that he ought to be whipped. I sent to the stable for a trace, and gave him a hundred and thirty with it, hard as I could lay on. I confess I did whip him unmercifully."

" Did he make no resistance ? "

" Oh, he knew better than that; my friends stood by to see me through. I was wrong, I know, but I was in a passion. That's the way we treat our servants, and shall treat them, until we can get used to the new order of things, — if we ever can."

" In the mean while, according to your own showing, it would seem that some restraint is necessary for you, and some protection for the negroes. On the whole, the Freedmen's Bureau is a good thing, is n't it ? "

He smiled: " May be it is ; yes, if the nigger is to be free, I reckon it is ; but it's a mighty bitter thing for us."

Then, speaking of secession: " I had never thought much about politics, though I believed our State was right when she went out. But when the bells were ringing, and everybody was rejoicing that she had seceded, a solemn feeling came over me, like I had never had in my life, and I could n't help feeling there was something wrong. I went through the war ; there were thousands like me. In our hearts we thought more of the Stars and Stripes than we did of the old rag we were fighting under."

He was going to Mississippi to look after some property left there before the war. But what he wished to do was to go North: " only I know I would n't be tolerated, — I know a man could n't succeed in business there, who was pointed out as a Rebel."

The same wish, qualified by the same apprehension, was frequently expressed to me by the better class of young Southern men ; and I always took pains to convince them that they would be welcomed and encouraged by all enlightened communities in the Northern States.

It was a dismal night in the cars. The weather changed, and it grew suddenly very cold. Now the stove was red hot ; and now the fire was out, with both car-doors wide open at some stopping-place.

At two in the morning we reached Corinth. A driver put me into his hack, and drove about town, through the freezing mud, to find me a lodging. The hotels were full. The boarding-houses were full, — all but one, in which, with a fellow-traveller, I was fortunate enough at last to find a room with two beds.

It was a large, lofty room, the door fifteen feet high from the floor, the walls eighteen feet. It had been an elegant apartment once; but now the windows were broken, the plastering and stucco-work disfigured, the laths smashed in places, there were bullet-holes through the walls, and large apertures in the wainscots. The walls were covered with devices, showing that Federal soldiers had been at home there ; such as a shield, admirably executed, bearing the motto : "The Union, it must be preserved"; "Heaven Bless our Native Land " ; " God of Battles, speed the Right " ; and so forth.

The beds were tumbled, some travellers having just got out of them to take the train. A black woman came in to make them. The lady of the house also came in, — a fashionably bred Southern woman, who had been reduced, by the fortunes of the Rebellion, from the condition of a helpless mistress of many servants, to that of a boarding-house keeper.

I asked for a single room, which I was somewhat curtly told I could n't have. I then asked for more bedclothes, — for the weather continued to grow cold, and the walls of the room offered little protection against it. She said, " I reckon you 're mighty particular ! " I replied that she was quite correct in

her reckoning, and insisted on the additional clothing. A·
last I got it, very fortunately; for my room-mate, who did
not make the same demand, nearly froze in the other bed before daylight.

In the morning a black man came in and made a fire. Then,
before I was up, a black girl came in to bring a towel, and to
break the ice in the wash-basin. That the water might not
freeze again before I could use it, (for the fire, as some one
has said, " could n't get a purchase on the cold,") I requested
her to place the basin on the hearth; also to shut the door;
for every person who passed in or out left all doors wide, affording a free passage from my bed to the street.

" You 're cold-natered, an't ye?" said the girl, to whose
experience my modest requests appeared unprecedented.

Afterwards I went out to breakfast in a room that showed
no chimney, and no place for a stove. The outer door was
open much of the time, and when it was shut the wind came
in through a great round hole cut for the accommodation of
cats and dogs. This, be it understood, was a fashionable
Southern residence; and this had always been the dining-
room, in winter the same as in summer, though no fire had
ever been built in it. The evening before, the lady had said
to me, " The Yankees are the cause that we have no better
accommodations to offer you," and I had cheerfully forgiven
her. But the Yankees were not the cause of our breakfasting
in such a bleak apartment.

Everybody at table was pinched and blue. The lady, white
and delicate, sat wrapped in shawls. She was very bitter
against the Yankees, until I smilingly informed her that her
remarks were particularly interesting to me, as I was a Yankee
myself.

" From what State are you, Sir?"

" From Massachusetts."

" Oh!" — with a shudder, — " they 're bad Yankees!"

" Bad enough, Heaven knows," I pleasantly replied;
" though, in truth, Madam, I have seen almost as bad people
in other parts of the world."

The lady's husband changed the conversation by offering me a piece of venison which he had killed the day before. Deer were plenty in that region. As in Tennessee and Alabama, game of all kinds — deer, foxes, wild turkeys, wolves, — had increased greatly in Mississippi during the war; the inhabitants having had something more formidable to hunt, or been hunted themselves.

Mr. M—— owned two abandoned plantations: this was his town residence. He left it just before the battle of Shiloh, and it was occupied either by the Rebels or Yankees till the end of the war. He was originally opposed to the secession-leaders, but he afterwards went into the war, and lost everything, while they kept out of it and made money.

The bullet-holes in the house were made by the Rebels firing at the Federals when they attacked the town.

The family consisted of three persons, — Mr. M——, his wife, and their little boy. Notwithstanding their poverty, they kept four black servants to wait upon them. They were paying a man fifteen dollars a month, a cook-woman the same, another woman six, and a girl six: total, forty-two dollars. It was mainly to obtain money to pay and feed these people that they had been compelled to take in lodgers. The possibility of getting along with fewer servants seemed never to have occurred to them. Before the war they used to keep seven or eight. It was the old wasteful habit of slavery: masters were accustomed to have many servants about them, and each servant must have two or three to help him.

The freedmen, I was told, were behaving very well. But the citizens were bitterly hostile to the negro garrison which then occupied Corinth. A respectable white man had recently been killed by a colored soldier, and the excitement occasioned by the circumstance was intense. It was called " a cold-blooded murder." Visiting head-quarters, I took pains to ascertain the facts in the case. They are in brief as follows : —

The said respectable citizen was drunk. Going down the street, he staggered against a colored orderly. Cursing him, he said, " Why don't you get out of the way when you see a white man coming?" The orderly replied, "There's room for you to pass." The respectable citizen then drew his revolver, threatening to "shoot his damned black heart out." This occasioned an order for his arrest. He drew his revolver, with a similar threat, upon another soldier sent to take him, and was promptly shot down by him. Exit respectable citizen.

Corinth is a bruised and battered village surrounded by stumpy fields, forts, earthworks, and graves. The stumpy fields are the sites of woods and groves cut away by the great armies. The graves are those of soldiers slain upon these hills. Beautiful woody boundaries sweep round all.

There is nothing about the town especially worth visiting; and my object in stopping there was to make an excursion into the country and visit the battle-field of Shiloh. I went to a livery-stable to engage a horse. I was told of frequent robberies that had been committed on that road, and urged by the stable-keeper to take a man with me; but I wished to make the acquaintance of the country people, and thought I could do better without a companion.

CHAPTER XLI.

ON HORSEBACK FROM CORINTH.

MOUNTING a sober little iron-gray, I cantered out of Corinth, in a northeasterly direction, past the angles of an old fort overgrown with weeds, and entered the solitary wooded country beyond.

A short ride brought me to a broken bridge, hanging its shaky rim over a stream breast-high to my horse. I paused on its brink, dubious; until I saw two ladies, coming to town on horseback to do their shopping (the fashion of the country), rein boldly down the muddy bank, gather their skirts together, hold up their heels, and take like ducks to the water. I held up my heels and did likewise. This was the route of the great armies; which whoso follows will find many a ruined bridge and muddy stream to ford.

It was a clear, crisp winter's morning. The air was elastic and sparkling. The road wound among lofty trunks of oak, poplar, hickory, and gum, striped and gilded with the slanting early sunshine. Quails (called partridges in the South) flew up from the wayside; turtle-doves flitted from the limbs above my head; the woodpeckers screamed and tapped, greeting my approach with merry fife and drum. Cattle were grazing on the wild grass of the woods, and a solitary cow-bell rang.

Two and a half miles from town I came to a steam saw-mill, all about which the forest resounded with the noise of axes, the voices of negroes shouting to their teams, the flapping of boards thrown down, and the vehement buzz of the saw. This mill had but recently gone into operation; being one of hundreds that had already been brought from the North, and set to work supplying the demand for lumber, and repairing the damages of war.

Near by was a new house of rough logs with the usual great opening through it. It was situated in the midst of ruins which told too plain a story. Tying my horse to a bush, I entered, and found one division of the house occupied by negro servants, the other by two lonely white women. One of these was young; the other aged, and bent with grief and years. She sat by the fire, knitting, wrapped in an ancient shawl, and having a white handkerchief tied over her head. The walls and roof were full of chinks, the wind blew through the room, and she crouched shivering over the hearth.

She offered me a chair, and a negro woman, from the other part of the house, brought in wood, which she heaped in the great open fireplace.

"Sit up, stranger," said the old lady. "I have n't the accommodations for guests I had once; but you 're welcome to what I have. I owned a beautiful place here before the war, — a fine house, negro quarters, an orchard, and garden, and everything comfortable. The Yankees came along and destroyed it. They did n't leave me a fence, — not a rail nor a pale. If I had stayed here, they would n't have injured me, and I should have saved my house; but I was advised to leave. I have come back here to spend my days in this cabin. I lost everything, even my clothes; and I 'm too old to begin life again."

Myself a Yankee, what could I say to console her?

A mile and a half farther on, I came to another log-house, and stopped to inquire my way of an old man standing by the gate. His countenance was hard and stern, and he eyed me, as I thought, with a sinister expression.

"You are a stranger in this country?" I told him I was. "I allow you 're from the North?" — eying me still more suspiciously.

"Yes," I replied; "I am from New England."

"I 'm glad to see ye. Alight. It 's a right cool morning: come into the house and warm."

I confess to a strong feeling of distrust, as I looked at him. I resolved, however, to accept his invitation. He showed me into a room, which appeared to be the kitchen and sleeping-room of a large family. Two young women and several children were crowded around the fireplace, while the door of the house was left wide open, after the fashion of doors in the South country. There was something stewing in a skillet on the hearth; which I noticed, because the old man, as he sat and talked with me, spat his tobacco-juice over it (not always with accuracy) at the back-log. I remarked that the country appeared very quiet.

" Quiet, to what it was," said the old man, with a wicked twinkle of the eye. " You 've probably heard of some of the murders and robberies through here."

I said I had heard of some such irregularities.

" I 've been robbed time and again. I 've had nine horses and mules stole."

" By whom ? "

" The bushwhackers. They 've been here to kill me three or four times ; but, as it happened, the killing was on t' other side."

" Who were these men ? "

" Some on 'em belonged in Massissippi, and some on 'em in Tennessy. They come to my house of a Tuesday night, last Feb'uary. They rode up to the house, and surrounded it, a dozen or fifteen of 'em. ' Old Lee ! ' they shouted, ' we want ye ! ' It had been cloudy 'arly in the evening, but it had fa'red up, and as I looked out thro' the chinks in the logs, I could see 'em moving around.

" ' Come out, Old Lee ! we 've business with ye ! '

" ' You 've no honest business this hour o' the night,' I says.

" ' Come out, or we 'll fire your house.'

" ' Stand back, then,' I says, ' while I open the doo'.'

" I opened it a crack, but instead of going out, I just put out the muzzle of my gun, and let have at the fust man.

" ' Boys ! I 'm shot ! ' he says. I 'd sent a slug plumb thro' his body. Whilst the others was getting him away, I loaded up again. In a little while they come back, mad as devils. I did n't wait for 'em to order me out, but fired as they come up to the doo'. I hit one of 'em in the thigh. After that they went off, and I did n't hear any more of 'em that night."

" What became of the wounded men ? "

" The one I shot thro' the body got well. The other died."

" How did you learn ? "

" They was all neighbors of mine. They lived only a few miles from here, over the Tennessy line. That was Tuesday night; and the next Sunday night the gang come again. I was prepared for 'em. I had cut a trap through the floo'; and I had my grandson with me, a boy about twelve year old; and he had a gun. We 'd just got comfortably to bed, when some men rode up to the gate, and hollah'd, ' Hello ! ' several times. I told my wife to ask 'em what they wanted. They said they was strangers, and had lost their road and wanted the man of the house to come out. I drapped thro' the hole in the floo', and told my wife to tell 'em I wa'n't in the house, and they must go somewhar else.

" ' We 'll see if he 's in the house,' they said. The house is all open underneath, and I reckoned I 'd a good position; but befo'e I got a chance at ary one, they 'd bust in. They went to rummaging, and threatening my wife, and skeering the children. I could hear 'em tramping over my head; till bimeby the clock struck; and I heerd one of 'em sw'ar, ' Ten o'clock, and nary dollar yet ! ' After that, I could see 'em outside the house; hunting around for me, as I allowed. I fired on one. ' My God ! ' I heered him say, ' he 's killed me ! ' I then took my grandson's gun, and fired again. Such a rushing and scampering you never heered. They run off, leaving one of their men lying dead right out here before the doo'. We found him thar the next morning. He laid thar nigh on to two days, when some of his friends come and took him and buried him."

" Why did those men wish to murder you ? "

" They had a spite agin me, because they said I was a Union man."

" They called him a Yankee," said one of the young women.

" But you are not a Yankee."

" I was born in Tennessy, and have lived either in Tennessy or Massissippi all my days. But I never was a secessioner ; I went agin the war ; and I had two son-in-law's in the Federal army. Both these girls' husbands was fighting the Rebels, and that 's what made 'em hate me. They was determined to kill me ; and after that last attempt on my life, I refugeed. I went to the Yankees, and did n't come back till the war wound up. There 's scoundrels watching for a chance to bushwhack me now."

" Old Lee 'd go up mighty quick, if they wa'n't afeared," remarked one of the daughters.

" I 'm on hand for 'em," said the old man, — and now I understood that wicked sparkle of his eye. " Killing is good for 'em. A lead bullet is better for getting rid of 'em than any amount of silver or gold, and a heap cheaper ! "

Two miles north of Old Lee's I came to the State boundary. While I was still in Mississippi, I saw, just over the line, in Tennessee, a wild figure of a man riding on before me. He was mounted on a raw-boned mule, and wore a flapping gray blanket which gave him a fantastic appearance. The old hero's story had set me thinking of bushwhackers, and I half fancied this solitary horseman — or rather mule-man — to be one of that amiable gentry. He had pursued me from Corinth, and passed me unwittingly while I was sitting in Old Lee's kitchen. He was riding fast to overtake me. Or perhaps he was only an innocent country fellow returning from town. I switched on, and soon came near enough to notice that the mule's tail was fancifully clipped and trimmed to resemble a rope with a tassel at the end of it ; also that the rider's face was mysteriously muffled in a red handkerchief.

I was almost at his side, when hearing voices in the woods behind me, I looked around, and saw two more mounted men coming after us at a swift gallop. The thought flashed through my mind that those were the fellow's accomplices. One to one had not seemed to me very formidable ; but three to one would not be so pleasant. I pressed my iron-gray immediately alongside the tassel-tailed mule, and accosted the rider, determined to learn what manner of man he was before the others arrived. The startled look he gave me, and the blue nose, with its lucid pendent drop, that peered out of the sanguinary handkerchief, showed me that he was as harmless a traveller as myself. He was a lad about eighteen years of age. He had tied up his ears, to defend them from the cold, and the bandage over them had prevented him from hearing my approach until I was close upon him.

"It's a kule day," he remarked, with numb lips, as he reined his mule aside to let me pass at a respectful distance, — for it was evident he regarded me with quite as much distrust as I had him.

At the same time the two other mounted men came rushing upon us, through the half-frozen puddles, with splash and clatter and loud boisterous oaths ; and one of them drew from his pocket, and brandished over the tossing mane of his horse, something so like a pistol that I half expected a shot.

"How are ye?" said he, halting his horse, and spattering me all over with muddy water. "Right cold morning! Hello, Zeek!" to the rider of the tassel-tailed mule. "I did n't know ye, with yer face tied up that fashion. Take a drink?" Zeek declined. "Take a drink, stranger?" And he offered me the pistol, which proved to be a flask of whiskey. I declined also. Upon which the fellow held the flask unsteadily to his own lips for some seconds, then passed it to his companion. After drinking freely, they spurred on again, with splash and laughter and oaths, leaving Zeek and me riding alone together.

CHAPTER XLII.

ZEEK.

" DID N'T I see your horse tied to Old Lee's gate?" said Zeek. And that led to a discussion of the old hero's character.

" Is he a Union man?"

" I kain't say; but that's the story they tell on him. One of the men he killed was one of our neighbors; a man we used to consider right respectable; but he tuke to thieving during the wa', and got to be of no account. That was the way with a many I know. You may stop at a house now whur they'll steal your horse, and like as not rob and murder ye."

Zeek told me he lived on the edge of the battle-field; and I engaged him to guide me to it. He thought I must be going to search for the body of some friend who fell there. When I told him I was from the North, and that my object was simply to visit the battle-field, he looked at me with amazement.

" I should think you'd be afraid to be riding alone in this country! If 't was known you was a Yankee, and had money about you, I allow you'd get a shot from behind some bush."

" I think the men who would serve me such a trick are very few."

" Thar was right smart of 'em befo'e the wa' closed. They 'd just go about robbing, — hang an old gray-haired man right up, till he'd tell whur his money was. They called themselves Confederates, but they was just robbers. They've got killed off, or have gone off, or run out, till, as you say, there an't but few left."

With these exceptions, Zeek praised highly the middling
class of people who inhabited that region.

" Some countries, a pore man ain't respected no mo'e 'n a
dog. 'Tan't so hyere. Man may be plumb pore, but if he 's
honest, he 's thought as much of as anybody. Mo'e 'n two
thirds of 'em can read and write." Before the war, they used
to have what they called "neighborhood schools." The
teacher was supported by the pupils, receiving two dollars a
month for each : he taught only in winter, and was fortunate
if he could secure forty pupils.

Flocks of sparrows flew up from the bushes or hopped along
the ground. There were bluebirds also ; and I noticed one
or two robins. " We never see robins hyere only in winter,"
said Zeek.

Green bunches of mistletoe grew on the leafless brown trees,
— a striking feature of Southern woods in winter. "It 's a
curiosity, the way it grows," said Zeek. "It just grows on
the tops of trees, without no rute, nor nothing. It 's a rare
chance you find it on the hills ; it grows mostly on the bottoms
whur thar 's mo'e moisture in the air." It was a beautiful
sight to me, riding under its verdant tufts, sometimes so low
on the boughs that, by rising in the stirrups, I could pluck
sprigs of it, with their translucent pearly berries, as I passed.
But Zeek was wrong in saying it had no root. It is supposed
to be propagated by birds wiping their bills upon the limbs of
trees, after eating the berries. A stray seed thus deposited
germinates, and the penetrating root feeds upon the juices that
flow between the bark and the wood of the tree.

We passed but few farm-houses, and those were mostly built
of logs. We crossed heavy lines of Beauregard's breastworks ;
and could have traced the route of the great armies by the
bones of horses, horned cattle, and mules we saw whitening in
the woods and by the roadside. A crest of hilly fields showed
us a magnificent sweep of level wooded country on the west
and south, like a brown wavy sea, with tossed tree-tops for
breakers.

" Mighty pore soil along hyere," observed Zeek. When I

told him that it was as good as much of the soil of New England, which farmers never thought of cultivating without using manures, he said, " When our land gits as pore as that, we just turn it right out, and cle'r again.   We don't allow we can afford to manure.   But No'th Car'linians come in hyere, and take up the land turned out so, and go to manuring it, and raise right smart truck on it."

As I was inclined to ride faster than Zeek, he looked critically at my horse, and remarked, " I don't reckon you give less 'n a dollar a day for that beast."   I said I gave more than that.   " I ride my beasts hard enough," he replied, " but I reckon if I paid a dollar a day for one, I 'd ride him a heap harder ! "

He had been down to the saw-mill, to get pay for a yoke of oxen his father had sold.   " I started by sun-up, and got thar agin nine o'clock."   It was now afternoon, and he was hungry and cold.   He therefore proposed to me to go home with him and get warm, before visiting the battle-field.

It was after two o'clock when we came to a hilly field covered with rotting clothes.

" Beauregard's troops come plumb up this road, and slept hyere the night befo'e the battle.   They left their blankets and knapsacks, and after they got brushed out by the Yankees, the second day, they did n't wait to pick 'em up again."

We entered the woods beyond, directing our course towards the western edge of the battle-field; and, after riding some distance, forded Owl Creek, — a narrow, but deep and muddy stream.   Zeek's home was in view from the farther bank; a log-house, with the usual great opening through the middle ; situated on the edge of a pleasant oak-grove strewn with rustling leaves, and enclosed, with its yard and out-houses, by a Virginia rail-fence.

20

CHAPTER XLIII.

ZEEK'S FAMILY.

" Alight ! " said Zeek, dismounting at the gate.

I remonstrated against leaving the animals uncovered in the cold, but he said it was the way people did in that country; and it was not until an hour later that he found it convenient to give them shelter and food.

We were met inside the gate by a sister of the young man's, a girl of fifteen, in a native Bloomer dress that fell just below the knees. As I entered the space between the two divisions of the house, I noticed that doors on both sides were open, one leading to the kitchen, where there was a great fire, and the other to the sitting-room, where there was another great fire, in large old-fashioned fireplaces.

Zeek took me into the sitting-room, and introduced me to his mother. There were two beds in the back corners of the room. The uncovered floor was of oak; the naked walls were of plain hewn logs; the sleepers and rough boards of the chamber floor constituted the ceiling. There were clothes drying on a pole stretched across the room, and hanks of dyed cotton thread on a bayonet thrust into a chink of the chimney. Cold as the day was, the door by which we entered was never shut, and sometimes another door was open, letting the wintry wind sweep through the house.

Zeek's mother went to see about getting us some dinner; and his father came in from the woods, where he had been chopping, and sat in the chimney-corner and talked with me: a lean, bent, good-humored, hard-working, sensible sort of man. He told me he had five hundred acres of land, but only thirty-six under cultivation. He and Zeek did the work; they had never owned negroes.

" Three or four niggers is too much money for a pore man to invest in that way : they may lie down and die, and then whur's yer money ? Thar was five niggers owned in Middle Tennessy," he added, " to one in this part of the State."

Speaking of his farm, he said it was mighty good land till it wore out. He had raised two bales of cotton on three and a half acres, the past season. It was equally good for other crops. "I make some corn, some pork, some cotton, and a mule or two, every year : I never resk all on one thing."

Looking at the open outside doors and the great roaring fires, I said I should think wood must be a very important item with Tennessee farmers.

" Yes, I reckon we burn two cords a week, such weather as this, just for fire, and as much more in the kitchen. We've wood enough. As we turn out old land, we must cle'r new ; then we have the advantage of the ashes for ley and soap."

" But the labor of chopping so much wood must be considerable."

" Oh, I can chop enough in a day, or a day and a half, to last a week. Winters, farmers don't do much else but feed and get wood."

I said I thought they would some day regret not having kept up their cleared fields by proper cultivation, and preserved their forests.

" I allow we shall. I've just returned from a trip up into Middle Tennessy " (accented on the first syllable), " whur I used to live ; they burnt up their timber thar, just as we 're doing hyere, and now they're setting down and grieving because they've no wood. They save everything thar, to the trunks and crotches. We just leave them to rot, or log 'em up in heaps and burn 'em, whur the land 's to be cle'red ; and use only the clean limbs, that chop easy and don't require much splitting." He broke forth in praise of a good warm fire. " Put on a big green back-log and build agin it, — that 's our fashion."

Zeek's mother came to announce our dinner. I crossed the open space, pausing only to wash my hands and face in a tin

basin half filled with water and pieces of ice, and entered the
kitchen.   It was a less pretentious apartment than the sitting-
room.   There was no window in it; but wide chinks between
the logs, and two open doors, let in a sufficiency of daylight,
and more than a sufficiency of cold wind.   There was a bed in
one corner, and a little square pine table set in the centre of
the room.   A gourd of salt hung by the chimney, and a home-
made broom leaned beside it.   I noticed a scanty supply of
crockery and kitchen utensils on pegs and shelves.

The table was neatly set, with a goodly variety of dishes for
a late dinner in a back-country farm-house.   I remember a
plate of fried pork; fricaseed gray squirrel (cold); boiled
" back of hog " (warmed up); a pitcher of milk; cold biscuit, cold corn bread, and " sweet bread " (a name given to a
plain sort of cake).

We could have dined very comfortably but for the open
doors.   Blowing in at one and out at the other, and circu-
lating through numberless cracks between the logs, the gale
frisked at will about our legs, and made our very hands numb
and noses cold while we ate.   The fire was of no more use
to us than one built out-of-doors.   The victuals that had
come upon the table warm were cold before they reached our
mouths.   The river of pork-fat which the kind lady poured
over my plate, congealed at once into a brownish-gray deposit,
like a spreading sand-bar.   I enjoyed an advantage over Zeek,
for I had taken the precaution to put on my overcoat and to
secure a back seat.   He sat opposite me, with his back towards the windward door, where the blast, pouncing in upon
him, pierced and pinched him without mercy.   He had not
yet recovered from the chill of his long winter-day's ride; and
his lank, shivering frame, and blue, narrow, puckered face
under its thin thatch of tow (combed straight down, and cut
square and short across his forehead from ear to ear), presented a picture at once astonishing and ludicrous.

" Have you got warm yet, Zeek? " I cheerfully inquired.

" No! " -- shuddering.   " I 'm plumb chilly !   I 'm so kule
I kain't eat."

" I should think you would be more comfortable with that door closed," I mildly suggested.

He slowly turned his head half round, and as slowly turned it back again, with another shiver. The possibility of actually shutting the door seemed scarcely to penetrate the tow-thatch. I suppose such an act would have been unprecedented in that country, — one which all conservative persons would have shaken their heads at as a dangerous innovation.

Zeek begged to be excused, he was so kule ; and taking a piece of squirrel in one hand, and a biscuit in the other, went and stood by the fire. I found that he was averse to going out again that day : it was now late in the afternoon, and our poor animals had not yet been fed, or even taken in from where they stood curled up with the cold by the gate : I accordingly proposed to the old folks to spend the night with them, and to take Zeek with me over the battle-field in the morning. This being agreed upon, the father invited me to go out and see his stock, and his two bags of cotton.

In the yard near the house was the smoke-house, or meat-house, a blind hut built of small logs, answering the purpose of a cellar, — for in that country cellars are unknown. In it the family provisions were stored. Under an improvised shelter at one corner was the cotton, neatly packed in two bales of five hundred pounds each, and looking handsome as a lady in its brown sacking and new hoops. The hoops were a sort of experiment, which it was thought would prove successful. Usually the sacking and ropes about a bale of cotton cost as much by the pound as the cotton itself; and, to economize that expense, planters were beginning to substitute hickory hoops for ropes. The owner was very proud of those two bales, picked by his own hands and his children's, and prepared for market at a gin and press in the neighborhood ; and he hoped to realize five hundred dollars for them when thrown upon the market. A planter of a thousand bales, made by the hands of slaves he was supposed to own, and ginned and pressed on his own plantation, could not have contemplated his crop with greater satisfaction, in King Cotton's haughtiest days.

Near the meat-house was a huge ash-leach. Then there was
a simple horse-mill for crushing sorghum, — for Mr. ——, like
most Southern farmers, made sufficient syrup for home con-
sumption, besides a little for market. Under a beech-tree was
a beautiful spring of water. A rail-fence separated the door-
yard from the cattle-yard, where were flocks of hens, geese,
ducks, and turkeys, cackling, quacking, and gobbling in such
old familiar fashion that I was made to feel strangely at home
in their company. There were bleating, hungry calves, and
good-natured surly bulls, and patient cows waiting to be milked
and fed, and a family of uncurried colts and young mules, and
beautiful spotted goats, with their kids, and near by a hog-lot
full of lean and squealing swine. Speaking of the goats,
Mr. —— said there was no money in them, but that he kept
them for the curiosity of the thing.

There was no barn on the place. The nearest approach to
it was the stable, or " mule-pen," constructed of logs with liberal openings between them, through one of which my lonesome iron-gray put his nose as I came near, and whinnied his
humble petition for fodder. There he was, stabled with mules,
unblanketed, and scarcely better off than when tied to the
gate-post, — for the wind circulated almost as freely through
the rude enclosure as it did in Mrs. ——'s kitchen. Such hospitalities were scarcely calculated to soothe the feelings of a
proud and well-bred horse ; but the iron-gray accepted them
philosophically.

" Where is your hay ? " I inquired.

" We make no hay in this country. Our stock feeds out on
the hills, or browses in the woods or cane-brakes, all winter.
When we have to feed 'em, we throw out a little corn, fodder,
and shucks."

A loft over the mule-pen was filled with stalks and unhusked
corn. Zeek went up into it, and threw down bundles of the
former, and filled baskets of the latter, for his father to feed
out to the multitude of waiting mouths.

I inquired particularly regarding the large quantities of natural manures which ought to accumulate in such a farm-yard.

"We just throw them out, and let them get trampled and washed away. We can't haul out and spread. It's the hardest work we ever did, and Tennesseans can't get used to it."

The yard was on a side hill, where every rain must wash it, and the mule-pen was conveniently situated near the brink of a gully, from which every freshet would sweep what was thrown into it. In vain I remonstrated against this system of farming: Mr. ——— replied that he was brought up to it, and could not learn another.

CHAPTER XLIV.

A NIGHT IN A TENNESSEE FARM-HOUSE

WE went into the house, and gathered around the sitting-room fire for a social evening's talk. As it grew dark, the doors were closed, and we sat in the beautiful firelight. And now I learned a fact, and formed a theory, concerning doors.

The fact was this : not a door on the premises had either lock or bolt.   Mule-pen, meat-house, and both divisions of the dwelling-house, were left every night without other fastening than the rude wooden latches of the country.   This was a very common practice among the small farmers of that region. " It was a rare chance we ever used to hear of anything being stolen.   My house was never robbed, and I never lost a mule or piece of meat till after war broke out."

The closing of the doors at dark, not because the weather had grown colder, but apparently because there was no longer any daylight to admit, suggested to my mind the origin of the universal Southern custom of leaving doors open during the severest winter weather.   The poor whites and negroes live very generally in huts and cabins without windows.   Even the houses of the well-to-do small farmers are scantily supplied with these modern luxuries.   The ancestors of the wealthier middle class dwelt not many years ago in similar habitations. Such is the strength of habit, and so strong the conservatism of imitative mankind, that I suppose a public statute would be necessary to compel now the shutting of doors of windowed houses against the piercing winds of the cold season ; just as, according to Charles Lamb, the Chinese people's method of obtaining roast pig by burning their dwellings over a tender suckling — that ravishing delicacy having been accidentally discovered to the world by the conflagration of a house with its adjoining pig-sty — had to be stopped by an imperial edict.

We sat without lamp or candle in the red gleaming firelight; and the faces of the little girls, who had been shrinking and shivering with the cold all day, took on a glow of comfort and pleasure, now that the house was shut. However, I could still feel gusts of the wintry air blowing upon me from openings between the logs. I have been in many Southern farmhouses; and I have heard the custom of open doors commended as necessary to give plenty of air and to toughen the inmates by wholesome exposure; but I do not now remember the habitation that was not more than sufficiently supplied with air, both for ventilating and toughening purposes, with every door closed.

Mr. —— talked quite sensibly of the origin and results of the war. He and the majority of the farmers in that region were originally Union men, and remained so to the last. " Some of the hottest secesh, too, got to be right good Union before the wa' was over, — they found the Yankees treated 'em so much better 'n they expected, and the Rebs so much wuss."

He accepted emancipation. " The way I look at it, the thing had growed up till it got ripe, and it fell on us in this age. It was the universal opinion before the wa', that the country would be a heap better off without niggers. But we could n't go with the Abolitionists of the No'th, nor with the secesh fire-eaters. We stood as it were between two fires. That was what made it so hard."

But he shared the common prejudice against permitting the negroes to remain and enjoy the land. " 'T won't do to have 'em settled among us. 'T would, if everybody was honest. But the whites, I 'm ashamed to say it, will just prey upon them. They 're bound to be the poorest set of vagabonds that ever walked the earth. O yes, they 'll work. It 's just this way, — they 'll work if they have encouragement; and no man will without, unless he 's driven. All around hyere, and up in Middle Tennessy, whur I 've been, they 're doing right smart. But it has seemed to bear on their minds that they wanted to rent land, and have a little place of their own. They get treated right rough by some unprincipled men, and by some that ought to know how to give 'em Christian treatment, now they 're free.   But the truth is, a white man can't take impudence from 'em.   It may be a long ways removed from what you or I would think impudence, but these passionate men call it that, and pitch in."

"Blair, an old nigger down to the saw-mill whur I went to-day," said Zeek, "got his head split open with an axe by a man two days ago.   He said Old Blair sassed him.   He fell plumb crossways of the fire, and they had to roll him off."

"That 's the way," said Mr. ——.   "Befo'e the wa' the owner of the nigger 'd have had the man arrested.   He was so much property.   It was as if you should kill or maim my horse.   But now the nigger has no protection."

"That 's very true, if the government does not protect him."

We talked of the depredations of the two armies.   "I never feared one party more than the other," said Mrs. ——.   "If anything, the Rebels was worst."

"Both took hosses and mules," said Mr. ——.   "At fust, I used to try to get my property back.   I 'd go to headquarters and get authority to take it whur I could find it; but always by that time 't would be hocus-pocussed out of the way. It was all an understood thing.   Aside from that, the regular armies, neither of them, did n't steal from us.   But as soon as they 'd passed, then the thieves would come in.   They 'd take what we had, and cus us for not having mo'e.   Sheep, chickens, geese, corn, watches, and money, — whatever they could lay hands on suffered.   Men never thought of carrying money about them, them times, but always give it to the weemun to hide.   Thar was scouts belonging to both armies, but which was mo'e robbers than scouts, that was the scourge of the country.   If a man had anything, they 'd be sure to h'ist it.   They 'd pretend to come with an order to search for gov'ment arms.   It was only an excuse for robbing.   They 'd search for gov'ment arms in a tin-cup.   They had what they called a cash rope. That was a rope to slip about a man's neck, and swing him up with, till he 'd tell whur his money was. They had a gimblet, which they said was for boring for treasures; and they always knew just whur to bore to find 'em. That was right hyere " (in a man's temples). " They 'd bore into him, till he could n't stand the pain, then if he had any money he 'd be only too glad to give it up. These was generally Confederates. We was pestered powerful by 'em. But Harrison's scouts was as bad as any. They pretended to be acting on the Union side. They was made up of Southern men, mostly from Mississippi, Alabama, and Tennessy. They was a torn-down bad set of men; bad as the Rebs. They 'd no respect for anybody or anything. One Sunday a neighbor of mine met them coming up the road. He knew them very well; and he said to them, it was Sunday, and he hoped thar 'd be no disturbances that day; the people, he said, had all gone to preaching. That 's right, they said; they believed in means of grace; and they asked whur the preaching was to be, and who was going to preach. He told them, and said he was going thar himself. They said they believed a man did right to go to preaching, though they was deprived of that privilege themselves. He told 'em he hoped they 'd look more after their eternal interest in futur', and they said they intended to, and inquired mo'e particular whur the preaching was to be, and thanked him, and rode on. They then just went to plund'ring, cl'aring out his house about the fust one. Then they said they thought they 'd take his advice, and look a little after their eternal interests, and go and hunt up the preaching. Then they just went over and robbed the meeting. There was seventeen horses with sidesaddles on 'em; the men generally went on foot, but the weemun rode. They tuke every horse, and left the weemun to walk home, and carry their saddles, or leave 'em."

" Some Rebel bushwhackers," said Mrs. ———, " went to the house of a woman I know as well as I know my own sisters, and because she would n't give 'em her money — she had it in a belt under her dress tied around her waist — they knocked her eye out ; then they took their knives, and cut right through to her flesh, cutting her money out."

Both Zeek and his father kept out of the war. The latter was too old, and the former too young, to be swept in by the conscription act. "Zeek escaped well!" said the mother, with a gleam of exultation. "But I was just in dread he'd be taken!" And I gathered that a little innocent maternal fiction, as to his years, had been employed to shield him.

"Some of the hardest times we saw, hyere in the Union parts of Tennessy, was when they come hunting conscripts. They got up some dogs now that would track a man. One of my neighbors turned and shot a hound that was after him, and got away. The men come up, and they was torn-down mad when they saw the dog killed. They pressed a man and his wagon to take the carcase back to town ; they lived in Adamsville, eight miles from hyere. They stopped to my house over night, going back."

"They just bemoaned the loss of that dog," said Mrs. ——. "They said they'd sooner have lost one of their company."

"They got back to town, and they buried that dog now with great solemnity. They put a monument over his grave, with an epitaph on it. But some of the conscripts they'd been hunting, dug him up, and hung him to a tree, and shot him full of bullets, and made a writing which they pinned to the tree, with these words on it : '*We'll serve the owners of the dogs the same way next.*' "

"Was Owl Crick swimming to-day, Zeek?" Mrs. —— asked ; meaning, was it so high that our beasts had to swim. And that led to a remark as to the origin of the name.

"Thar's right smart of owls on this Crick," said Mr. —— ; "sometimes we're pestered powerful by 'em ; they steal our chickens so."

Just then we heard a wild squawking in the direction of the hen-roost. "Thar's one catching a chicken now," quietly observed the farmer. I certainly expected to see either him or Zeek run out to the poor thing's rescue. But they sat unconcernedly in their chairs. It was the chicken's business, not theirs. The squawking grew fainter and fainter, and then ceased.

" The people all through this section I allow will never forget the battle," said Mr. ——. " Friday night Johnson's left wing was at Brooks's, — the last house you passed to-day befo'e you fo'ded Owl Crick. The woods was just full of men. They took Brooks, to make him show 'em the way. He said he did n't know the woods, and that was the fact ; but they swo'e he lied, and he must go with 'em, and they 'd shoot him if he led 'em amiss. He was in a powerful bad fix ; but, lucky for him they had n't gone fur when they met Dammern, an old hunter, that knew every branch and thicket in the country. So they swapped off Brooks for Dammern.

" The Federals was on the other side of us, and I allowed there was going to be a battle. And it looked to me as if it was going to be right on my farm."

" That was the awfulest night I ever had in my life," said Mrs. ——. " My husband was for leaving at once. But it did n't appear like I could bear the idea of it. Though what to do with ourselves if we staid? We 've no cellar, and if we 'd had one, and got into it, a shell might have set the house afire, and buried us under it. So I proposed we should dig a hole to get into. He allowed that might be the best thing. So the next morning I got off betimes, and went over and counselled with our neighbors through the grove, and told 'em I thought it would be a grand idee to dig a pit for both our families, and so they came over hyere and went to digging."

" You never see men work so earnest as we did till about 'leven o'clock," said Mr. ——. " Finally we got the pit dug, between the house and the spring. But when it was done it looked so much like a grave the weemun dreaded to get into it, and so much like a breastwork we men was afraid both armies would just play their artilleries onto it. So my wife give her consent we should take to the swamps. But what to do with the pit? for if it got shelled, the house would be destroyed ; and then thar was danger the armies would use the hole to bury their dead in, and the bodies would spoil our spring. And as we could n't take the pit with us, it appeared like thar was but one thing to do. So we put in and worked right earnest till we 'd filled it up again. A rain had come on Friday night, and bogged down some of Johnson's artillery be tween hyere and Corinth, and that 's my understanding why the fight did n't come off Saturday. That give us time to git off. I took my family three miles back to a cabin in the swamp, and thar they staid till it was all over; only Zeek and me come back for some loads of goods. We took one load Saturday, and come for another Monday. That was the second day of the fight. We found the place covered with Rebel soldiers. The battle was going on then. The roar of artillery was so loud you could n't converse at one end of the house, whur the echo was. The musketry sounded like a roaring wind; the artillery was like peals of thunder.

"Thar was one family caught on the battle-field. They had staid, because the man was laying dangerously sick, and they dreaded to move him. After the fighting begun, they started to get away. The little boy was shot through the head, and the horse killed. The weemun then just took up the sick man and run with him down into the swamp."

"We had a nephew living on the battle-field," said Mrs. ——. "The family was down with the measles at the time. But when they see thar was to be a fight, they just moved a plank in the ceiling over head, and hid up all their bacon, and lard, and corn-meal, and everything to eat they could n't take with 'em. Then they tuke up a child apiece and come on for us; we 'd done gone when they got hyere, and they come tearing through the swampy ground after us, toting their babes. They staid with us in the cabin till after the battle. But by that time his house was occupied by soldiers. He 'd been right ingenious hiding his provisions, so nobody could find 'em; but the soldiers went to tearing off ceilings to get planks to make boxes, and down come the corn-meal and bacon; so they had a pretty rich supply."

"After that," said Mr. ——, "his house got burnt. Nearly all the houses and fences for miles, on the battle-field, was burnt; so that it was just one common. Thar was nobody left. You never see such desolation. Then the armies moved off, leaving a rich pasture. I had my cattle pastured thar all that summer."

Mrs. —— proposed that the children should sing for me a little piece called "The Drummer Boy of Shiloh." Her husband favored the suggestion, saying it was "a right nice composed little song."

"I've plumb forgotten it," said Zeek. And the little girls, who blushingly undertook it after much solicitation, could remember only a few lines here and there, greatly to the parents' chagrin.

Mrs. —— was at times very thoughtful; and she told me a newly married elder daughter had that day left home with her husband.

"We'll go by their house in the morning, and I'll show it to you," said Zeek.

I congratulated the parents on having their child settled so near them; yet Mrs. —— could scarcely speak of the separation without rising tears. All were eloquent in their praises of the young husband. He was doing right well, when the war, the cruel, wasteful war, swept him in, and he fought for the slave despotism four years, without a dollar of pay. That left him plumb flat. But he was a right smart worker. He was a splendid hand to make rails. He could write also. After the surrender, he just let in to work, and made a crop; and after the crop was laid by, (*i. e.*, when the corn was hoed for the last time,) he pitched into writing. He employed himself as a teacher of that art. He had already taught nine schools, of ten successive lessons each, at two dollars a scholar. He had had as many as sixty pupils of an evening. I sympathized sincerely with the satisfaction they all felt in having their Maggie married to so smart a man. Indeed, I was beginning greatly to like this little family, and to feel a personal interest in all their affairs. It delights me now to recall that December evening, spent in the red firelight of that humble farm-house; and if I record their peculiarities of speech and manners, it is because they were characteristic and pleasing.

At eight o'clock, Zeek, weary with his long ride that day, said, " I believe I 'll lie down," and, without further ceremony, took off his clothes and got into one of the beds in the room. Mrs. —— thought I also must be tired, and said I could go to bed when I pleased.   Thinking it possible I might be assigned to the same apartment, I concluded to sit up until the audience became somewhat smaller.   The girls presently went up-stairs, lighted to their beds by the fire, which shone up the stairway and through the cracks in the chamber floor.   I took courage then to say that I was ready to retire ; and, to my gratification, saw a candle lighted to show me to my chamber, — though I marvelled where that could be, for I supposed I had seen every room in the house, except the loft to which the girls had gone, when I had seen the sitting-room and kitchen.

Mr. —— took me first out-doors, to a stoop on the side of the house opposite the great opening.   Thence a door opened into a little framed box of a room built up against the loghouse, as an addition.   There was scarcely space to turn in it. The walls consisted of the naked, rough boards.   There was not even a latch to the door, which opened into the universal night, and which the wind kept pushing in.   Mr. —— advised me to place the chair against it, which I did.   I set the candle in the chair, and blew it out after I had got into bed.   Then looking up, I saw with calm joy a star through the roof.   It was interesting to know that this was the bridal chamber.

The bed was deep and comfortable, and I did not suffer from cold, although I could feel the fingers of the wind toying with my hair.   The night was full of noises, like the reports of pistols.   It was the old house cracking its joints.

CHAPTER XLV.

THE FIELD OF SHILOH.

DAYLIGHT next morning shone in through the chinks of the bridal chamber (for window it had none), and I awoke refreshed, after sound sleep. The dawn was enlivened by pleasing old-time sounds, — the farmer chopping wood at the door, crowing cocks, gossiping geese, and the new-made fire snapping and crackling in the next room.

The morning was very cold. The earth was covered with white frost, like snow. We had breakfast at the usual hour. "Farmers commonly get their breakfases by sun-up," said mine host. At table (both doors open, and everybody shivering) Mrs. —— remarked that if it was any colder in my country she would not like to live there. I said to her, —

"We should call this cold weather, though we have some much colder. But, allow me to tell you, I have suffered more from the cold since I have been in Tennessee, than I have for ten years in the North. There, when we go out of doors in winter, we go clad to meet the inclemencies of the season; and we know how to make ourselves comfortable in our houses. Here your houses are open. The wind comes in through the cracks, and you do not even think of shutting the doors. My people at home would think they would perish, if they had to breakfast with the wind blowing on them, as you have it blowing on you here." In short, I said so much that I got one' of the doors closed, which I considered a great triumph.

Zeek brought our animals to the gate; and I called for my bill. Mr. —— said it appeared like he ought not to charge me anything; he had been very glad of my company. As I insisted on discharging my indebtedness, he named a sum so modest that I smiled. " You have n't heard of the rage for high prices, nor learned the art of fleecing the Yankees." I gave him twice the sum, but it was with difficulty I could prevail upon him to accept it, for he said it would trouble his conscience. A simple, thoroughly good and upright man, — would there were more like him !

I mounted my horse at the gate, and in company with Zeek and his mule, set out for the battle-field. We struck Owl Creek, but instead of crossing immediately, followed a cattle-path along its bank. On our right were woods, their tops just flushing with the new-risen sun ; on our left, corn-fields, in some of which the corn had not yet been gathered, while in others I noticed winter wheat, (ploughed in between the rows of stalks, still standing,) covering the ground with its green mat, now hoary with frost. Fording the creek at a safe place, and pushing in an easterly direction through the woods, we came to an army road, made by Wallace's division moving on towards Corinth, after the battle.

It was a pleasant, still morning, such as always brings to the susceptible spirit a sense of exhilaration. Leisurely we rode among the wooded hills, which I could scarcely believe were ever shaken by the roar of battle. Only the blue jay and the woodpecker made the brown vistas of the trees echo with their drumming and screaming, where had been heard the shriek and whiz of missiles and bullets tapping the trunks.

A little back from the cleared fields we came to a nice-look-ing new log-hut. It had no window, and but one door. This was closed ; by which token Zeek knew the folks were away. This was the abode of his sister and her interesting husband ; this the bridal home. Something tender and grateful swelled up in my heart as I looked at the little windowless log-cabin, and thought of the divine gift of love, and of happiness, which dwells in humble places as well as in the highest.

Quitting Wallace's road at its junction with a neighborhood road, we struck another cow-path, which led in a northeasterly direction through the woods. We soon came upon evidences of a vast encampment. Here our right wing had intrenched itself after the battle. In this place I may remark that the astonishing fact about this field is, that our army did not intrench itself *before* the battle. Three weeks it lay at Shiloh, menaced by the enemy; Grant himself pronounced an attack probable, and the sagacious Sherman expected it; yet when it came, it proved a perfect surprise; it found our lines badly arranged, weak, and undefended by a single breastwork.

Beyond was a magnificent field, swept of its fences, but stuck all over with abandoned tent-supports, showing where our finally victorious legions had lain. "This field was just like a city after the fight," said Zeek. I noticed that the trees in the surrounding groves were killed. "The Yankees skinned 'em for bark to lay on," Zeek explained.

Crossing Shiloh Branch, — a sluggish little stream, with low, flat shores, covered with yellow sedge and sentinelled by solemn dead trees, — we ascended a woody hill, along the crest of which a row of graves showed where Hildebrand's picket line was attacked, on that disastrous Sunday morning. Each soldier had been buried where he fell. The boughs, so fresh and green that April morning, waving over their heads in the sweet light of dawn, though dismantled now by the blasts of winter, had still a tranquil beauty of their own, gilded and sparkling with sunshine and frost. Fires in the woods had burned the bottoms of the head-boards. I stopped at one grave within a rude log-rail enclosure. "In memory of L. G. Miller," said the tablet; but the remainder of the inscription had been obliterated by fire. I counted eighteen graves in this little row.

We rode on to Shiloh Church, — formerly a mere log-cabin in the woods, and by no means the neat white-steepled structure on some village green, which the name of country church suggests to the imagination. There Beauregard had his headquarters after Sunday's battle. It was afterwards torn down for its timbers, and now nothing remained of it but half-burnt logs and rubbish.

Below the hill, a few rods south of the church, Zeek showed me some Rebel graves. There many a poor fellow's bones lay scattered about, rooted up by swine. I saw an old half-rotted shoe, containing a skeleton foot. But the most hideous sight of all, was a grinning skull pushed out of a hole in the ground, exposing the neck-bone, with a silk cravat still tied about it in a fashionable knot.

A short distance southeast of the church we visited the ruins of the Widow Ray house, burned to the ground in the midst of its blasted orchard and desolated fields. "A girl that lived hyere fell mightily in love with a Yankee soldier. Saturday night, he allowed there was going to be a battle, and come to bid her good-bye. He got killed; and she went plumb distracted. She's married now to a mighty clever feller."

Zeek had another romantic story to tell, as we returned to the church. "Hyere's whur the bale of hay was. When the Rebs was brushing out the Yankees, an old Reb found a Yankee soldier nigh about this spot, that had been wounded, and was perishing for a drink of water. He just took him, and got him behind a bale of hay that was hyere, and give him drink out of his canteen, just like he'd been his own brother. Some of the time he'd be nussing him behind the hay, and the rest he'd be shooting the Yankees over it. Some one asked him why he took such a heap of pains to save one Yankee life, while he was killing as many mo'e as he could. "They're fighting enemies," he said; "but a wounded man is no longer an enemy, he's a feller being."

Members of one family after all, though at war. Some were so in a literal sense. I recall the story of two Kentucky regiments that fought on this field, one for the bad cause and one for the good. Two brothers met, and the Federal captured the Rebel. The former recommenced firing, when the latter said, "Don't shoot there; that's daddy behind that tree."

Cantering over the hills towards the northeast, we came to the scene of a severe infantry fight in the woods. There was a wild burial-place, containing some fifty patriot graves, originally surrounded by a fence of stakes wattled with saplings

Both the fence and the head-boards had been broken down and partly burned. All around us were sheep feeding in the open woods ; and withdrawn to the seclusion of the little burial-ground was a solitary ewe and a pair of new-born lambs.

"All these hills are just lined with graves," said Zeek. Not far away was a fence surrounding the resting-places of "two officers and seventeen private Rebels," as an inscription cut in the side of a black-jack informed us. There was a story connected with these graves. A Federal soldier found on the dead body of one of the officers, a watch, his likeness, his wife's likeness, a letter from his wife, and a letter written by himself requesting that, in case he should fall, these relics might be sent to her. The soldier faithfully fulfilled this duty ; and at the close of the war the wife, following the directions he forwarded to her with them, came and found his grave.

We rode a mile due north through what Zeek termed "the long avenue," a broad, level opening through the woods, at the farther end of which, "on the elevatedest part," a Yankee battery had been posted, doing terrible execution, if one might judge by the trunks and boughs of trees lopped off by shot and shell. The Rebels charged this battery repeatedly, and it was captured and recaptured.

Leaving the sedgy hills, and pursuing our course towards the Landing, we were stopped by a trench in the woods. It was one hundred and fifty feet long, and four deep. For some reason both ends had been left open. Two feet from the bottom, planks were laid across, the trench being filled with earth over them. Beneath the planks the dead were buried. Their bones could be seen at one of the open ends of the trench. A row of head-boards indicated the graves of Illinois volunteers.

We rode on to the spot which has given the battle its northern name. Under high bluffs, on what Zeek called a "bench," — a shelf of land on the river bank, — approached from the land side by a road running down through a narrow ravine, stood the two log-huts, a dwelling and a grocery, which constituted the town of "Pittsburgh." There was not so much as a wharf there, but steamers made their landing against the natural bank. There was absolutely nothing there now, the two huts having been burned. Wild ducks sat afloat on the broad smooth breast of the river. It was not easy looking down from those heights upon the tranquil picture, to call up that other scene of battle-panic and dismay, — the routed Federal troops pouring through the woods, disorganized, beaten, seeking the shelter of the bluffs and the protection of the gunboats; the great conflict roaring behind them; the victorious Rebels in wild pursuit; God's solemn Sabbath changed to a horrible carnival of mad passions and bloodshed.

"The Rebels just fanned 'em out," said Zeek. "The Yankees put up white flags under the bluff, but the Rebels did n't come near enough to see 'em; they tuke a skeer, — the Federals fell back so easy, they was afraid of some trick. Thar was such a vast amount of 'em they could n't all get to the Landing. Some got drowned trying to swim Snake Creek. Numbers and numbers tried to swim the river. A Federal officer told me he saw his men swim out a little ways, get cold, then wind up together, and go to hugging each other, and sink." Such are the traditions of the fight which have passed into the memory of the country people; but they should be taken with considerable allowance.

On the level river bottom opposite the Landing we found an extensive corn-field, bounded by heavy timber beyond. Under that shore the gunboats lay where they shelled the advancing Rebels. It was there, emerging from the timber into the open field, that our defeated army saw, that Sunday evening, first the advanced cavalry, then a whole division of Buell's army coming to the rescue, — banners flying and bayonets glittering among the trees. Glad sight! No wonder the runaways under the bluffs made the welkin ring with their cheers! If Buell did not arrive in time to save that day, he was in time to save the next, and turn defeat into victory.

Taking the Hamburg Road up the river, we reached the scene of General Prentiss's disaster. The Rebels were in our camps that Sunday morning almost before the alarm of attack was given. First came the wild cries of the pickets rushing in, accompanied by the scattering shots of the enemy, and followed instantly by shells hurtling through the tents, in which the inmates were just rousing from sleep ; then, sweeping like an avalanche through the woods, the terrible resistless battle-front of the enemy.

" Into the just-aroused camps thronged the Rebel regiments, firing sharp volleys as they came, and springing towards our laggards with the bayonet. Some were shot down as they were running, without weapons, hatless, coatless, toward the river. Others fell as they were disentangling themselves from the flaps that formed the doors to their tents ; others as they were buckling on their accoutrements ; a few, it was even said, as they were vainly trying to impress on the cruelly-exultant enemy their readiness to surrender. Officers were wounded in their beds, and left for dead, who, through the whole two days' struggle, lay there gasping in their agony, and on Monday evening were found in their gore, inside their tents, and still able to tell the tale." [1]

The houses all along the road were burned. In Prentiss's front was a farm, all laid waste, the orchard shot to pieces and destroyed by balls. The woods all around were killed, perforated with countless holes, as by the bills of woodpeckers.

Striking the Hamburg and Purdy road, we went west to the spot where the Rebel General Sydney A. Johnston fell, pierced by a mortal wound. Zeek then piloted me through the woods to the Corinth Road, where, time pressing, I took leave of him, sorry I could not accept his invitation to go home with him to dinner. It was five miles to his father's house ; it was twenty miles to Corinth ; and the day was already half spent.

---

[1] "Agate," in the *Cincinnati Gazette*, who furnished the best contemporaneous account of this battle.

CHAPTER XLVI.

WAITING FOR THE TRAIN AT MIDNIGHT.

STOPPING occasionally to talk with the people along the road, and dining at a farm-house, I did not reach Corinth until sunset. The first thing I noticed, in passing the fortifications, was that the huts of the negro garrison were dismantled; and I found the citizens rejoicing over the removal of the troops. I returned to Mr. M——'s house, and was welcomed by Mrs. M——, who seemed almost to have forgotten that I was not only a Yankee, but a " bad Yankee" from Massachusetts. And here I may remark that, whatever hostility was shown me by the Southern people on account of my Northern origin, it usually wore off on a short acquaintance. Mrs. M—— had a private room for me this time; and she caused a great, glowing fire to be made in it for my comfort. After supper she invited me into her sitting-room, where we talked freely about the bad Yankees, the war, and emancipation.

Both her husband and father claimed to be Union men: but their Unionism was of a kind too common in the South. They hated the secession leaders almost as bitterly as they hated the Yankee government.

Mrs. M——: " Slavery was bad economy, I know; but oh, it was glorious! " — spoken with a kind of romantic enthusiasm. " I 'd give a mint of money right now for servants like I once had, — to have one all my own ! " — clasping her hands in the ardor of that passionate wish.

" Ladies at the North," she went on, " if they lose their servants, can do their own work; but we can't, we can't ! "

She bemoaned the loss of a girl she formerly owned; a bright mulattress, very pretty and intelligent. " She could read and write as well as I could. There was no kind of work

that girl could n't do.   And so faithful!—I trusted everything to her, and was never deceived."

I asked if she could feel in her heart that it was right to
own such a creature.

"I believed in it as much as I believed in the Bible.   We
were taught it from our infancy,—we were taught it with our
religion.   I still think it was right; but I think it was because
we abused slavery that it was taken from us.   Emancipation
is a worse thing for our servants than for us.   They can't take
care of themselves."

"What has become of that favorite girl of yours?"

"She is in St. Louis.   She works at her trade there; she's
a splendid dressmaker.   Oh, if I only had her to make my
dresses now, like she used to!   She owns the house and lot
where she lives; she has bought it with the money she has
earned.   She's married to a very fine mulatto man."

"It seems she can take care of herself a good deal better
than you can," I remarked.   "It is she who is independent;
it is you whom slavery has left helpless."

"Well, some of them have made money, and know how to
keep it.   But they are very few."

"Yet do not those few indicate what the race may become?
And, when we consider the bondage from which they have
just broken, and the childish improvidence which was natural
to them in that condition, is it not a matter of surprise that so
many know how to take care of themselves?"   She candidly
confessed that it was.

As an illustration of a practice Southern ladies too commonly indulge in, I may state that, while we were conversing,
she sat in the chimney-corner, chewing a dainty little quid,
and spitting into the fire something that looked marvellously
like tobacco juice.

As I was to take the train for Memphis at two o'clock in the
morning, I engaged a hackman to come to the house for me at
one.   Relying upon his fidelity, I went to bed, slept soundly,
and awoke providentially at a quarter past the hour agreed
upon.   I waited half an hour for him, and he did not appear.

Opening the door to listen for coming wheels, I heard the train whistle. Catching up my luggage, which luckily was not heavy, I rushed out to search, at dead of night, in a strange town, lampless, soundless, and fast asleep, for a railroad depot, which I should scarce have thought of finding even by daylight without inquiring my way. Not a living creature was abroad; not a light was visible in any house; I could not see the ground I was treading upon. Fortunately I knew the general direction in which the railroad lay; I struck it at last; then I saw a light, which guided me to the depot.

But where was the train? It was already over-due. I could hear it whistling occasionally down the track, where some accident had happened to it. The depot consisted of a little framed box just large enough for a ticket-office. You stood outside and bought your ticket through a hole. This box contained a stove, a railroad lantern, and two men. The door, contrary to the custom of the country, was kept scrupulously shut. In vain were all appeals to the two men within to open it. They were talking and laughing by their comfortable fire, while the waiting passengers outside were freezing. Two hours we waited, that cold winter's night, for the train which did not come. There was an express-office lighted up near by, but there was no admittance for strangers there either.

Seeing a red flame a short distance up the railroad track, and human forms passing at times before it, I went stumbling out through the darkness towards it. I found it an encampment of negroes. Twelve men, women, and children were grouped in gypsy fashion about a smoky fire. They were in a miserable condition, wretchedly clad, hungry, weary, and sleepy, but unable to sleep. One woman held in her arms a sick babe, that kept up its perpetual sad wail through the night. The wind seemed to be in every direction, blowing the smoke into everybody's eyes. Yet these suffering and oppressed creatures did for me what men of my own color had refused to do, — they made room for me at their fire, and hospitably invited me to share such poor comforts as they had. The incident was humiliating and touching. One man gave me an apple, for which I was but too glad to return him many times its cost.

They told me their story. They had been working all summer for a planter in Tishemingo County, who had refused to pay them, and they were now hunting for new homes. Two or three had a little money ; the rest had none. It made my heart sick to look at them, and feel that it was out of my power to do them any real, permanent service. But they were not discouraged. Said the spokesman of the party, cheerfully, — an old gray-haired man in tatters, — " I 'll drap my feet into de road in de mornin' ; I 'll go till I find somefin' ! "

Hearing the train again, whistling in earnest this time, I took leave of them, and reached the depot just as it arrived.

CHAPTER XLVII.

AT daylight we were running through the level lower counties of West Tennessee.   This is by far the most fertile division of the State.   Its soil is a rich black mould, adapted to the
culture of cotton, tobacco, and grains, which are produced in
great abundance.

Occasionally in the dim dawn, and later in the forenoon, we
passed out-door fires about which homeless negroes had passed
the night, and around which they still sat or stood, in wretched
plight, but picturesque and cheerful, — old men and women,
young children, and tall girls in tattered frocks, warming their
hands, and watching with vacant curiosity the train as it shot
by.

" That 's freedom ! that 's what the Yankees have done for
'em ! " was the frequent exclamation that fell from the lips of
Southern ladies and gentlemen looking out on these miserable
groups from the car windows.

" They 'll all be dead before spring."

" Niggers can't take care of themselves."

" The Southern people were always their best friends.   How
I pity them ! don't you ? "

" Oh, yes, of course I pity them !   How much better off they
were when they were slaves ! "

With scarcely one exception there was to be detected in
these expressions a grim exultation.   The slave-owners, having foretold that freedom would prove fatal to the bondman,
experienced a satisfaction in seeing their predictions come true.
The usual words of sympathy his condition suggested had all
the hardness and hollowness of cant.   Those who really felt

commiseration for his sufferings spoke of them in very different tones of voice.

But there was another side to the picture. At every stopping-place, throngs of well-dressed blacks crowded upon the train. They were going to Memphis to " buy Christmas," — as the purchase of gifts for that gay season is termed. Happier faces I have never seen. There was not a drunken or disorderly person among them, — which would have been a remarkable circumstance had the occasion been St. Patrick's day, or the Fourth of July, and had these been Irish or white American laborers. They were all comfortably clad, — many of them elegantly, — in clothes they had purchased with money earned out of bondage. They paid with pride the full fares exacted of free people, instead of the half fares formerly demanded for slaves. They had still left in their purses ample means to " buy Christmas " for their friends and relatives left at home. They occupied cars by themselves which they filled with the noise of cheerful conversation and laughter. And nobody said of *them*, " That is freedom ! That is what the Yankees have done for them ! "

Past cotton-fields and handsome mansions in the pleasant suburbs, we ran into Memphis, — a city which surprised me by its beautiful situation and commercial activity.

Memphis stands on a high bluff overlooking the Mississippi River. It is the emporium of West Tennessee, Eastern Arkansas, and Northern Mississippi, and is the most important town between New Orleans and St. Louis. Its growth has been rapid. Laid out in 1820, its population in 1840 was 8,839 ; in 1850, 16,000 ; in 1860, 50,000. Its present population is not known ; but it has immensely increased since the last census, and is still increasing. I was told that, at the time of my visit, the building of nineteen hundred new houses had been contracted for, and that only labor was wanted to complete them.

In the year ending September 1st, 1860, 400,000 bales of cotton were shipped from this port. During seven months of the year 1864, — May to November inclusive, — the shipments

amounted to only 34,316 bales. In 1865, from May, the month
when the cotton released by the fall of the Confederacy began to
pour in, to December 22d, the date of my visit, the shipments
were 138,615 bales. These last figures, furnished me by the
government assessors, do not include the government cotton,
which passed untaxed, and a considerable quantity which
came to Memphis after being taxed in interior districts.[1]

The view of the commerce of Memphis from the esplanade
overlooking the landing is one of the most animated imagina-
ble. You stand on the brow of the bluff, with the city behind
you, and the river below, — its broad, sweeping current severing the States. From the foot of the bluff projects an extensive shelving bank, with an understratum of sandstone ; forming a natural landing, commonly called a " levee," although
no levee is here, — the celebrated levee at New Orleans having
impressed its name upon all landings of any importance up the
river. You look down upon a superb array of steamers, lying
along the shore ; their elegantly ornamented pilot-houses and
lofty tiers of decks supported by slender pillars fully entitling
them to be named floating palaces. From the tower-like pipes
issue black clouds of smoke, with here and there rising white
puffs of steam. The levee is crowded with casks and cotton
bales, covering acres of ground. Up and down the steep way
cut through the brow of the bluff, affording access to the landing from the town, a stream of drays is passing and repassing.
Freights are going aboard, or coming ashore. Drays are loading and unloading. Bales of cotton and hay, casks, boxes,
sacks of grain, lumber, household furniture, supplies for plantations, mules, ploughs, wagons, are tumbled, rolled, carried,
tossed, driven, pushed, and dragged, by an army of laborers,
from the levee along the broad wooden stages to the steamers'
decks. The movement, the seeming confusion, the rattling of
drays, the ringing of boats' bells, the horrible snort of the
steam-whistle, the singing calls of the deck hands heaving at a

[1] Since March 15th, 1864, the government tax on cotton had been two cents a
pound. The average weight of a bale, which was latterly 460 or 465 pounds, is now
500 pounds. The tax on a bale was accordingly about ten dollars. There were in
Memphis at that time 30,000 bales.

rope or lifting some heavy weight, the multitudinous shouts, and wild, fantastic gesticulations of gangs of negroes driving on board a drove of frightened mules, the voices of the team-sters, the arriving and departing packets, drift-wood going down stream, and skiffs paddling up, — the whole forms an aston-ishing and amusing scene. Then over the immense brown sand-bar of the Arkansas shore, and behind its interminable line of dark forest boundaries, the sun goes down in a tranquil sea of fire, reflected in the river, — a wonderfully contrasting picture. Here all is life and animation; there all is softness and peace.

Evening comes, and adds picturesque effect to the scene. The levee is lighted by great smoking and flaring flambeaux. A grate swinging in a socket on the end of a pole is filled with bituminous coal and wood, the blaze of which is enlivened by flakes of oil-soaked cotton, resembling fat, laid on from a bucket. The far-illuminating flame shoots up in the night, while the ignited oil from the grate falls in little streams of dripping blue fire into the river. Until late at night, and often all night, amid darkness and fog and rain, the loading of freight goes on by this lurid illumination. The laborers are chiefly negroes, whose ebon, dusky, sallow and tawny faces, lithe attitudes, and sublime carelessness of attire, heighten the pic-torial effect of the scene. Bale after bale is tumbled from the drays, and rolled down the levee, — a negro at each end of it holding and guiding it with cotton-hooks. At the foot of the landing it is seized by two other negroes, who roll it along the plank to its place on the deck of the upward-bound boat. Here are fifty men rolling barrels aboard, each at the other's heels; and yonder is a long straggling file of blacks crossing the stage from the levee to the steamer, each carrying a box on his shoulder.

CHAPTER XLVIII.

FREEDMEN'S SCHOOLS AND THE FREEDMEN'S BUREAU.

BY a census taken in June, 1865, there were shown to be 16,509 freedmen in Memphis. Of this number 220 were indigent persons, maintained, not by the city or the Bureau, but by the freed people themselves. During the past three years, colored benevolent societies in Memphis had contributed five thousand dollars towards the support of their own poor.

There were three thousand pupils in the freedmen's schools. The teachers for these were furnished, here as elsewhere, chiefly by benevolent societies in the North. Such of the citizens as did not oppose the education of the blacks, were generally silent about it. Nobody said of it, " That is freedom ! That is what the Yankees are doing for them ! "

Visiting these schools in nearly all the Southern States, I did not hear of the white people taking any interest in them. With the exception of here and there a man or woman inspired by Northern principles, I never saw or heard of a Southern citizen, male or female, entering one of those humble school-rooms. How often, thinking of this indifference, and watching the earnest, Christian labors of that little band of refined and sensitive men and women and girls, who had left cheerful homes in the North and voluntarily exposed themselves to privation and opprobrium, devoting their noblest energies to the work of educating and elevating the despised race, — how often the stereotyped phrase occurred to me, " The Southern people were always their best friends ! "

The wonder with me was, how these " best friends " could be so utterly careless of the intellectual and moral interests of the freedmen. For my own part, I could never enter one of those schools without emotion.   They were often held in old buildings and sheds good for little else.   There was not a school-room in Tennessee furnished with appropriate seats and desks.   I found a similar condition of things in all the States. The pews of colored churches, or plain benches in the vestries, or old chairs with boards laid across them in some loft over a shop, or out-of-doors on the grass in summer, — such was the usual scene of the freedmen's schools.

In the branches taught, and in the average progress made, these do not differ much from ordinary white schools at the North.   In those studies which appeal to the imagination and memory, the colored pupil excels.   In those which exercise the reflective and reasoning faculties, he is less proficient.

But it is in the contrasts of age and of personal appearance which they present, that the colored schools differ from all others.   I never visited one of any size in which there were not two or three or half a dozen children so nearly white that no one would have suspected the negro taint.   From these, the complexion ranges through all the indescribable mixed hues, to the shining iron black of a few pure-blooded Africans, perhaps not more in number than the seemingly pure-blooded whites. The younger the generation, the lighter the average skin ; by which curious fact one perceives how fast the race was bleaching under the " peculiar " system of slavery.[1]

The contrast of features is no less than that of complexions. Here you see the rosy child, whose countenance shows a perfect Caucasian contour, shaded perhaps by light brown curls, reciting in the same class with thick-lipped girls and woolly-headed boys.

The difference in ages is even more striking.   Six years and sixty may be seen, side by side, learning to read from the same chart or book.   Perhaps a bright little negro boy or girl

---

[1] At Vicksburg, Miss., in one school of 89 children, only three were of unmixed African blood.   In another, there were two black and 68 mixed.   In a school for adults, there were 41 black to 50 mixed.   In a school of children on a Mississippi plantation, there were 46 black and 23 mixed.   In another plantation school, there were 30 black and 7 mixed.   These figures illustrate not only the rapid bleaching of the race, but also the difference in color between town and country.

is teaching a white-haired old man, or bent old woman in spectacles, their letters. There are few more affecting sights than these aged people beginning the child's task so late in life, often after their eyesight has failed. Said a very old man to a teacher who asked him his age, "I 'm jammed on to a hundred, and dis is my fust chance to git a start."

The scholars are generally well behaved. It is the restlessness and love of fun of the younger ones which prove the greatest trial to the teacher's patience. The proportion of vicious mischief-makers is no greater than in white schools. In the evening-schools, attended chiefly by adults, all is interest and attention. The older pupils are singularly zealous and assiduous in their studies. The singing is usually excellent. Never shall I forget the joyous blending of sweet, rich, exultant childish voices, to which I often listened. The voices of singing children are always delightful and touching: how especially so the musical choruses of children, once slaves, singing the glad songs of freedom!

At Memphis, as at Nashville and other points in Tennessee, I saw much of the operations of the Freedmen's Bureau.

General Fiske appeared to me peculiarly fitted for his position; and he was generally supported by firm and efficient officers; although, like all the Assistant - Commissioners I saw, he complained that the law establishing the Bureau did not permit him to choose his own agents. He had to take such army officers as were given him; some of whom were always found to be incompetent, or neglectful of their duties, or so prejudiced for or against the blacks that they were rendered incapable of administering justice. A few were in sympathy with slavery. Others, meaning to do right, were seduced from a straightforward course by the dinners to which they were invited by planters who had favors to ask. With such, the rights of the freedmen were sure to suffer, when into the opposite scale were thrown the aristocratic Rebel's flattering attentions and the smiles of his fair daughters.

It was the practice of the agents of the Bureau to make frequent tours of their counties, and General Fiske himself was

TEACHING THE FREEDMEN.

in the habit of running off every few days to visit some important point, where his organizing and conciliatory influence was
necessary. Often he would find the planters and the freedmen
separated by hedges of animosity and distrust. Usually his
first step was to call together as large an audience as could be
obtained of both classes, and explain to them the object of the
Bureau, and the duty each class owed the other. In nearly
every instance, earnestness and common sense prevailed; the
freedmen came forward and made contracts with the land-
owners, and the land-owners conceded to the freedmen advantages they had refused before.

Sometimes exciting and dramatic scenes occurred at these
meetings. "Not long ago," said General Fiske, "I addressed
a mixed audience of three thousand persons at Spring Hill.
The meeting was presided over by a black man. Rebel generals and Federal generals sat together on the platform. I
made a short speech, and afterwards answered questions for
anybody, white or black, that chose to ask them. I had said
that the intention of the Bureau was to do justice to all, without respect to color; when there rose up in the audience a
tall, well dressed, fine-looking woman, sallow, very pale, and
much agitated, and wished to know if *she* could have justice.
Said she, 'I was owned by a respectable planter in this neighborhood who kept me as his wife for many years. I have
borne him five children. Two of them are dead. A short
time ago he married another woman, and drove me and my
three children off.' The man was in the audience. Everybody
present knew him, and there were a hundred witnesses that
could vouch for the truth of the woman's story. I told her
justice should certainly be done in her case. The respectable
planter now supports her and her three children."

I have known many wrongs of this nature to be righted by
the Bureau; the late slave-owners learning that instead of
making their offspring by bondwomen profitable to them as
chattels, in the new order of things they were to be held responsible for their maintenance.

The freedmen's courts were designed to adjudicate upon

cases which could not be safely intrusted to the civil courts.[1] They are in reality military courts, and the law by which they are governed is martial law. I found them particularly efficient in Tennessee. The annoying technicalities and legal quibbles by which, in ordinary courts, the truth is so often inextricably embarrassed, were here swept aside, and justice reached with admirable directness. I have watched carefully scores of cases decided by these tribunals, and do not remember one in which substantial justice was not done. No doubt exceptions to this rule occur, but I am satisfied that they are no more frequent than those which occur in common-law courts; and they are insignificant compared with the wholesale wrong to which the unprotected freedman would be subjected in communities where old slave codes and immemorial prejudice deny to him human rights.

The freedmen's court is no respecter of persons. The proudest aristocrat and the humblest negro stand at its bar on an equal footing. I remember a case in which a member of the Tennessee Legislature was the defendant, and upwards of twenty freedmen hired by him were the plaintiffs. He had voted against the Negro Testimony Bill, which, if it had passed, would have placed his case in a civil court; and now he had the satisfaction of seeing eight of these blacks stand up and testify against him. He admitted that they were faithful and truthful men; and their testimony was so straightforward, I was astonished that he should have waited to have his accounts with them adjusted by the Bureau.

Many difficulties arise from honest misunderstandings be-

---

[1] See Paragraph VII. in Circular No. 5, issued by Major-General Howard, Commissioner of the Bureau, and approved by the President, June 2d, 1865: —

" In all places where there is an interruption of civil law, or in which local courts, by reason of old codes, in violation of the freedom guaranteed by the Proclamation of the President and the laws of Congress, disregard the negro's right to justice before the laws, in not allowing him to give testimony, the control of all subjects relating to refugees and freedmen being committed to this Bureau, the Assistant-Commissioners will adjudicate, either themselves or through officers of their appointment, all difficulties arising between negroes themselves, or between negroes and whites or Indians, except those in military service, so far as recognizable by military authority, and not taken cognizance of by the other tribunals, civil or military, of the United States."

tween the contracting parties. These are decided by the Bureau according to general rules of equity, and nearly always to the satisfaction of both. I was assured by several of the most experienced officers of the Bureau in Tennessee, that, in cases where contracts were fully understood, they were much less frequently broken by the freedmen than by the whites.

Complaints of assaults upon freedmen, and even upon women and girls, were very common. Here is a simple story of wrong related to me by a girl of fourteen whom I saw, weary and famished and drenched, after she had walked thirty-four miles to obtain the protection of the Bureau, bearing the marks of cruel beatings upon her back.

" My name is Milly Wilson ; I live in Wilson County ; my mistress's brother was my father. I have been kept a slave since Emancipation. I worked in de cornfield ; I had to hoe and drap corn ; I ho'ped gether the corn and shuck it. I had to cuke ; and I had spinning to do. I ho'ped sow, hoe, and pick cotton. I had to pick bolls and bring 'em into house, and pick cotton out o' bolls till chickens crowed for midnight. Dey never give me nothing. I did n't dare ax 'em for wages ; and dey said if I run away dey 'd shoot me. My mistress tried to whoop me, but she could n't ; I 'd run from her. Den her son Tom whooped me with a soap-paddle till he broke it. He struck me side of head with his fist, and knocked me down." (Her face was still discolored by the blow.) " His father said, ' That 's no way to beat 'em ; take 'em down and paddle 'em.' Dat night I lef'. I told Jennie to tell 'em I 'd gone to Murfreesboro', so dey would n't git on de right track ; and I started for Nashville. It was n't long till day when I lef'. I walked till sun-up ; and laid by de balance part of de day in an old barn. I had nothing to eat, but on'y jist de meat and bread I had for my supper I took and carried with me for de nex' day. De nex' night de moon riz. I could n't see de moon, but it give light enough so I could see how to walk. Two miles from Triune I found some friends, and dey give me breakfas'. Wednesday mornin' it was sleetin', and dey give me a shawl. Thursday I got to Nashville. Now I want to send for my clothes; for it was so dark when I lef' I could n't see to find 'em. I lef' my clothes, and a skillet and led, and a basket." The court sent not only for these, but for Master Tom who had paddled her, and for Master Tom's father who had abetted the outrage and held her enslaved after slavery was abolished. This is a very mild case compared with some that came to my knowledge, too horrible or too disgusting to be narrated.

The freedmen's affairs in West Tennessee were giving the Bureau daily less and less trouble, — both whites and blacks beginning to learn that contracts were made to be kept, and that their mutual interests depended upon mutual good-will. The most aggravated and embarrassing cases were from Mississippi. The farce of opening the civil courts to the blacks in that State had caused a discontinuance of the freedmen's courts, and the result was a stampede of wronged and outraged people across the line. During an hour I spent at the Bureau one morning, a stream of these cases kept coming in. The newly organized Mississippi militia, under pretence of searching for arms which the blacks were supposed to have provided for the forthcoming Christmas insurrections, had committed robberies, murders, and other outrages, against these unoffending and unprotected people. The Bureau at Memphis could do nothing but refer these cases to the Assistant-Commissioner at Vicksburg, who could do nothing but refer them to the civil courts, which let them alone. One case I recall, however, in which the officers at Memphis thought they could do something. A colored man, who had been managing a Mississippi plantation under contract for a quarter of the crop, came to Memphis for a redress of grievances. The owner had given him fifteen dollars, and refused to give him anything more for his labor. The cotton was baled, and ready for market. It would soon be in Memphis. " Keep watch of that cotton," said the agent; "and as soon as it arrives, we will attach it, and you shall have your share."

While I was there, two negroes came in from Parson Botts's

plantation, in De Soto County, (Mississippi,) bringing guns which they had run off with on the approach of the militia. The wife of one of these men had been beaten over the head with a pistol, and afterwards hung by the neck, to compel her to disclose where the guns were hidden. In this case there was no redress.

A great variety of business is brought before the Bureau. Here is a negro-man who has printed a reward offering fifty dollars for information to assist him in finding his wife and children, sold away from him in times of slavery: a small sum for such an object, you may say, but it is all he has, and he has come to the Bureau for assistance. Here is a free mulattress, who was stolen by a guerilla during the war, and sold into slavery in Arkansas, and she has come to enter a claim for wages earned during two years of enforced servitude. Yonder is a white woman, who has been warned by the police that she must not live with her husband because he is black, and who has come to claim protection in her marriage relation, bringing proof that she is in reality a colored woman. That poor old crippled negro was maimed for life when a slave by a cruel master, who will now be compelled to pension him. Yonder comes an old farmer with a stout colored boy, to get the Bureau's sanction to a contract they wish to make. "Pull off your hat, Bob," says the old man; "you was raised to that;" for he was formerly the lad's owner. He claims to have been a Union man. "I was opposed to secession till I was swep' plumb away." He is very grateful for what the officers do for him, and especially for the good advice they give the boy. "I'll do well by him, and larn him to read, if he'll do well by me."

As they go out, in comes a powerful, short-limbed black, in tattered overcoat, with a red handkerchief on his head, and with a lordly countenance, looking like a barbarian chief. He has made a crop; found everything — mules, feed, implements; hired his own help, — fifteen men and women; managed everything; by agreement he was to have one half; but, owing to an attempt to swindle him, he has had the cotton attached ; and now it is not on his own account he has come, but he is owing his men wages, and they want something for Christmas, which he thinks reasonable, and he desires the Bureau's assistance to raise three hundred dollars on the said cotton. " For I 'm bound," he says, " to be liberal with my men."

Here is a boy, who was formerly a slave, to whom his father, a free man, willed a sum of money, which the boy's owner borrowed, giving his note for it, but never repaid, — for did not the boy and all that he had belong to his master? The worn and soiled bit of paper is produced ; and now the owner will have that money to restore, with interest. Lucky for the boy that he kept that torn and dirty scrap carefully hidden all these years ! Such documents are now serving to right many an ancient wrong. I saw at the Freedmen's Bureau at Richmond a large package of wills, made in favor of slaves, usually by their white fathers, all which had been suppressed by the legitimate heirs. One, a mere rotten and jaundiced rag, scarcely legible, had been carried sewed in the lining of a slave-woman's dress for more than forty years, — the date of the will being 1823. Her son was legally emancipated by that instrument ; but her owner, who claimed to be his owner by inheritance, threatened to kill her if the will was not destroyed, and he believed that it had been destroyed. That boy was now a middle-aged man, having passed the flower of his years in bondage ; and his mother was an old woman, living to thank God that her son was free at last. The master, a rich man, had as yet no idea of the existence of that will, by which he was to be held responsible for the payment of over forty years' wages to his unlawful bondman.

From another of these documents, made by a white master, I copied the following suggestive paragraph : " It is also my last will and desire that *my beloved wife* SALLY DANDRIDGE, and *my son* HARRISON, and *my daughters* CHARITY and JULIA, should be free : and it is my wish and desire for them to be emancipated hereafter, and for them to remain as free people." Another paragraph gave them property. This will, like nearly all the rest, had been registered and proved; and, like them, it had been suppressed, — the beloved wife and son and daughters remaining in bondage, until the slave system went down with the Rebellion, and a day of judgment came with the Freedmen's Bureau.

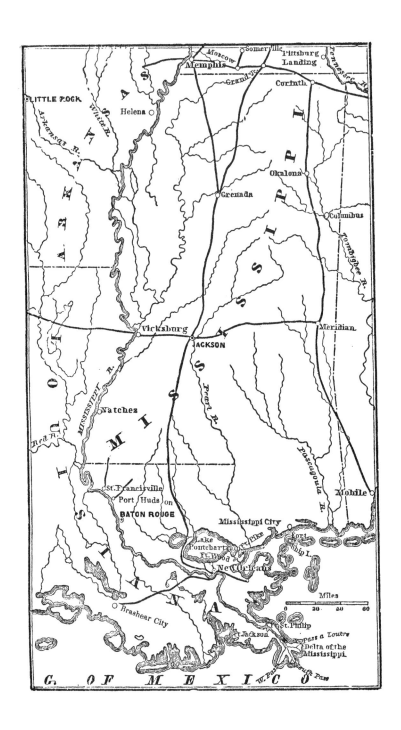

CHAPTER XLIX.

DOWN THE MISSISSIPPI.

At Memphis I took passage in a first-class Mississippi steam-packet for Vicksburg.   It was evening when I went on board. The extensive saloon, with its long array of state-rooms on each side, its ornamental gilt ceiling, and series of dazzling chandeliers, was a brilliant spectacle.   A corps of light-footed and swift-handed colored waiters were setting the tables, — bringing in baskets of table-cloths, and spreading them ; immense baskets of crockery, and distributing it ; and trays of silver, which added to the other noises its ringing and jingling accompaniment.   About the stove and bar and captain's office, at the end of the saloon, was an astonishing crowd of passengers, mostly standing, talking, drinking, buying tickets, playing cards, swearing, reading, laughing, chewing, spitting, and filling the saloon, even to the ladies' cabin at the opposite end, with a thick blue cloud which issued from countless bad pipes and cigars, enveloped the supper-tables, and bedimmed the glitter of the chandeliers.   In that cloud supper was to be eaten.

At a signal known only to the initiated I noticed that pipes were put out and quids cast out, and a mighty rush began. Two lines of battle were formed, confronting each other, with the table between them, each dauntless hero standing with foot advanced, and invincible right hand laid upon the back of a chair.   In this way every place was secured at least five minutes before the thundering signal was given for the beginning of the conflict.   At last the gong-bearing steward, poising his dread right hand, anxiously watched by the hostile hosts, till the ladies were fairly seated, beat the terrible roll and, instantly, every chair was jerked back with a simultaneous clash and clatter, every soldier plunged forward, every coat-tail was spread, and every pair of trousers was in its seat.

Then, rallied by the gong from deck and state-room and stove, came the crowd of uninitiated ones, (*quorum pars parva fui*,) hungry, rueful-faced, dismayed, finding themselves in the unhappy position of the fifth calf that suckled the cow with but four teats, — compelled to wait until the rest had fed.

After supper, there were music and dancing in the after-part of the saloon, and gambling, and clicking glasses, and everlasting talk about Yankees and niggers and cotton, in the other part. There were a few Federal officers in their uniforms, and a good many Rebel officers in civil dress. I recognized a thin sprinkling of Northern capitalists and business men. But the majority were Mississippi and Arkansas planters going down the river to their estates : a strongly marked, unrefined, rather picturesque class, — hard swearers, hard drinkers, inveterate smokers and chewers, wearing sad-colored linen for the most part, and clad in coarse " domestic," slouching in their dress and manners, loose of tongue, free-hearted, good-humored, and sociable. They had been to Memphis to purchase supplies for their plantations, or to lease their plantations, or to hire freedmen, or to " buy Christmas " for their freedmen at home. They appeared to have plenty of money, if the frequency with which they patronized the bar was any criterion. Liquors on board the Mississippi steamers were twenty-five cents a glass, and the average cost of such dram-drinking as I witnessed could not have been less than three or four dollars a day for each man. A few did not seem to be much attracted by the decanters ; while others made drafts upon them every hour, or two or three times an hour, from morning till bedtime, and were never sober, and never quite drunk.

How shall I describe the conversation of these men ? Never a word did I hear fall from the lips of one of them concerning literature or the higher interests of life ; but their talk was of mules, cotton, niggers, money, Yankees, politics, and the

Freedmen's Bureau, — thickly studded with oaths, and garnished with joke and story.

Once only I heard the subject of education indirectly alluded to. Said a young fellow, formerly the owner of fifty niggers, — "I've gone to school-keeping." — "O Lord!" said his companion, "you ha'n't come down to that!"

I judged that most were married men, from a remark made by one of them: "A married man thinks less of personal appearance than a bachelor. I've done played out on that since I got spliced."

There were a few Tennesseeans aboard, who envied the Mississippians their Rebel State government, organized militia, and power over the freedmen. "We might make a pile, if we could only regulate the labor system. But that can't be done in this dog-goned Brownlow State. In Mississippi, if they can only carry out the laws they've enacted, there'll be a chance." It was impossible to convince these gentlemen that the freedmen could be induced to work by any other means than despotic compulsion.

Leaving the gamblers over their cards, and the tipplers over their glasses, I went to bed, — to be awakened at midnight by an inebriated gentleman (weight two hundred, as he thickly informed me) climbing into the berth above me.

After a night of fog, Christmas morning dawned. In the cabin, the generous steward gave to each passenger a glass of egg-nog before breakfast; not because it was Christmas, but because passengers were human, and egg-nog (especially the whiskey in it) was one of the necessities of life.

The morning was warm and beautiful. Mists were chasing each other on the river, and clouds were chasing each other in the sky. A rival steamer was passing us. The decks of both boats were black with spectators watching the race, and making comments upon it: "Look how she piles the water up ahead of her!" "She'll open a gap of a mile between us in an hour!" and so forth.

The river was about half a mile in breadth. We were running down the broad current between high banks covered with forests, on one side, and sand-bars extending their broad yellow shelves out into the river, on the other. Sometimes the sand was on our right, then it shifted to our left; it was nearly always to be seen on one side, but never on both sides at once. The river is continually excavating one bank and making another opposite, — now taking from Arkansas to give to Mississippi, and now robbing Mississippi to pay Arkansas, and thus year after year forming and destroying plantations. I remember one point on the Arkansas shore where the bank rose forty feet above the water, and was covered with trees eighteen inches in thickness; of which a gentleman of the country said to me, "That is all a recent formation. Forty years ago the bed of the river was where that bank is." The water was now tearing away again what it had so suddenly built up, trying to get back into its old bed.

We were making landings at every plantation where passengers or freight were to be put off, or a signal was shown from the shore. Sometimes a newspaper or piece of cloth was fluttered by negroes among the trees on the bank; or a man who wished to come on board, stood on some exposed point and waved his handkerchief or hat. There was never a wharf, but the steamer, rounding to in the current, and heading up stream, went bunting its broad nose against the steep, yielding bank. The planks were pushed out; the passengers stepped aboard or ashore, and the deck-hands landed the freight.

Dirtier or more toilsome work than this landing of the freight I have seldom seen. Heavy boxes, barrels of flour and whiskey, had to be lifted and rolled up steep paths in the soft sand to the summit of the bank. Often the paths were so narrow that but one man could get hold of the end of a barrel and lift it, while another hauled it from above, their feet sinking deep at every step. Imagine a gang of forty or fifty men engaged in landing boxes, casks, sacks of corn and salt, wagons, live-stock, ploughs; hurrying, crowding, working in each other's way, sometimes slipping and falling, the lost barrel tumbling down upon those below; and the mate driving them with shouts and curses and kicks, as if they were so many brutes.

Here the plantations touched the river; and there the land-ing-place was indicated by blazed trees in the forest, where negroes and mules were in waiting.

Wooding-up was always an interesting sight. A long wood-pile lines the summit of the bank, perhaps forty feet above the river. The steamer lands; a couple of stages are hauled out: fifty men rush ashore and climb the bank; the clerk accompa-nies them with pencil and paper and measuring-rod, to take account of the number of cords; then suddenly down comes the wood in an amazing shower, rattling, sliding, bounding, and sometimes turning somersaults into the river. The bottom and side of the bank are soon covered by the deluge; and the work of loading begins in equally lively fashion. The two stages are occupied by two files of men, one going ashore at a dog-trot, empty-handed, and another coming aboard with the wood. Each man catches up from two to four sticks, accord-ing to their size or his own inclination, shoulders them, falls into the current, not of water, but of men, crosses the plank, and deposits his burden where the corded-wood, that stood so lately on the top of the bank, is once more taking shape, divided into two equally-balanced piles on each side of the boiler-deck.

The men are mostly negroes, and the treatment they re-ceive from the mate is about the same as that which they received when slaves. He stands on the shore between the ends of the two stages, within convenient reach of both. Not a laggard escapes his eye or foot. Often he brandishes a bil-let of wood, with which he threatens, and sometimes strikes; and now he flings it at the head of some artful dodger who has eluded his blow. And all the while you hear his hoarse, harsh voice iterating with horrible crescendo: " Get along, *get along!* Out o' the way 'th that wood! *out o' the way*, OUT O' THE WAY! OUT O' THE WAY! *Git on*, GIT ON, GIT ON!"

Meanwhile the men are working as hard as men can rea-sonably be expected to work; and how they discipline their souls to endure such brutality is to me a mystery.

Planters got off at every landing, by day and night; and although a few came aboard, the company was gradually thinning out.   At one plantation a colony of sixty negroes landed. They had a "heap of plunder."   Beds and bedding, trunks, tubs, hen-coops, old chests, old chairs, spinning-wheels, pots, and kettles, were put off under the mate's directions, without much ceremony.   The dogs were caught and pitched into the river, much to the distress of the women and children, who appeared to care more for the animals than for any other portion of their property.   These people had been hired for an adjoining plantation.   The plantation at which we landed had been laid waste, and the mansion and negro-quarters burned, leaving a grove of fifty naked chimneys standing, — "monuments of Yankee vandalism," said my Southern friends.

At one place a fashionably dressed couple came on board, and the gentleman asked for a state-room.   Terrible was the captain's wrath.   "God damn your soul," he said, "get off this boat!"   The gentleman and lady were colored, and they had been guilty of unpardonable impudence in asking for a state-room.

"Kick the nigger!"   "He ought to have his neck broke!" "He ought to be hung!" said the indignant passengers, by whom the captain's prompt and energetic action was strongly commended.

The unwelcome couple went quietly ashore, and one of the hands pitched their trunk after them.   They were in a dilemma: their clothes were too fine for a filthy deck passage, and their skins were too dark for a cabin passage.   So they sat down on the shore to wait for the next steamer.

"They won't find a boat that 'll take 'em," said the grim captain.   "Anyhow, they can't force their damned nigger equality on to me!"   He was very indignant to think that he had landed at their signal.   "The expense of running this boat is forty dollars an hour, — six thousand dollars a trip; — and I can't afford to be fooled by a nigger!"   I omit the epithets.

Afterwards I heard the virtuous passengers in calmer moments talking over the affair. "How would you feel," said one, with solemn emphasis, "to know that *your wife was sleeping in the next room to a nigger and his wife?*" The argument was unanswerable: it was an awful thought!

There is not a place of any importance on the river between Memphis and Vicksburg, a distance of four hundred miles. The nearest approach to an exception is Helena, on the Arkansas shore, a hastily built, high-perched town, looking as if it had flown from somewhere else and just lit. Another place of some note is Napoleon, which was burnt during the war. Here there is one of those natural "cut-offs" for which the Mississippi is remarkable ; the river having formed for itself a new channel, half a mile in length, across a tongue of land about which it formerly made a circuit of twelve miles. We passed through the cut-off, and afterwards made a voyage of six miles up the old channel, which resembles a long, placid, winding lake, to Beulah Landing, called after a novel of that name written by a Southern lady.

I remember Beulah as the scene of a colored soldier's return. He had no sooner landed from the steamer than his friends in waiting seized him, men, women, and girls, some grasping his hands, some clinging to his arms and waist, others hanging upon his neck, smothering him in their joyful embraces. All who could reach him hugged him ; while those who could not reach him hugged those who were hugging him, as the next best thing to be done on the happy occasion.

Below Napoleon, the cleared lands of many plantations extend to the river, while others show only a border of trees along the shore. The banks were continually caving, masses of earth flaking off and falling into the turbid current, as we passed. The levees, neglected during the war, were often in a very bad condition. The river, encroaching upon the shores upon which these artificial embankments were raised, had made frequent breaches in them, and in many places swept them quite away ; so that whole plantations lay at the mercy of the usual spring freshets, which render cotton culture on such unprotected lands impracticable.

23

The power and extent of these freshets is something astonishing. The river averages nearly half a mile in width. Its
depth is very great, often exceeding one hundred feet. Its
average velocity is something over two miles an hour. Yet
when come the sudden rains and thaws, and the great tributaries, with their thousand lesser streams, pour their floods
into the bosom of the Father of Waters, this huge artery becomes but an insignificant channel for them, and they spread
out into a vast lake inundating the valley. The course of the
river is then traceable only by the swifter current in its vicinity, and by the broad sinuous opening through the forests.
A gentleman of my acquaintance told me that in Bolivar
County, Mississippi, he had ridden thirty miles back from the
river, and seen all the way the marks of high water on the
trees as far up as he could reach with his riding-whip.

The crevasses, or breaks in the levees and banks, which
occur at such times, are often terrific. Plantations are destroyed, and buildings swept away. Boats are drawn into the
current and carried inland, to be landed, like the Ark, on the
subsidence of the waters, or lost among the trees of the deep
swamps.

The violence of these freshets is said to be on the increase
of late years, from two or three causes, — the drainage of
newly cultivated lands ; and the cut-offs and the levees, which
project the floods more directly upon the lower country, instead of retarding the water, and suffering it to spread out
gradually over the valley, naturally subject to its overflow.

The best-protected plantations are those which are completely surrounded by independent levees. " If my neighbor's
levee breaks, my land is still defended," said a planter to me,
describing his estate. " Inside of the levee is a ditch by which
the water that soaks in can all be drained to one place and
thrown over the embankment by a steam-pump."

I learned something of the planter's anxiety of mind during
the great floods. " Many is the time I 've sat up all night
just like these mates, looking after the levee on my plantation. Come a wind from the right direction, I 'd catch up a

lantern, and go out, and maybe find the water within three or four inches of the top. In some places a little more would send it over and make a break. My heart would be nigh about to melt, as I watched it. Sometimes I waited, all night long, to see whether the water would go an inch higher. If it did n't, I was safe; if it did, I was a ruined man."

On some of the levees negroes were at work making the necessary repairs; but I was told that many plantations would remain unprotected and uncultivated until another year.

I had heard much about the anticipated negro insurrections at Christmas time. But the only act of violence that came to my knowledge, committed on that day, was a little affair that occurred at Skipwith's Landing, on the Mississippi shore, a few miles below the Arkansas and Louisiana line. Four mounted guerillas, wearing the Confederate uniform, and carrying Spencer rifles, rode into the place, robbed a store kept by a Northern man, robbed and murdered a negro, and rode off again, unmolested. Very little was said of this trifling operation. If such a deed, however, had been perpetrated by freedmen, the whole South would have rung with it, and the cry of "Kill the niggers!" would have been heard from the Rio Grande to the Atlantic.

CHAPTER L.

IN AND ABOUT VICKSBURG.

ON the afternoon of the third day we came in sight of Vicksburg, — four hundred miles from Memphis by water, although not more than half that distance in a straight line, so voluminous are the coils of the Great River.

The town, seen across the intervening tongue of land as we approached it, — situated on a high bluff, with the sunlight on its hills and roofs and fortifications, — was a fine sight. It diverted my attention, so that I looked in vain for the famous canal cut across the tongue of land, which pushes out from the Louisiana shore, and about which the river makes an extensive curve.

"You could n't have found it without looking mighty close," said a native of the country. "It's a little small concern. The Yankees made just a big ditch to let the water through, thinking it would wash out, and make a cut-off. If it had, Farragut's fleet could have got through, and Vicksburg would have been flanked, high and dry. But, in the first place, they did not begin the ditch where the current strikes the shore; in the next place the water fell before the ditch was completed, and never run through it at all."

On the opposite shore, overlooking this peninsula and the winding river, stands Vicksburg, on the brow of a line of bluffs which sweep down from the north, here first striking the Mississippi. In this ridge the town is set, — to compare gross things with fine, — like a diamond in the back of a ring. It slopes up rapidly from the landing, and is built of brick and wood, not beautiful on a nearer view.

The hills are cut through, and their sides sliced off, by the deeply indented streets of the upper portion of the city. Here and there are crests completely cut around, isolated, and left standing like yellowish square sugar-loaves with irregular tops. These excavations afforded the inhabitants fine facilities for burrowing during the siege. The base of the hills and the cliff-like banks of the dug streets present a most curious appearance, being completely honey-combed with caves, which still remain, a source of astonishment to the stranger, who half fancies that a colony of large-sized bank-swallows has been industriously at work there.

The majority of the caves were mere " gopher-holes," as the soldiers call them. Others were quite spacious and aristocratic. The entrance was usually large enough to admit a person stooping slightly ; but within, the roofs of the best caves were hollowed sufficiently to permit a man to stand upright. The passage by which you entered commonly branched to the right and left, forming with its two arms a sort of letter Y, or letter T.

Every family had its cave. But only a few of the more extensive ones were permanently occupied. " Ours " (said a lady resident) " was very large and quite comfortable. There was first the entrance, under a pointed arch ; then a long cross-gallery. Boards were laid down the whole length and covered with carpets. Berths were put up at the sides, where we slept very well. At first we did not take off our dresses when we lay down ; but in a little while we grew accustomed to undressing and retiring regularly. In the morning we found our clothes quite wet from the natural dampness of the cave. Over the entrance there was built a little arbor, where our cooking was done, and where we sat and talked with our neighbors in the daytime, when there were no shells dropping. In the night the cave was lighted up. We lived this sort of life six weeks."

But few buildings were destroyed by the shells. Those that were partially injured had generally been patched up. After the twenty-sixth of May, when the bombardment became almost incessant, being continued night and day, it was estimated that six thousand shells were thrown into the city by the mortars on the river-side every twenty-four hours. Grant's siege guns, in the rear of the bluffs, dropped daily four thousand more along the Rebel lines. The little damage done by so great a bombardment is a matter of surprise. The soldiers had also their "gopher-holes," and laughed at the projectiles. Of the women and children in the town, only three were killed and twelve injured.

Both citizens and troops suffered more from the scarcity of provisions than from the abundance of shells. On both the river and land sides the city was completely cut off from supplies. The garrison was put upon fourteen-and-a-half-ounce rations; and in the town, mule-meat, and even dog-meat, became luxuries.

The day after my arrival I joined a small equestrian party, got up by Lieutenant E—— for my benefit, and rode out to visit the fortifications behind the city. We first came to the line of works thrown up by our troops after the capitulation. Exterior to these, zigzagging along the eastern brow of the bluffs, from the Mississippi, below Vicksburg, to the Yazoo River on the North, a distance of near fifteen miles, were the original Rebel defences, too extensive to be manned by less than a large army.

Three miles northeast of the city we passed Fort Hill, in the "crater" of which, after the Rebel bastions had been successfully mined and blown up, occurred one of the most desperate fights that marked the siege. Pushed up dangerously near to the Rebel position, is the advanced Federal line. Between the two, a little way down the slope from Fort Hill, is the spot rendered historic by the interview which terminated the long struggle for the key to the Mississippi. There, in full view of the confronting armies, the two commanding generals met under an oak-tree, and had their little talk.

Every vestige of the tree, root and branch, had long since disappeared, — cut up, broken up, dug up, and scattered over the country in the form of relics; and we found on the spot a monument, which bids fair to have a similar fate.

This was originally a neat granite shaft, erected by a private subscription among officers and soldiers of the national army, and dedicated on July 4th, 1864, the first anniversary of tho surrender of the city.   It bears the following inscription : —

SITE OF

INTERVIEW BETWEEN

MAJOR-GENERAL GRANT, U. S. A.,

AND

LIEUTENANT-GENERAL PEMBERTON,

JULY 4,

1863.

Nothing certainly could be more simple and modest.   Not a syllable is there to wound the sensibilities of a fallen foc.   Yet, since the close of the war, when the returning Confederates first obtained access to this monument, it had been shamefully mutilated.   The fact that it was never injured before, and the circumstance that the eagle and shield of the escutcheon surmounting the inscription had been nearly obliterated by persistent battering and grinding, showed that no mere relic-hunters had been hammering here, but that the mischief had been done by some enemy's hand.   The shaft was enclosed by a handsome iron fence, which we found broken and partly thrown down.

From the monument we rode northward over ridges crowned with zigzag fortifications, around steep crests and slopes, and past deep ravines green with tangled cane-brakes, — a broken and wild region ; crossing over through woods and hilly cotton-fields to the western brow of the bluffs, where Sherman made his unsuccessful assault in the gloomy last days of 1862.

We reined up our horses on a commanding point, and lookvd down upon the scene of the battle.   Away on our left was the Mississippi, its bold curve sweeping in from the west, and doub-ling southward toward the city.   Before us, under the bluff, was the bottom across which our forces charged, through the bristling abatis and their terrible entanglements, and in tho face of a murderous fire captured the Rebel rifle-pits, — a most heroic, bloody, but worse than useless work.

Finding a road that wound down the steep hill-sides, we galloped through the cotton-fields of the bottom to Chickasaw Bayou, which bounded them on the west,—a small stream flowing down through swamps and lagoons, from the Yazoo, and emptying into the Mississippi below the battle-field. We rode along its bank, and found one of the bridges by which our forces had crossed. Beyond were ancient woods, sombre and brown, bearded with long pendant moss.

Returning across the bottom, the Lieutenant guided us to three prominent elevations in the midst of the plain, which proved to be Indian mounds of an interesting character. The largest was thirty feet in height, and one hundred and fifty feet across the base. Leaving the ladies in the saddle, the Lieutenant and myself hitched our horses to a bush on one of the smaller mounds, and entered an excavation which he had assisted in making on a former visit.

We found the earth full of human bones and antique pottery. A little digging exposed entire skeletons sitting upright, in the posture in which they had been buried, — who knows how many centuries before ? Who were these ancient people, over whose unknown history the past had closed, as the earth had closed over their bodies ? Perhaps these burial-mounds marked the scene of some great battle on the very spot where the modern fight took place.

We found the surface of the mound, washed by the storms of centuries, speckled with bits of bones, yellowish, decayed, and often friable to the touch. Fragments of pottery were also exposed, ornamented in a variety of styles, showing that this ancient people was not without rude arts.

The cotton-fields on the bluffs and in the bottom were cultivated by a colony of freedmen, whose village of brown huts we passed, on the broad hill-side above the river, as we returned to the city.

The ride back over the western brow of the bluffs was one to be remembered. The sun was setting over the forests and plains of Louisiana, which lay dark on the horizon, between the splendid sky and the splendid, wide-spreading river reflecting it. Every cloud, every fugitive fleece, was saturated with fire. The river was a flood of molten gold. The ever-varying glory seemed prolonged for our sakes. The last exquisite tints had scarcely faded, leaving the river dark and melancholy, sweeping between its solitary shores, when we left the crests, with the half-moon sailing in a thinly-clouded sky above our heads, and descended, by the deep-cut, narrow streets, and through the open gates at the breastworks, into the city.

The next day, in company with Major-General Wood, in command of the Department of Mississippi, I visited the fortifications below Vicksburg. For a mile and a half we rode along beside banks perforated with "gopher-holes" dug by the Rebel soldiers, and lines of rifle-pits, which consisted often of a mere trench cut across the edge of a crest. These were the river-side defences. The real fortifications commenced with a strong fort constructed on a commanding bluff. This did not abut on the river, as maps I had seen, and descriptions I had read, had led me to expect. Below the city a tract of low bottom-land opens between the river and the bluffs, of such a nature that no very formidable attack was to be apprehended in that quarter. Standing upon the first redan, we saw a mile or two of low land and tangled and shaggy cypress swamps intervening between us and the glimpses of shining light which indicated the southward course of the Mississippi.

In this excursion, as in that of the previous day, I noticed on every side practical answers to the question, "Will the freedmen work?" In every broken field, in every available spot on the rugged crests, was the negro's little cotton patch.

Riding through the freedmen's quarter below the town the General and I called at a dozen or more different cabins, putting to every person we talked with the inquiry, — how large a proportion of the colored people he knew were shiftless characters. We got very candid replies : the common opinion being that about five out of twenty still had a notion of living without work. Yet, curiously enough, not one would admit that *he* was one of the five, — every man and woman acknowledging that labor was a universal duty and necessity.

CHAPTER LI.

FREE LABOR IN MISSISSIPPI.

COLONEL THOMAS, Assistant-Commissioner of the Freedmen's Bureau for the State of Mississippi, stationed at Vicksburg, gave the negroes more credit for industry than they gave each other. In the large towns, to which vagrancy naturally gravitates, one in four was probably a fair estimate of the proportion of colored people unable or unwilling to earn an honest livelihood. "But I am confident," said the Colonel, "there is no more industrious class of people anywhere than the freedmen who have little homesteads of their own. The colonies under my charge, working lands assigned them by the government, have raised this year ten thousand bales of cotton, besides corn and vegetables for their subsistence until another harvest."

Other well-informed and experienced persons corroborated this statement. Dr. Warren, Superintendent of Freedmen's Schools in Mississippi, told me of a negro family, consisting of one man, three women, and a half-grown girl, who took a lot of five acres, which they worked entirely with shovel and hoe, having no mule, and on which they had that season cleared five hundred dollars, above all expenses. I heard of numerous other well-authenticated instances of the kind.

Dr. Warren spoke of the great eagerness of the blacks to buy or lease land, and have homes of their own. This he said accounted in a great measure for their backwardness in making contracts. He said to one intelligent freedman : "The whites intend to compel you to hire out to them." The latter replied : "What if we should compel them to lease us lands?"

There were other reasons why the blacks would not contract. At Vicksburg, a gentleman who had been fifty miles

up the valley looking for a plantation, said to me : " The negroes everywhere I went have been shamefully abused. They
had been promised that if they would remain and work the
plantations, they should have a share of the crops ; and now
the planters refuse to give them anything. They have no
confidence in Southern men, and will not hire out to them ;
but they are very eager to engage with Northern men."

This was the universal testimony, not only of travellers, but
of candid Southern planters. One of the latter class explained
to me how it was that the freedman was cheated out of his
share of the crop. After the cotton is sent to market, the
proprietor calls up his negroes, and tells them he has " furnished them such and such things, for which he has charged
so much, and that there are no profits to divide. The darkey
don't understand it, — he has kept no accounts ; but he knows
he has worked hard and got nothing. He won't hire to that
man again. But I, and any other man who has done as he
agreed with his niggers, can hire now as many as we want."

Colonel Thomas assured me that two thirds of the laborers
in the State had been cheated out of their wages during the
past year.

Mr. C——, a Northern man who had taken a plantation at
——, (I omit names, for he told me that not only his property
but his life depended upon the good-will of his neighbors,) related to me his experience. He hired his plantation of a gentleman noted for his honesty : " He goes by the name of
' Honest M——' all through the country. But honesty
appeared to be a virtue to be exercised only towards white
people : it was too good to be thrown away on niggers. This
M—— has four hundred sheep, seventy milch cows, fifteen
horses, ten mules, and forty hogs, all of which were saved
from the Yankees when they raided through the country, by
an old negro who run them off across a swamp. Honest M——
has never given that negro five cents. Another of his slaves
had a cow of his own from which he raised a fine pair of
oxen : Honest M—— lays claim to those oxen and sells them.
A slave-woman that belonged to him had a cow she had raised

from a calf: Honest M—— takes that, and adds it to his herd. He promised his niggers a share of the crops this year; but he has sold the cotton, and locked up the corn, and never given one of them a dollar. And all this time he thinks he is honest: he thinks Northern capitalists treat free laborers in this way. You can't get it through the heads of these Southern planters that the laboring class has any rights.

" Honest M—— has two plantations," continued Mr. C——: " he rents me one of them. But he gave me notice at the start that he should take all the niggers from my plantation, and that I must look out for my own help. When I went to take possession I was astonished to find the niggers all there.

" ' How 's this ? ' I said. ' I thought these people were going with you ? '

" He said he could n't induce one of them to contract; and he had about given up the idea of running his other plantation, because the niggers would n't work. He had offered twenty-five dollars a month, with board and medical attendance, and they would n't engage to him even for that.

" ' Well,' said I, ' if you have got through I should like to hire them.'

" He said I was welcome to try. They knew me to be a Northern man, and when I called them around me for a talk, they all came with grinning faces. Said I: ' Mr. M—— offers you twenty-five dollars a month. That is more than I can afford to pay, and I think you 'd better hire to him.' They looked stolid: they could n't see it: they did n't want to work for him at any price.

" Then I said, ' If you won't work for him, will you work for me ? ' I never saw faces light up so in my life. ' Yes, master ! Yes, master ! ' ' But,' said I, ' ten dollars a month is all I can afford to pay.' That made no difference, they said ; they 'd rather work for ten dollars, and be sure of their pay, than for twenty-five dollars, and be cheated out of it. I gave them a day to think of it : then they all came forward and made contracts, with one exception. They went right to work with a will: I won't ask men to do any better than they have been doing. They are having their Christmas frolic now, and it's as merry a Christmas as ever you saw!"

I met with many planters in the situation of Honest M——. Having made arrangements to run their plantations, and got in the necessary supplies, they had discovered that "the niggers would n't contract." They were then trying to lease their lands to Northern capitalists.

I have seldom met a more anxious, panic-stricken set of men than the planters I saw on the steamer going down to Vicksburg to hire freedmen. Observing the success of Northern men, they had suddenly awakened to the great fact that, although slavery was lost, all was not lost, and that there was still a chance to make something out of the nigger. They could not hire their own freedmen, and were going to see what could be effected with freedmen to whom they were not known. Each seemed to fear lest his neighbor should get the start of him.

"They're just crazy about the niggers," said one, a Mississippian, who was about the craziest of the set, — "crazy to get hold of 'em."

"But," I remarked, "they say the freedmen won't work."

"Well, they won't," said my Mississippi friend, unflinchingly.

"Then what do you want of them?"

"Well, I found everybody else was going in for hiring 'em, and if anything was to be made, I did n't want to be left out in the cold." Adding with great candor and earnestness: "*If everybody else would have refused to hire 'em anyhow, that would have just suited me: I'd have been willing to let my plantation go to the devil for one year, just to see the free niggers starve.*"

I saw this gentleman afterwards in Vicksburg, and was not deeply grieved to learn that he had failed to engage a single freedman. "They are hiring to Northern men," said he, bitterly; "but they won't hire to Southern men anyhow, if they can help it."

"How do you account for this singular fact?" I asked.

"I don't know. They've no confidence in us; but they imagine the Yankees will do wonders by 'em. The Southern people are really their best friends." At which stereotyped bit of cant I could not forbear a smile.

The usual terms proposed by the planters were one hundred and fifty dollars, for a full hand, payable at the end of the year; together with doctors' bills, two hundred pounds of pork, and a peck of meal a week.

The terms most approved by Colonel Thomas were as follows: Fifteen dollars a month, with food, including flour, sugar, and molasses; a little patch of ground for each family, and Saturday afternoon, for the raising of their own vegetables; the freedmen to clothe themselves.

The planters insisted on furnishing all needful supplies, and charging the blacks for them when not stipulated for in the contract. The alleged reason for this was that the negroes, if allowed to buy their own supplies, would spend half their time in running about the country for knick-knacks. But the better class of planters admitted that the system was liable to gross abuse. "I have neighbors," said one, "who keep stores of plain goods and fancy articles for their people; and, let a nigger work ever so hard, and earn ever so high wages, he is sure to come out in debt at the end of the year."

Those who had given the free-labor system a fair trial admitted that the negro would work as well as ever before, while in the field, — some said better; but he would not work as many hours.

"How many hours did he formerly work?" I inquired; and received the following statement with regard to what was done on a well-regulated Mississippi plantation.

"Mr. P——'s niggers were in the field at daylight. It was so in the longest days of summer, as at other times of the year. They worked till six o'clock, when their breakfast was carried to them. They had just time enough allowed them to eat their breakfast; then they worked till noon, when their dinner was carried to them. They had an hour for their dinner. At six o'clock their supper was carried to them. Then they worked till dark. There were cisterns in the field, where they got their water. Nobody was allowed to leave the field from the time they entered it in the morning until work was over at night. That was to save time. The women who suckled babies had their babies carried to them. A little nigger-boy used to drive a mule to the field with a cart full of nigger babies; and the women gave the brats their luncheon while they ate their own. So not a minute was lost."

And this was the plantation of a "liberal" owner, worked by a "considerate and merciful overseer." It appeared, according to the planters' own statements, that their slaves used to work at least sixteen hours a day in summer, — probably more, for they had chores to do at home after dark. That they should not choose to keep up such a continual strain on their bodily faculties, now that they were free, did not appear to me very unreasonable, — but that was perhaps because I was prejudiced.

Under the old system, many plantations were left entirely to the management of overseers, the owners living in some pleasant town where they enjoyed the advantages of society for themselves and of schools for their children. The overseer who could produce the most cotton to the hand was in great request, and commanded the highest wages. The natural result was that both lands and negroes were often worked to a ruinous excess. But the occupation of these best overseers was now gone. Not a freedman would hire out to work on plantations where they were known to be employed. Some managed, however, to avoid being thrown out of business by attaching themselves to other plantations, and changing their title. With the negroes a name is imposing. Many would engage cheerfully to work under a "superintendent," who would not have entered the field under an "overseer."

But it is easier to change an odious name than an odious character. Said a candid Southern planter to me, "I should get along very well with my niggers, if I could only get my superintendent to treat them decently. Instead of cheering and encouraging them, he bullies and scolds them, and sometimes so far forgets himself as to kick and beat them. Now they are free they won't stand it. They stood it when they were slaves, because they had to. He can't get the notion out of his head that they are still somehow slaves. When I see things going right badly, I take him, and give him a good talking to. Then for about three days he'll use 'em better, and everything goes smooth. But the first I know, there's more bullying and beating, and there's more niggers bound to quit.'

Meanwhile the Christmas holidays were effecting a change in the prospects of free labor for the coming year. I never witnessed in so short a time so complete a revolution in public feeling. One day it seemed that everybody was in despair, complaining that the niggers would n't work ; the next, everybody was rushing to employ them. And the freedmen, who, before Christmas, had refused to make contracts, vaguely hoping that lands would be given them by the government, or leased to them by their owners, now came forward to make the best terms they could. The presence of the Bureau at this time in the South was an incalculable benefit to both parties. It inspired the freedmen with confidence, and persuaded them, with the promise of its protection, to hire out once more to the Southern planters. The trouble was, that there was not labor enough in the State to supply the demand. Many negroes had enlisted in the war; others had wandered back to the slave-breeding States from which they had been sold ; others had become small proprietors ; and others had died, in consequence of the great and sudden change in their circumstances which the war had brought about.

CHAPTER LII.

A RECONSTRUCTED STATE.

IT seemed impossible for the people of Mississippi — and the same may be said of the Southern people generally — to understand the first principle of the free-labor system. Their notions of it were derived from what they had seen of the shiftless poor whites about them, demoralized by an institution that rendered labor disreputable. They could not conceive of a man devoting himself voluntarily to hard manual toil, such as they had never seen performed except under the lash. Some compulsory system seemed to them indispensable. Hence the new black codes passed by the reconstructed legislatures of several States.

Mississippi, like South Carolina, on returning to the fold of the Union, from which those innocent lambs had strayed, made haste to pass apprentice laws, vagrant laws, and laws relating to contracts and labor, designed to bring back the freedmen under the planters' control. " An Act to regulate the Relation of Master and Apprentice," passed in November, 1865, provides that " all freedmen, free negroes, and mulattoes, under the age of eighteen, who are orphans," or are not maintained by their parents, shall be apprenticed " to some competent and suitable person," — the former owner to " have the preference ; " that " the said apprentices shall be bound by indenture, in the case of males until they are twenty-one years old, and in case of females until they are eighteen years old " ; that said master or mistress shall have power to inflict " moderate corporal chastisement " ; that in case the apprentice leaves them without their consent, he may be committed to jail, and "*punished as provided for the punishment of hired freedmen, as may be from time to time provided for by law,*" —

24

the meaning of which is clear, although the grammatical construction is muddy ; and that any person who shall employ,
feed, or clothe an apprentice who has deserted his master,
" shall be deemed guilty of a high misdemeanor," and so forth.

It will be seen that, by this act, (approved November 22d,
1865,) not merely children without means of support may be
thus bound out under a modified system of slavery, but that
young girls, and lads of from fourteen to eighteen, capable not
only of supporting themselves, but of earning perhaps the
wages of a man or woman, may be taken from the .employ-
ment of their choice and compelled to serve without wages
the master or mistress assigned them by the court.

" An Act to amend the Vagrant Laws of the State " provides that " all freedmen over the age of eighteen years, found
on the second Monday in January, 1866, or thereafter, with
no lawful employment or business," (as if no man was ever
honestly without employment,) " or found unlawfully assem-
bling themselves together either in the day or night time,
shall be deemed vagrants, and on conviction thereof shall be
fined in the sum of not exceeding fifty dollars, and imprisoned
at the discretion of the court not exceeding ten days " ; provided, however, that in case any freedman " shall fail for five
days after the imposition of said fine to pay the same, that it
shall be, and is hereby, made the duty of the sheriff of the
proper county to hire out said freedman to any person who
will for the shortest period of service pay said fine or forfeiture
and all costs."

A bill " To confer Civil Rights on Freedmen, and for other
Purposes," enacts " That all freedmen, free negroes, and mulattoes may sue and be sued, implead and be impleaded in all the
courts of law and equity of this State, and may acquire personal property and choses in action, by descent or purchase,
and may dispose of the same, in the same manner, and to the
same extent that white persons may : *Provided that the provisions of this section shall not be so construed as to allow any
freedman, free negro, or mulatto to rent or lease any lands or
tenements, except in incorporated towns and cities.*"

Not to speak of the gross injustice of this last provision, what shall be said of the wisdom of that legislation which prohibits an entire laboring class from acquiring real estate in the country, where their presence and energies are indispensable, and holds out an inducement for them to flock to the towns, which are crowded with them already, but where alone they can hope to become freeholders?

Another section of this bill enacts that freedmen shall be competent witnesses in all cases where freedmen are parties to the suit, or where a crime is alleged to have been committed by a white person upon the person or property of a freedman. But it does not give them the power to testify in cases in which only white persons are concerned. All the negro testimony bills which I have seen, passed by the legislatures of the reconstructed States under gentle pressure from Washington, are marked by this singular inconsistency. If the negro is a competent witness in cases in which his own or his fellow's interests are involved, he is certainly a competent witness in cases involving only the interests of white persons. He is permitted to give evidence when there may exist a temptation for him to swear falsely, and not when there is no such temptation. By the enactment of such laws the whites are in reality legislating against themselves. Even Governor Humphreys — late Rebel general, but now the reconstructed executive of the "loyal" State of Mississippi, elected for his services in the Confederate cause — in his message to this same legislature, favoring the admission of negroes into the courts as an indispensable step towards ridding the State of the military power, and of "that black incubus, the Freedman's Bureau," made this suggestive statement : —

" There are few men living in the South who have not known many white criminals to go ' unwhipt of justice ' because negro testimony was not permitted in the courts."

The act " To confer Civil Rights on the Freedmen," proceeds to make the following provisions, which look much more like wrongs: " That every freedman, free negro, and mulatto shall, on the second Monday of January, one thousand eight hundred and sixty-six, and annually thereafter, have a lawful home or employment," (of course on any terms that may be offered him,) " and shall have written evidence thereof, as follows, to wit : If living in any incorporated city, town, or village, a license from the Mayor thereof ; and if living outside of any incorporated city, town, or village, from the member of the Board of Police of his beat, authorizing him or her to do irregular and job work, or a written contract, as provided in section sixth of this act ; which licenses may be revoked for cause, at any time, by the authority granting the same."

Section sixth enacts : " That all contracts for labor made with freedmen, free negroes, and mulattoes, for a longer period than one month, shall be in writing and in duplicate ; . . . . and said contracts shall be taken and held as entire contracts ; and if the laborer shall quit the service of the employer before expiration of his term of service, without good cause, he shall forfeit his wages for that year up to the time of quitting." But who is to be the judge with regard to the " good cause ? " The white man, of course, and not the negro.

" Section 7. Be it further enacted, That every civil officer shall, and every person may, arrest and carry back to his or her legal employer any freedman, free negro, or mulatto, who shall have quit the service of his or her employer before the expiration of his or her term of service."

Section ninth provides that if any person " *shall knowingly employ any such deserting freedman, free negro, or mulatto, or shall knowingly give or sell to any such deserting freedman, free negro, or mulatto any food, raiment, or other thing, he or she shall be guilty of a misdemeanor, and upon conviction, shall be fined not less than twenty-five dollars, and not more than two hundred dollars and the costs.*"

These extracts — which I have made verbatim from an authorized copy of the recent State laws, with only such abridgments as were necessary to compress them within reasonable limits — show plainly enough what ideas prevail in the late Slave States on the subject of free labor. The design of all such enactments is simply to place both the labor and the laborer in the power of the employer, and to reorganize slavery under a new name. The fact that they are practically set aside and annulled by the military power and the Freedmen's Bureau, does not set aside or annul the spirit which dictated them. This still animates the people of the South; and I was often plainly told that as soon as the States were fully restored to their rights, just such laws as these would certainly be put in force. I remarked to a Mississippi planter, "Do you not think it was unwise for your Legislature to pass such a code of laws?" "Yes, it was unwise, *at this time*," he replied, not understanding the scope of my question. "*We showed our hand too soon.* We ought to have waited till the troops were withdrawn, and our representatives admitted to Congress; then we could have had everything our own way."

Since the admission of negro testimony in the civil courts of the State, the freedmen's courts had been discontinued, — greatly to the disadvantage of the colored race. The civil courts could hardly be induced to give the negro's cause a hearing. There were some exceptions; and at Vicksburg I found a judge who seemed inclined to administer justice without regard to the prejudice against color. This was Judge Yerger, an original Union man, — one of the seven (against seventy-eight) who voted No, on the adoption of the ordinance of secession in the Convention of 1861; the same who, when asked by a member what title should be given to that act, replied, "Call it *An Ordinance for the Abolition of Slavery and the Desolation of the South.*"

Yerger was the President of the new Convention that reconstructed the State. That Convention was animated by a very different temper from that shown by the new Legislature. The Convention was composed of the best men in Mississippi, who went prepared to do what the Government at Washington had a right to expect of rebellious States returning to their allegiance; the Legislature was made up of a different class, elected after the people of the South had been encouraged in their animosity and arrogance by the discovery that treason was not to be punished, nor made particularly odious. The Convention was governed by men of large influence and liberal views; the Legislature was controlled by narrow-minded intermeddlers, mostly from the poorer districts of the State, where the inhabitants hated the negroes the more by way of revenge for having owned so few.

It was claimed by the better class that the Legislature did not represent them, and there was talk of calling another State Convention. But the Legislature, although it did not carry out the views of the more enlightened and progressive citizens, nor reflect in any way the sentiments of the great mass of true Union men in the South, namely, the blacks, represented quite faithfully the majority by which it was elected.

I have already alluded to the organizing of the State militia, — an abuse that unfortunately received the sanction of the Administration. The only possible excuse for it was the cry raised regarding anticipated negro insurrections. To guard against danger from a class whose loyalty and good behavior during the war challenged the admiration of the world, arms were put into the hands of Confederate soldiers who had returned to their homes reeking with the blood of the nation. Power was taken from the friends of the government and put into the hands of its enemies. The latter immediately set to work disarming the former. They plundered their houses, under the pretence of searching for weapons; committing robberies, murders, and other atrocities, with authentic reports of which pages might be filled. Neither were white men, known to sympathize with the Union party of the North, safe from their violence. Governor Humphreys himself, startled by the magnitude of the evil that had been called into existence, told Colonel Thomas that he had been obliged to disband several militia companies already organized, "on learning that they were sworn to kill negroes asserting their independence, and to drive off Northern men."

Of what was being done by private parties outside of the militia organizations, a curious glimpse is given in the following "general order," published in the Holmesville (Miss.) "Independent" : —

" [General Order No. 1.]

" SUMMIT, MISS., Nov. 28, 1865.

" In obedience to an order of His Excellency, the Governor of Mississippi, I have this day assumed command of all the militia in this section of the State, with head-quarters at this place. And whereas it has been reported to me that there are various individuals, not belonging to any military organization, either State or Federal, who are engaged in shooting at, and sometimes killing, the freedmen on private account; and whereas there are other white men reported as the attendants of, and participants in, the negro balls, who, after placing themselves upon a social equality with the people of color, raise quarrels with the freedmen, upon questions of social superiority already voluntarily waived and relinquished by them in favor of the negro, by which the peace of the country is broken and the law disregarded; I therefore order the arrest of all such offenders, by the officers and soldiers under my command, and that they be taken before some civil officer having power to commit to the county jail, for the purpose of awaiting the action of the Grand Jury.

" Men must quit blacking themselves, and do everything legally.

" OSCAR J. E. STUART,

" Q. M. G. and Col. Com. Militia."

The objection here seems to be to shooting the freedmen " on private account," or doing anything " illegally," thus taking the proper work of the militia out of its hands.

There were no doubt serious apprehensions in the minds of the people on the subject of negro insurrections. But a great deal that was said about them was mere pretence and cant, with which I have not seen fit to load these pages. There was not, while I was in the South, the slightest danger from a rising of the blacks, nor will there be, unless they are driven to desperation by wrongs.

I remember two very good specimens of formidable negro insurrections. One was reported in Northern Mississippi, and investigated personally by General Fiske, who took pains to visit the spot and learn all the facts concerning it. According to his account, " a colored man hunting squirrels was magnified into a thousand vicious negroes marching upon their old masters with bloody intent."

The other case was reported at the hotel in Vicksburg where I stopped, by a gentleman who had just arrived in the steamer " Fashion " from New Orleans. He related an exciting story of a rising of the blacks in Jefferson Parish, and a great slaughter of the white population. He also stated that General Sheridan had sent troops to quell the insurrection. Afterwards, when at New Orleans, I made inquiry of General Sheridan concerning the truth of the rumor, and learned that it was utterly without foundation. The most noticeable phase of it was the effect it had upon the guests at the hotel table. Everybody had been predicting negro insurrections at Christmas-time ; now everybody's prophecy had come true, and everybody was delighted. A good deal of horror was expressed ; but the real feeling, ill-concealed under all, was exultation.

" What will Sumner & Co. say now ? " cried one.

" The only way is to kill the niggers off, and drive 'em out of the country," said another.

I was struck by the perfect unanimity with which the company indorsed this last sentiment. All the outrages committed by whites upon blacks were of no account ; but at the mere rumor of a negro insurrection, what murderous passions were roused !

Of the comparative good behavior of whites and blacks in a large town, the police reports afford a pretty good indication. Vicksburg, which had less than five thousand inhabitants in 1860, had in 1865 fifteen thousand. Of these, eight thousand were blacks. On Christmas-day, out of nineteen persons brought before the police court for various offences, fourteen were white and five colored. The day after there were ten cases reported, — nine white persons and one negro. The usual proportion of white criminals was more than two thirds.

An unrelenting spirit of persecution, shown towards Union men in Mississippi, was fostered by the reconstructed civil courts. Union scouts were prosecuted for arson and stealing. A horse which had been taken by the government, and afterwards condemned and sold, was claimed by the original owner, and recovered, — the quartermaster's bill of sale, produced in court by the purchaser, being pronounced null and void. The government had leased to McAlister, a Northern man, an abandoned plantation, with the privilege of cutting wood upon it, for which he paid forty cents a cord : the Rebel owner returns with his pardon, and sues the lessee for alleged damages done to his property by the removal of wood, to the amount of five thousand dollars ; a writ of attachment issues under the seal of the local court, and the defendant is compelled to give bonds to the amount of ten thousand dollars, or lie in jail. Such cases were occurring every day.

The beautiful effect of executive mercy upon rampant Rebels was well illustrated in Mississippi. A single example will suffice. The Reverend Dr. ——, an eloquent advocate of the Confederate cause, — who, as late as March 23d, 1865, delivered a speech before the State Legislature, urging the South to fight to the last extremity, — under strong pretences of loyalty, obtained last summer a full pardon, and an order for the restoration of his property. The —— House, in Vicksburg, belonging to this reverend gentleman, was at that time used as a hospital for colored persons by the Freedmen's Bureau. Returning, with the President's authority, he turned out the sick inmates with such haste as to cause the deaths of several ; and on the following Sunday preached a vehement sermon on reconstruction, in which he avowed himself a better friend to the blacks than Northern men, and declared that it was " the duty of the government to treat the South with magnanimity, because it was not proper for a living ass to kick a dead lion."

There was great opposition to the freedmen's schools. Dr. Warren, the superintendent for the State, told me that " if the Bureau was withdrawn not a school would be publicly allowed." There were combinations formed to prevent the leasing of rooms for schools ; and those who would have been willing to let buildings for this purpose were deterred from doing so by threats of vengeance from their neighbors. In

Vicksburg, school-houses had been erected on confiscated land, which had lately been restored to the Rebel owners, and from which they were ordered, with other government buildings, to be removed.

In the month of November there were 4750 pupils in the freedmen's schools, — the average attendance being about 3000. Of these, 2650 were advanced beyond the alphabet and primer ; 1200 were learning arithmetic, and 1000 writing.

The schools were mainly supported by the Indiana Yearly Meeting of Friends, the Ohio Yearly Meeting, the American Freedmen's Aid Commission, (composed of various denominations,) and the American Missionary Association, (Congregational.) Elkanah Beard, of the Indiana Yearly Meeting, was the first to organize a colony of colored refugees in Mississippi, and through him his society have furnished to the freedmen practical relief, in the shape of food, clothing, and shelter, to a very great amount. The United Presbyterian Body had fifteen teachers at Vicksburg and Davis's Bend. The Old School Presbyterian Church had a missionary at Oxford, introducing schools upon plantations, and the Moravian Church had a pioneer at Holly Springs.

CHAPTER LIII.

A FEW WORDS ABOUT COTTON.

THE best cotton lands in the States lie between 31° and 36° north latitude. Below 31° the climate is too moist, causing the plant to run too much to stalk, and the fibre to rot. Above 36° the season is too short and too cold. The most fertile tracts for the cultivation· of cotton are the great river bottoms. In the Mississippi Valley, twice or even three or four times as much may be raised to the acre as in Northern Alabama or Middle Tennessee. But in the Valley there is danger from floods and the army worm, by which sometimes entire crops are swept away. On the uplands there is danger from drought.

The life of the planter is one of care and uncertainty. It requires almost as extensive organization to run a large plantation as a factory. You never know, until the crop is picked, whether you are going to get fifty or five hundred pounds to the acre. Anxiety begins at planting-time. The weather may be too wet; it may be too dry; and the question eagerly asked is, "Will you have a stand?" If the "stand" is favorable, — that is, if the plants come up well, and get a good start, — you still watch the weather, lest they may not have drink enough, or the levees, lest they may have too much. Look out also for the destructive insects : kindle fires in your fields to poison with smoke the moths that lay the eggs ; and scatter corn to call the birds, that they may feed upon the newly-hatched worms. Perhaps, when the cotton is just ready to come out, a storm of rain and wind beats it down into the mud. Then, when the crop is harvested, it is liable to be burned; and you must think of your insurance.

Notwithstanding these disadvantages, there is great fascination in the culture, — the possibility of clearing in one season from a good plantation fifty or a hundred thousand dollars, causing you to take cheerfully all risks. The plausible figures dazzle you ; and to the Northern man the novelty of the life in prospect for a year or two is itself an inducement. You think little of the danger to health from the miasmas of the swamps ; or to property, from the midnight torch of an enemy ; or to life, from the ill-timed recreation of some bushwhacking neighbor. And you are quite insensible to what the Southern planter deems the greatest of all risks that beset your crop, — that some day your freedmen will desert, and leave it to destruction.

I found many Northern planters in the upland districts of Alabama and Tennessee, where lands are cheaper, plantations smaller, and the risks less, than in the Mississippi Valley. But the latter region proved the greater attraction to adventurous capital. Men from the Middle States and the great West were everywhere, buying and leasing plantations, hiring freedmen, and setting thousands of ploughs in motion.

From experienced cotton-growers I obtained various estimates of the cost and probable profits of a crop the present year. They usually differed little as to items of expense, but sometimes very widely as to profits, according to each man's conjectures regarding freedmen's willingness to work, and the price of cotton next fall, which one would place as low as fifteen cents, and another as high as fifty. The annexed statement, furnished by the Southern Land Agency at Vicksburg, is probably as good as any : —

"Sir : — The following is an estimate of the expense and cash capital required to cultivate 500 acres of cotton land within the scope of our agency, for the year 1866.

25 mules @ $150	$3,750
25 single sets plough harness @ $4	100
3 lumber wagons @ $75	225
25 single ploughs @ $13	325
10 double ploughs @ $18	180
700 bushels cotton-seed @ $1	700
Total outlay for stock, seed, and implements	$5,280

1200 bushels corn @ $0.75 ·	$900	
120 barrels of corn meal @ $6 (about 1¼ lb. per ration) ·	720	
84 barrels pork @ $35 (about ¾ lb. per ration) · · · · ·	2,940	
250 gallons molasses @ $0.75 (about ¼ gallon per ration each) ·	187	
5 barrels salt @ $3, for stock and hands · · · · · · · · · ·	15	
Wages of 60 hands for 10 months @ $15 per month · · ·	9,000	
Incidentals ·	1,000	
Total for supplies, wages, and incidentals · · · · · · · · ·		$14,762
Rent of 500 acres land @ $10 ·		5,000
Total outlay during the season · · · · · · · · · · · · · · · · ·		$25,042
Value of the articles on hand at the end of the year : —		
Amount paid for stock and implements, *less ¼ for usual wear* ·	3,435	
Amount paid for cotton-seed, which is replaced from the crop ·	700	$4,135
Leaving *total expenditure during the year* · · · · · · · ·		$20,907
For the actual amount of cash required up to the time a portion of the crop may be disposed of — say Sept. 30th — deduct ⅔ of the rent, which is not due until the crop is gathered · · · · · · · · · · · · · · ·	3,333	
Last quarter's expenditures for supplies, wages, &c. · · · ·	4,940	$8,273
		$16,769

" From which calculation we see that the *actual cash capital required* is $16,769, or about $33 per acre, and the *actual expense* about $42 per acre. But as men's financial abilities differ materially, we think it quite possible to cultivate land with smaller capital. Many are hiring men, agreeing to pay but a small portion of their wages monthly, and the balance at the end of the year; while others save the use of capital by procuring supplies on a short credit, or by allowing a portion of the crop for rent.

" The average crop on alluvial land is full one bale per acre; on second bottom or table lands, about ⅔ bale, and on uplands ½ bale.

" Clothing and extra supplies furnished to hands are usually charged against their wages.

" This calculation is considered by the most experienced cotton-growers in the country a fair and liberal estimate; and from it you may estimate the profit on any sized tract, as the difference in the amount of land tilled will not materially change the figures.

" Very respectfully," etc.

Here the cost of some articles is placed too low. Two hundred dollars each for mules would be nearer the actual price. The cotton-seed to be replaced by the crop should also be thrown out of the consideration if you expect to close up business at the end of the year, for although seed this season brought one dollar and upwards, it has no merchantable value in ordinary times. This you will take into account if intending to undertake a plantation next year.

But suppose we call the total expenditure for this year twenty-four thousand dollars. And suppose a full crop is produced, — five hundred acres yielding an equal number of bales. Taking twenty-five cents a pound as a safe estimate, you have for each bale (of five hundred pounds) $125 ; for five hundred bales, $62,500. From this gross amount deduct the total expenditure, and you have remaining $38,500. If you go to the uplands where less cotton is produced, you employ fewer hands, and have less rent to pay, — perhaps not more than four or five dollars for good land. Should cotton be as low as twenty cents, you have still a fair margin for profits ; and should it be as high as fifty, as many confidently maintain it will be, the resulting figures are sufficiently exciting.

In 1850 Mississippi produced 484,292 bales, of 400 pounds each ; in 1860, more than twice that quantity. The present year, notwithstanding the scarcity of labor and the number of unprotected and desolated plantations, there is a prospect of two thirds of an average crop, — say half a million bales. The freedmen are working well ; and cotton is cultivated to the neglect of almost everything else. If we have a good cotton season, there will be a large yield. If there is a small yield, the price will be proportionately high. So that in either case the crop raised in Mississippi this year bids fair to produce forty or fifty million dollars.

CHAPTER LIV.

DAVIS'S BEND. — GRAND GULF. — NATCHEZ.

DESCENDING the Mississippi, the first point of interest you pass is Davis's Bend, the former home of the President of the Confederacy.

A curve of the river encircles a pear-shaped peninsula twenty-eight miles in circumference, with a cut-off across the neck seven hundred yards in length, converting it into an island. There is a story told of a man who, setting out to walk on the levee to Natchez, from Mr. Joe Davis's plantation, which adjoins that of his brother Jeff, unwittingly made the circuit of this island, and did not discover his mistakè until he found himself at night on the spot from which he had started in the morning.

About a mile from the river stands the Jeff Davis Mansion, with its wide verandas and pleasant shade-trees. The plantation comprises a thousand acres of tillable land, now used as a Home Farm for colored paupers, under the superintendence of a sub-commissioner of the Bureau. Here are congregated the old, the orphaned, the infirm, and many whose energies of body and mind were prematurely worn out under the system which the Confederacy was designed to glorify and perpetuate.

Here you find the incompetent and thriftless. Some have little garden-spots, on which they worked last season until their vegetables were ripe, when they stopped work and went to eating the vegetables. The government cultivates cotton with their labor; and once, at a critical period, it was necessary to commence ejecting them from their quarters in order to compel them to work to keep the grass down.

The freedmen on the other plantations of the island represent other qualities of the race. Besides the Home Farm there are five thousand acres divided into farms and homesteads, cultivated by the negroes on their own account, and paying a large rent to the government. On these little farms twenty-five hundred bales of cotton were raised last year, besides large quantities of corn, potatoes, and other produce. Many of the tenants had only their naked hands to begin with : they labored with hoes alone the first year, earning money to buy mules and ploughs the next. The signal success of the colony perhaps indicates the future of free labor in the South, and the eventual division of the large plantations into homesteads to be sold or rented to small farmers This system suits the freedman better than any other ; and under it he is industrious, prosperous, and happy.

There were about three thousand people at the Bend. Some worked a few acres, others took large farms, and hired laborers. Fifty had accumulated five thousand dollars each during the past two years ; and one hundred others had accumulated from one to four thousand dollars. Some of these rising capitalists had engaged Northern men to rent plantations for the coming year, and to take them in as partners, — the new black code of Mississippi prohibiting the leasing of lands to the freedmen.

The colony is self-governing, under the supervision of the sub-commissioner. There are three courts, each having its colored judge and sheriff. The offender, before being put on trial, can decide whether he will be tried by a jury, or have his case heard by the judge alone. Pretty severe sentences are sometimes pronounced ; and it is found that the negro will take cheerfully twice the punishment from one of his own color that he will from a white court.

Some sound sense often falls from the lips of these black Solomons. Here is a sample. A colored man and his mother are brought up for stealing a bag of corn.

Judge : " Do you choose to be tried by a jury ? "

Culprit (not versed in the technicalities of the court) : " What 's dat ? "

Judge: "Do you want twelve men to come in and help me?"

Culprit, emphatically: "No, sah!" — for he thinks one man will probably be too much for him.

Judge, sternly: "Now listen you! You and your mother are a couple of low-down darkies, trying to get a living without work. You are the cause that respectable colored people are slandered, and called thieving and lazy niggers; when it's only the likes of you that's thieving and lazy. Now this is what I'll do with you. If you and your mother will hire out to-day, and go to work like honest people, I'll let you off on good behavior. If you won't, I'll send you to Captain Norton. That means, you'll go up with a sentence. And I'll tell you what your sentence will be : three months' hard labor on the Home Farm, and the ball and chain in case you attempt to run away. Now which will you do?"

Culprit, eagerly: "I'll hire out, sah!" And a contract is made for him and his mother on the spot.

The next point of interest is Grand Gulf; the only place that offered any resistance to our gunboats between Vicksburg and Port Hudson. It had before the war a thousand inhabitants, three churches, and several steam-mills. Water and fire appear to have conspired against it. The Yankees burned every vestige of the village, and the river has torn away a large section of the bank on which it stood. A number of cheap whitewashed wooden buildings have taken its place on the shore; above and 'behind which rises a steep rocky bluff, covered with sparse timber, sedge, and cane-brakes, and crowned by Rebel batteries.

There was formerly an extensive whirlpool below the confluence of the Big Black with the Mississippi, which had worn a gulf six hundred feet deep, just above this place : hence its name, Grand Gulf. This immense chasm has been filled, since the beginning of the war, by the river that excavated it; and where the whirlpool was there is now a solid sand-bar overgrown with cotton-wood bushes. Opposite the town, on the Louisiana side, there is another sand-bar, bare and low, occu-

25

pying the place of a fine plantation that flourished there before the war.

A hundred and twenty miles below Vicksburg is Natchez, one of the most romantically and beautifully situated cities in the United States. It is built on an almost precipitous bluff, one hundred and fifty feet above the river, which is overlooked by a delightful park and promenade along the city front. The landing is under the bluff.

The " Quitman " (in which I had taken passage) stopped several hours at Natchez getting on board a quantity of cotton. Above Vicksburg, I noticed that nearly all the cotton was going northward : below, it was going the other way, toward New Orleans. At every town, and at nearly every plantation landing, we took on board, sometimes a hundred bales and more, sometimes but two or three, until the " Quitman " showed two high white walls of ˜cotton all round her guards, which were sunk to the water's edge. She was constructed to carry forty-three hundred bales.

On the levee at Natchez I made the acquaintance of an old plantation overseer. He knew all about cotton raising. " I 've overseed in the swamps, and I 've overseed on the hills. You can make a bale to the acre in the swamps, and about one bale to two acres on the hills. I used to get ten to fifteen hundred dollars a year. I 'm hiring now to a Northern man, who gives me three thousand. A Northern man will want to get more out of the niggers than we do. Mine said to me last night, ' I want you to get the last drop of sweat and the last pound of cotton out of my niggers ; ' and I shall do it. I can if anybody can. There 's a heap in humbuggin' a nigger. I worked a gang this summer, and got as much work out of 'em as I ever did. I just had my leading nigger, and I says to him, I says, ' Sam, I want this yer crop out by such a time ; now you go a-head, talk to the niggers, and lead 'em off right smart, and I 'll give you twenty-five dollars.' Then I got up a race, and give a few dollars to the men that picked the most cotton, till I found out the extent of what each man could pick ; then I required that of him every day, or I docked his wages."

As we were talking, the mate of the " Quitman " took up an oyster-shell and threw it at the head of one of the deck-hands, who did not handle the cotton to suit him.   It did not hurt the negro's head much, but it hurt his feelings.

" Out on the plantations," observed my friend the overseer, " it would cost him fifty dollars to hit a nigger that way.   It cost me a hundred and fifty dollars just for knocking down three niggers lately, — fifty dollars a piece, by —— ! "

He thought the negroes were going to be crowded out by the Germans; and went on to say, with true Southern consistency, —

" The Germans want twenty dollars a month, and we can hire the niggers for ten and fifteen.   The Germans will die in our swamps.   Then as soon as they get money enough to buy a cart and mule, and an acre of land somewhar, whar they can plant a grape-vine, they 'll go in for themselves."

CHAPTER LV.

THE LOWER MISSISSIPPI.

WE were nearly all night at Natchez loading cotton. The next day, I noticed that the men worked languidly, and that the mate was plying them with whiskey. I took an opportunity to talk with him about them. He said, —

"We have a hundred and eighty hands aboard, all told. Thar's sixty deck-hands. That a'n't enough. We ought to have reliefs, when we're shipping freight day and night as we are now."

I remarked : "A gentleman who came up to Vicksburg in the 'Fashion,' stated, as an excuse for the long trip she made, that the niggers would n't work, — that the mates could n't make them work."

He replied : "I reckon the hands on board the 'Fashion' are about in the condition these are. These men are used up. They ha'n't had no sleep for four days and nights. I've seen a man go to sleep many a time, standing up, with a box on his shoulder. We pay sixty dollars a month, — more 'n almost any other boat, the work is so hard. But we get rid of paying a heap of 'em. When a man gets so used up he can't stand no more, he quits. He don't dare to ask for wages, for he knows he'll get none, without he sticks by to the end of the trip."

While we were talking, a young fellow, not more than twenty years old, came up, looking very much exhausted, and told the mate he was sick.

"Ye a'n't sick neither!" roared the mate at him, fiercely, "You're lazy! If you won't work, go ashore."

The fellow limped away again, and went ashore at the next landing.

" Is he sick or lazy ? " I asked.

" Neither. He's used up. He was as smart a hand as I had when he came aboard. But they can't stand it."

" Was it always so ? "

" No ; before the war we had men trained for this work. We had some niggers, but more white men. We could n't git all the niggers we wanted ; a fifteen hundred dollar man wore out too quick."

" The whites were the best, I suppose."

" The niggers was the best. They was more active getting down bales. They liked the fun. They stand it better than white men. Business stopped, and that set of hands all dropped off, — went into the war, the most of 'em. Now we have to take raw hands. These are all plantation niggers. Not one of 'm 'll ship for another trip ; they 've had enough of it. Thar 's no compellin' 'em. You can't hit a nigger now, but these d——d Yankee sons of b——s have you up and make you pay for it."

I told him if that was the case, I did n't think I should hit one.

" They 've never had me up," he resumed. " When I tackle a nigger, it 'll be whar thar an't no witnesses, and it 'll be the last of him. That 's what ought to be done with 'em, — kill 'em all off. I like a nigger in his place, and that 's a servant, if thar 's any truth in the Bible."

This allusion to Scripture, from lips hot with words of wrath and wrong, was especially edifying.

The " Quitman " was a fine boat, and passengers, if not deck-hands, fared sumptuously on board of her. The table was equal to that of the best hotels. An excellent quality of claret wine was furnished, as a part of the regular dinner fare, after the French fashion, which appears to have been introduced into this country by the Creoles, and which is to be met with, I believe, only on the steamboats of the Lower Mississippi.

On the " Quitman," as on the boat from Memphis to Vicksburg, I made the acquaintance of all sorts of Southern people. The conversation of some of them is worth recording.

One, a Mississippi planter, learning that I was a Northern man, took me aside, and with much emotion, asked if I thought there was " any chance of the government paying us for our niggers."

" What niggers ? "

" The niggers you 've set free by this abolition war."

" This abolition war you brought upon yourselves; and paying you for your slaves would be like paying a burglar for a pistol lost on your premises. No, my friend, believe me, you will never get the first cent, as long as this government lasts."

He looked deeply anxious. But he still cherished a hope. " I 've been told by a heap of our people that we shall get our pay. Some are talking about buying nigger claims. They expect, when our representatives get into Congress, there 'll be an appropriation made."

He went on : " I did one mighty bad thing. To save my niggers, I run 'em off into Texas. It cost me a heap of money. I came back without a dollar, and found the Yankees had taken all my stock, and everything, and my niggers was free, after all. '

Jim B——, from Warren County, ten miles from Vicksburg, was a Mississippi planter of a different type, — jovial, generous, extravagant in his speech, and, in his habits of living, fast. " My niggers are all with me yet, and you can't get 'em to leave me. The other day my boy Dan drove me into town ; when we got thar, I says to him, ' Dan, ye want any money ? ' ' Yes, master, I'd like a little ? ' I took out a ten-dollar bill and give him. Another nigger says to him, ' Dan, what did that man give you money for ? ' ' That man ? ' says Dan ; ' I belongs to him.' ' No, you don't belong to nobody now ; you 're free.' ' Well,' says Dan, ' he provides for me, and gives me money, and he 's my master, any way.' I give my boys a heap more money than I should if I just hired 'em. We go right on like we always did, and I pole 'em if they don't do right. This year I says to 'em, ' Boys, I 'm going to make a bargain with you. I 'll roll out the ploughs and the mules and the feed, and you shall do the work; we'll make a crop of cotton, and you shall have half. I'll provide for ye, give ye quarters, treat ye well, and when ye won't work, pole ye like I always have. They agreed to it, and I put it into the contract that I was to whoop 'em when I pleased."

Jim was very enthusiastic about a girl that belonged to him. "She's a perfect mountain-spout of a woman!" (if anybody knows what that is.) "When the Yankees took me prisoner, she froze to a trunk of mine, and got it out 'of the way with fifty thousand dollars Confederate money in it."

He never wearied of praising her fine qualities. "She's black outside, but she's white inside, shore!" And he spoke of a son of hers, then twelve years old, with an interest and affection which led me to inquire about the child's father. "Well," said Jim, with a smile, "he's a perfect little image of me, only a shade blacker."

An Arkansas planter said: "I've a large plantation near Pine Bluff. I furnish everything but clothes, and give my freedmen one third of the crop they make. On twenty plantations around me, there are ten different styles of contracts. Niggers are working well; but you can't get only about two thirds as much out of 'em now as you could when they were slaves" (which I suppose is about all that ought to be got out of them). "The nigger is fated: he can't live with the white race, now he's free. I don't know one I'd trust with fifty dollars, or to manage a crop and control the proceeds. It will be generations before we can feel friendly towards the Northern people."

I remarked: "I have travelled months in the South, and expressed my sentiments freely, and met with better treatment than I could have expected five years ago."

"That's true; if you had expressed abolition sentiments then, you'd have woke up some morning and found yourself hanging from some limb."

Of the war he said: "Slavery was really what we were fighting for, although the leaders didn't talk that to the people. They saw the slave interest was losing power in the Union, and trying to straighten it up, they tipped it over."

A Louisiana planter, from Lake Providence, — and a very intelligent, well-bred gentleman, — said: "Negroes do best when they have a share of the crop; the idea of working for themselves stimulates them. Planters are afraid to trust them to manage; but it's a great mistake. I know an old negro who, with three children, made twenty-five bales of cotton this year on abandoned land. Another, with two women and a blind mule, made twenty-seven bales. A gang of fifty made three hundred bales, — all without any advice or assistance from white men. I was always in favor of educating and elevating the black race. The laws were against it, but I taught all my slaves to read the Bible. Each race has its peculiarities: the negro has his, and it remains to be seen what can be done with him. Men talk about his stealing: no doubt he'll steal: but circumstances have cultivated that habit. Some of my neighbors could n't have a pig, but their niggers would steal it. But mine never stole from me, because they had enough without stealing. Giving them the elective franchise just now is absurd; but when they are prepared for it, and they will be some day, I shall advocate it."

Another Louisianian, agent of the Hope Estate, near Water-Proof, in Tensas Parish, said: "I manage five thousand acres, — fourteen hundred under cultivation. I always fed my niggers well, and rarely found one that would steal. My neighbors' niggers, half-fed, hard-worked, they'd steal, and I never blamed 'em. Nearly all mine stay with me. They've done about two thirds the work this year they used to, for one seventh of the crops. Heap of niggers around me have never received anything; they're only just beginning to learn that they're free. Many planters keep stores for niggers, and sell 'em flour, prints, jewelry and trinkets, and charge two or three prices for everything. I think God intended the niggers to be slaves; we have the Bible for that:" always the Bible. "Now since man has deranged God's plan, I think the best we can do is to keep 'em as near a state of bondage as possible. I don't believe in educating 'em."

"Why not?'

" One reason, schooling would enable them to compete with white mechanics."

" And why not ? "

" It would be a *disadvantage* to the whites," he replied, — as if that was the only thing to be considered by men with the Bible in their mouths ! " In Mississippi, opposite Water-Proof, there 's a minister collecting money to buy plantations in a white man's name, to be divided in little farms of ten and fifteen acres for the niggers. He could n't do that thing in my parish : he 'd soon be dangling from some tree. There is n't a freedman taught in our parish ; not a school ; it would n't be allowed."

He admitted that the war was brought on by the Southern leaders, but thought the North " ought to be lenient and give them all their rights." Adding : " What we want chiefly is to legislate for the freedmen. Another thing : the Confederate debt ought to be assumed by the government. We shall try hard for that. If we can't get it, if the North continues to treat us as a subjugated people, the thing will have to be tried over again," — meaning the war. " We must be left to manage the nigger. He can 't be made to work without force." (He had just said his niggers did two thirds as much work as formerly.) " My theory is, feed 'em well, clothe 'em well, and then, if they won't work, d—n 'em, whip 'em well ! "

I did not neglect the deck-passengers. These were all negroes, except a family of white refugees from Arkansas, who had been burnt out twice during the war, once near Little Rock, and again in Tennessee, near Memphis. With the little remnant of their possessions they were now going to seek their fortunes elsewhere, — ill-clad, starved-looking, sleeping on deck in the rain, coiled around the smoke-pipe, and covered with ragged bedclothes.

The talk of the negroes was always entertaining. Here is a sample, from the lips of a stout old black woman : —

" De best ting de Yankees done was to break de slavery chain. I should n't be here to-day if dey had n't. I 'm going to see my mother."

" Your mother must be very old."

" You may know she 's dat, for I 'm one of her baby chil'n, and I 's got 'leven of my own. I 've a heap better time now 'n I had when I was in bondage. I had to nus' my chil'n four times a day and pick two hundred pounds cotton besides. My third husband went off to de Yankees. My first was sold away from me. Now I have my second husband again ; I was sold away from him, but I found him again, after I 'd lived with my third husband thirteen years."

I asked if he was willing to take her back.

" He was willing to have me again *on any terms*," — emphatically — " for he knowed I was Number One ! "

Several native French inhabitants took passage at various points along the river, below the Mississippi line. All spoke very good French, and a few conversed well in English. One, from Point Coupée Parish, said : " Before the war, there were over seventeen thousand inhabitants in our parish." (In Louisiana a county is called a parish.) " Nearly thirteen thousand were slaves. Many of the free inhabitants were colored ; so that there were about four colored persons to one white. We made yearly between eight and nine thousand hogsheads of sugar, and fifteen hundred bales of cotton. The war has left us only three thousand inhabitants. We sent fifteen hundred men into the Confederate army. All the French population were in favor of secession. The white inhabitants of these parishes are mostly French Creoles. We treated our slaves better than the Americans treated theirs. We did n't work them so hard ; and there was more familiarity and kindly feeling between us and our servants. The children were raised together ; and a white child learned the negroes' *patois* before he learned French. The patois is curious : a negro says ' *Moi pas connais* ' for ' *Je ne sais pas* ' (I do not know) ; and they use a great many African words which you would not understand. Our slaves were never sold except to settle an estate. Besides these two classes there was a third, quite separate, which did not associate with either of the others. They were the free colored, of French-African descent, some almost or quite white, with many large property holders and slave-owners among them ; a very respectable class, forming a society of their own."

The villages and plantation dwellings along here, with their low roofs and sunny verandas, on the level river bank, had a peculiarly foreign and tropical appearance.

The levees of Louisiana form a much more extensive and complete system than those of Mississippi. In the latter State there is much hilly land that does not need their protection, and much swamp land not worth protecting ; and there is, I believe, no law regarding them. In the low and level State of Louisiana, however, a large and fertile part of which lies considerably below the level of high water, there is very strict legislation on the subject, compelling every land-owner on the river to keep up his levees. This year the State itself had undertaken to repair them, issuing eight per cent. bonds to the amount of a million dollars for the purpose, — the expense of the work to be defrayed eventually by the planters.

For a long distance the Lower Mississippi, at high water, appears to be flowing upon a ridge. The river has built up its own banks higher than the country which lies back of them ; and the levees have raised them still higher. Behind this fertile strip there are extensive swamps, containing a soil of unsurpassed depth and richness, but unavailable for want of drainage. Three methods are proposed for bringing them under cultivation. First, to surround them by levees, ditch them, and pump the water out by steam. Second, to cut a canal through them to the Gulf. Third, to turn the Mississippi into them, and fill them with its alluvial deposit. This last method is no doubt the one Nature intended to employ ; and it is the opinion of many that man, confining the flow of the stream within artificial limits, attempted the settlement of this country several centuries too soon.

A remarkable feature of Louisiana scenery is its forests of cypress-trees growing out of the water, heavy, sombre, and shaggy with moss.

The complexion of the river water is a light mud-color,

which it derives from the turbid Missouri, — the Upper Mis
sissippi being a clear stream. Pour off a glass of it after it
has been standing a short time, and a sediment of dark mud
appears at the bottom. Notwithstanding this unpleasant peculiarity, it is used altogether for cooking and drinking purposes
on board the steamboats, and I found New Orleans supplied
with it.

A curious fact has been suggested with regard to this wonderful river, — that it *runs up hill.* Its mouth is said to be
two and a half miles higher — or farther from the earth's centre — than its source. When we consider that the earth is a
spheroid, with an axis shorter by twenty-six miles than its equatorial diameter ; and that the same centrifugal motion which
has caused the equatorial protuberance tends still to heap up
the waters of the globe where that motion is greatest ; the
seeming impossibility appears possible, — just as we see a re-
volving grindstone send the water on its surface to the rim.
Stop the grindstone, and the water flows down its sides. Stop
the earth's revolution, and immediately you will see the Mississippi River turn and flow the other way.

Some years ago I made a voyage of several days on the
Upper Mississippi, to the head of navigation. It was difficult
to realize that this was the same stream on which I was
now sailing day after day in an opposite direction, — six days
in all, from Memphis to New Orleans. From St. Anthony's
Falls to the Gulf, the Mississippi is navigable twenty-two hundred miles. Its entire length is three thousand miles. Its
great tributary, the Missouri, is alone three thousand miles in
length : measured from its head-waters to the Gulf, it is four
thousand five hundred miles. Consider also the Ohio, the
Arkansas, the Red River, and the hundred lesser streams that
fall into it, and well may we call it by its Indian name, Michi-
Sepe, the Father of Waters.

CHAPTER LVI.

THE CRESCENT CITY.

ON the morning of January 1st, 1866, I arrived at New Orleans.

It was midwinter; but the mild sunny weather that followed the first chill days of rain, made me fancy it May. The gardens of the city were verdant with tropical plants. White roses in full bloom climbed upon trellises or the verandas of houses. Oleander trees, bananas with their broad drooping leaves six feet long, and Japan plums that ripen in February, grew side by side in the open air. There were orange-trees whose golden fruit could be picked from the balconies which they half concealed. Magnolias, gray-oaks and live-oaks, some heavily hung with moss that swung in the breeze like waving hair, shaded the yards and streets. I found the roadsides of the suburbs green with grass, and the vegetable gardens checkered and striped with delicately contrasting rows of lettuce, cabbages, carrots, beets, onions, and peas in blossom.

The French quarter of the city impresses you as a foreign town transplanted to the banks of the Mississippi. Many of the houses are very ancient, with low, moss-covered roofs projecting over the first story, like slouched hat-brims over quaint old faces. The more modern houses are often very elegant, and not less picturesque. The names of the streets are Pagan, foreign, and strange. The gods and muses of mythology, the saints of the Church, the Christian virtues, and modern heroes, are all here. You have streets of " Good Children," of " Piety," of " Apollo," of " St. Paul," of " Euterpe," and all their relations. The shop-signs are in French, or in French and English. The people you meet have a foreign air and speak a foreign tongue. Their complexions range through all hues, from the dark Creole to the ebon African. The anomalous third class of Louisiana — the respectable free colored people of French-African descent — are largely represented. Dressed in silks, accompanied by their servants, and speaking good French, — for many of them are well educated, — the ladies and children of this class enter the street cars, which they enliven with the Parisian vivacity of their conversation.

The mingling of foreign and American elements has given to New Orleans a great variety of styles of architecture ; and the whole city has a light, picturesque, and agreeable appearance. It is built upon an almost level strip of land bordering upon the left bank of the river, and falling back from the levee with an imperceptible slope to the cypress and alligator swamps in the rear. The houses have no cellars. I noticed that the surface drainage of the city flowed *back* from the river into the Bayou St. John, a navigable inlet of Lake Ponchartrain. The old city front lay upon a curve of the Mississippi, which gave it a crescent shape : hence its poetic *soubriquet.* The modern city has a river front seven miles in extent, bent like the letter S.

The broad levee, lined with wharves on one side and belted by busy streets on the other, crowded with merchandise, and thronged with merchants, boatmen, and laborers, presents always a lively and entertaining spectacle. Steam and sailing crafts of every description, arriving, departing, loading, unloading, and fringing the city with their long array of smoke-pipes and masts, give you some idea of the commerce of New Orleans.

Here is the great cotton market of the world. In looking over the cotton statistics of the past thirty years, I found that nearly one half the crop of the United States had passed through this port. In 1855–1856 (the mercantile cotton year beginning September 1st and ending August 31st) 1,795,023 bales were shipped from New Orleans, — 986,622 to Great Britain (chiefly to Liverpool) ; 244,814 to France (chiefly to Havre) ; 162,657 to the North of Europe ; 178,812 to the South of Europe, Mexico, &c. ; and 222,100 coastwise, –

151,469 going to Boston and 51,340 to New York. In 1859–1860, 2,214,296 bales were exported, 1,426,966 to Great Britain, 313,291 to France, and 208,634 coastwise, — 131,648 going to Boston, 62,936 to New York, and 5,717 to Providence. This, it will be remembered, was the great cotton year, the crop amounting to near 5,000,000 bales.

One is interested to learn how much cotton left this port during the war. In 1860–1861, 1,915,852 bales were shipped, nearly all before hostilities began ; in 1861–1862, 27,627 bales ; in 1862–1863, 23,750; in 1863–1864, 128,130 ; in 1864–1865, 192,351. The total receipts during this last year were 271,015 bales. From September 1st, 1865, to January 1st, 1866, the receipts were 375,000 bales ; and cotton was still coming. The warehouses on the lower tributaries of the Mississippi were said to be full of it, waiting for high water to send it down. There had been far more concealed in the country than was supposed : it made its appearance where least looked for ; and such was the supply that experienced traders believed that prices would thenceforth be steadily on the decline.

A first-class Liverpool steamer is calculated to take out 3000 500-pound bales, the freight on which is 7-8ths of a penny per pound, — not quite two cents. The freight to New York and Boston is 1 1-4th cents by steamers, and 7-8ths of a cent by sailing-vessels.

I put up at the St. Charles, famous before the war as a hotel, and during the war as the head-quarters of General Butler. It is a conspicuous edifice, with white-pillared porticos, and a spacious Rotunda, thronged nightly with a crowd which strikes a stranger with astonishment. It is a sort of social evening exchange, where merchants, planters, travellers, river-men, army men, (principally Rebels,) manufacturing and jobbing agents, showmen, overseers, idlers, sharpers, gamblers, foreigners, Yankees, Southern men, the well dressed and the prosperous, the rough and the seedy, congregate together, some leaning against the pillars, and a few sitting about the stoves, which are almost hidden from sight by the concourse of people standing or moving about in the great central space. Numbers of citizens regularly spend their evenings here, as at a club-room. One, an old plantation overseer of the better class, told me that for years he had not missed going to the Rotunda a single night, except when absent from the city. The character he gave the crowd was not complimentary.

"They are all trying to get money without earning it. Each is doing his best to shave the rest. If they ever make anything, I don't know it. I've been here two thousand nights, and never made a cent yet."

I inquired what brought him here.

"For company; to kill time. I never was married, and never had a home. When I was young, the girls said I smelt like a wet dog; that's because I was poor. Since I've got rich, I'm too old to get married."

What he was thinking of now was a fortune to be made out of labor-saving machinery to be used on the plantations: "I wish I could get hold of a half-crazy feller, to fix up a cotton planter, cotton-picker, cane-cutter, and a thing to hill up some."

He talked cynically of the planters. "They're a helpless set. They're all confused. They don't know what they're going to do. They never did know much else but to get drunk. If a man has a plantation to rent or sell, he can't tell anything about it; you can't get any proposition out of him."

He complained that Northern capital lodged in the cotton belt; but little of it getting through to the sugar country. He did not know any lands let to Northern men. "They hav'n't got sugar on the brain; it's cotton they're all crazy after."

He used to oversee for fifteen hundred dollars a year: he was now offered five thousand. He was a well-dressed, rather intelligent, capable man; and I noticed that the planters treated him with respect. But his manner toward them was cool and independent: he could not forget old times. "I never was thought anything of by these men, till I got rich. Then they began to say 'Dick P—— is a mighty clever feller;' and by-

and-by it got to be ' Mr. P———.' Now they all come to me, because I know about business, and they don't know a thing."

Like everybody else, he had much to say of the niggers. "A heap of the planters wants 'em all killed off. But I believe in the nigger. He 'll work, if they 'll only let him alone. They fool him, and tell him such lies, he 's no confidence. I 've worked free niggers and white men, and always found the niggers worked the best. But no nigger, nor anybody else, will work like a slave works with the whip behind him. You can't make 'em. I was brought up to work alongside o' niggers, and soon as I got out of it, nothing, no money, could induce me to work so again."

Speaking of other overseers, he said : " I admit I was about as tight on the nigger as a man ought to be. If I 'd been a slave, I should n't have wanted to work under a master that was tighter than I was. But I wa'n't a priming to some. You see that red-faced feller with his right hand behind him, talking with two men ? He 's an overseer. I know of his killing two niggers, and torturing another so that he died in a few days." (I omit the shocking details of the punishment said to have been applied.) " The other night he came here to kill me because I told about him. He pulled out his pistol, and says he, ' Dick P———, did you tell so-and-so I killed three niggers on Clark's plantation ? ' ' Yes,' I says, ' I said so, and can prove it ; and if there 's any shooting to be done, I can shoot as fast as you can.' After that he bullied around here some, then went off, and I hav'n't heard anything about shooting since."

Among the earliest acquaintances I made at New Orleans was General Phil. Sheridan, perhaps the most brilliant and popular fighting man of the war. I found him in command of the Military Division of the Gulf, comprising the States of Louisiana, Texas, and Florida. In Florida he had at that time seven thousand troops ; in Louisiana, nine thousand ; and in Texas, twenty thousand, embracing ten thousand colored troops at Corpus Christi and on the Rio Grande, watching the French movements.

26

It was Sheridan's opinion that the Rebellion would never be ended until Maximilian was driven from Mexico. Such a government on our borders cherished the seeds of ambition and discontent in the minds of the late Confederates. Many were emigrating to Mexico, and there was danger of their uniting either with the Liberals or the Imperialists, and forming a government inimical to the United States. To prevent such a possibility, he had used military and diplomatic strategy. Three thousand Rebels having collected in Monterey, he induced the Liberals to arrest and disarm them. Then in order that they should not be received by the Imperialists, he made hostile demonstrations, sending a pontoon train to Brownsville, and six thousand cavalry to San Antonio, establishing military posts, and making extensive inquiries for forage. Under such circumstances, Maximilian did not feel inclined to welcome the Rebel refugees. It is even probable that, had our government at that time required the withdrawal of the French from Mexico, the demand, emphasized by these and similar demonstrations, would have been complied with. Maximilian is very weak in his position. Nineteen twentieths of the people are opposed to him. There is no regular, legitimate taxation for the support of his government, but he levies contributions upon merchants for a small part of the funds he requires, and draws upon France for the rest. His "government" consists merely of an armed occupation of the country; with long lines of communication between military posts, which could be easily cut off and captured one after another by a comparatively small force.

The Southern country, in the General's opinion, was fast becoming "Northernized." It was very poor, and going to be poorer. The planters had no enterprise, no recuperative energy: they were entirely dependent upon Northern capital and Northern spirit. He thought the freedmen's affairs required no legislation, but that the State should leave them to be regulated by the natural law of supply and demand.

Phil. Sheridan is a man of small stature, compactly and somewhat massively built, with great toughness of constitu-

tional fibre, and an alert countenance, expressive of remarkable energy and force. I inquired if he experienced no reaction
after the long strain upon his mental and bodily powers occasioned by the war.

" Only a pleasant one," he replied. " During my Western
campaigns, when I was continually in the saddle, I weighed
but a hundred and fifteen pounds. My flesh was hard as iron.
Now my weight is a hundred and forty-five."

He went over with me to the City Hall, to which the
Executive department of the State had been removed, and
introduced me to Governor Wells, a plain, elderly man, affa-
ble, and loyal in his speech. I remember his saying that the
action of the President, in pardoning Governor Humphreys,
of Mississippi, after he had been elected by the people on
account of his services in the Confederate cause, was doing
great harm throughout the South, encouraging Rebels and
discouraging Union men. " Everything is being conceded to
traitors," said he, " before they have been made to feel the
Federal power." He spoke of the strong Rebel element in
the Legislature which he was combating ; and gave me copies
of two veto messages which he had returned to it with bills
that were passed for the especial benefit of traitors. The new
serf code, similar to that of Mississippi, engineered through
the Legislature by a member of the late Confederate Congress,
he had also disapproved. After this, I was surprised to hear
from other sources how faithfully he had been carrying out
the very policy which he professed to condemn, — even going
beyond the President, in removing from office Union men appointed by Governor Hahn and appointing Secessionists and
Rebels in their place ; and advocating the Southern doctrine that the Government must pay for the slaves it had
emancipated. Such discrepancies between deeds and pro-
fessions require no comment. Governor Wells is not the
only one, nor the highest, among public officers, who, wishing
to reconcile the irreconcilable, and to stand well before the
country whilst they were strengthening the hands and gaining
the favor of its enemies, have suffered their loyal protestations
to be put to some confusion by acts of doubtful patriotism.

At the Governor's room I had the good fortune to meet the Mayor of the city, Mr. Hugh Kennedy, whom I afterwards called upon by appointment. By birth a Scotchman, he had been thirty years a citizen of New Orleans, and, from the beginning of the Secession troubles, had shown himself a stanch patriot. He was appointed to the mayoralty by President Lincoln ; General Banks removed him, but he was afterwards reinstated.

I found him an almost enthusiastic believer in the future greatness of New Orleans. "It is certain," he said, "to double its population in ten years. Its prosperity dates from the day of the abolition of slavery. Men who formerly lived upon the proceeds of slave-labor are now stimulated to enterprise. A dozen industrial occupations will spring up where there was one before. Manufactures are already taking a start. We have two new cotton-mills just gone into operation. The effect upon the whole country will be similar. Formerly planters went or sent to New York and Boston and laid in their supplies ; for this reason there were no villages in the South. But now that men work for wages, which they will wish to spend near home, villages will everywhere spring up."

Living, in New Orleans, he said, was very cheap. The fertile soil produces, with little labor, an abundance of vegetables the year round. Cattle are brought from the extensive prairies of the State, and from the vast pastures of Texas : and contractors had engaged to supply the charitable institutions of the city with the rumps and rounds of beef at six cents a pound.

The street railroads promised to yield a considerable revenue to the city. The original company paid only $130,000 for the privilege of laying down its rails, and an exclusive right to the track for twenty-five years. But two new roads had been started, one of which had stipulated to pay to the city government eleven and a half per cent. of its gross proceeds, and the other twenty-two and a half per cent. "In two or three years an annual income from that source will not be less than $200,000."

From Mr. Kennedy I learned that free people of color owned property in New Orleans to the amount of $15,000,000.

He was delighted with the working of the free-labor system. " I thought it an indication of progress when the white laborers and negroes on the levees the other day made a strike for higher wages. They were receiving two dollars and a half and three dollars a day, and they struck for five and seven dollars. They marched up the levee in a long procession, white and black together. I gave orders that they should not be interfered with as long as they interfered with nobody else; but when they undertook by force to prevent other laborers from working, the police promptly put a stop to their proceedings."

CHAPTER LVII.

POLITICS, FREE LABOR, AND SUGAR.

THROUGH the courtesy of the Mayor I became acquainted with some of the radical Union men of New Orleans. Like the same class in Richmond and elsewhere, I found them extremely dissatisfied with the political situation and prospects. " Everything," they said, " has been given up to traitors. The President is trying to help the nation out of its difficulty by restoring to power the very men who created the difficulty. To have been a good Rebel is now in a man's favor ; and to have stood by the government through all its trials is against him. If an original secessionist, or a time-serving, half-and-half Union man, ready to make any concession for the convenience of the moment, goes to Washington, he gets the ear of the administration, and comes away full of encouragement for the worst enemies the government ever had. If a man of principle goes to Washington, he gets nothing but plausible words which amount to nothing, if he is n't actually insulted for his trouble."

I heard everywhere the same complaints from this class. And here I may state that they were among the saddest things I had to endure in the South. Whatever may be thought of the intrinsic merits of any measures, we cannot but feel misgivings when we see our late enemies made jubilant by them, and loyal men dismayed.

The Union men of New Orleans were severe in their strictures on General Banks. " It was he," they said, " who precipitated the organization of the State government on a Rebel basis. Read his *General Orders No.* 35, issued March 11th, 1864, concerning the election of delegates to the Convention. Rebels who have taken the amnesty oath are admitted to the polls, and loyal colored men are excluded. Section 4th reads, 'Every free white man,' &c. Since his return to Massachusetts he has been making speeches in favor of negro suffrage. He is in favor of it there, where it is popular as an abstraction, and a man gets into Congress on the strength of it; but he was not in favor of it here, where there was a chance of making it practical. His excuse was, that if black men voted white men would take offence, and keep away from the polls. Very likely some white men would, but loyal white men would n't. That he had the power to extend the franchise to the blacks, or at least thought he had, may be seen by his apology for not doing so, in which he says: 'I did not decide upon this subject without very long and serious consideration,' and so forth. So he let the great, the golden opportunity slip, of organizing the State government on a loyal basis, — of demonstrating the capacity of the colored man for self-government, and of setting an example to the other Rebel States."

Being one day in the office of Mr. Durant, a prominent lawyer and Union man, I was much struck by the language and bearing of a gentleman who called upon him, and carried on a long conversation in French. Having understood that the Creoles were nearly all secessionists, I was surprised to hear this man give utterance to the most enlightened Republican sentiments. After he had gone out, I expressed my gratification at having met him.

" That," said Mr. Durant, " is one of the ablest and wealthiest business men in New Orleans. He was educated in Paris. But there is one thing about him you do not seem to have suspected. He belongs to that class of Union men the government has made up its mind to leave politically bound in the hands of the Rebels. That man, whom you thought refined and intelligent, has not the right which the most ignorant, Yankee-hating, negro-hating Confederate soldier has. He is a colored man, and has no vote."

There were six daily newspapers published in New Orleans, — five in English and one in English and French, — besides several weeklies. There was but one loyal sheet among them, and that was a " nigger paper," the *Tribune*, not sold by any newsboy, and, I believe, by but one news-dealer.

I called on General T. W. Sherman, in command of the Eastern District of Louisiana, who told me that, in order to please the people, our troops had been withdrawn from the interior, and that the militia, consisting mostly of Rebel soldiers, many of whom still wore the Rebel uniform, had been organized to fill their place. The negroes, whom they treated tyrannically, had been made to believe that it was the United States, and not the State government, that had thus set their enemies to keep guard over them.

Both Governor Wells and General Sherman had received piles of letters from " prominent parties " expressing fears of negro insurrections. The most serious indications of bloody retribution preparing for the white race had been reported in the Teche country, where regiments of black cavalry were said to be organized and drilled. The General, on visiting the spot, and investigating the truth of the story, learned that it had its foundation in the fact that some negro boys had been playing soldier with wooden swords. No wonder the Rebel militia was thought necessary !

From General Baird, Assistant-Commissioner, and General Gregg, Inspecting-Agent of the Freedmen's Bureau, I obtained official information regarding the condition of free labor in Louisiana. A detailed account of it would be but a recapitulation, with slight variations, of what I have said of free labor in other States. The whites were as ignorant of the true nature of the system as the blacks. Capitalists did not understand how they could secure labor without owning it, or how men could be induced to work without the whip. It was thought necessary to make a serf of him who was no longer a slave. To this end the Legislature had passed a code of black laws even more objectionable than that enacted by the Legislature of Mississippi. By its provisions freedmen were to be arrested as vagrants who had not, on the 10th of January, 1866, entered into contracts for the year. They were thus left little choice as to employers, and none as to terms. They were also subjected to a harsh system of fines and punishments for loss of time and the infraction of contracts; and made responsible for all losses of stock on the plantation, until they should be able to prove that they had not killed it. Although these laws had not been approved by the Governor, there was no doubt but they would be approved and enforced as soon as the national troops were removed.

A majority of the Southern planters clamored for the withdrawal of the troops and the Freedmen's Bureau. But Northern planters settled in the State as earnestly opposed the measure. " If the government's protection goes, we must go too. It would be impossible for us to live here without it. Planters would come to us and say, ' Here, you 've got a nigger that belongs to us ; ' they would claim him, under the State laws, and compel him to go and work for them. Not a first-class laborer could we be sure of."

Here, as elsewhere, the fact that the freedmen had no independent homes, but lived in negro-quarters at the will of the owner, placed him under great disadvantages, which the presence of the Bureau was necessary to counteract. The planters desired nothing so much as to be left to manage the negroes with or without the help of State laws. " With that privilege," they said, " we can make more out of them than ever. The government must take care of the old and worthless niggers it has set free, and we will put through the able-bodied ones." The disposition to keep the freedmen in debt by furnishing their supplies at dishonest prices, and to impose upon their helplessness and ignorance in various other ways, was very general.

Fortunately there was a great demand for labor, and the freedmen, with the aid of the Bureau, were making favorable contracts with their employers. When encouraged by just treat ment and fair wages, they were working well. But they were observed to be always happier, thriftier, and more comfortable, living in little homes of their own and working land on their own account, than in any other condition. " I believe," said General Gregg, " the best thing philanthropic Northern cap-

italists can do both for the freedmen and for themselves, is to
buy up tracts of land, which can be had in some of the most
fertile sections of Louisiana at two, three, and five dollars an
acre, to be leased to the freedmen."

The more enlightened planters were in favor of educating
the blacks. But the majority were opposed to it; so that in
many parishes it was impossible to establish schools, while in
others it had been very difficult. In January last there were
278 teachers in the State, instructing 19,000 pupils in 143
schools. The expenses, $20,000 a month, were defrayed by
the Bureau from the proceeds of rents of abandoned and confiscated estates. But this source of revenue had nearly failed,
in consequence of the indiscriminate pardoning of Rebel owners and the restoration of their property. In New Orleans,
for example, the rents of Rebel estates had dwindled, in October, 1865, to $8,000; in December, to $1,500; and they were
still rapidly diminishing. The result was, it had been necessary to order the discontinuance of all the schools in the State
at the end of January, the funds in the treasury of the Bureau
being barely sufficient to hold out until that time. It was
hoped, however, that they would soon be reëstablished on a
permanent basis, by a tax upon the freedmen themselves. For
this purpose, the Assistant Commissioner had ordered that five
per cent. of their wages should be paid by their employers to
the agents of the Bureau. The freedmen's schools in New
Orleans were not in session at the time I was there; but I
heard them highly praised by those who had visited them.
Here is Mr. Superintendent Warren's account of them: —

" From the infant which must learn to count its fingers, to the
scholar who can read and understand blank-verse, we have grades
and departments adapted and free to all. Examinations, promotions,
and gradations are had at stated seasons. The city is divided into
districts; each district has its school, and each school the several departments of primary, intermediate, and grammar. A principal is
appointed to each school, with the requisite number of assistants.
Our teachers are mostly from the North, with a few Southerners,
who have heroically dared the storm of prejudice to do good and

right. The normal method of teaching is adopted, and object teaching is a specialty.

" There are eight schools in the city, with from two to eight hundred pupils each, which, with those in the suburbs, amount to sixteen schools with nearly six thousand pupils and one hundred teachers."

It was estimated that there were at least fifty thousand Northern men in Louisiana. Some were in the lumber business, which had been stimulated to great activity throughout the South. Many were working cotton plantations with every prospect of success ; a few had purchased, others were paying a fixed rent, while some were furnishing capital to be refunded by the crop, of which they were to have a third or a half.

Occasionally I heard of one who had taken a sugar plantation. Mr. ——, a merchant of New York, told me he had for two years been working the Buena Vista plantation, in St. James Parish. He employed an agent, and visited the place himself once a year. There were twelve hundred acres under cultivation, for which he paid an annual rent of sixteen thousand dollars. There was one hundred thousand dollars' worth of machinery on the plantation. He employed sixty freedmen. They worked faithfully and well, but needed careful management. During the past year but one had deserted, while two had been discharged. They received one third of their wages monthly, and the remainder at the end of the year. " If they were paid in full as fast as their work was done, when sugar-making season comes they would be apt to quit, the labor is so hard, — though we pay them then fifty cents a night extra."

I inquired concerning profits. " The first year we lost money. This year we have made it up, and more. Next year we shall be in full blast."

It takes three years from the start to get a sugar plantation going ; and in two years, if neglected, the cane will run out. This is the case in Louisiana, — although I was told that in the West Indies some kinds of cane would yield twenty or thirty successive crops, without replanting. In some parts of the State, where the soil is too dry, or the climate too cold for the most profitable cultivation, it requires replanting every year for the subsequent year's crop.

The majority of the plantations in Lower Louisiana, said to be good for little else but sugar and sweet potatoes, were waste and unavailable. St. Mary's Parish had been almost entirely abandoned. The cane had run out; seed-cane was not to be had; and to recommence the culture an outlay of capital was necessary, from which no such immediate, bountiful returns could be anticipated as from the culture of cotton.

The sugar region and the cotton belt overlap each other. Cane may be cultivated to some extent as far north as 34°, while cotton ranges as far south as 30°, although it can scarcely be considered a safe or profitable crop much below 31°. In 1850 there were in Louisiana 4205 cotton and 1558 sugar plantations. This year cotton is not only king, but a usurper, holding with uncertain tenure much of the special province of sugar.

Good cotton plantations in Louisiana yield a bale (of five hundred pounds) to the acre. The sugar crop varies from five hundred to thirty-five hundred pounds, according to the fitness of the soil, the length of the season, and the mode of culture. A hogshead of eleven hundred and fifty pounds to the acre, is about an average crop.

Five different varieties of cane are used by the planters of Louisiana. The cuttings from which it is propagated are called "seed-cane." They are cut in September, and laid in "mats," — a sort of stack adapted to protect them from frost. Cane is usually planted between the months of October and March. Two or three stalks are laid together in prepared rows seven feet apart, and covered by five or six inches of soil. This is called the "mother-cane." In cold soil it rots, and is eaten by vermin. The first year's growth is called "plant-cane," and is ploughed and hoed like corn. On being cut, new stalks spring up from the roots. These subsequent year's stalks are called rattoons, — a West Indian word, derived from the Spanish retoñó, (retoñar, to sprout again,) which was probably imported into Louisiana, together with the Creole cane, by the refugees from St. Domingo, in 1794.

"There's nothing handsomer," said my friend Dick P——, the overseer, "than a field of cane on the first of June, high as your head, all green, a thousand acres, waving and shining in the wind." It is a lively scene when a gang of fifty or sixty negroes, armed with knives, enter such a field in the fall, and the cutting begins.

I was desirous of seeing a sugar-mill in operation, but could hear of none within convenient visiting distance. The scene is thus described in a letter written by a Northern lady whose husband was last year working a Louisiana plantation : —

"I am sitting in the gallery of a building two hundred and fifty feet long. This gallery was made expressly for the white overseer, and overlooks all that is going on in the main building. There is a sleeping-room in each end of it, and a large open space in the middle which serves as a dining-room ; here I am writing. In the opposite end of the building I can see the engine which carries all the machinery ; just this side of it are the great rollers that crush the cane, and the apron, or feed-carrier, that carries the cane from the shed outside up to the crushers.

"Just this side of the crushers are four large vats that receive the juice. From these it is carried into two large kettles, where the lime is put in, and the juice is raised to the boiling-point, and then skimmed. From these kettles the juice is transferred by means of a bucket attached to a long pole, to the next kettle, where it is worked to the right consistency for clarifying.

"This done, it is conveyed, by means of a steam-pump, to the filtering room, where it is passed into large vats filled with burnt bones, called bone black, through which it is filtered, and thus freed from all impurities. From these filters it is run off into a large cistern, and pumped up by the same steam-pump into tanks, where, by means of faucets, it is drawn into the sugaring-off pan. In this pan it is heated by means of a coil of pipe that winds round and round till it fills the bottom of the pans and carries the steam which, in from fifteen to twenty minutes, finishes the boiling process. From this pan it is let off into a box car, set on a railroad track which runs up and down between the coolers, which are ranged along each side of this end of the building, like pews in a church.

"The Creoles along the coast have looked with amazement all sum-

mer upon our success with free black laborers, and have been obliged
to acknowledge that they never saw a more cheerful, industrious set
of laborers in all their experience. 'But wait till sugar-making
comes,' they have said, 'and then see if you can get off your crop
without the old system of compulsion. Your niggers will flare up
when you get off your ten-hour system. They are not going to work
night and day, and you cannot get off the crop unless they do.'

" White sugar-makers presented themselves, telling us, in all so-
briety, ' Niggers cannot be trusted to make sugar,' and offering, with
great magnanimity, to oversee the matter for five hundred dollars.
J—— declined all such friendly offers, and last Monday morning
commenced grinding cane. The colored men and women went to work
with a will, — no shirking or flinching. The cutters pushed the
handlers, the handlers pushed the haulers, and so on, night and day,
each gang taking their respective watches, and all moving on with
the regularity of clock-work.

" And so the business went on with black engineers, black crushers, black filterers, black sugar-makers, — all black throughout, —
but the sugar came out splendid in quantity and quality. Sixty
hogsheads of sugar, finished by Saturday night, and things in readiness for the Sabbath's rest, is acknowledged by old planters to be the
largest run ever made in this sugar-house for the first week of the
sugar season. So they gape and stare, and wonder that humanity
and justice can bring forth more profitable results than the driver's
whip."

Louisiana has been the great sugar-growing State of the
Union. For several years before the war, the annual crop
varied from 100,000 to 450,000 hogsheads. In 1864 less than
nine thousand hogsheads were produced. In 1865 the crop
amounted to between sixteen and seventeen thousand hogsheads, less than was raised in 1860 on four plantations !

Attempts were being made to introduce white laborers into
Louisiana. While I was there, one hundred Germans, who
had been hired in New York for a sugar plantation, were
landed in New Orleans. Within twenty-four hours thirty of
them deserted for higher wages ; by which trifling circumstance planters, who had hoped to exchange black for white
labor, were very much disgusted.

CHAPTER LVIII.

THE BATTLE OF MOBILE BAY.

LEAVING New Orleans for Mobile at half-past four o'clock, by the usual route, I reached Lake Ponchartrain by railroad in time to take the steamer and be off at sunset.

The lake, with its low, dark-wooded shores, and its placid, glassy waters, unruffled by a breeze, outspread under the evening sky, was a scene of solitary and tranquil beauty. Here its breast was burnished with the splendors of a reflected cloud, which faded, leaving upon the darkening rim of the lake the most delicate belts of green, and blue, and violet, until these faded in their turn, and the gloomy surface appeared sprinkled all over with molten stars. Strange constellations rose in the Southern hemisphere; while others about the opposite pole, which never set in the latitude of the Northern States, were below the horizon. The "Dipper" was dipped in the lake. I had never seen the North Star so low before.

I walked the deck with the mate, who had been a good Rebel, and was concerned in the capture of the United States steamer "Water Witch."

"I had command of one of the boats," said he. "There was a consultation of officers, and it was proposed to make the attack that night at eleven o'clock; we would have the tide with us then. 'For that very reason,' I said, 'I would postpone it until two. Then we shall have the tide against us. It will be harder pulling down to her, but we can board better, and if we miss grappling the first time we shan't drift by and get fired upon; and if we fail, we can come back on the tide.'"

The steamer was surprised, and the boarding was a success. "The officer in command of our party was killed, and the command devolved upon me. I got three wounds, one through this arm, one across my stomach, and one through the fleshy part of my thigh. But I laid out a man for each wound. I got to the cabin, and had my sword at the captain's throat, and would have run him through, if he had n't been mighty glib in his speech: 'I surrender! I surrender!' He did n't stammer a bit! 'Do you surrender your command?' 'Yes, yes! I do!' And in a minute I stopped the fighting."

This is the style of story one hears travelling anywhere in the South. Lying in my berth in the cabin, I was kept awake half the night by Rebel soldiers relating similar adventures.

The next morning we were in the Gulf of Mexico. We had entered by the South Pass, the tide being unfavorable for an inside passage between the islands and the coast. It was a summer-like, beautiful day. Gulls and pelicans were sailing around and over the steamer and sporting on the waves. On

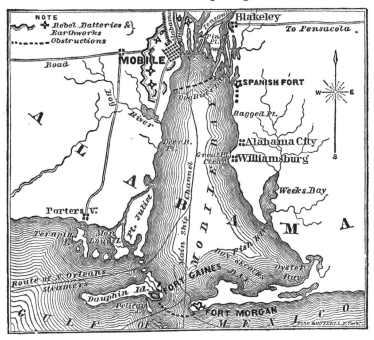

the south was the open Gulf; on our left, a series of low, barren, sandy islands, — Ship Island among them, reminding one of Butler's Expedition.

All the morning we sailed the lustrous, silken waters of the Gulf; approaching in the afternoon the entrance to Mobile Bay. Porpoises were tumbling, and pelicans diving, all around us. Flocks of gulls followed, picking up the fragments of our dinner thrown overboard by the cook. Sometimes a hundred would be fighting in the air for a morsel one of them had picked up, — chasing the bird that bore it, snatching it, dropping it, and darting to catch it as it fell, — until left far behind, and almost lost to sight on the horizon; then they would come up again, flapping low along our white wake, until another fragment attracted and detained them.

We passed the curious, well-defined line, where the yellowish river-water from the Bay and the pure liquid crystal of the Gulf met and mingled. On our left, the long, smooth swells burst into white breakers on the shoals below Pelican Island. On the point of Dauphin Island beyond was Fort Gaines, while close upon our right, as we passed up, was Fort Morgan, on a point of the main land, — its brick walls built upon a sheet of sand white as snow.

Having kept the outside passage, instead of the usual route of the New Orleans steamers, our course lay between these forts, up the main ship-channel, past the scene of Farragut's famous fight. I thought of Brownell's ringing lyric of that day: —

> " Gaines growled low on our left,
> Morgan roared on our right:
> Before us, gloomy and fell,
> With breath like the fume of hell,
> Lay the Dragon of iron shell,
> Driven at last to the fight !
>
> . . . .
>
> " Every ship was drest
> In her bravest and her best,
> As if for a July day;
> Sixty flags and three,
> As we floated up the Bay;
> Every peak and mast-head flew

27

> The brave Red, White, and Blue :
> We were eighteen ships that day.
>
> . . . .
>
> " On in the whirling shade
>   Of the cannon's sulphury breath,
> We drew to the Line of Death
> That our devilish Foe had laid ;
> Meshed in a horrible net,
>   And baited villanous well,
> Right in our path were set
>   Three hundred traps of hell ! "

These were the torpedoes, one of which destroyed the iron clad " Tecumseh," Commander T. A. M. Craven.

> " A moment we saw her turret,
>   A little heel she gave,
> And a thin white spray went o'er her,
>   Like the crest of a breaking wave ;
> In that great iron coffin,
>   The Channel for their grave,
>   The Fort their monument,
> (Seen afar in the offing,)
> Ten fathom deep lie Craven,
>   And the bravest of our brave."

We passed very near to the spot where that " great iron coffin " still lies at the bottom of the stream.
But the ships went in undismayed.

> " Right abreast of the Fort,
>   In an awful shroud they lay,
>   Broadsides thundering away,
> And lightnings in every port, —
>   Scene of glory and dread !
> A storm-cloud all aglow
>   With flashes of fiery red,
> The thunder raging below,
>   And the forest of flags overhead !
>
> . . . .
>
> " Fear ? a forgotten form !
>   Death ? a dream of the eyes !
> We were atoms in God's great storm
>   That roared through the angry skies."

The combat with the Rebel ram " Tennessee," the " Dragon of iron shell," commanded by Admiral Buchanan, (the same who commanded the " Merrimac " in her brief but brilliant career in Hampton Roads,) was as fierce as any of the old sea-fights, but wholly unique and modern.

> " Half the fleet, in an angry ring,
> Closed round the hideous Thing,
> Hammering with solid shot,
> And bearing down, bow on bow :
> He has but a minute to choose ;
> Life or Renown ? — which now
> Will the Rebel Admiral lose ?

> " Cruel, haughty, and cold,
> He was ever strong and bold :
> Shall he shrink from a wooden stem ?
> He will think of that brave band
> He sank in the ' Cumberland,' —
> Ay, he will sink like them !

> " Nothing left but to fight
> Boldly his last sea-fight !
> Can he strike ? By Heaven, 't is true !
> Down comes the traitor Blue,
> And up goes the captive White !

> " Up went the White ! Ah, then,
> The hurrahs that once and again
> Rang from three thousand men
> All flushed and savage with fight !
> Our dead lay cold and stark,
> But our dying, down in the dark,
> Answered as best they might, —
> Lifting their poor lost arms,
> And cheering for God and Right ! "

CHAPTER LIX.

ABOVE the forts the merchant fleet lies at anchor, twenty-five miles from Mobile, — the shallowness of the bay preventing at all times vessels drawing more than ten feet of water from going up to the city. The extensive gulf coast of Louisiana, Mississippi, and Alabama, presents not a single first-class harbor. The first you meet with is that of Pensacola.

Steamers were plying between the ships and the city, receiving and delivering cargoes. We met or passed them as we kept on our course. Blueish lines of forests enclosed the Bay. Four miles below the city we came in sight of the Rebel defences. On our right were the bastion and extensive fortifications of Spanish Fort, commanding Minetta Bay and several miles of the coast of Mobile Bay. This work, originally built by De Soto more than three centuries ago, was finally invested by our fleet and land forces on the day of the fall of Richmond. It surrendered on the ninth of April, and on the eleventh Mobile was evacuated. The water approaches to this fort, and to the other defences of the city, were strewn with torpedoes, by which four or five vessels of our fleet were blown up.

We passed a line of obstructions, consisting of piles and sunken wrecks thrown across the channel; and Mobile, a smoking, sunlit city, lay before us on the low shore. By the direct channel it was less than three miles distant; but, in order to reach it, we were compelled to ascend Spanish River to the Mobile River, and descend that stream, a circuit of over twenty miles. It was four o'clock when we reached the wharf.

Mobile is a level, shady town, regularly laid out, and built on a dry, sandy plain. It is the principal city of Ala-

EXPLOSION AT MOBILE.

bama, and the second city in importance in the Gulf States ; its commerce ranking next to that of New Orleans. For several years before the war its annual exports of cotton were between six and seven hundred thousand bales. It endured a four years' blockade, falling into Federal hands only at the latter end of the war.

But its great catastrophe did not occur until some time after the termination of hostilities. It would seem as if the genius of Destruction was determined to strike a final blow at the city. The explosion of the lately captured Confederate ammunition was one of the most terrible disasters of the kind ever known. It was stored in a large three-story warehouse one street back from the river. The last of Dick Taylor's shells were going in, when, it is supposed, one of them accidentally ignited. Twenty brick blocks, and portions of other blocks, were instantly blown to atoms. Four or five hundred persons were killed, — it was never known how many. A black volcanic cloud of smoke and fragments went up into the sky: " It was big as a mountain," said one. It was succeeded by a fearful conflagration sweeping over the field of ruins. Ten thousand bales of cotton were burned. The loss of property was so immense that nobody ventured to estimate it.

In the vicinity of the explosion, citizens were thrown off their feet, chimneys knocked down, and windows and doors demolished. Lights of glass were broken all over the city, a mile or more from the scene of the explosion.

" I was lifted from the ground, and my hat thrown off," said one. " Then I looked up, and there were great black blocks of something in the air, high as I could see, and shells exploding."

Said another: " I was riding out a mile and a half from the city. I heard a sound, and at the same time my head and shoulders were thrown forward on my horse's neck, as if I had dodged. ' That 's the first time I 've dodged a cannon,' I said, ' and that 's after the war is over.' I looked around, and saw the strangest cloud going up slowly over the city. Then I knew it was the shock that had thrown me down."

The town had neither the means nor the material to rebuild: " We made no bricks during the war." I found the scene of the disaster a vast field of ruins. Where had stood the warehouse in which the ammunition was stored, there was a pit twenty feet deep, half filled with water, and surrounded by fragments of iron and bricks, and unexploded shells. A large brick block, containing a cotton-press, which stood between the magazine and the river, had entirely disappeared. " The bricks were all blown into the water, and we never saw them any more."

Business was brisk. " There are more goods on Dauphin Street to-day," an old merchant told me, " than I have ever before seen in the whole of Mobile." And the captain of the Mobile steamer, who took me up the Alabama to Selma, said : " There was never such a trade on this river before. Nobody ever expected such a freight on this boat : her guards are all under water." Her upward-bound lading consisted mostly of supplies for plantations and provincial stores, — barrels of Western flour and whiskey that had come down the Mississippi, and boxes of fine liquors, soap, starch, and case goods, from the North Atlantic ports. Her downward freight was chiefly cotton.

CHAPTER LX.

ALABAMA PLANTERS.

THE Alabama River steamers resemble those of the Mississippi, although inferior in size and style. But one meets a very different class of passengers on board of them. The Alabamians are a plain, rough set of men, not so fast as the Mississippi-Valley planters, but more sober, more solid, more loyal. They like their glass of grog, however, and some of them are very sincere in their hatred of the government. I found the most contradictory characters among them, which I cannot better illustrate than by giving some specimens of their conversation.

Here is one of the despairing class. " The country is ruined; not only the Southern country, but the Northern country too. The prosperity of our people passed away with the institution of slavery. I shall never try to make another fortune. I made one, and lost it in a minute. I had a hundred and fifty thousand dollars in niggers. I am now sixty years old. I'll bet a suit of clothes against a dime, there'll be no cotton crop raised this year. If there's a crop grown, the hands that raise it won't pick it. Some few niggers go on, and do well, just as before; but they're mighty scarce. They never will be as well off again as they have been, and some of 'em see it. A nigger drayman came to me the other day and asked me to buy him. He said, 'I want a master. When I had a master, I had nothing to do but to eat and drink and sleep, besides my work. Now I have to work and think too.' When I said the law would n't allow me to buy him, he looked very much discouraged."

I heard of a few such cases as this drayman's, but they

were far less common than one would have expected. Poor fellow, he did not know that if he was ever to be anything but an animal, a beast of burden, it was necessary for him to begin to think.

Mr. J——, of Marengo County, also an old man, talked in a different spirit.

" The trouble with the freedmen is, they have not yet learned that living is expensive. They never before had any idea where their clothes came from, except that ' Master gave 'em to me.' In my county, I find them generally better disposed than the whites. I don't know of a case where they have been treated kindly and justly, and have deserted their masters. A few restless ones are exceptions. I noticed one of my boys that I had asked to make a contract for the coming year, packing up his things; and I said to him, ' Warren, what are you doing ? ' He replied, ' Master, they say if we make contracts now, we 'll be branded, and made slaves again.' I had always treated him well. I don't remember that I ever struck him, but he says I did strike him once, and he 's a truthful boy. Another old man that I was raised with, said, ' Master, all the contract I want with you is that you shall bury me, or I 'll bury you.' He said he would go on and work for me like he always had ; and he 'll do it, for he 's an honest man."

Mr. J—— related the case of one of his neighbors who contracted with his freedmen to furnish their supplies and give them one fifth of the crop. He gave them provisions for a year at the start ; and deducted a dollar a day for lost time. " He raised the largest crop of corn he ever did; but when he came to harvest it, he owed them nothing, though he had kept his contract. He was honest, but he had managed badly. I give my hands a share of the crop," added Mr. J——. " But I do not give them provisions any faster than they need them, for if I did they would call in their friends, make a great feast, and eat up everything, — they are so generous and improvident. I deduct a dollar a day for lost time, but instead of putting it into my own pocket, I give the lazy man's dollar to those who do the lazy man's work. I find that encourages them, and the consequence is, there are few lost days."

This genial old gentleman, whom I found to be well known and highly esteemed throughout the country, justified the North in its course during the war, and expressed confidence in the future of the South under the free-labor system.

Mr. G———, one of the bitterest Yankee-haters I met, became nevertheless one of my most intimate steamboat acquaintances. I cull the following from many talks I had with him.

"I owned a cotton factory in Dallas County, above Selma. I had two plantations besides, and an interest in a tan-yard. Wilson's Thieves came in, and just stripped me of everything. They burned eight hundred bales of cotton for me. That was because I happened to be running my mill for the Confederate government. I was making Osnaburgs for the government for a dollar a yard, when citizens would have paid me four dollars a yard; and do you imagine I'd have done that except under compulsion? But the Yankee rascals didn't stop to consider that fact. They skipped my neighbors' cotton and burned mine.

"In other respects they treated them as bad as they did me. They robbed our houses of everything they could find and carry away. I should n't have had a thing left, if it had n't been for my niggers. Some of 'em run off my mules and saved 'em. I gave all my gold and silver to an old woman who kept it hid from the raiders. On one of my plantations a colored carpenter and his wife barrelled up three barrels of fine table crockery and buried it. One of the Yankee officers rode up and said to this woman, 'Where 's your husband?' 'There 's my husband,' she said, pointing to the mulatto. 'You 're a sight whiter 'n he is,' he said,—for she is white as anybody, and he had taken her for the lady of the house. An old negro saved the tannery by pleading with the vandals, and lying to 'em a little bit.

"Three hundred and fifty thousand dollars in gold would n't cover my losses. I never can feel towards this government like I once did. I got started to leave the country ; I swore

I wouldn't live under a government that had treated me in this way. I made up my mind to go to Brazil. I got as far as Mobile, and changed my mind. Now I've concluded to remain here, like any alien. I'm a foreigner. I scorn to be called a citizen of the United States. I shall take no oath, so help me God! Unless," he added immediately, " it is to enable me to vote. I want to vote to give the suffrage to the negro."

As I expressed my surprise at this extraordinary wish, he went on: " Because I think that will finish the job. I think then we'll have enough of the nigger, North and South, and all will combine to put him out of the country."

" It seems to me," I said, " you are a little ungrateful after all you say your negroes have done for you."

" There are a few faithful ones among them," he replied. " If all were like some of mine I wouldn't say anything. They're as intelligent and well behaved as anybody. But I can't stand free niggers, any how ! "

" I notice," said I, " that every man who curses the black race, and prays for its removal or extermination, makes exceptions in favor of negroes he has raised or owned, until I am beginning to think these exceptions compose a majority of the colored population."

G—— made no reply to the remark, but resumed, —

" I want this country filled up with white men. I want the large plantations cut up, and manufactories established. We never had any manufactories for this reason : Southern capitalists all jammed their money into niggers and land. As their capital increased, it was a few more niggers, a little more land. The few factories we had were consequently one-horse concerns, that couldn't compete with those at the North. They were patronized by men who wanted to buy on credit. If a man had cash, he went to the North to buy goods ; if he was short, he bought here. Consequently, to carry on a business of a hundred thousand dollars, a capital of three hundred thousand dollars was necessary. Two thirds of it was sunk ; below the water, like the guards of this boat.

"Now I want the old system played out. But," continued G——, "if the Freedmen's Bureau is withdrawn, things will work back again into their old grooves. The nigger is going to be made a serf, sure as you live. It won't need any law for that. Planters will have an understanding among themselves : ' You won't hire my niggers, and I won't hire yours ; ' then what 's left for them ? They 're attached to the soil, and we 're as much their masters as ever. I 'll stake my life, this is the way it will work. The country will be no better off than it ever was. To make a farming and manufacturing country, like you have at the North, we must put the nigger out of the way. For this reason, I hope the cotton crop this year will be a failure. And I not only hope, but I know it will. There a'n't labor enough in the country ; the planters are going to bid against each other, and make contracts they won't be able to keep, and that 's going to put the Old Harry into the freedmen."

I remarked that, as long as the demand for labor exceeded the supply, planters would continue to bid against each other, and that the plan he had suggested, by which the freedman was to be made a serf without the aid of legislation, would thus be defeated.

"Let the Bureau be taken away," he replied, "and planters will come into the arrangement. That is, all honorable ones will ; and if a man has n't honor enough to come in, he 'll be scared in. If he hires my niggers, or yours, he 'll be mobbed."

Mr. H——, of Lowndes County, often joined in our conversation. "I don't believe my friend G—— here believes half he says. I am sure the South is going to make this year a million bales, — probably much more. One thing planters have got to learn : the old system is gone up, and we must begin new. It won't do to employ the old overseers ; they can't learn to treat the freedmen like human beings. I told my overseer the old style would n't do, — the niggers would n't stand it, — and he promised better fashions ; but it was n't two days before he fell from grace, and went to whipping

again. That just raised the Old Scratch with them; and I
don't blame 'em."

H—— went on to say that it was necessary now to treat
the negroes like men. "We must deal justly with them;"
he had a great deal to say about justice. "We must reason
with them, — for they are reasonable beings;" and he repeated some of the excellent homilies with which he had
enlightened their consciences and understandings.

"'Formerly,' I said to them, 'you were my slaves; you
worked for me, and I provided for you. You had no thought
of the morrow, for I thought of that for you. If you were
sick, I had the doctor come to you. When you needed
clothes, clothes were forthcoming; and you never went hungry for lack of meal and pork. You had little more responsibility than my mules.

"'But now all that is changed. Being free men, you
assume the responsibilities of free men. You sell me your
labor, I pay you money, and with that money you provide for
yourselves. You must look out for your own clothes and
food, and the wants of your children. If I advance these
things for you, I shall charge them to you, for I cannot give
them like I once did, now I pay you wages. Once if you
were ugly or lazy, I had you whipped, and that was the end
of it. Now if you are ugly and lazy, your wages will be paid
to others, and you will be turned off, to go about the country
with bundles on your backs, like the miserable low-down
niggers you see that nobody will hire. But if you are well-
behaved and industrious, you will be prosperous and respected
and happy.'

"They all understood this talk," added H——, "and liked
it, and went to work like men on the strength of it. If every
planter would begin that way with his freedmen, there 'd be
no trouble. There 's everything in knowing how to manage
them."

"If anybody knows how to manage them, you do," said
G——. Then turning to me: "H—— is the shrewdest
manager in this country. There 's a good story about his
managing a nigger and a horse; — shall I tell it, H——?"

"Go ahead," said H——, laughing.

"An old nigger of his picked up a horse the Yankee raiders had turned loose in the country, and brought him home to H——'s plantation. The old nigger gave the horse to his son Sip, and died. The horse had been used up, but he turned out to be a mighty good one, — just such an animal as H—— wanted; so he laid claim to him, and Sip had to go to the Freedmen's Bureau for an order to compel my friend here to give him up. He told his story, got the order, and brought it home, and showed it to H——, who looked at it, then looked at Sip, and said, 'Do you know what this paper says?' 'It says I'm to have de hoss; dat's what dey told me.' 'I'll tell you what it says,' and H—— pretended to read the order: '*If this boy troubles you any more about that horse, give him a sound thrashing!*' 'Fore God,' says Sip, 'I done went to de wrong man!'"

I looked to see H——, the just man, who treated his freed people like rational beings, deny the truth of this story.

"G—— has told something near the fact; but there's one thing he has left out. *I just put my Spencer to Sip's head, and told him if he pestered me any more about that horse, I'd kill him.* He knew I was a man of my word, and he never pestered me any more."

I thought G—— must have intended the story as a hard hit at H——'s honesty; but I now saw that he really meant it as a compliment to his "shrewd management," and that as such H—— received it with satisfaction.

"But," said I, "as you relate the circumstance, it seems to me the horse belonged to Sip."

"A nigger has no use for a horse like that," replied H——.

"He had been brought on to the plantation and fed there at H——'s expense," explained G——.

"Hadn't he done work enough to pay for his keeping?"

"Yes, and ten times over," said H——, frankly. "I foresaw in the beginning there was going to be trouble about the ownership of that horse. So I told my driver to kill him, — with hard work, I mean. He tried his best to do it; but he was such a tough beast, he did the work and grew fat all the time."

I was still unable to see why the horse did not belong rightfully to Sip, instead of his master. But one thing I did see, more and more plainly: that it was impossible for the most honorable men who had been bred up under the institution of slavery to deal at all times and altogether honorably with those they had all their lives regarded as chattels. Mr. H——— was one of the fairest and most sensible men in his speech whom I chanced to meet ; and I believe that he was sincere, — or at least meant to be sincere. I made inquiries concerning him of his neighbors fifty miles around, — for every large planter knows every other, at least by reputation, within a circuit of several counties, — and all spoke of him as a just and upright man. No doubt if I had had dealings with him I should have found him so. He meant to give the freedmen their rights, but he was only beginning dimly to perceive that they had any rights ; and when it came to treating a black man with absolute justice, he did not know the meaning of the word.

Mr. B———, of Monroe County, was a good sample of the hopeful class.

" We 're brushed out, and must begin new. I 've lost as much as any other man, but it 's foolish to sit down and complain of that. I believe if Southern men will only take courage, and do their best, in five years the country will be more prosperous than ever. When you hear it said the country is ruined, and the niggers won't work, the trouble is in them that make the complaint, and not in the niggers. My niggers say to me, ' Massa Joe, we ought to work mo'e 'n we ever did befo'e ; for once, we just worked for our victuals and clothes, and now we 're getting wages besides.' And they 'll do it, — they *are* doing it. If you want a freedman to do what he promises, you 've only to set him the example, and do by him just what you promise. I 've a negro foreman on my plantation that has been with me twenty years ; and I can trust him to manage just as far as I can trust myself.

"Talk about the country being ruined!" B—— went on: "I'm sick of such nonsense. Just look at it. I hire my freedmen by the year; I give four and five dollars a month to women, and seven and eight to men. A woman will do about two thirds as much work ploughing, hoeing, and picking as a man. For two months now I shall keep my women spinning and making clothes, and my men cutting and hauling wood to the steamboats, for which I get four dollars a cord. That will pay their wages and more. Then what have we got to do the rest of the year? Make a crop of cotton. If we don't make more than a quarter of a crop, it will pay handsomely, at present prices; but it's my opinion we shall make a good crop. I used to find it profitable to pay a hundred and fifty dollars a year for slaves, with cotton at ten cents a pound; and if I can't make money now, I'm a fool."

A Mobile merchant, overhearing this talk, remarked: "You are the most hopeful man, Mr. B——, I ever saw. I don't know but what you say is true; but it won't do to talk it very loud, so they'll hear it on the other side of the water. It's our policy to talk the other way, and keep the prices up."

B—— assured me that the majority of the planters in Monroe County were of his way of thinking. They had formed an Agricultural Association, the object of which was "to protect and preserve the colored population, by furnishing them employment and ministering to their wants and necessities." The constitution adopted by this association breathes such a different spirit from the serf-codes of Mississippi, Louisiana, and South Carolina, that it is refreshing and encouraging to refer to it. I quote some of its provisions:—

"ARTICLE 6th. It shall be the duty of the Executive Committee to look after the welfare of the freedmen, in their respective beats, to inspect and sanction each and every contract made between the freedmen and their employers, and to see that said freedmen are not deceived or overreached in any contract made with the employer. . . . And when any contract, as aforesaid, shall be fairly and understandingly made, it shall be the law between the parties thereto, and when any difficulty arises between any freedman and his white employer, relative to the construction or performance of any contract, said com mitteeman may act as arbitrator between the parties, and his decision shall be final, unless one or both of the parties desire an appeal.

" ART. 8th.   It shall be the duty of all the officers of this Association, to see that the freedman shall receive from his employer his wages or earnings, and in case such employer refuses to pay promptly such wages and earnings, to aid the freedman by their full power in the collection of the same.

" ART. 9th.   It shall also be the duty of this Association, and particularly the officers thereof, to see that the freedman shall comply with his contracts with his employer unless he can show some good or reasonable excuse for the non-performance.

" ART. 13th.   It shall be the duty of the said Association to provide a home for the aged and helpless freedmen of the county, and for such others as are unable to make an honest support, and to see that they are provided with the necessaries of life, — to devise ways and means for their permanent relief and support.

" ART. 15th.   It shall be the duty of this Association, and all the officers thereof, to favor, as much as possible, the education and schooling of the colored children in said county, and to aid in devising ways and means, and making arrangements for having said children properly taught and their general morals taken care of."

The association taxed itself for the purpose of carrying out the provisions of its constitution.   Every planter in Monroe County had joined it.   General Swayne, Assistant-Commissioner of the Freedmen's Bureau for Alabama, had approved its action, and appointed its president superintendent of freedmen for that county.   " The thing is working admirably," said B——.   " The planters are encouraged, and the freedmen are contented and at work."

I said to him : " If all the members of the association are as sincere as yourself, and will perform what they promise ; if all the counties in the State will follow the example of Monroe ; and if other States will follow the example of Alabama, there will be no longer any trouble about reconstruction : the great problem of the country will be solved."

He said he believed so, and was sure the association would act in good faith.   And I heard afterwards that Conecuh County had already followed the example of Monroe.

CHAPTER LXI.

WILSON'S RAID.

WE had lovely weather, sailing up the Alabama River. The shores were low, and covered with canebrakes, or with growths of water-oak, gum, sycamore, and cotton-wood trees, with here and there dark and shaggy swamps. Then plantations began to appear, each with its gin-house and cotton-press, planter's house, corn-crib, and negro-quarters, on the river's bank.

The sycamores, with their white trunks covered all over with small black spots, and heavily draped with long moss, presented a peculiar appearance. Green tufts of the mistletoe grew upon the leafless tree-tops. Clouds of blackbirds sometimes covered the shore, casting a shadow as they flew. The second day, the low shores disappeared, replaced by pleasantly wooded bluffs and elevated plantations.

Nearly all the planters I met had been down to Mobile to purchase their supplies for the season. Freight went ashore at every landing. Recent rains had made the steep clayey banks as slippery as if they had been greased; and it was quite exciting to see the deck-hands carry up the freight, — many a poor fellow getting a perilous fall. The wood for the steamboat was sometimes shot from the summit of the bluff down a long wooden spout which dropped it at the landing.

Seeing some heavy bars of iron going ashore at one place, I asked an old gentleman to what use they were put on the plantation.

" They are to make ploughs of, sir."

" Does every plantation make its own ploughs ? "

" Do we make our own ploughs ? " he repeated, regarding

28

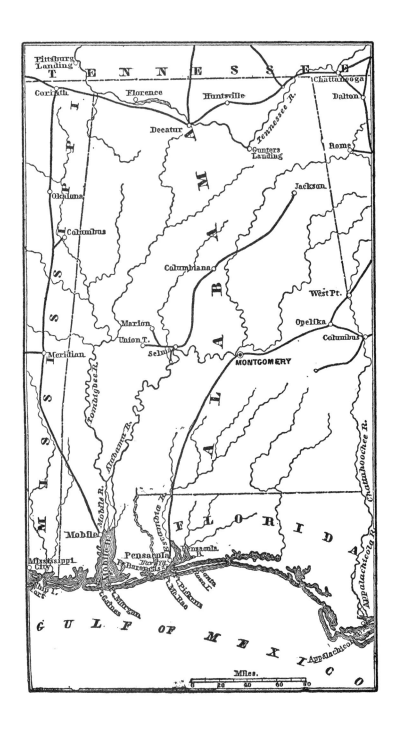

me with astonishment and indignation. " Why, sir, it would n't be a civilized country, if we did n't. How do you think, sir, we should get our ploughs ? "

" Buy them, or have them made for you."

" Buy our ploughs ! It would impoverish us, sir, if we had to buy our ploughs."

" On the contrary, I should think a plough-factory could furnish them for less than they now cost you, — that, like boots and shoes, it would be cheaper to buy them than to make them."

" No, sir ! I 've a black man on my plantation who can make as good a plough, at as little cost, as can be made anywhere in the world."

After that I had nothing to say, having already sufficiently exposed my ignorance.

On the third day (it was the slowest trip, our captain said, which he had made in twenty years) we reached Selma, three hundred miles above Mobile, — a pleasantly situated town, looking down from the level summit of a bluff that rises almost precipitously from the river. Before the war it had three thousand inhabitants, and exported annually near a hundred thousand bales of cotton. It is connected by railroads with the North and West, and by railroad and river with Montgomery and the East. It was a point of very great importance to the Confederacy.

I found it a scene of " Yankee vandalism " and ruin. The Confederate arsenal, founderies, and rolling-mills, — the most important works of the kind in the South, covering many acres of ground, furnished with coal and iron by the surrounding country, — together with extensive warehouses containing ammunition and military stores, were burned when Wilson captured the place. A number of private stores and dwellings were likewise destroyed ; and the work of rebuilding them was not yet half completed.

Climbing the steps from the landing to the level of the town, the first object which attracted my attention was a chain-gang of negroes at work on the street; while a number of white persons stood looking on, evidently enjoying the sight, and saying to one another, "That's the beauty of freedom! that's what free niggers come to!"

On inquiring what the members of the chain-gang had done to be punished in this ignominious manner, I got a list of their misdemeanors, one of the gravest of which was "using abusive language towards a white man." Some had transgressed certain municipal regulations, of which, coming in from the country, they were very likely ignorant. One had sold farm produce within the town limits, contrary to an ordinance which prohibits market-men from selling so much as an egg before they have reached the market and the market-bell has rung. For this offence he had been fined twenty dollars, which being unable to pay, he had been put upon the chain. Others had been guilty of disorderly conduct, vagrancy, and petty theft, which it was of course necessary to punish. But it was a singular fact that no white men were ever sentenced to the chain-gang, — being, I suppose, all virtuous.

The battle of Selma was not a favorite topic with the citizens, most of whom were within the stockade, or behind the breastworks, captured by an inferior force of the Yankee invaders. But on the subject of the burning and pillaging that ensued they were eloquent.

A gray-haired old gentleman said to me : "I was in the trenches when Wilson came. Everybody was. I just watched both ways, and when I saw how the cat was jumping, I threw my musket as far as I could, dropped down as if I was killed, and walked into town atter the Yankees. I stood by my own gate, when four drunken fellows came up, slapped me on the shoulder, and said, 'This old man was in the stockade, — he's a Rebel!' 'Of course I'm a Rebel,' I said, 'if I'm ketched in a Rebel trap.'

"They was taking me away when an officer rode up. 'Old man,' says he, 'can you show me where the corn depot is?' 'I reckon I kin, if these gentlemen will let me,' I says. So I got off; and when I had showed him the corn he let me go.

"The fire was first set by our own men: that was in the

cotton yards. They blazed up so quick, the Yankees could n't have got thar without they went on wires. The next was the post-office ; that they burned. The next was a drug store ; the other drug store they did n't burn, but they smashed everything in it. The Arsenal was owing me and my family fifteen hundred dollars, when they destroyed it.

" They just ruined me. They took from me six cows, four mules, fifteen hogs, fifteen hundred pounds of bacon, eight barrels of flour, and fifty-five sacks of corn. They took my wife's and daughters' clothing to carry away flour in. I saw a man take my wife's best dress, empty into it all the flour he could tote, tie it up, clap it on his shoulder, and march off. Another went off with an elegantly embroidered petticoat full of flour swung on his arm. Another would take a pair of ladies' drawers, fill the legs with flour, and trot off with 'em riding straddle of his neck. It made me feel curi's ! It made me feel like if I had 'em down in the squirrel woods, I could shoot a right smart passel of 'em with a will ! "

There were one hundred and fifty dwellings burned ; some caught from the shops and warehouses, and others were said to have been set by marauders. These robbed everybody, even the negroes in the streets and the negro-women in their houses. Charles Mencer, a well-known and respectable colored man, related to me the following : —

" I worked here in a saddle-shop, at the time of Wilson's raid. I hired my time of my master, and had laid up two hundred dollars in gold and silver : I had invested my earnings in specie, and in two watches, because I knew the Confederacy could n't last. The Yankees came in on Sunday evening ; they robbed my house and stole my gold and silver, and one of my watches. Four of them stopped me in the street, and took my other watch, and my pocket-book, with all my Confederate money in it."

The rest of this man's story possesses a semi-historical interest.

" The next Tuesday General Wilson sent for me ; he wanted somebody that he could trust to carry despatches for him down the river to General Canby, and I had been recommended to him by some colored people. I said I would take them; and I sewed them up in my vest collar. Then I went to my master, and told him there was no chance for work since the Yankees had come in, and got a pass from him to go down to Mobile and find work. Tuesday night I started in a canoe, and paddled down the river. I dodged the Rebel guard when I could, but I was taken and searched twice, and got off by showing my master's pass. I paddled night and day, and got to Montgomery Hill on Sunday. There I saw Federal troops, and went ashore, and delivered myself up to the captain. He took me to General Lucas, who sent me with a cavalry escort to General Canby at Blakely."

For this service Mencer was paid three hundred dollars in greenbacks, which he had recently invested in a freedmen's newspaper, " The Constitutionalist," just started in Mobile.

The negroes everywhere sympathized with the Federal cause, and served it when they could; but they would seldom betray a master who had been kind to them. Many stories were told me by the planters, illustrating this fidelity. Here is one, related by a gentleman of Lowndes County : —

" The Yankees, when they left Selma, passed through this side of the river, on their way to Montgomery. The streams were high; that hindered them, and did us a sight of damage. I got the start of 'em, and run off my horses and mules. I gave a valise full of valuable papers to my negro boy Arthur, and told him to hide it. He took it, and put it in his trunk, — threw out his own clothes to hide my property; for he did n't suppose the Yankees would be mean enough to rob niggers. But they did: after they robbed my house, they went to the negro-quarters, and pilfered them. They found my valise, took out my old love-letters, and had a good time reading 'em for about an hour. Then they said to Arthur, —

" ' You are your master's confidential servant, a'n't you ? '

" ' Yes, sir,' says Arthur, proud of the distinction.

" ' You know where he has gone with his mules and horses ? '

" ' Yes, sir, I know all about it.'

" ' Jump on to this horse, and go and show us where he is, and we 'll give you five dollars.'

" ' I don't betray my master for no five dollars,' says Arthur.

" ' Then,' says they, ' we 'll shoot you if you won't show us ! ' And they put their carbines to his head.

" He never flinched. ' You can shoot me if you like,' he says, ' but I sha'n't betray my master ! '

" They were so struck with his courage and fidelity that they just let him go. So I saved my horses. He don't know it, but I 'm going to give that boy a little farm and stock it for him."

Another planter in Lowndes County, an old man, told me his story, which will pass as a sample of a hundred others.

" The Yankees burnt my gin-house and screw. They did n't burn my house, for they made it a rule to destroy none but unoccupied dwellings. But they took everything from my house they wanted, and ruined about everything they did n't want. They mixed salt with the sugar, emptied it on the floor, and poured vinegar on it. They took a great fancy to a little grandson of mine. They gave him a watch, and told him they 'd give him a little pony to ride if he would go to camp with them. ' I won't go with you,' says he, ' for you 're taking away all the flour that we make biscuit of.' They carried him a little ways, when they stopped to burn a school-house. ' Here ! You must n't burn that ! ' he says ; ' for that 's our school-house.' And they did n't burn it."

" The Confederates used me as bad as the Yankees," said Mr. M——, a planter whom I saw in Macon County. " They had taken twenty-six horses from me, when Wilson came and took thirty more. I ran off six of my best horses to a piny hill ; and there I got on a high stump, and looked over the bushes, to see if the Yankees were coming. I was n't near as happy as I 'd been some days in my life ! All I thought of was to get my horses off down one side of the hill, if I saw the raiders coming up the other."

This gentleman had been extensively engaged in the culture

of the grape, — to which, by the way, the soil and climate of Alabama are admirably adapted. He had in his cellar twenty thousand dollars' worth of wine, when Wilson came. His wife caused it all to be destroyed, to prevent it from falling into the hands of the soldiers. The last cask was scarcely emptied when they arrived. " She thought she 'd sooner deal with men sober than drunk," said M——. " They treated her very well and took nothing from the house they did n't need."

The route of Wilson's cavalry can be traced all the way, by the burnt gin-houses with which they dotted the country. At Montgomery they destroyed valuable founderies and machine-shops, after causing the fugitive Rebels to burn a hundred thousand bales of cotton, with the warehouses which contained it. I followed their track through the eastern counties of Alabama, and afterwards recrossed it in Georgia, where the close of hostilities terminated this, the most extensive and destructive raid of the war.

CHAPTER LXII.

NOTES ON ALABAMA.

MONTGOMERY, the capital of Alabama, and originally the capital of the Confederacy, is a town of broad streets and pleasant prospects, built on the rolling summits of high bluffs, on the left bank of the Alabama, one hundred miles above Selma. Before the war it had ten thousand inhabitants.

Walking up the long slope of the principal street, I came to the Capitol, a sightly edifice on a fine eminence. On a near view, the walls, which are probably of brick, disguised to imitate granite, had a cheap look ; and the interior, especially the Chamber of Representatives in which the Confederate egg was hatched, appeared mean and shabby. This was a plain room, with semicircular rows of old desks covered with green baize exceedingly worn and foul. The floor carpet was faded and ragged. The glaring white-washed walls were offensive to the eye. The Corinthian pillars supporting the gallery were a cheap imitation of bronze. Over the Speaker's chair hung a sad-looking portrait of George Washington, whose solemn eyes could not, I suppose, forget the scenes which Treason and Folly had enacted there.

I remained two days at Montgomery ; saw General Swayne and other officers of the Bureau ; visited plantations in the vicinity ; and conversed with prominent men of the surrounding counties. Both there, and on my subsequent journey through the eastern part of the State, I took copious notes, which I shall here compress within as small a space as possible.

I have already sketched the class of planters one meets on steamboats and railroads. These are generally men who mix with the world, read the newspapers, and feel the current of progressive ideas. Off the main routes of travel, you meet with a different class, — men who have never emerged from their obscurity, who do not read the newspapers, and who have not yet learned that the world moves. Many of them were anti-secessionists ; which fact renders them often the most troublesome people our officers now have to deal with. Claiming to be Union men, they cannot understand why their losses, whether of slaves or other property, which the war occasioned, should not be immediately made up to them by the government.

As in Mississippi and Tennessee, the small farmers in the Alabama legislature were the bitterest negro-haters in that body ; while the more liberal-minded and enlightened members were too frequently controlled by a back-country constituency, whom they feared to offend by voting for measures which ignorance and obstinacy were sure to disapprove.

In Alabama, as in all the Southern States, the original secessionists were generally Democrats and the Union men Old Line Whigs. The latter opposed the revolution until it swept them away ; when they often went into the war with a zeal which shamed the shirking policy of many who were very hot in bringing it on, and very cool in keeping out of it. I found them now the most hopeful men of the South. If a planter said to me, " I 'm going to raise a big crop of cotton this year, — my negroes are working finely," — I needed no other test that he belonged to this class.

Concerning the loyalty of the people I shall give the testimony of a very intelligent young man of Chambers County, — whose story will in other respects prove instructive.

" I enlisted in the Confederate Army for one year ; and before my time was up I was conscripted for two years ; then, before these expired, I was conscripted for two more. I was made prisoner at Forest Hill, in Virginia, and taken to Harrisburg, in Pennsylvania. At the end of the war I was paroled. I knew that my people were ruined, and all my property gone. That consisted in twelve slaves ; their labor supported me before the war, but now I had nothing but my own hands to depend upon. I made up my mind to stay where I was and go to work. I hired out to a farmer for six dollars a month. I had never done a stroke of labor in my life, and it came hard to me at first. But I soon got used to it.

"One day a merchant of Harrisburg was riding by, and he asked me some questions which I answered. A few days after he came that way again, got into conversation with me, and proposed to me to go into his store. He offered me eighteen dollars a month. I said to him, ' You are very kind, sir, but you probably do not know who I am, or you would not want me : I am a Rebel soldier, just out of prison.' He said he believed I was an honest fellow, and would like to try me. I went into his store, and after the first month he raised my wages to thirty dollars.' After the second month, he gave me forty, and after the third month he gave me fifty. I had been a wild boy before the war ; I had plenty of money with no restrictions upon my spending it. But I tell you I was never so happy in my life as when I was at work for my living in that store. My employer liked me, and trusted me, and I liked the people.

"I have now come home on a visit. My relations and neighbors are very much incensed against me because I tell them plainly what I think of the Yankees. I know now that we were all in the wrong, and that the North was right, about the war ; and I tell them so. I have met with the most insulting treatment on this account. They feel the bitterest animosity against the government, and denounce and abuse the Yankees, and call me a Yankee, as the worst name they can give me. To you, a Northern man, I suppose they won't say much ; but they talk among themselves and to me."

" How large a proportion of your people express such sentiments ? "

" Well, sir, there are fifteen hundred voting men in the county ; and all but about a hundred and eighty feel and talk the way I tell you. They can't be reconciled to living under the old government, and those who are able are preparing to emigrate. A fund has already been raised to send agents to select lands for them in Mexico."

" Did you find in the North any such animosity existing towards the people of the South ? "

" Very little ; and there was this difference : In the North it is only a few ignorant people, of the poorer class, who hate the South : I believe the mass of the Northern people, while they hate treason and rebellion, have only kind feelings towards the Southern people. But with us it is the wealthy and influential class that hates the North, while only the poor whites and negroes have any loyalty at heart. I wish," he added, " that for every Northern man now settling in the South, a Southern man would go into business at the North, and see for himself, as I have done, just what sort of people and institutions we have all our lives been taught to misunderstand and slander."

The editors of the southern half of the State were nearly all disloyal, judged by their prints. The same may be said of the ministers of the aristocratic churches, judged by their words and works.

There is a wide difference between the people of Northern and Southern Alabama. The inhabitants of many of the upper counties were as loyal as those of East Tennessee. In some it was necessary for the Davis government to maintain a cavalry force in order to keep the people in subjection. Such a county was Randolph, whose inhabitants were as strongly opposed to secession, as those of Chambers County, its next neighbor on the South, were in favor of it.

" The commanders discriminated in their foraging against the Union people. The fact that a man was absent in the service of the United States, or was opposed to the rebellion, was deemed a sufficient warrant to take the last piece of meat from his smoke-house, and the last ear of corn and bundle of fodder from his barns, leaving his family to starve. Randolph alone furnished nearly five hundred men who actually took up arms in the service of the United States, enlisting in whatever organization they found convenient as they made their escape from the Rebel conscripting officers into our lines. Their graves are upon every battle-field, attesting their bravery, their patriotism, and their sacrifices."

Thus wrote, in a private letter to General Swayne, Lieutenant R. T. Smith, himself a loyal Alabamian who served in the Union army. The county was impoverished by the absence of its men in both armies, and by the troopers who preyed upon it. There was still great suffering at the time of my visit.

" Much destitution also exists," said the lieutenant, " among the families of the late Rebels ; for the soldiery, who had come in the beginning partly at their instance, consumed their substance when the means of the Union people were exhausted. Like Actæon, they were eaten by their own dogs."

" It is a common, an every-day sight in Randolph County, to see women and children, most of whom were formerly in good circumstances, begging for bread from door to door. They must have immediate help, or perish. Fifteen hundred families, embracing five thousand persons, are in need of immediate aid." This was in January, 1866.

The destitution here described was not confined to a portion of the country, nor was it a new thing. In 1863, the shortness of the crops, the depreciation of the currency, and the consequent high prices of provisions, produced a famine among the poorer classes. The families of soldiers, fighting the battles of a confederacy which paid them in worthless paper, were left to suffer the extremes of want, while many, who helped to bring on the war, were growing rich by speculating upon the misery it occasioned. In Mobile there were insurrections of women, driven by starvation to acts of public violence. The State was finally awakened to the necessity of ameliorating these sufferings ; and during the last year of the war it fed with meal and salt one hundred and forty thousand white paupers.

This charity, inherited, in a manner, by the government which feeds the enemy it subjugates, was continued, after the war had closed, with the aid of the United States Commissary Department. At the same time the emancipation of four hundred and fifty thousand slaves, — nearly half the population of the State, — threw a large number of black paupers upon the community.

In these circumstances, the Freedmen's Bureau proved an instrument of inestimable good. Its mediatory and organizing influence prevented outbreaks, and saved thousands from perishing. It assumed the care of homeless blacks and of white refugees. It colonized the former upon abandoned lands, and thence supplied many plantations with labor.

In the month of August, 1865, there were at one of these colonies thirty-four hundred freedmen. "I have been sending paupers to it ever since," said General Swayne; "and there are now but one hundred and fifty persons there." This was in January. At that time the Bureau was feeding less than twenty-five hundred blacks, and the number was rapidly diminishing.

No freedmen's courts had been established by the Bureau in Alabama. "We had not officers enough to establish more than ten courts," General Swayne told me. "And when those were withdrawn, the negro would have been left defenceless. I therefore preferred to educate the civil courts to do the freedmen justice." He had displayed considerable diplomatic skill in securing the coöperation of the Convention, and getting an ordinance passed by it, which authorized civil officers to try freedmen's cases and receive negro testimony. If an officer failed of his duty towards the blacks, his commission as an agent of the Bureau was revoked. General Swayne thought the system was working well; but he confessed that these officers required close watching; and some of his special agents, who came more directly in contact with the people, and with the actual crude state of affairs, while he saw them too much perhaps through the atmosphere of influential State officials, assured me that the justice obtained by the freedmen from these courts was but scanty. "At the outset," said one, "they meet with obstacles. If they enter a complaint, they must give bail to appear as witnesses, or be lodged in jail. As no white man will give bail for a negro to appear as a witness against a white man, and as they don't fancy lying perhaps weeks in jail in order to be heard, they prefer to suffer wrong rather than seek redress."

There were but two freedmen's schools in the State, one at Montgomery, and another at Mobile, with an aggregate of fifteen teachers and nine hundred pupils.

Everywhere I heard complaints of the demoralization of the people occasioned by the war. There were throughout the South organized bands of thieves. In Alabama, cotton-stealing had become a safe and profitable business. I was told of men, formerly respectable, and who still held their heads high in society, who were known to have made large fortunes by it. These men employ negroes to do the work, because negroes cannot give legal evidence against a white man. During the last three months of 1865, it was estimated that, on the line of the Mobile and Ohio Railroad, ten thousand bales of cotton had been stolen.

Crimes of every description, especially upon the property and persons of the freedmen, were very common. General Swayne told me that he stood greatly in need of a force of cavalry, without which it was almost impossible to arrest the offenders.

There was every prospect of a good cotton crop the present year. Since the invention of the spinning-jenny by Arkwright, and of the gin by Whitney, the culture of this great staple has received no such impulse as the recent high prices have given it. The planters were taking courage, the freedmen were at work, and a large amount of Northern capital was finding investment in the State. Even the poor whites, who never before would consent to degrade themselves by industrious labor in the field, seemed inspired by the general activity, and many of them, for the first time in their lives, were preparing to raise a few bales of cotton. Labor was not abundant. "Our best young men went off with the Yankee army; and our best girls followed the officers." Men of sense and reputation had not much difficulty, however, in securing laborers. "When I got all ready to hire," said one, "I just turned about four hundred hogs into a field near the road. Every freedman that came that way stopped; and in a week I had as many as I wanted. They all like to hire out where there is plenty of pork." Others, to fill their quota of hands, were paying the fines of stout negroes on the chain-gangs, and bailing those who were lying in jail.

All sorts of contracts were entered into ; and various devices were used to stimulate the energies of the freedmen. Some paid wages ; some gave a share in the crop ; and I heard of planters who defrayed all expenses, and gave five cents a pound for the cotton raised on their lands. One man, who hired sixty freedmen at moderate wages, divided them into six gangs of ten each, and offered a premium of three hundred dollars to the gang which should produce the greatest number of bales.

General Swayne estimated that there were five thousand Northern men in the State, engaged in planting and trading. Many of them were late army-officers. Business in the principal towns had been paying large profits ; and Northern merchants, who purchased their goods at the North, were, notwithstanding the popular prejudice against them, enabled to compete with, and undersell, native traders who bought in smaller quantities and at second hand.

The hilly northern part of Alabama falls off gradually through the rolling prairies and alluvial bottoms of the central, to the low, flat southern portion of the State. Much of this latter region is sandy and barren, producing little besides poor whites and sweet potatoes. There are fertile bottom lands, however, adapted to the sugar-cane ; and rice has also been successfully cultivated near the coast.

All through the lower half of the State, the long tree-moss grows with great luxuriance. It flourishes in a warm, moist climate ; and the forests of the entire Southern country, below thirty-three degrees, are festooned by it. It likes the dank and heavy shade of swamps, which it darkens still more with its pendant shrouds. In favorable localities it grows to a great length, till its long-fibred masses appear dripping from the trees. One can imagine the effect when the great winds move through the woods, and to their solemn roaring is added the weird, unearthly aspect of a myriad gloomy banners, waving and beckoning from every limb.

Gathered by means of hooks attached to long poles, and seasoned by a simple process, this moss becomes a valuable article of merchandise, being principally used in the manufacture of mattresses. I saw many bales of it going down the rivers to New Orleans, Mobile, and Savannah. Its color on the boughs is a dull greenish gray ; but when prepared for market, it resembles black crinkled horse-hair. A gentleman of Charleston told me that just before the war he tried the experiment of sending a bale of it to France, where it was not permitted to pass the custom-house until his factor had obtained from him a properly attested certificate, showing that it was to be taxed, not as hair, but as a vegetable substance. The French called it " vegetable horse-hair."

The best cotton lands of Alabama lie between the Alabama and Tombigbee rivers, where a bale to the acre is the usual yield. The valleys of the Black Warrior and some lesser streams are scarcely inferior.

The general fertility of the great central portion of the State is offset by two or three disadvantages. One is the mud of the " black lime land," which, in the rainy season, is often of such depth and tenacity that travel on the roads by means of wheeled vehicles is impracticable. A greater inconvenience is the scarcity of wells. In the northern portion of the State good water is abundant ; but in other parts plantations are supplied only by means of house and field cisterns. In some towns excellent Artesian wells have been constructed ; a few reaching a depth of a thousand feet, and throwing water in sufficient volume and force to carry machinery. At Selma there were lately two very good flowing wells, but on an attempt being made to bore a third, a rock was split, which injured materially the condition of the two first. In the large public square at Montgomery, the broad circular basin of the Artesian well, surrounded by an iron railing on a stone curb,

29

visited by throngs of citizens, descending the steps, dipping up the water, or catching it as it gushes from the spout, and filling their pails and casks, forms an interesting feature of the place.

In the northern part of Alabama there are beautiful and fertile valleys adapted to the culture of both cotton and grain. On the other hand, there are hills unfit for cultivation. Between these two extremes there are upland tracts of moderate fertility, capable of producing a third or a quarter of a bale to the acre. This is the region of small farms and few negroes.

The climate throughout the elevated portions of the State is healthy and delightful. On the low river bottoms there is much suffering from fevers and mosquitoes.

The common-school system of Alabama is very imperfect. The wealthy planters send their children to private schools, and object to taxation for the education of the children of the poor. The poor, on the other hand, take no interest in schools, to which they will not send their children as long as money is to be paid for tuition, or as long as there is cotton to pick and wood to cut at home. The isolation of the inhabitants on plantations, or in widely scattered log-cabins, and the presence of an uneducated race forming nearly one half the population, have been great obstacles in the way of popular education.

Alabama has a common-school fund, derived principally from lands, comprising the sixteenth section in each township, given for educational purposes by the United States. This fund has never been consolidated, but each township enjoys the income, by sale or rent, of its own allotted portion. The system works badly. The sixteenth section is valueless in many of the townships where both the land and the inhabitants are poor, and where there is consequently most need of educational assistance; while in townships occupied by planters who have grown rich on the richness of the soil, and who need no such assistance, it has generally proved very valuable. Mr. Taylor, the State Superintendent of Schools, told me that in one of these wealthier townships, in Montgomery County, there was for some years but a single child to whose education the sixteenth-section fund could be properly applied. She was a girl; and the independent planters performed their duty faithfully in her case. They sent her to a boarding-school, where she received a fashionable education; and, when she came to marry, furnished her wedding-outfit, and presented her with a piano.

Alabama is comparatively a new State. Admitted into the Union in 1819, her rise in importance has kept pace steadily with the progress of modern cotton cultivation. It sounds strange to hear planters still young refer to their experiences in the early days of cotton in regions which are now celebrated for its production. "I came to Montgomery County in 1834," said one. "I raised my first cotton crop in 1836. I had nine negroes, and I made a bale to the hand. They did n't know how to pick it. So I hired thirty Indian girls to pick, — as handsome young creatures as ever you saw. Cotton was then eighteen cents a pound. The Indian war disturbed us some; but I and a dozen more settlers went out and killed more Indians than all Scott's army. I have now two large plantations; this year I work a hundred and ten hands, and fifty-five mules and horses, on thirteen hundred acres of cotton and five hundred of corn; and I intend to make more money than ever before."

The principal railroads of the State were all in running condition; although the rolling stock was generally shabby and scarce. The Montgomery and West Point Road, which Wilson's raiders damaged to the amount of several millions, had been temporarily repaired. Depots were never plenty in the South, and where our forces had passed, not one was left; — a great inconvenience, especially to single gentlemen, going to take the train at two or three o'clock in the morning, finding the cars locked and guarded until the ladies should all be seated, and compelled to wait perhaps an hour, in the cold, for them to be opened.

CHAPTER LXIII.

IN AND ABOUT ATLANTA.

THE railroad runs eastward from Montgomery, forks at Opelika, and enters Georgia by two divergent routes, — the south branch crossing the Chattahoochee at Columbus, and the north branch at West Point.

Wilson, the Raider, paid his respects to both these roads. The main body of his troops proceeded to Columbus, (one of the principal towns of Georgia,) which they carried by assault, with a loss of but thirty men, capturing fifteen hundred prisoners, twenty-four pieces of artillery, and immense military stores. At the same time Lagrange's Brigade took West Point. These were the closing battles of the great war of the rebellion. Pushing on towards Macon, Wilson's advance was met, not by bloody opposition, but by a flag of truce announcing the surrender of Lee and the armistice between Sherman and Johnston.

Concerning our loss at West Point I was not able to obtain very exact information. A citizen, who claimed to have been in the fight, said to me, "We had seven men killed, and we just slaughtered over three hundred Yankees." A negro said: "I saw five dead Yankees, and if there was any more nobody knows what was done with 'em." A returned Confederate soldier, who regarded with great contempt the little affair the citizens bragged so much about, said it was no fight at all; the militia gave up the fort almost without a struggle; and there were not over a dozen men killed on both sides. The fort was situated on a high hill; and one old man, who was in it, told me they could not hold it because they could n't use the guns effectively, — they "could n't elevate 'em down enough."

The Yankees had the credit of behaving very well at West Point. "They were going to burn the railroad depot, full of rolling stock; but a lady told 'em that would set her house, so they just run the cars off down the track, over a hundred of 'em, and fired 'em there," — the black ruins remaining to attest the fact.

Leaving West Point at noon I reached Atlanta at seven o'clock in the evening. It was a foggy night; the streets were not lighted, the hotels were full, and the mud, through which I tramped from one to the other, with a dark guide and a very dark lantern, was ankle deep on the crossings. I was at length fortunate enough to find lodgings, with a clergyman and a cotton-speculator, in an ancient tavern-room, where we were visited all night by troops of rats, scampering across the floor, rattling newspapers, and capering over our beds. In the morning, it was discovered that the irreverent rogues had stolen the clergyman's stockings.

A sun-bright morning did not transmute the town into a place of very great attractiveness. Everywhere were ruins and rubbish, mud and mortar and misery. The burnt streets were rapidly rebuilding; but in the mean while hundreds of the inhabitants, white and black, rendered homeless by the destruction of the city, were living in wretched hovels, which made the suburbs look like a fantastic encampment of gypsies or Indians. Some of the negro huts were covered entirely with ragged fragments of tin-roofing from the burnt government and railroad buildings. Others were constructed partly of these irregular blackened patches, and partly of old boards, with roofs of huge, warped, slouching shreds of tin, kept from blowing away by stones placed on the top. Notwithstanding the ingenuity displayed in piecing these rags together, they formed but a miserable shelter at the best. "In dry weather, it's good as anybody's houses. But they leaks right bad when it rains; then we have to pile our things up to keep 'em dry." So said a colored mother of six children, whose husband was killed "fighting for de Yankees," and who supported her family of little ones by washing. "Sometimes I gits along tolerable ; sometimes right slim ; but dat's de way wid everybody ; — times is powerful hard right now."

Every business block in Atlanta was burned, except one. The railroad machine-shops, the founderies, the immense rolling-mill, the tent, pistol, gun-carriage, shot-and-shell factories, and storehouses, of the late Confederacy, disappeared in flames and explosions. Half a mile of the principal street was destroyed. Private residences remained, with a few exceptions. The wooden houses of the suburbs had been already torn down, and their materials used to construct quarters for Sherman's men. The African Methodist Episcopal Church, built by the colored people with their hard earnings, and viewed by them with as much pride and satisfaction as the Jews felt in the contemplation of the great Temple at Jerusalem, was also demolished by our soldiers, — at the instigation, it is said, of a white citizen living near, who thought the negro's religious shoutings a nuisance.

"When I came back in May," said a refugee, "the city was nothing but piles of brick and ruins. It did n't seem it could ever be cleared. But in six weeks new blocks began to spring up, till now you see more stores actually in operation than we ever had before."

The new business blocks were mostly one-story structures, with cheap temporary roofs, designed to be rebuilt and raised in more prosperous times. Nine stores of this description had just been put up by a Connecticut man ; each costing three thousand dollars, and renting for twenty-five hundred. "He run a rolling-mill for the Confederate Government during the war ; sold out when Sherman was coming ; called himself a good Union man ; — a mighty shrewd fellow!" said one who knew him.

Here and there, between the new buildings, were rows of shanties used as stores, and gaps containing broken walls and heaps of rubbish.

Rents were enormous. Fifteen and twenty dollars a month were charged for huts which a respectable farmer would hardly consider good enough for his swine. One man had crowded into his backyard five of these little tenements, which rented for fifteen dollars a month each, and a very small brick house that let for thirty dollars. Other speculators were permitting the construction, on their premises, of houses that were to be occupied rent-free, for one year, by the poor families that built them, and afterwards to revert to the owners of the land.

The destitution among both white and black refugees was very great. Many of the whites had lost everything by the war; and the negroes that were run off by their masters in advance of Sherman's army, had returned to a desolate place, with nothing but the rags on their backs. As at nearly every other town of any note in the South which I visited, the small-pox was raging at Atlanta, chiefly among the blacks, and the suffering poor whites.

I stopped to talk with an old man building a fence before the lot containing the ruins of his burnt house. He said: "The Yankees did n't generally burn private dwellings. It's my opinion these were set by our own citizens, that remained after Sherman's order that all women who had relatives in the Southern army should go South, and all males must leave the city except them that would work for government. I put for Chattanooga. My house was plundered, and I reckon, burnt, by my own neighbors, — for I 've found some of my furniture in their houses. Some that stayed acted more honorably; they put out fires that had been set, and saved both houses and property. My family is now living in that shebang there. It was formerly my stable. The weather-boards had been ripped off, but I fixed it up the best I could to put my little 'uns in till we can do better."

Another old man told me the story of his family's sufferings, with tears running down his cheeks. "During the battle of July, I had typhoid fever in my house. One of my daughters died, and my other three were down with it. The cemeteries were being shelled, and I had to take out my dead child and bury her hastily in my backyard. My house was in range of the shells; and there my daughters lay, too sick to be moved." His description of those terrible days I shall not repeat. At length his neighbors came with ambulances, and the sick daughters were removed. They were scarcely out of the house when a shell passed through it.

Walking out, one Sunday afternoon, to visit the fortifications, I stopped to look at a negro's horse, which had been crippled by a nail in his foot. While I was talking with the owner, a white man and two negroes, who had been sitting by a fire in an open rail-cabin close by, conversing on terms of perfect equality, came out to take part in the consultation, around the couch of the sick beast. One proffered one remedy ; another, another.

" If ye had some tare," said the white man (meaning tar) ; — " open his huf, and bile tare and pour int' it."

His lank frame and slouching dress, — his sallow visage, with its sickly, indolent expression, — his lazy, spiritless movements, and the social intimacy that appeared to exist between him and the negroes, indicated that he belonged to the class known as " Sand Hillers " in South Carolina, " Clay-eaters " in North Carolina, " Crackers " in Georgia, and " white trash " and " poor whites " everywhere. Among all the individuals of this unfortunate and most uninteresting class, whom I have seen, I do not remember a specimen better worth describing. I give his story in his own words.

He told me his name was Jesse Wade. " I lived down in Cobb," (that is, Cobb County,) — seating himself on the neap of the negro's wagon, and mechanically scraping the mud from it with his thumb-nail. " I was a Union man, I was that, like my daddy befo'e me. Thar was no use me bein' a fule 'case my neighbors was. The Rebel army treated us a heap wus 'n Sherman did. I refugeed, — left everything keer o' my wife. I had four bales o' cotton, and the Rebs burnt the last bale. I had hogs, and a mule, and a hoss, and they tuk all. They did n't leave my wife narry bedquilt. When they 'd tuk what they wanted, they put her out the house and sot fire to 't. Narry one o' my boys fit agin the Union ; they was conscripted with me, and one night we went out on guard together, we did, and jest put for the Yankees. All the men that had a little property went in for the wa', but the po' people was agin it. Sherman was up yer to Kenesaw Mountain then, and I left, I did, to jine him."

Wade claimed to have acted as a scout, and referred me to the quartermaster : " This one that 's yer," (the quartermaster at Atlanta,) " you ax him what Wade done, if you don't reckon I tell the truth." He pronounced the division of the Federal forces a great stroke of strategy. " Atter we split the army, the Rebels could n't hold us no hack."

He was very poor. " I 've got two hosses and a wagon, and I should n't have them if Sherman had n't gin 'em tu me." He held up his feet, and looked at his toes protruding through great gaps in his shoes. " I kain't git money enough to buy me a new pair, to save my life."

" I beat ye, then," said the owner of the crippled horse, showing a very good pair of boots.

" *You* 're drayin'," said Wade. " *I* haul. I 'm gittin' wood to the halves. The owner 's as strong an old secessioner as ever lived. I kain't make but tu loads a day, and one 's mine, and one 's the feller's ; I give one load for t' other. Takes me three loads to git a cord ; I git a dollar and a half, and some-time tu, for a load. I 've got one boy that helps, — he 's about as high as hand boy standin' hander," (yond' boy standing yonder,) — pointing to a negro lad of fourteen.

I asked Wade how old he was. " I 'm in my fifty-one year old," he replied ; " and thar 's eight on us in the family, and tu hosses."

I inquired concerning education in his county. "Thar 's a heap o' po' men in Cobb that kain't read nor write. I 'm one. I never went to skule narry time, and I was alluz so tight run I never could send my chil'n, only 'tween crap time."

" What do you mean by ' *'tween crap time* ' ? "

" When I 'd laid by my crap," (that is, stopped hoeing it, as corn,) " till fodder pullin'. I alluz had to make a little cotton, to keep up. I could alluz rent land befo'e the wa', by givin' half to the owners, — them a pound o' cotton, and me a pound o' cotton ; them a load and me a load. That 's tu much ; but

I kain't git it for that now. You might as well try to git their eyes as their land."

Wade's theory of reconstruction was simple, and expressed in few words : " We should tuk the land, as we did the niggers, and split it, and gin part to the niggers and part to me and t' other Union fellers. They 'd have had to submit to it, as they did to the niggers." I also found the freedmen, who had gathered about us, unanimously of this opinion.

" Wade," I said, " you 're a candid man : now tell me which you think will do the most work, — a white man, or a nigger ? "

" The nigger," said Wade, surprised at so simple a question.

" Do you mean to say that one of these black men will do more work than you ? "

" Yes, sho'e," (sure.)

" What 's the reason of that ? "

" 'Case they was allus put mo'e at ıt."

He went on to complain that he could n't always get pay for the work he did. " A man owes me money for wood. If he don't pay me soon, I 'll take a stick and beat it out on him."

" That 'll be to work for it twict, and not git it then," observed a negro, very wisely ; and I trust Wade was persuaded not to try the stick.

" Ought to have such laws yer as dey has up in Tennessee," said another negro. " Dar you 'd git yer money ! Laws is strick in Tennessee ! Ebery man chalks a line up dar. A man owes you money, de probo' marshal make him toe de line. I 's been round, since de wa' busted, and I han't seen no whar laws like dey got up dar in Tennessee."

By this time a large number of negroes had assembled on the spot, dressed in their Sunday clothes ; and such an animated discussion of their political rights ensued, that, concluding I had strayed by mistake into an out-door convention of the freed people, I quietly withdrew, — followed by my friend Wade, who wished to know if I could accommodate him to a " chaw of tobacker."

Atlanta is the centre of a " perfect crow's-foot of railroads,"

CONVENTION OF FREEDMEN DISCUSSING THEIR POLITICAL RIGHTS.

which have given it its business and military importance. The Western and Atlantic Road, connecting it with Chattanooga, forms a main trunk, with tributaries running into it from all parts of the North and West, and with branches from Atlanta running to all parts of the South. This road was constructed by the State, which in past years derived from it a large revenue. The war left it in a bad condition, with a dilapidated track, and merely temporary bridges in place of those which had been destroyed; — without machine-shops, or materials for the repair of what little remained of the old, worn-out rolling-stock. A purchase of four hundred thousand dollars' worth of indispensable stock from the government, had sufficed to put it in operation, and it was contributing something, by its earnings, towards the great outlay still necessary to refurnish it and place it in thorough repair. The other railroads in the State, built by private companies, were nearly all doing well, by reason of the great amount of freight and travel passing over them. Those destroyed by Sherman belonged to corporations which could best afford to rebuild them; and work upon them was going forward with considerable vigor. All these roads had heavy claims against the Confederate Government; some of them amounting to several millions.

Georgia, before the war, had over twelve hundred miles of railroad in operation, forming the most extensive and complete system south of Tennessee and Virginia, — Alabama having but five hundred miles, and Mississippi seven hundred.

The best of the old Georgia banks were connected with the railroads. The bills of the Georgia Railroad and Banking Company were still worth, after the war had swept over the State, ninety-five per cent. of their par value. Those of the Central Railroad and Banking Company were selling for about the same. The issues of the other banks were worth from five to seventy-five per cent.; the stock being sacrificed.

CHAPTER LXIV.

DOWN IN MIDDLE GEORGIA.

As my first view of Atlanta was had on a dismal night, (if view it could be called,) so my last impression of it was received on a foggy morning, which showed me, as I sat in the cars of the Macon train, waiting at the depot, groups of rain-drenched negroes around out-door fires ; the dimly seen trees of the Park ; tall ruins looming through the mist ; Masonic Hall standing alone (having escaped destruction) ; squat wooden buildings of recent, hasty construction, beside it ; windrows of bent railroad iron by the track ; piles of brick ; a small mountain of old bones from the battle-fields, foul and wet with the drizzle ; a heavy coffin-box, marked " glass," on the platform ; with mud and litter all around.

A tide of negro emigration was at that time flowing westward, from the comparatively barren hills of Northern Georgia to the rich cotton plantations of the Mississippi. Every day anxious planters from the Great Valley were to be met with, inquiring for unemployed freedmen, or returning home with colonies of laborers, who had been persuaded to quit their old haunts by the promise of double wages in a new country. Georgia planters, who raise but a bale of cotton on three, four, or five acres, could not compete with their more wealthy Western neighbors : they higgled at paying their freedmen six or seven dollars a month, while Arkansas and Mississippi men stood ready to give twelve and fifteen dollars; and the expenses of the journey. As it cost no more to transport able-bodied young men and women than the old and the feeble, the former were generally selected and the latter left behind. Thus it happened that an unusually large proportion of poor families remained about Atlanta and other Georgia towns.

There were two such families huddled that morning under
the open shed of the depot. They claimed that they had
been hired by a planter, who had brought them thus far, and,
for some reason, abandoned them. They had been at the
depot a week or more, sleeping in piles of old rags, and sub-
sisting on rations issued to them by the Bureau : stolid-looking
mothers, hardened by field-labor, smoking short black pipes ;
and older children tending younger ones, feeding them out of
tin cups, and rocking them to sleep in their arms. It was
altogether a pitiful sight, — although, but for the rain which
beat in upon them, I might have thought their freely venti-
lated lodgings preferable to some of the tavern-rooms I had
lately slept in. But to me the most noticeable feature of the
scene was the spirit manifested towards these poor creatures
by spectators of my own color.

" That baby's going to die," said one man. " Half your
children will be dead before spring."

" How do you like freedom ? " said another.

" Niggers are fated," said a third. " About one out of fifty
will take care of himself; the rest are gone up."

" The Southern people are the niggers' best friends," resumed the first speaker. " They feel a great deal of sympathy
for them. There are many who give them a heap of good
advice when they leave them."

Good advice is cheap ; but nobody gave these homeless ones
anything else, nor even that, — with a single exception : there
was one who gave them kind words and money, but he was a
Yankee.

The remarks of the ladies in the car were equally edifying.

" How much better they were off with somebody to take
care of 'em ! "

" Oh dear, yes ! I declare it makes me hate an Abolitionist ! "

" The government ought to have given them houses ! " —
(sneeringly.) " If I had seven children to take care of, I 'd
go back and sell 'em to my old master."

" Do see that little bit of a baby ! it 's a-kicking and screaming! I declare, it's white! one of the young Federals', I reckon."

From Atlanta, until within about twenty-five miles of Macon, the railroad runs upon a ridge, from which the waters of the country flow each way, — those of the west side, through the Flint River and the Appalachicola to the Gulf; those of the east, through the Ocmulgee and Altamaha to the Atlantic. The soil of this ridge is sandy, with a mixture of red clay; much of it producing little besides oaks and pines. The doorways of the log-huts and shabby framed houses we passed, were crowded with black, yellow, and sallow-white faces, — women, children, and slatternly, barefoot girls, with long, uncombed hair on their shoulders, — staring at the train. The country is better, a little back from the railroad, as is frequently the case in the South.

Macon, at the head of steamboat navigation on the Ocmulgee River, and the most important interior town in the State, is a place of broad, pleasant streets, with a sandy soil which exempts it from mud. It had in 1860 eight thousand inhabitants. As it was a sort of city of refuge, "where everybody was run to," during the latter years of the war, its population had greatly increased. Hundreds of white refugees from other parts of the country were still crowded into it, having no means of returning to their homes, or having no homes to return to. The corporation of Macon showed little disposition to relieve these unfortunate people, and the destitution and suffering among them were very great. They were kept from starvation by the government. "To get rid of feeding them," said Colonel Lambert, Sub-Assistant-Commissioner of the Freedmen's Bureau, "we are now giving them free transportation wherever they wish to go."

By a recent census, taken with a view to catching vagrants and setting them to work, the colored population of Macon was shown to be four thousand two hundred and seventy-three. "All those who are not now employed will soon be taken by the planters. If any will not hire out, they will be set to earning their living on the public streets. I have now on hand applications from Alabama and Mississippi planters for three hundred laborers; I could fill the orders if I chose to, for the negroes are much disposed to emigrate. But all the freedmen in the counties of my district are needed here, and I encourage them to remain."

Colonel Lambert had on hand sixteen cases of murder and felonious shooting by white persons, negroes being the victims. The seventeenth case was reported from Twiggs County, while I was at Macon. A chivalrous sportsman, apparently for the fun of the thing, took a shot at a negro walking peaceably along the street, and killed him. The Colonel sent out twenty-five mounted men to hunt the murderer; but it was almost impossible to make arrests in such cases. There were in every place unprincipled men who approved the crime and helped to shield the criminal. Warned by them of the approach of blue uniforms, he would betake himself to the canebrakes, or to some friendly garret, where he would lie safely concealed until the scouts had given up their search for him and retired from the neighborhood. These negro-shooters and their accomplices were no doubt a small minority of the people, but they were a very dangerous minority, whom the better class did not deem it prudent to offend by assisting the officers of justice.

Crimes of this description were more or less frequent in districts remote from the military posts. In some places the freedmen were shot down in mere wantonness and malice. In others, the very men who had been wishing them all dead or driven out of the country, had become enraged at seeing them emigrate for higher wages than they were willing to pay, and sworn to kill any that attempted to leave the State.

Said Colonel Lambert: "To prevent these outrages, we need a much greater military force than we have. But the force we have is being reduced by the mustering out of more troops. We are thus prevented from carrying out the intentions of the government; and there is danger that before long the continuance of its authority here will be regarded as a mere farce. What we need is cavalry; but our troops are all

infantry. I mount them in a case of emergency, where some
desperado is to be hunted, by seizing horses at the first livery-
stable, which we return after we have got through with them,
politely thanking the proprietor in the name of the government."

The southwestern part of Georgia is one of the most fertile
sections of the South: it is the region of large plantations and
rich planters. The northern half of the State is comparatively unproductive : it is the region of small planters, and of
farmers who do their own work with the aid of their sons.
Much of the northwestern part is barren. The fertile Southwest suffered little damage from the war; it came out of it with
its plantations unimpaired, and a large stock of cotton on hand.
Northern and Middle Georgia were ploughed with the furrows
of desolation. Sherman's army left nothing in its track but
poverty and ruin. Plantations were wasted, provisions taken,
stock killed or driven away, buildings and farming implements
destroyed. The people were left very poor : they raised no
crops in '65, and a famine was very generally anticipated.

In this condition, all the better class of planters recognized
the sincere efforts of the Freedmen's Bureau to aid them, and
to organize a labor system which should prove beneficial to
both employers and employed. They generally spoke of its
officers with respect ; and many acknowledged that it would
be a great injury to the country to have it immediately removed. Others were bitter in their opposition to it; and I
often heard such remarks as this : " The idea of a *nigger* having the power of bringing a *white man* before a tribunal ! The
Southern people a'n't going to stand that."

The negro of Middle Georgia is a creature in whom the
emotions entirely predominate over the intellectual faculties.
He has little of that shrewdness which town life cultivates in
the black race. The agents of the Bureau complained that
they had sometimes great difficulty in persuading him to act
in accordance with his own interests. If a stranger offered
him twelve dollars a month, and a former master in whom he
had confidence, appealing to his gratitude and affection, offered

him one dollar, he would exclaim impulsively, " I work for you, Mass'r Will!" Sometimes, when he had been induced by his friends to enter a complaint against his master or mistress for wrongs done him, ludicrous and embarrassing scenes occurred in the freedmen's courts. " Now, Thomas," says the good lady, " can you have the heart to speak a word against your old, dear, kind mistress ? " " No, missus, I neber will ! " blubbers Thomas; and that is all the court can get out of him.

The reverence shown by the colored people toward the officers of the Bureau was often amusing. They looked to them for what they had formerly depended upon their masters for. If they had lost a pig, they seemed to think such great and all-powerful men could find it for them without any trouble. They cheered them in the streets, and paid them at all times the most abject respect.

I was told that the blacks were quite as apt to keep their contracts as the whites ; and that often, when they broke them, it was through the persuasion of some planter who lacked laborers. " Look here, Sam, I 'm giving two dollars a month more than this man you are at work for ; why don't you come and live with me ? " A respectable planter was fined a hundred and fifty dollars for this offence, by the Bureau, whilst I was at Macon. " It is one of the worst offences we have to deal with," said Colonel Lambert, " and one that we punish most severely."

It was the popular belief that the agents of the Bureau had control of funds arising from such fines, and that they appropriated them pretty freely to their own use. On the contrary, they were required at the end of each month to make returns and forward all funds on hand to the chief quartermaster of the State, who alone was authorized to apply them in necessary expenditures.

There were four freedmen's schools in Macon, with eleven teachers and a thousand pupils. There was a night-school of two hundred children and adults, where I saw men of my own age learning their letters, (and thought, " What if *I* was now first learning *my* letters?") and gray-haired old men and women forming, with slowness and difficulty, by the aid of spectacles, the first characters in the writing-book. The teachers were furnished by the American Missionary Association, — the freedmen paying for their own books, (an item with the booksellers,) and for the necessary fuel and lights.

Mr. Eddy, the superintendent, and an old experienced teacher, said to me: "The children of these schools have made in a given time more progress in the ordinary branches of education than any white schools I ever taught. In mathematics and the higher sciences they are not so forward. The eagerness of the older ones to learn is a continual wonder to me. The men and women say, 'We work all day, but we'll come to you in the evening for learning, and we want you to make us learn; we're dull, but we want you to beat it into us!'"

I was much interested in a class of young clergymen who recited in the evening to the young matron of the " teachers' home." One of them told me with tears of gratitude how kind and faithful all the teachers had been to them.

" Are you not mistaken?" I said. "I have been told a hundred times that the Southern people are your best friends."

He replied: " Georgia passed a law making it a penitentiary offence, punishable with five years' imprisonment, to teach a slave to read. Now we are no longer slaves, and we are learning to read. They may deceive you, but *we* know who are our best friends."

I was repeatedly assured by earnest secessionists that there were no Union men in Georgia; that, soon or late, all went into the rebellion. But one day I met an old man who denied the charge with indignation.

" I am sixty-five years old. I fought for the spot where Macon now stands, when it was Indian territory. I don't know what they mean by no Union men. If to fight against secession from first to last, and to oppose the war in every way, makes a Union man, I was that. Of course I paid taxes, because I couldn't help it. And when Stoneman

raided on us, and every man that could bear arms was pressed,
I went with the rest, and was all day behind the breastworks.
But I 've always spoke my mind, and being an old citizen, I
never got hung yet. A majority of the people of Macon were
with me, if they had only dared to say so. They hate the
secessionists now worse than they hate the Yankees : no comparison ! The secessionists now cry, ' No party ! ' but never
a party stuck together closer than they do.

" The Confederates," he went on, " injured us ten times
more than the Yankees did. When Wilson came in last
April, he put a guard at my house, who stayed with me seven
weeks, and did his duty faithfully."

CHAPTER LXV.

ANDERSONVILLE.

JUST across the railroad track below Macon, in a pleasant pine grove, is the Fair Ground, where was located that thing of misery known to us as the Macon Prison. It was the " Yankee Prison," down here.

I visited the spot one bright morning after a shower, when the breezes and the sunshine were in the pine-tops overhead. The ground was covered with a thin growth of brown grass, wet with the rain : stepping along which I came suddenly to a quadrangular space, as arid as the hill of Golgotha. No marks were necessary to show where the stockade had stood, with its elevated scaffolding on which walked the Rebel guard. The stockade had been removed ; but the blasted and barren earth remained to testify of the homesick feet that had trodden it into dreary sterility.

A little stream runs through a hollow below the Fair Ground, carrying off much of the filth of the town. From that stream our prisoners drank. The tub set in the side of the bank at the foot of the hill, and the ditch that conducted into it the water for their use, were still there. Guarded, they came down from the stockade, to this tub, of the contents of which they were not always permitted to have enough. " I used to hear 'em yell for water," said a negro living near. " I was bad off as a slave, but I never begun to be so bad off as they was. Some of 'em had no shoes for winter, and almost no clothes."

In the pine woods on the hill above the area of the stockade is " Death's Acre," — the prison burying-ground, enclosed by a plain board fence, and containing little rows of humble graves marked with stakes, and numbered. I noticed numbers as high as two hundred and thirty. How many national soldiers lie buried in this lot I do not know.

I shall not dwell upon the sufferings endured by the inmates of this prison. They shrink into insignificance compared with the horrors of the great military prison of Georgia and the South. Neither of these do I purpose to say much. Enough, and more than enough has been spoken and written about them. The infamy of Andersonville is world-wide.

Passing through Washington in August, 1865, I one morning looked into the hot and steaming court-room where Captain Henry Wirz was on trial. In a somewhat worn broadcloth coat, with his counsel at his side occasionally whispering him, his elbow on a table, and his thin uneasy hand fingering his dark beard or supporting his chin; attenuated, bent, and harassed with the most terrible anxieties, — for, however indifferent he may have been to the lives of other and better men, there was one life to which he was not indifferent, and which was now at stake; down-looking for the most part, but frequently glancing his quick sharp eye at the court or the witnesses; there sat the miserable man, listening to minutely detailed accounts of the atrocities of which he had been the instrument. The cause he had served with such savage fidelity, had perished; and the original authors of the enormities he had been employed to commit, stalked at large, or lay in temporary confinement, confidently expecting the executive clemency; while this wretched hireling, whose sin consisted in having done their work too well, was to suffer, not the just for the unjust, but the guilty dog for the still more guilty masters.

Fifty-eight miles below Macon, by the Southwestern Railroad, is the scene of the crimes against humanity for which Henry Wirz was punished with death. The place is set down as *Anderson* on maps and in guide-books; and that is the name by which it was known to the inhabitants of the country, until the immense hideous business the war brought to it dignified it with the title of *ville*.

It is a disagreeable town, with absolutely no point of interest about it except the prison. Before the war it had but five buildings : a church without a steeple ; a small railroad depot ; a little framed box in which was the country post-office ; and two dwellings, — a log-cabin, and a house with a saw- and grist-mill attached. There were other dwellings within a mile.

Such was Anderson. Anderson*ville* contains some forty additional cheap-looking, unpainted buildings, of various sizes, all of which were constructed with reference to the prison ; such as officers' houses, large or small according to the rank of the occupants, government storehouses, hospital buildings, (for the troops on duty,) and so forth. The hospital is now used as a hotel. The entire aspect and atmosphere of the place are ugly and repulsive.

The village lies on the railroad and west of it. Between a third and one half of a mile east of it, is the prison.

The space enclosed by the rough stockade contains twenty-five acres, divided by a sluggish stream flowing through it. It looks like a great horse-yard. Much of the land is swampy, but the rest is elevated, rising on the south side gradually, and on the north side quite steeply from the brook. It was from this shallow stream, defiled with refuse from the camp of the Georgia Reserves, which it received before entering the stockade, that the thirty thousand prisoners, who were sometimes crowded into this broken oblong space, drew their chief supply of water. There were a few little springs in the banks, very precious to them.

The walls of the stockade are of upright logs about a foot in diameter, twenty feet high above the ground, in which they are set close together, deep enough to be kept firmly in their position. There are an outer and an inner wall of this description, with a space some fifty yards in breadth between them. There were sentry-boxes for the soldiers on guard, hung like birds'-nests near the top of the inner wall. These were reached by ladders. For further security, the stockade was partly surrounded by a deep ditch ; and on portions of two sides there is an unfinished third line of upright logs.

The outer wall of the stockade has but one entrance.

Through this the newly arrived prisoners were marched, and along the space between the two walls, to one of two gates which gave admission to the interior of the prison. How many thousands of brave and stalwart soldiers entered these infernal doors, from which only ghostly skeleton-men, or the corpses of skeleton-men, ever issued forth again!

The prisoners were of course confined within the inner wall. And not only so, but they were prevented from approaching within twenty feet of it by the dead line. Or if not prevented, — for much of the way this fatal boundary was marked only by posts set at intervals of six or seven yards, — he who, in blindness and sickness and despair, perhaps jostled out of his way by the blind, sick, despairing multitude crowded within, set his foot one inch beyond the strict limits, as some Rebel on guard chose to *imagine* them, crack went a musket, a light puff of smoke curled up from one of the birds'-nests, and the poor wretch lay in his blood, groaning out the last of many groans, which ended his long misery.

I learned that when the stockade was first built the ground it encloses was covered with forest-trees. Why were they not left — at least a few of them — to bless with their cooling shade the unfortunate captives, in the heat of those terrible prison summers? Not a tree remained. Near by were forests of beautiful timber, to which they were not even permitted to go and cut wood for fuel and huts.

One can imagine nothing more dreary and disheartening than the interior view of the stockade as it is to-day, except the stockade as it was during the war. The holes in which the prisoners burrowed for protection from the weather, have been mostly destroyed by the washing rains. Nearly all the huts are in ruins. The barrack sheds, in which but a mere handful of the thirty thousand prisoners could find place, still remain, marked with sad relics, — bunks with the names of the occupants cut upon them, or fragments of benches, knives, old pipes, and old shoes.

Between the outer and inner walls were the bakehouse, the pen for sick-call, and the log-sheds in which the stocks were kept. The cookhouse was outside.

Besides the great stockade, there was a small stockade for officers, and a hospital stockade containing some eight acres, and surrounded by upright logs ten or twelve feet high.

In pleasant pine woods, about a hundred rods north of the stockade, is the original burying-ground of the Andersonville prison, enlarged and converted into a national cemetery since the war. A whitewashed picket-fence encloses a square space of near fifty acres, divided into four main sections by two avenues crossing it and cutting each other at right angles. Two of these sections — those south of the east-and-west road — are subdivided by alleys into five smaller sections, where the dead lie in long, silent rows, by hundreds. Here are about seven thousand graves. The northeast quarter of the cemetery is undivided; and here, in a single vast encampment, sleep five thousand men. There are in all near thirteen thousand graves, each with its little white head-board commemorating the name, rank, company, regiment, and date of death, of its inmate. The records show that the first death occurred on February 27th, 1864, and the last on April 28th, 1865. From April 1st, 1864, to April 1st, 1865, the average rate of mortality was over a thousand a month. It sometimes reached a hundred a day.

Apart from the rest, in the northwestern corner of the cemetery, are the graves of the Georgia Reserves who died while on duty here, — one hundred and fifteen out of four regiments. The mortality among them appears also to have been great; and indeed one cannot conceive how it should be otherwise, living as they did within the pestiferous influence of the prison atmosphere.

At the entrance to the cemetery, on the south side, appears the following inscription, — the same I noticed above the graves at Spottsylvania, and which might with propriety be placed before every national soldiers' cemetery : —

> " On Fame's eternal camping-ground
> Their silent tents are spread,
> And Glory guards with solemn round
> The bivouac of the dead."

At the alley-crossings stand the following : —

> " The hopes, the fears, the blood, the tears,
>   That marked the battle strife,
>   Are now all crowned by Victory
>   That saved the Nation's life."

> " Whether in the prison drear,
>   Or in the battle's van,
>   The fittest place for man to die,
>   Is where he dies for man."

> " A thousand battle-fields have drunk
>   The blood of warriors brave,
>   And countless homes are dark and drear
>   In the land they died to save."

> " Then shall the dust
>   Return to the earth as it was ;
>   And the spirit shall return
>   Unto God who gave it."

Over the encampment of five thousand is raised the following : —

> " Through all Rebellion's horrors
>   Bright shines our Nation's fame :
>   Our gallant soldiers, perishing,
>   Have won a deathless name."

At the intersection of the avenues rises the flag-staff planted here by Miss Clara Barton's party, who laid out the Cemetery Grounds in the summer of 1865. Here, on the soil of Georgia, above the graves of our dead, waves the broad symbol of the Nation's power and victory; while all round this sanctified ground stand the ancient pines, Nature's serene and solemn priesthood, waving their green arms, and murmuring softly, by day and all through the starry night, — whilst thou, O mother! O wife! art mourning in thy desolated Northern home, — the requiems of the weary ones at rest.

The Rebel owner of the land occupied by the prison had been pardoned by the President; and I learned of the Freedmen's Bureau that he had asked for the restoration of his property, — demanding even that the cemetery grounds should be turned over to him.

In conclusion I may state that citizens of Georgia, living at a distance from Andersonville, said to me that they knew of the atrocities permitted there at the time of their occurrence, and that they did not think it possible for the Rebel leaders to have been ignorant of them.

CHAPTER LXVI.

SHERMAN IN MIDDLE GEORGIA.

ACCORDING to a tradition which I found current in Middle Georgia, General Sherman remarked, while on his grand march through the State, that he had his gloves on as yet, but that he should take them off in South Carolina. Afterwards, in North Carolina, I heard the counterpart of this story. As soon as he had crossed the State line, " Boys," said he to his soldiers, " remember we are in the old North State now; " which was equivalent to putting his gloves on again.

At the mere mention of these anecdotes, however, many good Georgians and North Carolinians blazed up with indignation : " If he had his gloves on here, I should like to know what he did with his gloves off ! " — and it was not easy to convince them that they had suffered less than their neighbors in South Carolina.

A Confederate brigadier-general said to me : " One could track the line of Sherman's march all through Georgia and South Carolina by the fires on the horizon. He burned the gin-houses, cotton-presses, railroad depots, bridges, freight-houses, and unoccupied dwellings, with some that were occupied. He stripped our people of everything. He deserves to be called the Great Robber of the nineteenth century. He did a sort of retail business in North Carolina, but it was a wholesale business, and no mistake, in Georgia, though perhaps not quite so smashing as his South Carolina operations."

Confederate soldiers delight in criticisms and anecdotes of this famous campaign. Here are two or three samples.

" When we were retreating before old Sherman, he sent word to Johnston that he wished he would leave just a horse-shoe, or something to show where he had been. Hood always left enough; but Johnston licked the ground clean behind him."

" Did n't we have high old times laying in the water, nights when we had a chance to lay down at all! I remember, one of our boys was told he must move his position, one night, after we 'd just got comfortably settled down in the wet. Says he, ' I 've got my water hot, and I be d——d if I 'm going to move for anybody ! ' "

" The approach to Savannah was defended by splendid, proud forts, bristling with long old cannon, and our cowardly militia just run from them without firing a shot ! "

" You should have seen Washington's statue, at Columbia, after Sherman burned the city ! Nose broke, eyes bunged, face black and blue, and damaged miscellaneously, the Father of his Country looked like he 'd been to an Irish wedding."

The citizens talked with equal freedom, but with less hilarity, of the doings of the " Great Robber." A gentleman of Jones County said : —

" I had a nob field of corn, not yet harvested. Old Sherman came along, and turned his droves of cattle right into it, and in the morning there was no more corn there than there is on the back of my hand. His devils robbed me of all my flour and bacon and corn meal. They took all the pillow-slips, ladies' dresses, drawers, chemises, sheets, and bed-quilts, they could find in the house, to tie up their plunder in. You could n't hide anything but they 'd find it. I sunk a cask of molasses in a hog-wallow; that I think I should have saved, but a nigger boy the rascals had with 'em said he 'lowed there was something hid there ; so he went to feeling with a stick, and found the molasses. Then they just robbed my house of every pail, cup, dish, what-not, that they could carry molasses off to their camping-ground in. After they 'd broke open the cask, and took what they wanted, they left the rest to run in a river along the ground. There was one sweet hog-wallow, if there never was another ! "

A lady, living near Milledgeville, was the president of a soldiers' aid society. At the time of Sherman's visit she had in her house a dry-goods box full of stockings knit by the fair hands of patriotic ladies for the feet of the brave defenders of their country. This box she caused to be buried in a field which was afterwards ploughed, in order to obliterate all marks of its concealment. A squadron of cavalry arriving at this field, formed in line, charged over it, and discovered the box by a hollow sound it gave forth under the hoofs of the horses. The box was straightway brought to light, to the joy of many a stockingless invader, who had the fair ladies of Milledgeville to thank for his warm feet that winter.

The Yankees took special delight in killing dogs, many an innocent cur having to atone with his life for the sins committed by bloodhounds used in hunting down negroes, conscripts, and escaped Yankee prisoners.

Sherman's field-orders show that it was not his intention to permit indiscriminate destruction and plundering.[1] Yet these

---

[1] See, in *Special Field-Orders, No.* 120, issued Nov. 24th, 1864, the following paragraphs: —

" IV. The army will *forage liberally on the country during the march.* To this end, each brigade commander will organize a good and sufficient foraging party, under the command of one or more discreet officers, who will gather near the route travelled corn or forage of any kind, meat of any kind, vegetables or corn-meal or whatever is needed by the command; aiming at all times to keep in the wagon trains *at least ten days' provisions for the command, and three days' forage. Soldiers must not enter the dwellings* of the inhabitants, or commit any trespass during the halt or a camp; they may be permitted to gather turnips, potatoes, and other vegetables, and drive in stock in front of their camps. To regular foraging parties must be intrusted the gathering of provisions and forage at any distance from the road travelled.

" V. To army-corps commanders is intrusted the power *to destroy mills, houses, cotton-gins, &c.*, and for them this general principle is laid down: In districts and neighborhoods *where the army is unmolested no destruction* of such property should be permitted; but should guerillas or bushwhackers molest our march, or should the inhabitants burn bridges, obstruct roads, or otherwise manifest local hostility, then army-corps commanders should order and *enforce a devastation more or less relentless according to the measure of such hostility.*

" VI. As for horses, mules, wagons, &c., belonging to the inhabitants, the cavalry and artillery may appropriate freely and without limit, discriminating, however, between the rich, who are usually hostile, and the poor or industrious, usually neutral or friendly. Foraging parties may also take mules or horses to replace the jaded animals of their trains, or to serve as pack-mules for the regiments or brigades. In all foraging, of whatever kind, the parties engaged will refrain from abusive or threatening language, and may, when the officer in command thinks proper, give written certificates of the facts, but no receipts; and they will endeavor to leave with each family a reasonable portion for their maintenance."

orders appear to have been interpreted by his men very liberally. A regiment was usually sent ahead with instructions to
guard private dwellings ; but as soon as the guards were removed, a legion of stragglers and negroes rushed in to pillage ; and I am convinced that in some cases even the guards
pilfered industriously.

Wilson's men, when they seized fresh horses for their use,
turned the jaded ones loose in the country. Sherman's army-
corps acted on a different principle. The deliberate aim
seemed to be to *leave no stock whatever in the line of march.*
Whenever fresh horses were taken, the used-up animals
were shot. Such also was the fate of horses and mules found
in the country, and not deemed worth taking. The best herds
of cattle were driven off ; inferior herds were slaughtered in
the fields, and left. A company of soldiers would shoot down
a drove of hogs, cut out the hind-quarters, and abandon what
remained.

" The Federal army generally behaved very well in this
State," said a Confederate officer. " I don't think there was
ever an army in the world that would have behaved better, on
a similar expedition, in an enemy's country. Our army certainly would n't. The destruction of railroads, mills, and gin-
houses, if designed to cripple us, was perfectly justifiable.

" But you did have as mean a set of stragglers following
your army as ever broke jail. I 'll do you the credit to say,
though, that there were more foreigners than Yankees among
them.

" A lot of these rascals came to my house, and just about
turned it inside out. They would n't wait for my wife to give
them the keys of the bureau, but smashed in the drawers
with the butts of their muskets, and emptied them.

" My sister, living near me, gave her plate and valuables,
locked up in a trunk, to a negro, who took it and hid it in the
woods. Then, to avoid suspicion, he joined the Yankees, and
was gone with 'em several days. She felt great anxiety about
the trunk, until one morning he came home, by the way of
the woods, grinning, with the trunk on his shoulder.

" My wife did like my sister. She gave her money and plate to a negro, who hid it ; but he did n't get off so well as the other darkey. The Yankees suspected him, and threatened to hang him if he did n't give it up. They got the rope around his neck, and actually did string him up, till they found he would die sooner than tell, when they let him down again.

" Your fellows hung several men in my neighborhood, to make 'em tell where their money was. Some gave it up after a little hanging ; but I know one man who went to the limb three times, and saved his money, and his life too. Another man had three hundred dollars in gold hid in his garden. He is very fat ; weighs, I suppose, two hundred and fifty pounds. He held out till they got the rope around his neck, then he caved in. ' I 'm dogged,' says he, ' if I 'm going to risk my weight on a rope around my neck, just for a little money ! ' "

An old gentleman in Putnam County, near Eatonton, related the following : —

" Sherman's men gave my son-in-law sut ! He had made that year thirty-two hundred gallons of syrup, — more than he had casks for ; so he sunk a tank in the ground, and buried it. The Yankee soldiers all came and helped themselves to it. He had the finest flower-garden in the country ; they made his own slaves scatter salt, and corn-on-the-cob, all over it, then they turned their horses on, and finished it. They made my own daughter wait on them at table. She said she kept servants for such work ; but they replied : ' You are none too good.' They robbed all the houses through here of all the jewels, watches, trinkets, and hard metals the people did n't put out of their way ; and stripped us of our bedding and clothing."

Sherman's invasion of the South cannot properly be called a raid : even Wilson's brilliant expedition with twelve thousand cavalry is belittled by that epithet.

Sherman had under his command four infantry corps and a corps of cavalry, pursuing different routes, their caterpillar tracks sometimes crossing each other, braiding a belt of devastation from twenty-five to fifty miles in breadth, and upwards of six hundred miles in extent. The flanking parties driving the light-footed Rebel cavalry before them ; bridges fired by the fugitives ; pontoon trains hurrying to the front of the advancing columns, when streams were to be crossed ; the hasty corduroying of bad roads ; the jubilant foraging parties sweeping the surrounding country of whatever was needful to support life and vigor in those immense crawling and bristling creatures, called army-corps ; the amazing quantity and variety of plunder collected together on the routes of the wagon-trains, — the soldiers sitting proudly on their heaped-up stores, as the trains approached, then, in lively fashion, thrusting portions into each wagon as it passed, — for no halt was allowed ; the 'ripping up of railroads, the burning and plundering of plantations ; the encampment at evening, the kindling of fires, the sudden disappearance of fences, and the equally sudden springing up of shelter-tents, like mushrooms, all over the ground ; the sleep of the vast, silent, guarded hosts ; and the hilarious awakening to the toil and adventures of a new day ; such are the scenes of this most momentous expedition, which painters, historians, romancers, will in future ages labor to conceive and portray.

Warned by the flying cavalry, and the smoke and flames of plantations on the horizon, the panic-stricken inhabitants thought only of saving their property and their lives from the invaders. Many fled from their homes, carrying with them the most valuable of their possessions, or those which could be most conveniently removed. Mules, horses, cattle, sheep, hogs, were driven wildly across the country, avoiding one foraging party perhaps only to fall into the hands of another. The mother caught up her infant ; the father, mounting, took his terrified boy upon the back of his horse behind him ; the old man clutched his money-bag and ran ; not even the poultry, not even the dogs were forgotten ; men and women shouldering their household stuffs, and abandoning their houses to the mercies of the soldiers, whose waving banners and bright steel were already appearing on the distant hill-tops.

FLEEING BEFORE SHERMAN'S GRAND MARCH.

Such panic flights were often worse than useless. Woe unto that house which was found entirely deserted! To the honor of Southern housewives be it recorded, that the majority of them remained to protect their homes, whilst their husbands and slaves ran off the live stock from the plantations.

The flight from Milledgeville, including the stampede of the Rebel State legislators, who barely escaped being entrapped by our army, — the crushing of passengers and private effects into the overloaded cars, the demand for wheeled vehicles, and the exorbitant prices paid for them, the fright, the confusion, the separation of families, — formed a scene which neither the spectators nor the actors in it will soon forget.

The negroes had all along been told that if they fell into the hands of the Yankees they would be worked to death on fortifications, or put into the front of the battle and shot if they did not fight, or sent to Cuba and sold ; and that the old women and young children would be drowned like cats and blind puppies. And now the masters showed their affection for these servants by running off the able-bodied ones, who were competent to take care of themselves, and leaving the aged, the infirm, and the children, to the "cruelties" of the invaders. The manner in which the great mass of the remaining negro population received the Yankees, showed how little they had been imposed upon by such stories, and how true and strong their faith was in the armed deliverance which Providence had ordained for their race.

CHAPTER LXVII.

PLANTATION GLIMPSES.

In travelling through the South one sees many plantations ruined for some years to come by improper cultivation. The land generally washes badly, and where the hill-sides have been furrowed up and down, instead of being properly "horizontalized," the rains plough them into gulleys, and carry off the cream of the soil. Or perhaps neglect, during four years of war, has led to the same result. Many worn-out plantations are in this condition, the gulleys cutting the slopes into ridges and chasms.

In Georgia, as in parts of Alabama, one becomes weary of tracts of poor-looking country, overgrown with sedge-grass, or covered with oaks and pines. The roads, never good, in bad weather are frightful. Never a church steeple relieves the monotony of the landscape. Occasionally there is a village, its houses appearing to be built upon props. If standing upon a ridge above the highway or railroad by which you pass, the sight of the blue sky *under* them gives them a singular appearance.

It is customary, all through the South, to build country-houses in this manner, and rarely with cellars. The props, which are sometimes of brick, but oftener of fat pine, which makes an underpinning almost as durable as brick, lift the building a few feet from the earth and allow a free circulation of air under it. This peculiarity, which strikes a stranger as unnecessary, is not so. A Northern man of my acquaintance, settled in North Carolina, told me that he built his house in the New-England style, with a close underpinning; but soon discovered that the dampness of the earth was causing the lower timbers to rot badly. By opening the underpinning, and ventilating the foundation, he succeeded in checking the decay. Let Northern men emigrating to the South take a hint from his experience. No doubt many Southern customs, which appear to us irrational or useless, will thus be found to have originated in common sense and necessity.

I was too late to see the cotton-picking, and too early for the chopping-out and hoeing, but in season to witness the preparation of the ground for planting. Sometimes, in a gang of fifty or sixty laborers running as many ploughs on the fields of a large plantation, there would be twenty or thirty women and strong girls. The sight of so many ploughs in motion, each drawn by a single mule, and scratching its narrow furrow three inches deep, was of itself interesting; and the presence with the ploughmen of the stout black ploughwomen added to it a certain picturesqueness.

I have already related how my ignorance was enlightened with regard to the manufacture of ploughs on Alabama plantations. I afterwards saw the blacksmiths at work upon these somewhat rude implements, and learned that some of the larger plantations manufactured their own carts and wagons. The plantation harness is a simple affair, and is nearly always made on the place. While the negro women are spinning and weaving cloth in rainy weather, the men are bending hames, braiding mule-collars of corn husks, and making back-bands of leather or bagging.

I found that some of the large plantations had, besides a white superintendent, two black overseers, — one whose sole business was to take care of the ploughs and hoes, and one who looked after the mules and other live stock.

The buildings of a first-class plantation form a little village by themselves. There is first the planter's house, which is commonly a framed dwelling of good size, with two or four brick chimneys built outside. There is not a closet in the house. The pantry and dairy form a separate building. The kitchen is another; and the meat-house still another. Next in importance to the planter's house is the overseer's house. Then come the negro quarters, which, on some plantations I have seen, are very comfortable and neat-looking little framed houses. They are oftener mere huts. A barn is a rare exception. The corn is kept in cribs, and other grain in out-door bins framed with roof-like covers that shut down and lock. Then there are the mule-pens ; the gin-house (if it has not been burned) ; and the mill for crushing sorghum. Orchards are rare, planters thinking of little besides cotton, and living, like their negroes, chiefly on hog and hominy.

Travelling by private conveyance from Eatonton — the northern terminus of the Milledgeville and Eatonton Railroad — over to Madison on the Georgia road, on my way to Augusta, I passed a night at a planter's house of the middle class. It was a plain, one-and-a-half story, unpainted, weather-browned framed dwelling, with a porch in front, and two front windows. The oaken floors were carpetless, but clean swept. The rooms were not done off at all ; there was not a lath, nor any appearance of plastering or whitewash about them. The rafters and shingles of the roof formed the ceiling of the garret-chamber ; the sleepers and boards of the chamber-floor, the ceiling of the sitting-room ; and the undisguised beams, studs, and clapboards of the frame and its covering, composed the walls. The dining-room was a little detached framed box, without a fireplace, and with a single broken window. There was a cupboard, a wardrobe, and a bed in the sitting-room ; a little bedroom leading off from it ; and two beds in the garret.

There was a glowing fire in the fireplace, beside which sat a neatly-attired, fine-looking, but remarkably silent grandmother, taking snuff, or smoking.

The house had three other inmates, — the planter and his wife, and their son, a well-educated young man, who sat in the evening reading " Handy Andy " by the light of pitch-pine chips thrown at intervals upon the oak-wood fire. No candle was lighted except for me, at bed-time.

This, be it understood, was not the house of a small farmer, but of the owner of two plantations, of a thousand acres each. He had fifty-nine negroes before the war.

There was a branch running through his estate, on the

bottom-land of which he could make a bale of cotton to the acre. On the uplands it took three or four acres to make a bale. This year his son had undertaken to run the plantation we were on, while he was to oversee the other.

The young man was far more hopeful of success than his father.

The old man said : " You can't get anything out of the niggers, now they 're free."

" I never knew them to work any better," said the young man.

" Just now they are showing a little spirit, maybe," said the father ; " but it won't continue."

" I believe mine will do more work this year than ever," said the son.

" Perhaps they will for you, but they won't for me."

The old man went away early in the evening to spend the night on his other plantation. After he was gone, the young man looked up from the pages of " Handy Andy," and re-marked emphatically : —

" The great trouble in this country is, the people are mad at the niggers because they 're free. They always believed they would n't do well if they were emancipated, and now they maintain, and some of them even hope, they won't do well, — that too in the face of actual facts. The old planters have no confidence in the niggers, and as a matter of course the niggers have no confidence in them. They have a heap more confidence in their young masters, and they work well for us. They have still more confidence in the Yankees, and they work still better for them. They have the greatest affec-tion for the Yankees ; they won't steal from them, like they will from us. I had forty-seven hogs in one lot when I took the plantation ; and in two weeks there were only twenty-six left. The same thing happened to my turnip patch. I don't reckon it is my freedmen that steal from me ; but the country is full of thieving darkeys that think it 's no wrong to take from a Southern white man."

" I wish we older ones had the faculty you say you have for

making the free niggers work," said the young man's mother. " I always kept two women just to weave. The same women are with me now. Before they were declared free, they could weave six and eight yards of cloth a day, easy. Now the most they do is about one yard."

The house was on the main road traversed by the 15th corps, belonging to the left wing of Sherman's army, on its way from Madison to Milledgeville.

" I never would have thought I could stay home while the Yankees were passing," said the young man's mother, " but I did. They commenced passing early in the morning, and there was n't an hour in the day that they were not as thick as blue pigeons along the road.

" I was very much excited at first. My husband was away, and I had nobody with me but our negroes. A German soldier came into the house first of any. He was an ugly-looking fellow as ever I saw ; but I suppose any man would have looked ugly to me under such circumstances. Said he, ' I 've orders to get a saddle from this house.' I told him my husband had done gone off with the only saddle we had. Then he said, ' A pistol will do.' I said I had no pistol. Then he told me he must have a watch of me. I had a watch, but it was put out of the way where I hoped no Yankee could find it ; so I told him I had none for him.

" He then looked all around the room, and said, ' Madam, I have orders to burn this house.' I replied that I hoped the Federals were too magnanimous to burn houses over the heads of defenceless women. He said, ' I 'll insure it for fifty dollars ; ' for that 's the way they got a heap of money out of our people. I said, ' I 've no fifty dollars to pay for insuring it ; and if it depends upon that, it must burn.'

" Soon as he saw he could n't frighten me into giving him anything, he went to plundering. He had found a purse, with five dollars in Confederate money in it, when he saw an officer coming into the front door, and escaped through the back door. He was a very great villain, and the officer said if he was caught he would be punished.

" I don't know what I should have done if it had n't been for the Yankee officers. They treated me politely in every way. They could n't prevent my meal and bacon from being taken by the foraging parties, — all except what I had hid; but they gave me a guard to keep soldiers from plundering the house, and when one guard was taken away I had another in his place. Some families on this road, who had no guard, were so broken up they had nothing left to keep house with.

" When the foragers were carrying off our provisions, I said to an officer, ' That's all the corn meal I have,' — which was n't quite true, for I had some hid away; but he ordered the men to return me a sack. I did n't make anything by the lie; for the next party that came along took the sack the others had left. But I did save a pot of lard. I said to an officer, ' They 've done taken all my turkeys and cows and hogs, and you will leave me without anything.' ' Take back that pot of lard to the lady,' said he; and I soon had it where it was n't seen again that day.

" What was out doors nothing could prevent the soldiers from taking. I had bee-gum, and they just carried it off, hives and all. A soldier would catch up a hive, and march right along, with it on his head, and with the bees swarming all about him. They did n't care anything for the bees. I reckon they would n't sting Yankees."

During the evening, I paid a visit to the freedmen's quarters. The doors of the huts were all open, in a row, and I could see a dozen negro families grouped around cheerful fires within, basking in the yellow light, and looking quite happy and comfortable.

CHAPTER LXVIII.

POLITICS AND FREE LABOR IN GEORGIA.

At Milledgeville, — a mere village (of twenty-five hundred inhabitants before the war), surrounded by a beautiful hilly and wooded country, — I saw something of the Georgia State Legislature. It was at work on a cumbersome and rather useless freedmen's code, which, however, contained no very objectionable features. In intelligence and political views this body represented the State very fairly. I was told that its members, like the inhabitants of the State at large, were, with scarce an exception, believers in the right of secession. The only questions that ever divided them on that subject, were not as to the right, but as to the policy; and whether the State should secede separately, or coöperate with the other seceding States.

Since the Rebel State debt had been repudiated, there existed a feeling among both legislators and people that all debts, public and private, ought to be wiped out with it. I remember well the argument of a gentleman of Morgan County. " Two thirds of the people in this county are left hopelessly involved by the loss of the war debt. There is a law to imprison a man for paying what the act of the convention takes from him the power of paying. The more loyal portion of our citizens would not invest in Confederate scrip, but put their money into State bonds, which they thought safe from repudiation. A large number of debts are for negro property. Now, since slavery is abolished, all debts growing out of slavery ought to be abolished. Four or five men in this county," he added, " have the power to ruin over thirty families, whose obligations they bought up with Confederate money. As that money turns out to have never been legally good for anything, all such obligations should be cancelled."

Throughout the State I heard the bitterest complaints against the Davis despotism. " There was first a tax of ten per cent. levied on all our produce ; then of twelve per cent. on all property. Worse still, our property was seized at the will of the government, and scrip given in exchange, which was not good for taxes or anything else. There was public robbery by the government, and private robbery by the officers of the government. The Secretary of War, Seddon, had grain to sell ; so he raised the price of it to forty dollars a bushel, when it should have sold for two dollars and a half. The conscript act was executed with the most criminal partiality. A man of an influential family had no difficulty in evading it. During the last year of the war, there were one hundred and twenty-two thousand young Confederates in bomb-proof situations. But an ordinary conscript was treated like a prisoner, thrown into jail, and often handcuffed."

The value of slave property was the subject of endless debate. Said a Georgia planter : " I owned a hundred niggers : their increase paid me eight per cent., their labor four per cent. ; and I 've sixty thousand dollars' worth of property buried in that lot," — pointing to the plantation graveyard. The convention that reconstructed the State had not the grace to accept emancipation without inserting in the new Bill of Rights the proviso " that this acquiescence in the action of the United States Government is not intended as a relinquishment, or waiver or estoppel of such claim for compensation of loss sustained by reason of the emancipation of his slaves as any citizen of Georgia may hereafter make upon the justice and magnanimity of that government." And there existed in most minds a growing hope that, when the Southern representatives got into Congress, measures would be carried, compelling the government not only to pay for slaves, but for all other losses occasioned by the war.

Not one of the men elected as members of Congress could take the Congressional test-oath. The mere fact that a man could take that oath was sufficient to insure his defeat.

Georgia has no common-school system. The poor, who can

show that they are unable to pay for the tuition of their children, are permitted to send them to private schools on the credit of the county in which they reside. Few, however, take advantage of a privilege which involves a confession of poverty. There is great need of Northern benevolent effort to bring forward the education of the poor whites in all these States.

I found the freedmen's schools in Georgia supported by the New-England Freedmen's Aid Society, and the American Missionary Association. These were confined to a few localities, — principally to the large towns. There were sixty-two schools, with eighty-nine teachers, and six thousand six hundred pupils. There were in other places, self-supporting schools, taught by colored teachers, who did not report to the State Superintendent. The opposition to the freedmen's schools, on the part of the whites, was generally bitter; and in several counties school-houses had been burned, and the teachers driven away, on the withdrawal of the troops. Occasionally, however, I would hear an intelligent planter make use of a remark like this: " The South has been guilty of the greatest inconsistency in the world, in sending missionaries to enlighten the heathen, and forbidding the education of our own servants."

At Augusta, I visited a number of colored schools; among others, a private one kept by Mr. Baird, a colored man, in a little room where he had secretly taught thirty pupils during the war. The building, containing a store below and tenements above, was owned and occupied by persons of his own race; the children entered it by different doors, the girls with their books strapped under their skirts, the boys with theirs concealed under their coats; all finding their way in due season to the little school-room. I was shown the doors and passages by which they used to escape and disperse, at the approach of white persons.

Mr. Baird told me that during ten years previous to the war, he taught a similar school in the city of Charleston, South Carolina. The laws prohibited persons of color from teaching; and accordingly he employed a white woman to assist him.

She sat and sewed, and kept watch, until the patrol looked in, when she appeared as the teacher, and the real teacher (a small man) fell back as a pupil.   It was ostensibly a school for free colored children, the teaching of slaves to read being a criminal offence ; yet many of those were taught.

On the road to Augusta, my attention was attracted by the conversation of two gentlemen, a Georgian and a Mississippian, sitting behind me in the car.

We had just passed Union Point, where there was considerable excitement about an unknown negro found lying out in the woods, sick with the small-pox.   Nobody went to his relief, and the citizens, standing with hands in their pockets, allowed that, if he did not die of his disease, he would soon perish from exposure and starvation.

" The trouble is just here," said the Georgian behind me. " The niggers have never been used to taking care of their own sick.   Formerly, if anything was the matter with them, their masters had them taken care of; and now they don't mind anything about disease, except to be afraid of it.   If they've a sick baby, they let it die.   They're like so many children themselves, in respect to sickness."

" How much better off they were when slaves ! " said the Mississippian.   " A man would see to his own niggers, like he would to his own stock.   But the niggers now don't belong to anybody, and it's no man's business whether they live or die."

" I exercise the same care over *my* niggers I always did," replied the Georgian.   " They are all with me yet.   Only one ever left me.   He was a good, faithful servant, but sickly.   He said one day he thought he ought to have wages, and I told him if he could find anybody to do better by him than I was doing, he'd better go.   He went, and took his family ; and in six weeks he came back again.   ' Edward,' I said, ' how's this ? '   ' I want to come and live with you again, master, like I always have,' he said.   ' I find I ain't strong enough to work for wages.'   ' Edward,' I said, ' I am very sorry ; you wanted to go, and I got another man in your place; now I have nothing for you to do, and your cabin is occupied.' He just burst into tears. ' I 've lived with you all my days, master,' he said, ' and now I have no home ! ' I could n't stand that. ' Take an ax,' I said ; ' go into the woods, cut some poles, and build you a cabin. As long as I have a home, you shall have one.' He was the happiest man you ever saw ! "

" A Yankee would n't have done that," said the Mississippian. " Yankees won't take care of a poor white man. I 've travelled in the North, and seen people there go barefoot in winter, with ice on the ground."

" Indeed ! " said I, turning and facing the speaker. " What State was that in ? "

" In the State of New York," he replied. " I 've seen hundreds of poor whites barefoot there in the depth of winter."

" That is singular," I remarked. " I am a native of that State ; I lived in it until I was twenty years old, and have travelled through it repeatedly since ; and I never happened to see what you describe."

" I have seen the same thing in Massachusetts too."

" I have been for some years a resident of Massachusetts, and have never yet seen a man there barefoot in the snow."

The Mississippian made no direct reply to this, but ran on in a strain of vehement and venomous abuse of the Yankees, in which he was cordially joined by his friend the Georgian. Although not addressed to me, this talk was evidently intended for my ear ; but I had heard too much of the same sort everywhere in the South to be disturbed by it. At length the conversation turned upon the Freedmen's Bureau.

" General Tillson " (Assistant Commissioner for the State) " has done a mighty mean thing ! " said the Georgian. " I 've just made contracts to pay my freedmen seventy-five and a hundred dollars a year. And now he is going to issue an order requiring us to pay them a hundred and forty-four dollars. That will ruin us. Down in South-western Georgia they can afford to pay that ; but in my county the land is so poor we can't feed our people at that rate. I 'm going to

Augusta now to see about it. If Tillson insists upon it, I shall throw up my contracts: I can't do it: I'll sell out: I won't live in a country that's ruled in this way."

" From what county are you, sir?" I inquired.

" Oglethorpe ; my name is C——. Are you an agent of the Bureau?"

" No, sir." But from some remark I made, he got the impression that I was connected with it. His abuse of the Yankees ceased ; and after a while he said : —

" I believe General Tillson is a very fair man ; and I understand why he intends to issue such an order. To one planter who is willing to do right by the freedmen, there are five that will be unjust towards them. I would n't accept the agency of the Bureau in my county, because so many contracts have been made that I could n't approve ; and they would get me into trouble with my neighbors. One man has hired a good fair field hand, his wife, who is a good cook, his sister, a good field hand, and his daughter, a good house servant, all for a hundred dollars a year, — twenty-five dollars apiece ; and he does n't clothe them, either. That's a specimen. I think the Bureau ought to interfere in such cases. But it a'n't fair to make honest men suffer for the conduct of these sharpers."

I said I thought so too.

" Then I hope you'll tell General Tillson so."

" I'll tell him so, if you wish me to."

" And tell him you think I'm an honest man."

" I am inclined to think you are an honest man, and I'll tell him that too."

" But see here : don't mention what I said about the Yankees, will you?"

" Certainly not: that's of no consequence."

C—— appeared quite anxious on that point. After serious reflection, he said : —

" If you overheard me damn the Yankees, you'll forgive me, when I tell you how they treated me. It was after the war was over, and that's what made it hurt so. Seven of

Stoneman's men came to my house, and put a carbine to my breast, and demanded my watch. 'You may shoot me,' I said, ' but you can't have my watch.' 'Then give us some dinner,' they said. I got dinner for them, and waited on them with my own hands. They paid me for my trouble by stealing seven of my horses. While I was absent from home, trying to get back my horses, some more Yankees came and robbed my house ; they broke open the bureau with a chisel, and injured more than they took. You don't blame me for cursing 'em, do you ? "

" Not in the least. According to your story, they were very great rascals."

After another interval of silence, C—— resumed : —

" Tell General Tillson I am willing to pay my laborers every dollar they 're worth; and that I treat them well. I 've one boy that has always been with me, and is a better overseer than any white man I ever had. He looks after my interest better than I can myself, for he is younger. I trust everything in his hands, — all my keys, and sometimes money." He could not forbear adding, — " Your fanatics at the North would n't believe I treat this man so well."

" Very likely. But it seems you have good reason for treating him well. What do you pay him ? "

" I pay him two hundred dollars a year."

" And what would you have to pay a white overseer ? "

" I could n't get a white man to do for me what he does, for eight hundred dollars."

" I am quite sure," I said, " that our fanatics at the North would *not* see your extraordinary kindness to this man in the same light you do. They would think him worth considerably more than you pay him. If he does the work of a white overseer, they would say he ought to have the salary of a white overseer. They are such an unreasonable set, they would consider six hundred dollars, the difference between his wages and a white man's, a pretty heavy tax to pay on the color of his skin."

C—— did not seem inclined to pursue the subject, bu'

commenced talking in a very candid, sensible manner, of the old Southern methods.

" If the war only breaks them up, it will have done some good. Our large planters generally gave no attention to business. The men were fast and reckless ; the women, helpless and luxurious. We gave so much attention to cotton and niggers we could n't stop to think of the comforts of life. And after all we were just working to enrich Northern capitalists. There are no millionaires amongst us. Three hundred thousand dollars is a rare and large fortune in Georgia."

Arriving in Augusta that night, I went the next morning to call on General Tillson. In our conversation, I took early occasion to speak to him of my yesterday's acquaintance, Mr. C——, of Oglethorpe County. " He will be here soon, and explain to you why it is that planters in Northern Georgia cannot afford to pay the twelve dollars a month you insist upon."

" He will not be the first who has come to me on that business," replied the clear-headed general. " I shall give him a patient hearing, and if he convinces me that I am wrong, he will do more than any have done yet. When it was white man against white man, these planters paid one hundred and fifty and two hundred dollars a year for first-class field-hands. Now they are not willing to pay the negro for his labor one half what they formerly paid his owner. When I took charge of the Bureau's affairs in this State, last September, I found the ordinary wages to be from two to seven dollars a month, — sometimes as low as twelve bushels of corn for a year's labor. And the planters complained that the freedman would n't work for those prices. Now all I ask is that they should pay what his labor is worth in the open market. Men from Alabama, Mississippi, Arkansas, say it is worth fifteen dollars, and stand ready to give it. Since that is the case, to permit him to make contracts for very much less, is to permit him to be swindled. A little while ago many of these men were wishing the negroes all driven out of the State ; and now they are in a great panic, because I am allowing them to go. They come to me to remonstrate against sending off any more laborers. 'Gentlemen,' I say, 'if you cannot afford to pay the freedman what his services are worth, it is not his fault, but your misfortune.'

"But they *can* afford it. Here is a careful statement of facts relating to free labor in Wilkes County, which adjoins Oglethorpe. 'One field-hand will cultivate nine acres of cotton, on which he will raise three and a half bales, worth — say three hundred and seventy-five dollars. The same hand will also cultivate nine acres of corn, raising one hundred and eight bushels, worth one hundred and eight dollars. Total, four hundred and eighty-three dollars.

"'Expenses: — Board, fifty-two dollars. Rent of cabin, six. Fuel, six. Wages, one hundred forty-four. Total, two hundred and eight dollars.' Deducting two hundred and eight from four hundred and eighty-three, you have a clear profit of two hundred and seventy-five dollars on each man; that, too, at the rate of wages I prescribe.

"These, understand, are the planters' own estimates. In South-western Georgia, where the land is much richer than in this section, the most extravagant charges against the plantation show a nett income of three hundred and twenty-five dollars from the labor of a full field freedman. This estimate is from data furnished by several of the most popular and extensive planters in that region.

"Now," added the Commissioner, "when your friend, Mr. C——, of Oglethorpe, comes to make his complaint, if he is the honest man you represent him to be, I will show him, by his own figuring, that so far from being impoverished by paying his men twelve dollars a month, he will make a handsome profit from them."

As I went out, I found Mr. C——, of Oglethorpe, in the ante-room, waiting to see the General. He regarded me with a curious, uneasy expression, fearing no doubt lest I had reported to the Commissioner his indiscreet remarks of yesterday concerning the Yankees and the Bureau. I introduced him to General Tillson, however, in a manner that seemed to reassure him, and left them closeted together.

That evening, by appointment, I saw the General at his residence. " Well," I asked, " how did you and my friend C—— get along ? " and received from him the following statement, which he had kindly had copied for me.

" *Statement of —— —— C——, of Oglethorpe County, leading planter of that county.*

" Good hands in county will work 8½ acres
in cotton — 2 bales................ $300 00
8½ acres in corn — 85 bush.......... 85 00

                                Gross Income, $385 00
" Expenses.
3 lbs. bacon a week, 60 cts. ⎞
1 peck meal, ...25 " ⎠
Board of hand for year.............. $44 20
Rent of Cabin...................... 10 00
Fuel 25 00
Wages............................ 144 00

                        Total Expenses, $223 20
        Nett Income from each hand,.... $161 80."

" Here," said General Tillson, " the profits of the labor are placed as low, and the expenses as high, as Mr. C—— could figure them, after considerable study. From the labor of a hundred freedmen, on his two plantations, he would clear, according to his own account, upwards of sixteen thousand dollars, — sufficient to cover all risks, and all other expenses of the plantation, and leave him a little fortune at the end of the year."

Mr. C—— had repeated to General Tillson his statement to me, regarding the dishonest contracts made with the freed-men in his county. " The truth is," said the General, " he wants to hire them himself for about half what they are worth, and he is indignant because others have hired them for less. He can really afford to pay his help twice what I demand, and then make two hundred dollars a year from the labor of each freedman. The other day some leading planters from South-

32

western Georgia made the same complaint with regard to wages. ' Very well,' I said, ' if you can't pay twelve dollars a month, give your laborers a part of the crops.' They thought one seventh of the cotton was more than they ought to give, declaring that the negro would get rich on that. ' If sixty freedmen,' I said, ' can get rich on one seventh of a crop, the planter, I am sure, can get rich on six sevenths.'

" The trouble is, these men wish to make everything there is to be made, and leave the freedman nothing. They resort to the meanest schemes to cheat him. They tell the negroes that if they go with the agents of the Bureau to other places, the able-bodied among them will be carried off and sold into Cuba, and the women and children drowned in the Mississippi.[1]

" I have not yet sent a thousand negroes out of the State," continued General Tillson. " But I have sent off enough to alarm the people, and raise the rate of wages. I told the planters on the coast of Georgia, that they must pay the women twelve dollars a month, and the men fifteen, or I would take the colored population out of their counties. That brought them to terms, after all their talk about wanting to get rid of the niggers.

[1] Since my return from the South, I have received a letter from a gentleman of character, late an officer in the Federal army, from which I make the following extract bearing on this subject : —

" After leaving you at Grand Gulf, I rode twenty or thirty miles into the interior, but could find little inducement for a Northern man to settle in that portion of the South. The further you go from main routes, the more hostile you find the inhabitants. I finally determined to locate on or near the Mississippi, and recent experience only confirms my earlier impressions. I am now located on the river, one hundred and sixty miles below Memphis, on the Arkansas side, and am making preparations to plant one thousand acres of cotton. It has been very difficult to secure help here, and I determined to make a trip to Georgia for the purpose of obtaining the requisite number of hands. I succeeded tolerably well, and could have hired many more than I needed, had not the people induced the negroes to believe that we were taking them to Cuba to sell them. I award the palm to the Georgians, as the meanest and most despicable class of people it was ever my misfortune to meet. While they are constantly urging that the negro will not work, they use every means to dissuade him from securing honorable and profitable employment. I was never so grossly insulted as when in Georgia. They fear the powerful arm of the government, but are to-day as bitter Rebels as at any time during the war. The consequences would ne most disastrous if the military force scattered through the South should be at once removed."

" The freed people in most parts of the State are still so ignorant of their condition, that they are glad to make contracts to work for only their food and clothes. There are many, however, who will live vagrant lives, if permitted. It is necessary to compel such to enter into contracts." Firmly convinced of this necessity, General Tillson had issued an order directing his agents to make contracts for all freedmen without other means of support, who should neglect to make contracts for themselves after a given time. The Commissioner at Washington disapproved the order, for what reason I cannot divine, unless it was feared that the over-zealous friends of the negro at the North might be alarmed by it. No contracts were made for the vagrant blacks under it; but its effect, in inducing them to make contracts for themselves, was immediate, wholesome, and very gratifying.

The officers of the Bureau were everywhere subject to the temptation of bribes; and I often heard planters remark that they could do anything with the Bureau they pleased, if they had plenty of money. General Tillson said, " I could make a million dollars here very shortly, if I chose to be dishonest. Only to-day I was offered a thousand dollars for one hundred freedmen, by a rich planter." He had made it a rule of the Bureau to receive no personal fees whatever for any services.

Over three thousand dollars had been paid in fines by the people of Georgia for cruelties to the freedmen during the past three months. " It is considered no murder to kill a negro. The best men in the State admit that no jury would convict a white man for killing a freedman, or fail to hang a negro who had killed a white man in self-defence."

The General added : " As soon as the troops were withdrawn from Wilkes County, last November, a gang of jayhawkers went through, shooting and burning the colored people, holding their feet and hands in the fire to make them tell where their money was. It left such a stigma on the county that the more respectable class held a meeting to denounce it. This class is ashamed of such outrages, but it does not prevent them, and it does not take them to heart; and I could name a dozen cases of murder committed on the colored people by young men of these first families."

General Tillson, by his tact, good sense, business capacity, freedom from prejudice for or against color, and his uniform candor, moderation, and justice, had secured for the Bureau the coöperation of both the State Convention and the Legislature, and was steadily winning the confidence and respect of the planters. The most serious problem that remained to be solved was the Sea-Island question, of which I shall speak hereafter.

The prospect was favorable for a good cotton crop in Georgia, although anxiety was felt with regard to the vitality of the seed, much of which, being several years old, had no doubt been injured by keeping.

CHAPTER LXIX.

SHERMAN IN EASTERN GEORGIA.

THE track of the Central Railroad, one hundred and ninety-one miles in length, was destroyed with conscientious thoroughness by Sherman's army. From Gordon, twenty miles below Macon, to Scarborough Station, nine miles below Millen, a distance of one hundred miles, there was still an impassable hiatus of bent rails and burnt bridges, at the time of my journey; and in order to reach Savannah from Macon, it was necessary to proceed by the Georgia road to Augusta, either returning by railroad to Atlanta, or crossing over by railroad and stage to Madison, between which places the Georgia road, destroyed for a distance of sixty-seven miles, had been restored. From Augusta I went down on the Augusta and Savannah road to a station a few miles below Waynesboro', where a break in that road rendered it necessary to proceed by stages to Scarborough. From Scarborough to Savannah the road was once more in operation.

The relaid tracks were very rough; many of the old rails having been straightened and put down again. "General Grant and his staff passed over this road a short time ago," said a citizen; "and as they went jolting along in an old box-car, on plain board seats, they seemed to think it was great fun: they said they were riding on Sherman's *hair-pins*," — an apt name applied to the most frequent form in which the rails were bent.

"Sherman's men had all sorts of machinery for destroying the track. They could rip it up as fast as they could count. They burnt the ties and fences to heat the iron; then two men would take a bar and twist it or wrap it around a tree or a telegraph post. Our people found some of their iron-benders, and they helped mightily about straightening the rails again. Only the best could be used. The rest the devil can't straighten."

Riding along by the destroyed tracks, it was amusing to see the curious shapes in which the iron had been left. Hair-pins predominated. Corkscrews were also abundant. Sometimes we found four or five rails wound around the trunk of a tree, which would have to be cut before they could be got off again. And there was an endless varity of most ungeometrical twists and curves.

The Central Railroad was probably the best in the State. Before the war its stock paid annual dividends of fifteen per cent., — one year as high as twenty seven and a half per cent. It owned property to the amount of a million and a half dollars, mostly invested in Europe. This will be nearly or quite sunk in repairing the damage done by Sherman. Then the road will have all of its bent iron, — for Sherman could not carry it away or burn it ; — and this was estimated to be worth two thirds as much as new iron. The track, composed partly of the T and partly of the U rail, was well laid ; and the station-houses were substantially built of brick. I was told that the great depot building at Millen, although of wood, was equal in size and beauty to the best structures of the kind in the North. Sherman did not leave a building on the road, from Macon to Savannah. For warehouses, I found box-cars stationed on the side tracks.

The inhabitants of Eastern Georgia suffered even more than those of Middle Georgia from our army operations, — the men having got used to their wild business by the time they arrived there, and the General having, I suspect, slipped one glove off. Here is the story of an old gentleman of Burke County : —

" It was the 14th Corps that came through my place. They looked like a blue cloud coming. They had all kinds of music, — horns, cow-bells, tin-pans, everything they could pick up that would make a hideous noise. It was like Bedlam broke loose. It was enough to frighten the old stumps in the dead-

enings, say nothing about the people. They burned everything but occupied dwellings. They cut the belluses at the
blacksmith-shops. They took every knife and fork and cooking utensil we had. My wife just saved a frying-pan by
hanging on to it; she was considerable courageous, and they
left it in her hands. After that they came back to get her to
cook them some biscuit.

" ' How can I cook for you, when you 've carried off everything ? ' she said.

" They told her if she would make them a batch of biscuit
they would bring back a sack of her own flour, and she should
have the balance of it. She agreed to it; but while the biscuit was baking, another party came along and carried the
sack off again.

" The wife of one of my neighbors, — a very rich family,
brought up to luxuries, — just saved a single frying-pan, like
we did. Their niggers and all went off with Sherman; and
for a week or two they had to cook their own victuals in that
frying-pan, cut them with a pocket-knife, and eat them with
their fingers. My folks had to do the same, but we had n't
been brought up to luxuries, and did n't mind it so much.

" General Sherman went into the house of an old woman
after his men had been pillaging it. He sat down and drank
a glass of water. Says she to him, ' I don't wonder people
say you 're a smart man; for you 've been to the bad place and
got scrapings the devil would n't have.' His soldiers heard of
it, and they took her dresses and hung them all up in the
highest trees, and drowned the cat in the well.

" A neighbor of mine buried all his gold and silver, and
built a hog-pen over the spot. But the Yankees were mighty
sharp at finding things. They mistrusted a certain new look
about the hog-pen, ripped it away, stuck in their bayonets, and
found the specie.

" Another of my neighbors hid his gold under the brick
floor of his smoke-house. He put down the bricks in the
same place ; but the rascals smelt out the trick, pulled up the
floor, got the gold, and then burnt the smoke-house. They

made him take off his boots and hat, which they wore away They left him an old Yankee hat, which he now wears. He swears he never 'll buy another till the government pays him for his losses.

" My wife did the neatest thing. She took all our valuables, such as watches and silver-spoons, and hid them in the corn-field. With a knife she would just make a slit in the ground, open it a little, put in one or two things, and then let the top earth down, just like it was before. Then she 'd go on and do the same thing in another place. The soldiers went all over that corn-field sticking in their bayonets, but they did n't find a thing. The joke of it was, she came very near never finding them again herself.

" One of my neighbors, a poor man, was stopped by some cavalry boys, who demanded his watch. He told 'em it was such a sorry watch they would n't take it. They wanted to see it, and when he showed it, they said, ' Go along! — we won't be seen carrying off such a looking thing as that!' "

The following story was related to me by a Northern man, who had been twenty-five years settled in Eastern Georgia : —

" My neighbors were too much frightened to do anything well and in good order. But I determined I 'd save as much of my property as I could drive on its own feet or load on to wagons. I took two loads of goods, and all my cattle and hogs, and run em off twenty miles into Screven County. I found a spot of rising ground covered with gall bushes, in the middle of a low, wet place. I went through water six inches deep, got to the knoll, cut a road through the bushes, run my wagons in, and stuck the bushes down into the wet ground where I had cut them. They were six or eight feet high, and hid everything. My cattle and hogs I turned off in a bushy field. After that, I went to the house of a poor planter and staid. That was Friday night.

"Sunday, the soldiers came. I lay hid in the woods, and saw 'em pass close by the knoll where my goods were, running in their bayonets everywhere. The bushes were green yet, and they did n't discover anything, though they passed right by the edge of them.

" All at once I heard the women of the house scream murder.   Thinks I, ' It won't do for me to be lying here looking
out only for my own interests, while the soldiers are abusing the
women.'   I crawled out of the bushes, and was hurrying back
to the house, when five cavalrymen overtook me.   They put
their carbines to my head, and told me to give 'em my money.

" As soon as I 'd got over my fright a little, I said, ' Gentlemen, I 've got some Confederate money, but it will do you no
good.'

" ' Give me your pistol,' one said.   I told him I had no
pistol.   They thought I lied, for they saw something in my
pocket ; but come to snatch it out, it was only my pipe.   Then
they demanded my knife.

" ' I 've nothing but an old knife I cut my tobacco with ; —
you won't take an old man's knife ! '

" They let me go, and I hurried on to the house.   It was
full of soldiers.   I certainly thought something dreadful was
happening to the women ; but they were screeching because
the soldiers were carrying off their butter and honey and corn-
meal.   They were making all that fuss over the loss of their
property ; and I thought I might as well have stayed to watch
mine.

" That night the army camped about a mile from there ; and
the next morning I rode over to see if I could get a safeguard
for the house.   But the officers said no ; — they were bound
to have something to eat.   I went back, and left my horse at
the door while I stepped in to tell the women if they wished
to save anything that was left they must hide it.   Before I
could get out again my horse was taken.   I went on after it ;
the army was on the march again, and I was told if I would
go with it all day, I should have my horse come night.   I
marched a few miles, but got sick of it, and went back.   I
could see big fires in the direction of my house, and I knew
that the town was burning.

" I got back to the poor planter's house, and found a new
misfortune had happened to him.   The night before, all his
hogs and mine came together to his door, — the soldiers having

let the fences down. 'This won't do,' I said; 'I'm going to make another effort to save my hogs.' But he was true Southern; he had n't energy; he said, 'No use!' and just sat still. I tolled my hogs off with corn, and scattered corn all about in the bushes to keep them there. The next day it was hot, and they lay in the shade to keep cool; so the soldiers did n't find them.

" But when, as I said, I got back to his house, I found the soldiers slaughtering his hogs right and left. They killed every one. So much for his lack of faith. But the worst part of the joke was, they borrowed his cart to carry off his own hogs to the wagon-train which was passing on another road half a mile away. They said they'd bring it back in an hour. As it did n't come, he went for it, and found they'd piled rails on to it and burnt it. I had taken care of my wagons, and he might have done the same with his. But that's the difference between a Northern and a Southern man.

" Monday I returned home, and found my family living on corn-meal bran. They had been robbed of everything. The soldiers had even taken the hat off from my little grandson's head, six years old. They took a mother-hen away from her little peeping chickens. There were fifty or a hundred soldiers in the house all one day, breaking open chests and bureaus; and those that come after took what the first had left. My folks asked for protection, being Northern people; and there was one officer who knew them; but he could control only his own men. So we fared no better than our neighbors."

The staging to Scarborough was very rough; but our route lay through beautiful pine woods, carpeted with wild grass. It was January, but the spring frogs were singing.

The best rolling-stock of the Central Road had been run up to Macon on Sherman's approach, and could not be got down again. So I had the pleasure of riding from Scarborough to Savannah in an old car crowded full of wooden chairs, in place of the usual seats.

The comments of the passengers on the destruction wrought

by Sherman were sometimes bitter, sometimes sentimental. A benevolent gentleman remarked: "How much good might be done with the millions of property destroyed, by building new railroads elsewhere!" To which a languishing lady replied: "What is the use of building railroads for *slaves* to ride on? I'd rather be free, and take it afoot, than belong to the Yankees, and ride."

Our route lay along the low, level borders of the Ogeechee River, the soil of which is too cold for cotton. We passed immense swamps, in the perfectly still waters of which the great tree-trunks were mirrored. And all the way the spring frogs kept up their shrill singing.

At some of the stations I saw bales of Northern hay that had come up from Savannah. "There is a commentary on our style of farming," said an intelligent planter from near Millen. "This land, though worthless for cotton, could be made to grow splendid crops of grass, — and we import our hay."

CHAPTER LXX.

A GLANCE AT SAVANNAH.

On the 16th of November, 1864, Sherman began his grand march from Atlanta. In less than a month his army had made a journey of three hundred miles, consuming and devastating the country. On December 13th, by the light of the setting sun, General Hazen's Division of the 15th Corps made its brilliant and successful assault on Fort McAlister on the Ogeechee, opening the gate to Savannah and the sea. On the night of the 20th, Savannah was hurriedly evacuated by the Rebels, and occupied by Sherman on the 21st. The city, with a thousand prisoners, thirty-five thousand bales of cotton, two hundred guns, three steamers, and valuable stores, thus fell into our hands without a battle. Within forty-eight hours a United States transport steamer came to the wharf, and the new base of supplies, about which we were all at that time so anxious, was established.

The city was on fire during the evacuation. Six squares and portions of other squares were burned. At the same time a mob collected and commenced breaking into stores and dwellings. The destroyers of railroads were in season to save the city from the violence of its own citizens.

A vast multitude of negroes had followed the army to the sea. This exodus of the bondmen from the interior had been permitted, not simply as a boon to them, but as an injury to the resources of the Confederacy, like the destruction of its plantations and railroads. What to do with them now became a serious problem. Of his conference with Secretary Stanton on the subject at Savannah, General Sherman says : " We agreed perfectly that the young and able-bodied men should be enlisted as soldiers or employed by the quartermaster in the necessary work of unloading ships, and for other army purposes ; but this left on our hands the old and feeble, the women and children, who had necessarily to be fed by the United States. Mr. Stanton summoned a large number of the old negroes, mostly preachers, with whom he held a long conference, of which he took down notes. After this confer-ence, he was satisfied the negroes could, with some little aid from the United States by means of the abandoned plantations on the sea islands and along the navigable rivers, take care of themselves." Sherman's " General Orders No. 15 " were the result, giving negro settlers " possessory titles " to these lands. Thus originated the knotty Sea-Island controversy, of which more by-and-by.

The aspect of Savannah is peculiarly Southern, and not without a certain charm. Its uniform squares, its moist and heavy atmosphere, the night fogs that infest it, the dead level of its sandy streets, shaded by two and four rows of moss-draped trees, and its frequent parks of live-oaks, water-oaks, wild-olives, and magnolias, impress you singularly. The city, notwithstanding its low, flat appearance, is built on a plain forty feet above the river. The surrounding country is an almost unbroken level. Just across the Savannah lie the low, marshy shores of South Carolina. It is the largest city of Georgia, having something like twenty-five thousand inhab-itants. Here, before the war, dwelt the aristocracy of the country, living in luxurious style upon the income of slave labor on the rice and cotton plantations.

Trade was less active at Savannah than in some of the interior towns, owing to its greater isolation. A flood of business passed through it, however. The expense of trans-portation was very great. Every bale of cotton brought down the river from Augusta, two hundred and thirty miles, cost eight dollars ; and the tariff on returning freights was two cents a pound.

There were sixteen hundred colored children in Savannah, twelve hundred of whom attended school. Three hundred and fifty attended the schools of the Savannah Educational

Association, organized and supported by the colored population. I visited one of these schools, taught by colored persons, in a building which was a famous slave-mart, in the good old days of the institution. In the large auction-room, and behind the iron-barred windows of the jail-room over it, the children of slaves were now enjoying one of the first, inestimable advantages of freedom.

If you go to Savannah, do not fail to visit the Bonaventure Cemetery, six miles from the city. You drive out southward on the Thunderbolt Road, past the fortifications, through fields of stumps and piny undergrowths, whose timber was cut away to give range to the guns, to the fragrant, sighing solitude of pine woods beyond. Leaving the main road, you pass beneath the low roof of young evergreen oaks overarching the path. This leads you into avenues of indescribable beauty and gloom. Whichever way you look, colonnades of huge live-oak trunks open before you, solemn, still, and hoary. The great limbs meeting above are draped and festooned with long fine moss. Over all is a thick canopy of living green, shutting out the glare of day. Beneath is a sparse undergrowth of evergreen bushes, half concealing a few neglected old family monuments. The area is small, but a more fitting scene for a cemetery is not conceivable.

CHAPTER LXXI.

CHARLESTON AND THE WAR.

1 HE railroad from Savannah to Charleston, one hundred and four miles in length, running through a country of rice-plantations, was struck and smashed by Sherman in his march *from* the sea. As it never was a paying road before the war, I could see no prospect of its being soon repaired. The highway of the ocean supplies its place. There was little travel and less business between the two cities, two or three small steamers a week being sufficient to accommodate all. Going on board one of these inferior boats at three o'clock one afternoon, at Savannah, I awoke the next morning in Charleston harbor.

A warm, soft, misty morning it was, the pale dawn breaking through rifts in the light clouds overhead, a vapory horizon of dim sea all around. What is that great bulk away on our left, drifting past us ? That is the thing known as Fort Sumter : it does not float from its rock so easily : it is we who are drifting past it. We have just left Fort Moultrie on our right ; the low shores on which it crouches lie off there still visible, like banks of heavier mist. That obscure phenomenon ahead yonder looms too big for a hencoop, and turns out to be Fort Ripley. The dawn brightens, the mist clears, and we see, far on our right, Castle Pinckney ; and on our left a gloomy line of pine forests, which we are told is James Island.

This is historic ground we are traversing, — or rather historic water. How the heart stirs with the memories it calls up ! What is that at anchor yonder ? A monitor ! A man on its low flat deck walks almost level with the water. Two noticeable objects follow after us : one is a high-breasted, proud-beaked New York steamer ; the other, the wonderful light of dawn dancing upon the waves.

Before us all the while, rising and expanding as we approach, its wharves and shipping, its warehouses and church steeples, gradually taking shape, on its low peninsula thrust out between the two rivers, is the haughty and defiant little city that inaugurated treason, that led the Rebellion, that kindled the fire it took the nation's blood to quench. And is it indeed you, city of Charleston, lying there so quiet, harmless, half asleep, in the peaceful morning light? Where now are the joy-intoxicated multitudes who thronged your batteries and piers and house-tops, to see the flag of the Union hauled down from yonder shattered little fortress? Have you forgotten the frantic cheers of that frantic hour? Once more the old flag floats there! How do you like the looks of it, city of Charleston?

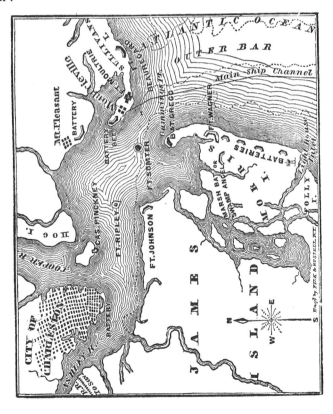

I gave my travelling-bag to a black boy on the wharf, who took it on his head and led the way through the just awakened streets to the Mills House.

The appearance of the city in the early morning atmosphere, was prepossessing. It is a well built, light, and airy city. It lacks the broad streets, the public squares, and the forest of trees, which give to Savannah its charm; but it strikes one as a more attractive place for a residence. You are not at all oppressed with a sense of the lowness of the situation; and yet it is far less elevated than Savannah, the flat and narrow peninsula on which it is built rising but a few feet above high water.

Charleston did not strike me as a very cleanly town, and I doubt if it ever was such. Its scavengers are the turkey buzzards. About the slaughter-pens on the outskirts of the city, at the markets, and wherever garbage abounds, these black, melancholy birds, properly vultures, congregate in numbers. There is a law against killing them, and they are very tame. In contrast with these obscenities are the gardens of the suburban residences, green in midwinter with semi-tropical shrubs and trees.

Here centred the fashion and aristocracy of South Carolina, before the war. Charleston was the watering-place where the rich cotton and rice planters, who lived upon their estates in winter, came to lounge away the summer season, thus inverting the Northern custom. It has still many fine residences, built in a variety of styles; but, since those recent days of its pride and prosperity, it has been wofully battered and desolated.

The great fire of 1861 swept diagonally across the city from river to river. A broad belt of ruin divides what remains. One eighth of the entire city was burned, comprising much of its fairest and wealthiest quarter. No effort had yet been made to rebuild it. The proud city lies humbled in its ashes, too poor to rise again without the helping hand of Northern Capital.

The origin of this stupendous fire still remains a mystery.

33

It is looked upon as one of the disasters of the war, although it cannot be shown that it had any connection with the war. When Eternal Justice decrees the punishment of a people, it sends not War alone, but also its sister terrors, Famine, Pestilence, and Fire.

The ruins of Charleston are the most picturesque of any I saw in the South. The gardens and broken walls of many of its fine residences remain to attest their former elegance. Broad, semicircular flights of marble steps, leading up once to proud doorways, now conduct you, over their cracked and calcined slabs, to the level of high foundations swept of everything but the crushed fragments of their former superstructures, with here and there a broken pillar, and here and there a windowless wall. Above the monotonous gloom of the ordinary ruins rise the churches, — the stone tower and roofless walls of the Catholic Cathedral, deserted and solitary, a roost for buzzards ; the burnt-out shell of the Circular Church, interesting by moonlight, with its dismantled columns still standing, like those of an antique temple ; and others scarcely less noticeable.

There are additional ruins scattered throughout the lower part of the city, a legacy of the Federal bombardment. The Scotch Church, a large structure, with two towers and a row of front pillars, was rendered untenantable by ugly breaches in its roof and walls, that have not yet been repaired. The old Custom-House and Post-Office building stands in an exceedingly dilapidated condition, full of holes. Many other public and private buildings suffered no less. Some were quite demolished ; while others have been patched up. After all, it would seem that the derisive laughter with which the Charlestonians, according to contemporaneous accounts in their newspapers, received the Yankee shells, must have been of a forced or hysterical nature. Yet I found those who still maintained that the bombardment did not amount to much. A member of the city fire department said to me : —

" But few fires were set by shells. There were a good many fires, but they were mostly set by mischief-makers.

LEAVING CHARLESTON ON THE CITY BEING BOMBARDED.

The object was to get us firemen down in shelling range. There was a spite against us, because we were exempt from military duty."

The fright of the inhabitants, however, was generally frankly admitted. The greatest panic occurred immediately after the occupation of Morris Island by General Gillmore. " The first shells set the whole town in commotion. It looked like everybody was skedaddling. Some loaded up their goods, and left nothing but their empty houses. Others just packed up a few things in trunks and boxes, and abandoned the rest. The poor people and negroes took what they could carry on their backs or heads, or in their arms, and put for dear life. Some women put on all their dresses, to save them. For a while the streets were crowded with runaways, — hurrying, hustling, driving, — on horseback, in wagons, and on foot, — white folks, dogs, and niggers. But when it was found the shells only fell down town, the people got over their scare; and many who went away came back again. Every once in a while, however, the Yankees would appear to mount a new gun, or get a new gunner; and the shells would fall higher up. That would start the skedaddling once more. One shell would be enough to depopulate a whole neighborhood."

A Northern man, who was in Charleston during the war, told me that he was lying sick in a house which was struck by a shell early during the bombardment. " A darkey that was nursing me took fright and ran away, and left me in about as unpleasant a condition as I was ever in. I could n't stir from my bed, and there was much more danger that I might die from neglect, than from Gillmore's shells. Finally a friend found me out, and removed me to another house a few streets above. It was nine months before the shells reached us there."

The shelling began in July, 1863, and was kept up pretty regularly until the surrender of the city, on the 18th of February, 1865. This last event occurred just four years after the inauguration of Jefferson Davis as President of the Confederate States. How did the people of Charleston keep that last glorious anniversary?

Sherman's northward marching army having flanked the city, its evacuation was not unexpected; but when it came, confusion and dismay came with it. The Rebel troops, departing, adhered to their usual custom of leaving ruin behind them. They fired the upper part of the city, burning an immense quantity of cotton, with railroad buildings and military stores. While the half-famished poor were rushing early in the morning to secure a little of the Confederate rice in one of the warehouses, two hundred kegs of powder blew up, killing and mutilating a large number of those unfortunate people. Here also it devolved upon the Union troops to save the city from the fires set by its own friends.

Of the sixty-five thousand inhabitants which the city contained at the beginning of the secession war, only about ten thousand remained at the time of the occupation by our troops. Those belonged mostly to the poorer classes, who could not get away. Many people rushed in from the suburbs, got caught inside the intrenchments, and could not get out again. Others rushed out panic-stricken from the burning city, and when they wished to return, found that they could not. Charleston, from the moment of its occupation, was a sealed city. Families were divided. Husbands shut within the line of fortifications drawn across the neck of the peninsula, could not hear from their families in the country; and wives in the country could not get news from their husbands. "It was two months before I could learn whether my husband was dead or alive," said a lady, who took refuge in the interior. And some who remained in Charleston, told me it was a month before they heard of the burning of Columbia; that they could not even learn which way Sherman's army had gone.

CHAPTER LXXII.

A VISIT TO FORT SUMTER.

ONE morning I went on board the government supply steamer "Mayflower," plying between the city and the forts below. As we steamed down to the rows of piles, driven across the harbor to compel vessels to pass under the guns of the forts, I noticed that they were so nearly eaten off by worms that, had the war continued a year or two longer, it would have been necessary to replace them. There is in these Southern waters an insect very destructive to the wood it comes in contact with. It cannot live in fresh water, and boats, the bottoms of which are not sheathed, or covered with tar, are taken occasionally up the rivers, to get rid of it. Only the palmetto is able to resist its ravages; of the tough logs of which the wharves of Charleston are constructed.

Fort Sumter loomed before us, an enormous mass of ruins. We approached on the northeast side, which appeared covered with blotches and patches of a most extraordinary description, commemorating the shots of our monitors. The notches in the half-demolished wall were mended with gabions. On the southeast side not an angle, not a square foot of the original octagonal wall remained, but in its place was an irregular steeply sloping bank of broken bricks, stones, and sand, — a half-pulverized mountain, on which no amount of shelling could have any other effect than to pulverize it still more.

I could now readily understand the Rebel boast, that Fort Sumter, after each attack upon it, was stronger than ever. Stronger for defence, as far as its walls were concerned, it undoubtedly was; but where were the double rows of portholes for heavy ordnance, and the additional loopholes on the south side for musketry? Our guns had faithfully smashed everything of that kind within their range.

On the northwest side, facing the city, the perpendicular lofty wall stands in nearly its original condition, its scientific proportions, of stupendous solid masonry, astonishing us by their contrast with the other sides.   Between this wall and the wreck of a Rebel steamer, shot through and sunk whilst bringing supplies to the fort, we landed.   By flights of wooden steps we reached the summit, and looked down into the huge crater within.   This is a sort of irregular amphitheatre, with sloping banks of gabions and rubbish on all sides save one. On the southeast side, where the exterior of the fort received the greatest damage from the guns on Morris Island, the interior received the least.   There are no casemates left, except on that side.   In the centre stands the flagstaff, bearing aloft the starry symbol of the national power, once humbled here, and afterwards trailed long through bloody dust, to float again higher and haughtier than ever, on those rebellious shores.   Who, that loves his country, can look upon it there without a thrill ?

The fort is built upon a mole, which is flooded by high-water.   It was half-tide that morning, and climbing down the slope of the southeast embankment, I walked upon the beach below, — or rather upon the litter of old iron that strewed it thick as pebble-stones.   It was difficult to step without placing the foot upon a rusty cannon-ball or the fragment of a shell. The curling waves broke upon beds of these iron debris, extending far down out of sight into the sea.   I suggested to an officer that this would be a valuable mine to work, and was told that the right to collect the old iron around the fort had already been sold to a speculator for thirty thousand dollars.

The following statement of the cost to the United States of some of the forts seized by the Rebels, and of others they would have been glad to seize, but could not see their way clear to do so, will interest a few readers.

Fort Moultrie, $87,601.   (Evacuated by Major Anderson Dec. 26th, 1860.)

Castle Pinckney, $53,809.   (Seized by South Carolina State troops, Dec. 27th, 1860.)

Fort Sumter, $977,404.

Fort Pulaski, at the mouth of the Savannah River, $988,-
859. (Seized by order of Governor Brown, Jan. 3d, 1861.)

Fort Morgan, Mobile Harbor, $1,242,552. (Seized Jan.
4th, 1861.)

Fort Gaines, opposite, $221,500. (Same fate.)

Fort Jackson, on the Mississippi, below New Orleans, $837,-
608. Its fellow, Fort St. Philip, $258,734. (Both seized
Jan. 10th, 1861.)

Fort Warren, Boston Harbor, $1,208,000. (Not conve-
nient for the Rebels to appropriate.)

Fortress Monroe, the most expensive, as it is the largest of
our forts, $2,476,771. (Taken by Jeff Davis in May, 1865,
under peculiar circumstances, and still occupied by him at this
date, May, 1866.)

I found eighty-five United States soldiers in Sumter: a
mere handful, yet they were five more than the garrison that
held it at the time of Beauregard's bombardment in April,
1861. My mind went back to those earlier days, and to that
other little band. How anxiously we had watched the newspapers, week after week, to see if the Rebels would *dare* to
execute their threats! Even the children caught the excitement, and asked eagerly, as papa came home at night with the
news, " Is Fort Sumter attackted ? " At last the defiant act
was done, and what a raging, roaring fire it kindled all over
the land! How our hearts throbbed in sympathy with Major
Anderson and his seventy-nine heroes! Major, Colonel, General Anderson, — well might he step swiftly up the degrees of
rank, for he was already atop of our hearts.

It was so easy for a man to blaze forth into sudden glory of
renown at that time! One true, loyal, courageous deed, and
fame was secure. But when the hurricane howl of the storm
was at its height, when the land was all on fire with such
deeds, glory was not so cheap. Only the taller flame could
make itself distinguished, only the more potent voice be heard
amid the roar. So many a hero of many a greater exploit
than Anderson's passed on unnoted.

And looking back coolly at the event from the walls of Sumter to-day, it is not easy to understand how a patriot and a soldier, who knew his duty, could have sat quiet in his fortress while Rebel batteries were rising all around him. He was acting on the defensive, you say, — waiting for the Rebels to commence hostilities. But hostilities had already begun. The first spadeful of earth thrown up, to protect the first Rebel gun, within range of Sumter, was an act of war upon Sumter. To wait until surrounded by a ring of fire, which could not be resisted, before opening the guns of the fort, appears, by the light both of military duty and of common sense, absurd. But fortunately something else rules, in a great revolution, besides military duty and common sense ; and in the plan of that Providence which shapes our ways, I suppose Major Anderson did the best and only thing that was to be done. Besides, forbearance, to the utmost verge of that virtue, and sometimes a little beyond, was the policy of the government he served.

Reëmbarking on the steamer, and running over to Morris Island, I noticed that Sumter, from that side, looked like nothing but a solitary sandy bluff, heaved up in the middle of the harbor.

CHAPTER LXXIII.

A PRISON AND A PRISONER.

" Is this your first visit to Charleston ? " I asked General S——, one day as we dined together.

" My first visit," he replied, " occurred in the summer of 1864, considerably against my inclination. I was lodged at the expense of the Confederate Government in the Work-House, — not half as comfortable a place as this hotel ! "

Both visits were made in the service of the United States Government ; but under what different circumstances ! Then, a helpless, insulted prisoner ; now, he came in a capacity which brought to him as humble petitioners some of the most rebellious citizens of those days. When sick and in prison, they did not minister unto him ; but since he sat in an office of public power, nothing could exceed their polite, hat-in-hand attentions.

Dinner over, he proposed that we should go around and look at his old quarters in the Work-House. I gladly assented, and, on the way, drew from him the story of his capture.

He was taken prisoner at the battle of July 22d, before Atlanta, and placed on a train, with a number of other prisoners, to be conveyed to Macon.

" When we were about ten or a dozen miles from Macon, I went and sat on the platform with the guard. To prevent his suspecting my design, I told him I was disabled by rheumatism, and complained of pain and weakness in my back. He presently leaned against the car, and closed his eyes ; like everybody else after the battles of July, he was pretty well used up, and in a few minutes he appeared to be asleep. His gun was cocked, ready to shoot any prisoner that attempted to escape; and I quietly took the cap off, without disturbing him. Then I did n't dare wait a minute for a better opportunity, but jumped when I could. We were five or six miles from Macon, and the train was running about ten miles an hour. As I took my leap, I felt my hat flying from my head, and instinctively put up my hand and caught it, knowing if it was lost it might give a clew that would lead to my recapture. All this passed through my mind while I went rolling down an embankment eighteen or twenty feet high. I thought I never should strike the bottom. When I did, the concussion was so great that I lay under a fence, nearly senseless, for I don't know how long : I could n't have moved, even if I had known a minute's delay would cause me to be retaken.

" After a while I recovered, got up, crossed the fields, and found a road on the edge of some woods. It was then just at dusk. I walked all night, and in the morning found myself where I started. I had been walking around a hill, on a road made by woodmen.

" I was very tired, but I made up my mind I must leave that place. I got the points of the compass by the light in the east, and started to walk in a northerly direction, hoping to strike our lines somewhere near Atlanta. I soon passed a field of squealing hogs. I ought to have taken warning by their noise ; but I kept on, and presently met a man with a bag of corn on his shoulder, going to feed them. I was walking fast, with my coat on my arm ; and we passed each other without saying a word. My whole appearance was calculated to excite suspicion. Besides, one might know by my uniform that I was a Yankee officer. I suppose, by the law of self-defence, I ought to have turned about and put him out of the way of doing me any mischief. It would have been well for me if I had. I was soon out of sight; but I could hear the hogs squealing still, so I knew he had not stopped to give them the corn; I knew he had dropped his bag and run, as well as if I had watched him.

" I crossed the fields to the road, where I saw somebody coming very fast on a horse. I hid in some weeds, and presently saw this same man riding by at a sharp gallop towards a neighboring plantation.

" Then I knew I had a hard time before me. I first sat down and rubbed pine leaves and tobacco on the soles of my boots ; then took once more to the fields. It was n't an hour before I heard the blood-hounds on my track. I can never tell what I suffered during the next three days. I did not sleep at all ; I travelled almost incessantly. Sometimes when I stopped to rest the dogs would come in sight ; and often I could hear them when I did not see them. I baffled them continually by changing my course, walking in streams, and rubbing tobacco and pine leaves on my boot-soles."

" What did you live on all this time ? "

" I will tell you what I ate : three crackers, which I had with me when I jumped from the cars, one water-melon, and some raw green corn I picked in a field. The third day I got rid of the dogs entirely. I saw a lonely looking house on a hill, and went to it. It was occupied by a widow. I asked for something to eat, and she cooked me a dinner while I kept watch for the dogs. Perhaps she was afraid to do differently ; but she appeared very kind. When the dinner was ready I was so sick from excitement and exhaustion that I could n't eat. I managed to force down an egg and a spoonful of peas, and that was all. The Rebels had taken my money, and I could pay her only with thanks.

" I travelled nearly all that night again. Towards morning I lay by in a canebrake, and slept a little. It was raining hard. The next day I started on again. As I was crossing a road, suddenly a man came round a steep bank, on horse-back. I did n't see him until he was right upon me. I felt desperate. He asked me some question, and I gave him a surly answer. I thought I would n't leave the road until he had gone on ; but he checked his horse, and rode along by my side.

" ' You look like you are in trouble,' he said.

" ' I am,' I said.

" ' Can I be of any service to you ? '

" ' Yes. I want to go to Crawford's Station. How far is it ? '

" He said it was three miles, and told me the way to go. Crawford's is only fifteen miles from Macon ; so you see I had not got far whilst running from the dogs.

" Suddenly a terrible impulse took me. I turned upon him ; I felt fierce ; I could have murdered him, if necessary.

" ' I told you a lie,' said I. ' I am not going to Crawford's. I am a Federal soldier trying to escape.'

" He turned pale. ' I am the provost-marshal of this district,' he said, after we had looked each other full in the face for about a minute, ' and do you know it is my duty to arrest you ? '

" Then a power came upon me such as I never felt before in my life ; and I talked to him. I laid open the whole question of the war with a clearness and force which astonishes me now when I think of it. I believe I convinced him. Then I told him that if *I* had been doing *my* duty, it was *his* duty to help me escape, instead of arresting me. And then I prophesied : — ' This war is going to end,' I said ; ' and it is going to end in only one way. As true as there is a heaven above us, your Confederate Government is going to be wiped from the earth ; and then where will you be ? then what will you think of the duty of one man to arrest another whose only fault is that he has been fighting for his country ? The time is coming, sir, when it may make a mighty difference with you, whether you help me now, or send me to a Rebel prison.'

" He looked at me in perfect amazement. He did not answer me a word ; only when I got through he said, ' I 'd give a thousand dollars if I had not met you ! ' I got down to drink from a ditch by the road. Then he said, ' I 've got a canteen at the house which you might have.' That was the first intimation I received that he would help me.

" He told me to stay where I was and he would bring me something better to drink than ditch-water. I looked him through. ' I 'll trust you,' I said ; for no man ever looked as he did who was n't sincere. Yet there was danger he might change his mind; and I waited with great anxiety to see whether he would bring the canteen or a guard of soldiers. At last he came — with the canteen ! It was full of the most delicious spring water. I can't begin to tell you how good that water tasted ! The nectar of the gods was nothing to it.

" That night he hid me between two bales of cotton in his gin-house. He brought me bacon and biscuits enough to last me two or three days. What was more to the purpose, he gave me a suit of citizens' clothes to put on. While it was yet early, he brought me out, and went with me a mile or so on my way. He gave me the names of several citizens of the country, so that I could claim to be going to see them if anybody questioned me. I carried my uniform with me tied up in a bundle, which I intended to drop in the first piece of woods at a safe distance from his house. I never parted with a man under more affecting circumstances. An enemy, he had risked his life to save me, — for we both knew that if the part he took in my escape was discovered, his reward would be the halter.

" I had a valuable gold watch, which the Rebels had not taken from me, and I urged him to accept it. ' If I am recaptured,' I said, ' some Confederate soldier will get it. If I escape, it will be the greatest source of satisfaction I can have to know that you keep this token of my gratitude.' At last he consented to accept it, and we parted.

" I travelled due north all that day, and lay by at night in a canebrake. How it rained again ! The next day, in avoiding the main roads, as I had been careful to do whenever I could, I got entangled among streams that put into the Ocmulgee River. I came to a large one, and as I was turning back from it, I saw a squad of soldiers going down to it to bathe. I was in a complete *cul de sac*, and I must either run for the river or meet them. I put on a bold face, and went out towards them. As it was an extraordinary situation for a stranger to be in, they naturally suspected everything was not right. They asked me where I was from, and where I was going. I said I came from near Macon, and that I was going to visit my uncle, Dr. Moore, in De Kalb County. I suppose my speech betrayed me. They did n't suspect me of being an escaped prisoner; but their captain said, 'I believe you 're a damned Yankee spy.'

" That sealed my fate. I was taken to Forsyth, on the Macon and Western Railroad, where I was finally recognized by the guard I had escaped from.

" While I was sitting in the depot, in my citizens' clothes, a half-drunken Confederate soldier came in, flourishing a loaded pistol, and inquiring for the 'damned Yankee.' 'What do you want of him?' I asked. 'To shoot his heart out!' said he. 'What!' said I, 'would you shoot a prisoner? I hope you are too chivalrous to do that.' 'It 's a part of my chivalry to kill every Yankee I find,' said he. 'Just show him to me, and you 'll see.' 'I 'll show him to you. I am the man. Now let 's see you shoot him.'

" He swore I was joking. He would n't believe I was the Yankee, even when the guard told him I was; and he went blustering away again. I suspect that he was a fellow of more talk than courage.

" Meanwhile Mr. T——, who gave me my citizens' dress, heard of my recapture, and came over to Forsyth, in great anxiety lest I should betray him. I pretended not to recognize him, but gave him to understand by a look that his secret was safe. He said it was very important to ascertain how I came by my clothes, and questioned me. I said I obtained them of a good and true man, whom I should never name to his injury; but that I would tell where I left my uniform, because I wished to get it again. When I described the spot, he said he believed he recognized it, and, if so, that it was on one of his neighbors' plantations. He sent to search, and the next day I received my uniform. I forgot to state that when I was retaken, my drawers were mildewed from my lying out in the canebrakes in the rain.

" From Forsyth I was sent to the stockade at Macon, where I found my companions from whom I separated when I jumped from the car. I had n't been there three days when I formed a new plan of escape. I got the other prisoners enlisted in it, and we went to tunnelling the ground under the stockade. Each man worked with a knife, or a piece of hoop, — anything that he could scratch with, — and filled a haversack with the dirt, which was brought out and scattered over the ground. As prisoners exposed to the weather were always burrowing in caves, our design was not suspected. It was exceedingly toilsome work, and it was carried on principally by night. You would be astonished to see how much a man will accomplish, with not much· besides his finger-nails to do with, when his liberty is at stake. We worked six tunnels, three feet high, and extending well out beyond the stockade. The very night when we were going to open them up on the outside, one of the prisoners, a Kentuckian, betrayed us. If we had found out who he was, he would n't have lived a minute. Then, just as I was maturing another plan, I was sent here."

We were at the Work-House, a castle-like building, flanked by two tall towers ; built of brick, but covered with a cement in imitation of freestone. Before the war it was used as a safe place of deposit for that description of property known as slaves. Negroes for sale and awaiting the auction-day, negroes who had or had not merited chastisement not convenient for their city masters or mistresses to administer at home, negroes who had run away, or were in danger of running away, were sent here for safe-keeping or scientific flogging, as the case might be. It was a mere jail, with cells and bolts and bars, like any other. During the war, the negroes were transferred to another building near by, and the " Work-House " became a Yankee prison, in which officers were confined.

In the same block was the City Jail, likewise turned into a prison for Federal officers. The Roper and Marine Hospitals, not far off, were put to the same use.

It was a dungeon-like entrance, dark and low and damp, to which we gained admittance through a heavy door that creaked harshly on its hinges.

" When I first entered here," said General S——, " a cold

shudder ran over me. I looked around for a chance to escape, and saw behind and on each side of me two rows of bayonets, not encouraging to the most enterprising man ! "

We walked through the empty, foul, and dismal passages, up-stairs and down-stairs; visited the various cells, the old negro whipping-room, the room in which General Stoneman, the captured raider, was confined ; and at length came to a room in the second story of the west tower, which was occupied by General S—— and a dozen more Federal officers. There were several wooden bunks in it, on which they slept; from among which the General singled out his own. " This is the old thing I lay on ! Here is my mark ! "

He looked up : " Do you see that patched place in the roof ? A shell came in there one day, when we were lying on our bunks. It made these holes in the floor. But it hurt no one."

He took me to the window. " That other tower was knocked by a shell. It was one of our amusements to watch the shells as they came up from Morris Island, rose over the ruined Cathedral yonder, and passed diagonally across these streets, until they fell. They were dropping all the time ; but the gunners knew where we were, and avoided us. At night we could watch them from the time they rose, until, after describing a beautiful curve, they fell and exploded. Our guard was much more afraid of them than we were. Every day there was a fire set by them. This burnt section near the Work-House was set by a shell while I was here."

We went down into the yard. " I never got outside of this enclosure but once. Then I went through that gate for a load of wood. I had a taste of the pure air, and I can't tell you how good it was ! It exhilarated me like wine."

On the other side of the yard was the building to which the negroes were transferred. " Every day we could hear the yells of those who were being whipped."

In the yard is a wooden tower of observation, which we climbed, and had a view of the city. It was occupied as a lookout by the Rebel guard.

" Near the foot of this tower," said General S——, " was

a small mountain of offal, — fragments of food, old bones, and the like, thrown out from the prison ; a horrible heap, — all a moving mass of maggots, — left to engender disease. Luckily for us, the men on guard were made sick by it, and it was finally removed.

" The officer who had control of the prison has been appointed United States Marshal for the State of South Carolina, for his kindness to us," he continued. " It is strange I never heard of his kindness when I was here. We were not whipped like the negroes ; but in other respects our treatment was no better than they received. Out of curiosity I once measured my rations for ten days, and counted just fifty-five spoonfuls, — five and a half spoonfuls a day !

" I believe the prisoners at the Roper Hospital were treated very well. They had the run of the garden, and the privilege of trading with the negroes through the fence. But those who went there took an oath not to try to get away. I could have gone there, if I would have consented to take such an oath. But I would n't sell the hope of escaping at any price.

" I had n't been here a week before we had three schemes on foot for getting out. One was to cut through a board in the yard fence ; but we found we were watched too closely for that. Another was to make a tunnel to the sewer in the street in front of the prison, as I will show you."

Descending the tower, he took me to an iron grating that covered a dark cavity in the ground under one of the prison passages.

"Here is a large cistern, which we had exhausted of its contents. One day I pulled up this grate, dropped down into the hole, lighted a candle which I had in my pocket, and made an exploration. On coming out I gave a favorable report, and that night we went to digging. We tunnelled first through the cistern wall, then through the foundation wall of the prison, and got into the sand under the street. We half filled the old cistern with the stones and dirt we dug out with sticks, old bones, and any bits of iron we could lay our hands on. We worked like rats. Two or three of us were constantly

34

in the tunnel, while others kept watch above. A friend outside had given us information with regard to the position of the sewer; we had already struck it, and the next night we should have got into it, and into the street beyond the prison guard, when once more we were betrayed by the same Kentuckian who exposed our scheme at Macon. This time we found him out, and he had to be removed from the prison to save his life.

" We had our third and great plan in reserve.

" There were at that time six hundred prisoners in the Work-House, three hundred in the City Jail adjoining, and one thousand in the Roper and Marine Hospitals, within an arrow's shot. These were officers. At the Race-Course prison, on the outskirts of the town, there were four thousand enlisted men. Our guard, here at the Work-House, consisted of three reliefs of thirty-three men each. They were mere militia, that had never seen service. Old soldiers like us were not afraid of such fellows ; and we knew that if we made a demonstration they would be afraid of us. Our plan was, for two prisoners, at a given signal, to leap on the back of each one of the guard in the prison, and disarm him. Possibly some of us might get hurt, but we were pretty sure of success. Then, with the arms thus secured, we could easily capture the second relief guard as it marched in. Then we were to rush out immediately and seize the third relief. This would give us ninety-nine guns. With these we were to march directly upon the arsenal, capture it, and provide ourselves with all the arms and ammunition we needed. Then to release the thirteen hundred officers at the jail and hospitals, and the four thousand privates at the Race-Course, would have been easy ; and we should have had a force of near six thousand men. With these, the city would have been in our power.

" Our plan then was, to set fires clear across it, from river to river, to make a barricade of burning buildings against the Rebel artillery that would have been coming down to look after us. Of course the panic and confusion of the citizens would have been extreme, and the military would hardly have known what we were about ; while our plans were laid with mathematical precision. Our friend outside had smuggled in to us, done up in balls of bread, a map of Charleston, with complete explanations of every point about which we needed information ; and through him we had communicated with our friends on Morris Island. We were to seize the shipping, capture the water-batteries, and hold the lower part of the town until our friends, under cover of a furious bombardment, could come to our assistance. My whole heart was in this scheme, and the time was set for its execution. The very day before the day appointed, I was exchanged, together with the principal leaders in it. To be let out just on the eve of what promised to be such a brilliant exploit, was almost a disappointment."

" I am still interested to know one thing," I said. " Have you ever heard from the Rebel who gave you the citizen's dress ? "

" After the breaking up of the rebellion I wrote to him, making inquiries concerning his condition. He replied, saying that he had come out of the war a poor man, and that he did not know how he was to relieve the destitution of his family. I immediately made application in his behalf to the War Department, and obtained for him a pardon, and a place under the government, in his own county, which he now fills, and which yields him a liberal income."

CHAPTER LXXIV.

THE SEA ISLANDS.

THE plantation negro of the great cotton and rice-growing States is a far more ignorant and degraded creature than the negro of Virginia and Tennessee. This difference is traceable to a variety of causes. First, the farmers of the slave-breeding States were formerly accustomed to select, from among their servants, the most stupid and vicious class, to be sold in the Southern market. To the same destination went all the more modern importations of raw savages from the coast of Africa. The negro is susceptible to the influences of civilization; and in the border States his intelligence was developed by much intercourse with the white race. His veins also received a generous infusion of the superior blood. The same may be said of house and town servants throughout the South. The slaves of large and isolated plantations, however, enjoyed but limited advantages of this sort; seeing little of civilized society beyond the overseer, whose lessons were not those of grace, and the poor whites around them, scarcely more elevated in the scale of being than themselves.

In South Carolina the results of these combined causes are more striking than in any other State. The excess of her black population, and the unmitigated character of slavery within her borders, afford perhaps a sufficient explanation of this fact. In 1860 she had 291,388 white, 402,406 slave, and 9,914 free colored inhabitants. Even these figures do not indicate the overwhelming predominance of black numbers in certain localities. In the poorer districts, as counties are here called, the whites are in a majority; while in certain others there were three and four times as many negroes as white persons. Herded together in great numbers, and worked like cattle, the habits of these wretched people, their comforts and enjoyments, were little above those of the brute. Under such circumstances it was hardly possible for them to make any moral or intellectual advancement, but often, even to the third generation, they remained as ignorant as when brought from the wilds of Africa.

It was owing much no doubt to this excessive black population and its degraded character, that labor appeared to be more disorganized, and the freedmen in a worse condition in South Carolina, than elsewhere. The Sea-Island question, however, had had a very marked and injurious effect upon labor in the State, and should be taken into consideration.

The most ignorant of the blacks have certain true and strong instincts, which stand them in the place of actual knowledge. Their faith in Providence has a depth and integrity which shames the halting belief of the more enlightened Christian. Next to that, and strangely blended with it, is the faith in the government which has brought them out of bondage. Along with these goes the simple and strong conviction, that, in order to be altogether free, and to enjoy the fruits of their freedom, they must have homes of their own. The government encouraged them in that belief and hope. Conscious of their own loyalty, and having a clear understanding of the disloyalty of their masters, they expected confidently, long after the war had closed, that the forfeited lands of these masters would be divided among them. It was only after earnest and persistent efforts on the part of the officers of the Bureau, to convince them that this hope was futile, that they finally abandoned it.

But by this time it had become known among the freed people of South Carolina and Georgia, that extensive tracts of land on the coast of these States had been set aside by military authority for their use. There the forty thousand bondmen who followed Sherman out of Georgia, together with other thousands who had preceded them, or come after, were established upon independent farms, in self-governing communities from which all white intruders were excluded. These settlements were chiefly upon the rich and delightful Sea Islands, which the Rebel owners had abandoned, and which now became the paradise of the freedmen's hopes. "Go there," they said, "and every man can pick out his lot of forty acres, and have it secured to him."

With such fancies in his brain, the negro of the interior was not likely to remain contented on the old plantation, after learning that no acre of it was to be given him. He was naturally averse to accepting a white master, when he might be his own master elsewhere. His imaginative soul sang too, in its rude way : —

> " Oh, had we some sweet little isle of our own,
> In a blue summer ocean, far off and alone ! "

And so the emigration to the coast set in.

In October, 1865, orders were issued that no more allotments of land should be made to the Freedmen. But this did not avail to stop entirely the tide of emigration; nor did it inspire with contentment those who remained in the interior. " If a freedman has forty acres on the coast," they reasoned, " why should n't we have as much here ? " Hence one of the most serious troubles the officers of the Bureau had to contend against.

In October, General Howard visited the Sea Islands with the intention of restoring to the pardoned owners the lands on which freedmen had been settled, under General Sherman's order. According to the President's theory, a pardon entitled the person pardoned to the immediate restoration of his property. Hence arose a conflict of authority and endless confusion. Secretary Stanton had approved of Sherman's order, and earnestly advised the freedmen to secure homesteads under the government's protection. General Saxton, Assistant Commissioner of the Bureau, had in every way encouraged them to do the same. So had General Hunter. Chief Justice Chase had given them similar counsel. General Howard found the land-owners urgent in pressing their claims, and the freedmen equally determined in resisting them.

Impressed by the immense difficulty of the problem, he postponed its immediate solution by a compromise, leaving the main question to be settled by Congress. Congress settled it, after a fashion, in the provisions of the Freedmen's Bureau Bill ; but that, in consequence of the President's veto, did not become a law.

By General Howard's plan, abandoned lands on which there were no freedmen settled under Sherman's order, or only " a few," were to be restored to pardoned owners. Other estates, on which there were more than "a few," were also to be restored, provided arrangements could be made, satisfactory to both the owners and the freedmen. So nothing was settled. The owners claimed the lands, and wished the freedmen to make contracts to work for them. The freedmen claimed the lands, and positively refused to make contracts.

The freedmen's crops for the past year had generally proved failures, or nearly so. Their friends argued that this result was owing to causes that could not be controlled, — the lack of capital, of seed, of mules and farming implements, and the lateness of the season when most of them commenced work. The owners of the lands contended that the negro, under the best conditions, could not make a crop of cotton. The truth probably lies between these two extremes. The freedmen lacked experience in management, as well as planting capital ; and I have no doubt but many of them thought more of a gun and a fishing-rod, sources of a pleasure so new to them, than of hard work in the field, which was anything but a novelty.

I regret to add that the freedmen's prospects for the coming year did not appear flattering. The uncertainty of their titles caused them deep trouble and discouragement, and they did not exhibit much energy in improving lands which might be taken from them at any moment. The feeling, " This is my home and my children's," seemed no longer to inspire them. The majority were at work ; but others were sullenly waiting to see what the government would do.

This whole question is one of great embarrassment and

difficulty, and it is not easy to say how it should be decided. The plan proposed by Congress, of securing to the freedmen the possession of the lands for three years, did not seem to me a very wise one. It would take them about three years, under the most favorable circumstances, to overcome the obstacles against which their poverty and inexperience would have to struggle; and the knowledge that, after all, those homes were not to be permanently their own, would tend to discourage industry and promote vagabondism. It would be better to remove them at once, if they are to be removed at all; but then the question presents itself, can a great and magnanimous government afford to break its pledges to these helpless and unfortunate people?

On the other hand, to make their titles perpetual, is to give over to uncertain cultivation, by a race supposed to exist only for the convenience of another, the most valuable cotton-lands of those States, — for it is here alone that the incomparable long-fibred "Sea-Island" staple is produced, — a conclusion deemed inadmissible and monstrous, especially by the Rebel owners of the lands.

CHAPTER LXXV.

A VISIT TO JAMES ISLAND.

A COMPANY of South Carolina planters, who were going over to look at their estates on James Island, and learn if any arrangements could be made with the freedmen, invited me to accompany them ; and on the morning of the day appointed, I left my hotel for the purpose.

Finding I was too early for the boat, I took a stroll along the wharves, and visited the colonies of homeless plantation negroes who had sought shelter under the open coal-sheds.

There were at that time in Charleston fifteen hundred freed people of this class waiting for transportation back to their former homes, or to the plantations of new masters who had hired them. A more wretched and pitiable herd of human beings I never saw ; nor had I witnessed anything like it out of South Carolina.

Families were cooking and eating their breakfasts around smoky fires. On all sides were heaps of their humble household goods, — tubs, pails, pots and kettles, sacks, beds, barrels tied up in blankets, boxes, baskets, bundles. They had brought their live-stock with them ; hens were scratching, pigs squealing, cocks crowing, and starved puppies whining.

One colony was going to Beaufort. "Mosser told we to go back. We 'se no money, and we 'se glad to git on gov-'ment kindness, to git off." But the government was not yet ready to send them.

Many seemed deeply to regret that they were so much trouble to the government. " We wants to git away to work on our own hook. It 's not a good time at all here. We does nothing but suffer from smoke and ketch cold. We wants to begin de planting business."

Another colony had been two weeks waiting for transportation back to their old homes in Colleton District. Their sufferings were very great. Said an old woman, with a shawl over her head : " De jew and de air hackles we more 'n anyting. De rain beats on we, and de sun shines we out. My chil'n so hungry dey can't hole up. De Gov'ment, he han't gib we nottin'. Said dey would put we on board Saturday. Some libs and some dies. If dey libs dey libs, and if dey dies dey dies." Such was her dim philosophy. I tried to converse with others, who spoke a wild jargon peculiar to the plantations, of which I understood hardly one word in ten.

General Scott, who had recently succeeded General Saxton as Assistant Commissioner of the Bureau in South Carolina, was hastening measures for the relief of these poor people, and to prevent any more from coming to the city.

I walked around by the delightful residences on East Bay and South Bay, commanding fine views of the harbor and Ashley River; and reached the wharf from which we were to embark.

Opposite lay James Island, with its marshy borders, and its dark-green line of pines. Boats — mostly huge cypress dugouts, manned by negroes — were passing to and fro, some coming from the island with loads of wood, others returning, heavily laden, with families of freedmen going to their new homes, and with household goods and supplies.

" This is interesting," said one of the planters, whom I found in waiting. " That wood comes from our plantations. The negroes cut it off, bring it over to the city, and perhaps sell it to the actual owners of the land they have taken it from. We are buying our own wood of the darkey squatters. The negroes are still going to the island, picking their lands, and staking out forty-acre lots, though the Bureau is giving no more titles."

A large cypress dug-out came to the wharf, rowed by a black man and his son.

" These boats all belonged to the planters, till the negroes took possession of them. Now a man has to hire a passage in his own canoe, and like as any way of one of his own negroes."

The grim, silent boatman seemed to understand well that he was master of the situation. There were seven individuals in our party, and his charge for taking us over to the Island and back was ten dollars. He made no words about it : we could accept his terms, or find another boat. The gravity and taciturnity of this man indicated decided character, and no mean capacity for self-ownership. As he and his son rowed us across the river, he attended strictly to his business, hearing the talk of the planters about the race he represented — talk by no means complimentary — with an impenetrability of countenance quite astonishing.

This was the third visit of the planters to the island, since the war. On the first occasion, they were met by a party of negroes, about forty in number, who rushed down to the landing, armed with guns, and drove them away, with threats to kill them if they came to disturb them in their homes again ; whereupon they discreetly withdrew. On their second visit they were accompanied by Captain Ketchum, special agent of the Bureau for the Sea Islands, to whose influence they probably owed their lives. They were met as before, surrounded by fierce black faces and levelled guns, captured, and not permitted to regain their boat until their leaders, who could read a little, became satisfied, from an examination of the Captain's papers, that he was an officer of the government. " We are ready to do anything for gov'ment," they said. " But we have nothing to do with these men."

They asked the Captain, who were the real owners of the land, — they who had been placed there by the government, or the planters who had been fighting against the government ?

" That is uncertain," replied the conscientious Captain.

The planters, who had hoped for a different reply, well aware that the negroes could not be brought to terms without a positive assurance from an officer of the Bureau that they had no good title to the lands, were very much disgusted. " We may as well go back now," said they. And scarcely any effort was made to induce the negroes to abandon their claims and make contracts.

This was now their third visit, and it remained to be seen how they would be received. We rowed a short distance down Wappoo Creek, which separates the island from the main land, and disembarked at a plantation belonging to three orphan children, whose guardian was a member of our party. The freedmen, having learned that the mere presence of the planters on the soil could effect nothing, had changed their tactics, and now not one of them was to be seen. Although there were twenty-two hundred on the island, it appeared as solitary and silent as if it had not an inhabitant.

We found the plantation house occupied as head-quarters by an officer of the Bureau, recently sent to the island. The guardian of the three orphans took me aside, showed me the desolated grounds without, shaded by magnificent live-oaks, and the deserted chambers within.

"You can understand my feelings coming here," he said. "My sister expired in this room. She left her children to me. This estate, containing seventeen hundred acres, and worth fifty thousand dollars, is all that remains to them ; and you see the condition it is in. Why does the Government of the United States persist in robbing orphan children? They have done nothing ; they have n't earned the titles of Rebels and traitors. Why not give them back their land?"

I sympathized sincerely with this honest gentleman and his orphan wards. "But you forget," I said, "that such a war as we have passed through cannot be, without involving in its calamities the innocent as well as the rest. It would have been well if that fact had not been overlooked in the beginning."

He made no reply. I afterwards learned from his friends that he was one of the original and most fiery secessionists of Charleston. He made a public speech, early in 'sixty-one, — printed in the newspapers at the time, — in which he expressly pledged his life and his fortune to the Confederate cause. His life he had managed to preserve ; and of his fortune sufficient remained for the elegant maintenance of his own and his sister's children ; so that it appeared to me quite unreasonable for him to complain of the misfortune which he himself had been instrumental in bringing upon the orphans.

The party separated, each man going to look at his own estate. I accompanied one who had three fine plantations in the vicinity. A Northern man by birth, his sympathy had been with the government, while he found his private interest in working for the Confederate usurpation under profitable contracts. By holding his tongue and attending to business he had accumulated a handsome fortune, — wisely investing his Confederate scrip in real estate, which he thought somewhat more substantial. These plantations were a part of his earnings. Being a Northern man, and at heart a Union man, he deemed it hard that they should not be at once restored to him. The fact that they were his reward for aiding the enemies of his country, — rich gains, so to speak, snatched from the wreck of a pirate ship on board which he had served, — did not seem to have occurred to him as any bar to his claims.

At first we found all the freedmen's houses shut up, and as silent as if the inhabitants had all gone to a funeral. By pressing into some of them, we discovered a 'few women and children, but the men had disappeared. Since they were not to resist our coming, it seemed their policy to have nothing whatever to do with us. At last we found an old negro too decrepit to run away, who sullenly awaited our approach.

" What is your name, uncle ? "

" Samuel Butler."

" Where are you from ? "

" From St. John."

" How did you come here ? "

" Yankees fotch me."

" Don't you want to go back to St. John ? "

" Yankees fotch me here," repeated the old man, " and I won't go back widout de Yankees send me back."

We inquired about his family and his prospects.

" My chil'n 's out in soldiering. I made corn, peas, and

potatoes; I got enough to carry me out de year. I had to bought my own clo'es, besides. Gov'ment don't help me none."

He had his forty-acre lot, and would not peril his claim to it by talking about a contract.

In one cabin we found a very old negro lying on the floor, miserably sick with the dropsy. He had been " a faithful old family servant," as the phrase is; and was accounted a wise head by the planters. When asked if he thought the freedmen could be prevailed upon to contract, he replied :

" What little we do will be sarvice to we-self. We don't want to work for rest," — meaning the planters.

Speaking of himself, he said :

" My time is all burnt out." He said there was a heap of idlers on the island. " Dey 'm on a full spree now. Dey got a sort of frolic in de brains." There had been considerable destitution even among the industrious ones the past year ; but many of them had made fair crops, and had corn sufficient to keep them till another harvest. " Dey 'm more situated better now." The small-pox had raged on the island, and " a sight of our people had died."

We lingered at these cabins, waiting for a guard the officer at head-quarters thought it prudent to send with us. At last he arrived, — a shining black youngster in soldier-clothes, overflowing with vanity and politeness. " I 'm waiting on your occupation, gentlemen," he said ; and we started on.

We passed a field in which there were several women at work. As they had no mule, they did everything by hand, chopping up the turf and weeds with their great awkward hoes, and scraping them, with the surface soil, into little ridges, on which cotton or corn was to be planted. This process of preparing the ground is called " listing " ; it answers the purpose of ploughing, and the refuse stuff scraped together, rotting, serves instead of manure.

My companion inquired on what terms they would consent to give up their forty-acre lot. One of them, poising her formidable hoe, replied in accents that carried conviction with them :

"Gov'ment drap we here. Can't go 'till Gov'ment take we off."

As we were now proceeding to a more remote part of the island, our colored guard walked proudly on to protect us from danger. " Dey can't make no raid on you, widout dey makes raid on me fus' ! "

He evidently felt himself vastly superior to these low-down plantation niggers. And I noticed that when we stopped to talk with any of them, and my friend recorded their names and numbers, and I also took notes, this shining black fellow in blue likewise produced a piece of card and a pencil, and appeared to be writing down very interesting and amusing memoranda.

A mile or so from head-quarters we found negro men and women working in the fields.

" Is this your farm ? " my friend inquired of one of them.

" I calls it mine. General Saxton told me to come and stake out my forty acres, and he'd give me a ticket for it."

" Would n't it be better for you to contract for good wages, than to work in this way ? "

" No, I don't want to contract. I 'll eat up my corn and peas fus'."

" Did you raise much last year ? "

" I begun too late. Den de drought hit us bad. Heap of places didn't raise much. But I got a little."

Observing a strange looking thing of skin and bones standing in the weeds, I asked, " Is that a horse ? "

" Dat 's a piece o' one. When he gits tired, I can take my arms ; I 've good strong arms."

Upon that one of the women struck in vehemently :

" I can plough land same as a hoss. Wid dese hands I raise cotton dis year, buy two hosses ! "

Seeing the immense disadvantage under which these poor people labored, without teams, without capital, and even without security in the possession of their little homesteads, I urged them to consider well what the planters had to offer.

" If I contract, what good does my forty acres do me ? "

"But you are not sure of your forty acres. This year or next they may be given back to the former owner. Then you will have nothing; for you will have spent all your time and strength in trying to get a start. But if you work for wages, you will have, if you are prudent, a hundred and fifty dollars in clear cash at the end of the year. At that rate it will not be long before you will be able to buy a little place and stock it handsomely; when you will probably be much better off than you would be working here in this way."

I could see that this argument was not without its weight with the men. They appeared troubled by it, but not convinced. The women clamored against it, and almost made me feel that I was an enemy, giving them insidious ill advice. And when I saw the almost religious attachment of these people to their homes, and their hope and ambition bearing up resolutely against poverty and every discouragement, it would have caused me a pang of remorse to know that I had persuaded any of them to give up their humble but worthy and honest aims. Then the children came around us, carrying primers, out of which they read with pleased eagerness, either for the fun of the thing, or to show us what they could do. The parents, forgetting the disheartening words we had spoken, said cheerily, "Richard, Helen, time for school!" and the little ones scampered away; the older ones resumed their work, and we walked on.

I was pleased to see some of the forty-acre lots enclosed by substantial new fences. But every question of benefit has two sides. The other side to this was that the fine old plantation shade-trees had been cut down and split into rails; a circumstance which made my friend the planter look glum.

The island is level, with handsome hedged avenues running through it in various directions. It is nine miles in length and three in breadth. We extended our walk as far as Fort Pemberton, on Stono River, which bounded my friend's plantations in that direction. On our return, he thought he would try one more freedman with the offer of a contract.

The man was working with his wife on a little farm of indefinite extent. "I don't know how much land I have. I guessed off as near as I could forty acres."

He said he had "a large fambly," and that he came from Charleston. "I heard there was a chance of we being our own driver here; that's why we come." He could get along very well if he only had a horse. "But if I can git de land, I'll take my chances."

"But if you can't get the land?"

"If a man got to go crost de riber, and he can't git a boat, he take a log. If I can't own de land, I'll hire or lease land, but I won't contract."

"Come, then," said my friend, "we may as well go home."

35

CHAPTER LXXVI.

SHERMAN IN SOUTH CAROLINA.

" THE march of the Federals into our State," says a writer in the " Columbia Phœnix," " was characterized by such scenes of license, plunder, and conflagration as very soon showed that the threats of the Northern press, and of their soldiery, were not to be regarded as a mere *brutum fulmen.* Daily long trains of fugitives lined the roads, with wives and children, and horses and stock and cattle, seeking refuge from the pursuers. Long lines of wagons covered the highways. Half-naked people cowered from the winter under bush-tents in the thickets, under the eaves of houses, under the railroad sheds, and in old cars left them along the route. All these repeated the same story of suffering, violence, poverty, and nakedness. Habitation after habitation, village after village, — one sending up its signal flames to the other, presaging for it the same fate, — lighted the winter and midnight sky with crimson horrors.

" No language can describe, nor can any catalogue furnish, an adequate detail of the wide-spread destruction of homes and property. Granaries were emptied, and where the grain was not carried off, it was strewn to waste under the feet of the cavalry, or consigned to the fire which consumed the dwelling. The negroes were robbed equally with the whites of food and clothing. The roads were covered with butchered cattle, hogs, mules, and the costliest furniture. Valuable cabinets, rich pianos, were not only hewn to pieces, but bottles of ink, turpentine, oil, whatever could efface or destroy, were employed to defile and ruin. Horses were ridden into the houses. People were forced from their beds, to permit the search after hidden treasures.

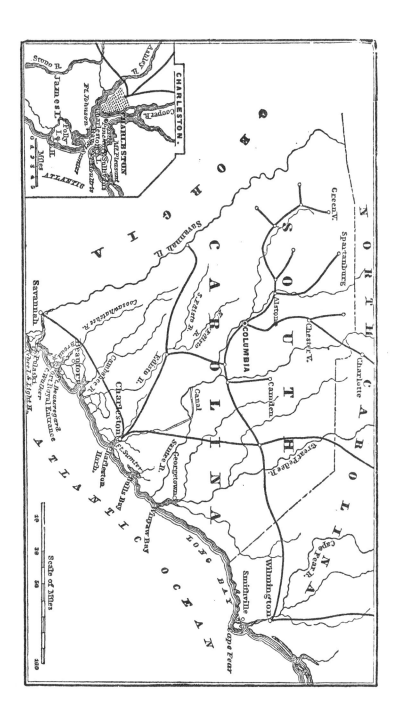

"The beautiful homesteads of the parish country, with their wonderful tropical gardens, were ruined ; ancient dwellings of black cypress, one hundred years old, which had been reared by the fathers of the Republic, — men whose names were famous in Revolutionary history, — were given to the torch as recklessly as were the rude hovels ; choice pictures and works of art from Europe, select and numerous libraries, objects of peace wholly, were all destroyed. The inhabitants, black no less than white, were left to starve, compelled to feed only upon the garbage to be found in the abandoned camps of the soldiers. The corn scraped up from the spots where the horses fed, has been the only means of life left to thousands but lately in affluence. The villages of Buford's Bridge, of Barnwell, Blackville, Graham's, Bamberg, Midway, were more or less destroyed ; the inhabitants everywhere left homeless and without food. The horses and mules, all cattle and hogs, whenever fit for service or for food, were carried off, and the rest shot. Every implement of the workman or the farmer, tools, ploughs, hoes, gins, looms, wagons, vehicles, was made to feed the flames."

Passing northward through the State, by the way of Orangeburg, Columbia, and Winnsboro', I heard, all along the route, stories corroborative of the general truthfulness of this somewhat highly colored picture. The following, related to me by a lady residing in Orangeburg District, will serve as a sample of these detailed narratives.

"The burning of the bridges by the Confederates, as the Yankees were chasing them, did no good, but a deal of harm. They could n't stop such an army as Sherman's, but all they could do was to hinder it, and keep it a few days longer in the country, eating us up.

"It was the best disciplined army in the world. At sundown, not a soldier was to be seen, and you could rest in peace till morning. That convinces me that everything that was done was permitted, if not ordered.

"I had an old cook with me, — one of the best old creatures you ever saw. She had a hard master before we bought her,

and she carried the marks on her face and hands where he had thrown knives at her. Such treatment as she got from us was something new to her; and there was nothing she would n't do for us, in return.

"'For heaven's sake, missus,' says she, 'bury some flour for the chil'n!' I gave her the keys to the smoke-house, and told her to do what she pleased. 'Send all the niggers off the place but me and my son,' she says, 'for I don't trust 'em.' Then she and her son buried two barrels of flour, the silver pitcher and goblets, and a box of clothes. But that night she dreamed that the Yankees came and found the place; so the next morning she went and dug up all the things but the flour, which she had n't time to remove, and buried them under the hog-pen. Sure enough, when the Yankees came, they found the flour, but her dream saved the rest. She was afraid they would get hold of her son, and make him tell, so she kept him in the chimney-corner, right under her eyes, all day, pretending he was sick.

"Some of the negroes were very much excited by the Yankees' coming. One of our black girls jumped up and shouted, 'Glory to God! de Yankees is comin' to marry all we niggers!' But they generally behaved very well. A black man named Charles, belonging to one of our neighbors, started with a load of goods, and flanked the Yankees for three days, and eluded them.

"A good many houses were burned in our neighborhood. Some that were occupied were set on fire two or three times, and the inhabitants put them out. The Yankees set the woods on fire, and we should have all been burnt up, if our negroes had n't dug trenches to keep the flames from reaching the buildings. General Sherman and his staff stopped at the house of a man of the name of Walker, in Barnwell District. While Mr. Walker was thanking him for protecting his property, he turned around, and saw the house on fire. General Sherman was very indignant. Said he, 'If I could learn who did that, he should meet with condign punishment!'

"The foragers broke down all the broadside of our barn,

and let the corn out ; then they broke down all the broadside of the garden, and drove in. We had three hundred bushels of corn ; and they took all but fifty bushels; they told me to hide that away. We had three barrels of syrup, and they took all but one gallon. They took eight thousand pounds of fodder, and three barrels of flour, all we had. We had twelve hundred pounds of bacon, and the soldiers took all but three pieces, which they said they left for the rest to take. We had twelve bushels of rough-rice ; they left us three ; and afterwards soldiers came in and threw shot in it, and mixed all up with sugar.

" They loaded up our old family carriage with bacon and sweet potatoes, and drove it away, — and that hurt me worse than all.

" They took our last potatoes. Three or four had just been roasted for the children : ' Damn the children ! ' they said ; and they ate the potatoes.

" Out of forty hogs, they left us six. We had twenty-one head of cattle, and they left us five. The officers were very kind to us, and if we could have had them with us all the time, we should have saved a good deal of stuff. One Yankee lieutenant was with us a good deal, and he was just like a brother to me. He reprimanded the soldiers who spoke saucily to us, telling them to remember that they had mothers and sisters at home. He wanted me to put out a white flag, because my husband is a Northern man. But I said, ' I 'll see this house torn to pieces first, for I 'm as good a Rebel as any of them ! ' He took three wagon-loads of corn from us : I thought that was mighty hard, if he cared anything for me." It was he, however, who left her the fifty bushels, which nobody took.

" The soldiers were full of fun and mischief. Says one, ' I 'm going to the smoke-house, to sweeten my mouth with molasses, and then I 'm coming in to kiss these dumb perty girls.' They emptied out the molasses, then walked through it, and tracked it all over the house. They dressed up their horses in women's clothes. They tore up our dresses and tied them to their horses' tails. They dressed up the negroes that followed them. They strung cow-bells all around their horses and cattle. They killed chickens and brought them into the house on their bayonets, all dripping.

"Two came into the house drunk, and ordered the old cook to get them some dinner. She told them we had nothing left. 'Go and kill a weasel!' said they. She boiled them some eggs. They took one, and peeled it, and gave it to my little boy. 'Here, eat that!' said one. 'But I've a good mind to blow your brains out, for you're a d——d little Rebel.' This man was from Connecticut, a native of the same town my husband came from. It would have been curious if they had met, and found that they were old acquaintances!

"Some behaved very well. One was handling the fancy things on the what-not, when another said, 'It won't help crush the Rebellion to break them.' 'I ain't going to break them,' he said, and he did n't.

"My husband had moved up a large quantity of crockery and glass-ware from his store in Charleston, for safety. The Yankees smashed it all. They would n't stop for keys, but broke open every drawer and closet. There wasn't a lock left in the neighborhood.

"For three nights we never lay down at all. I just sat one side of the fireplace and another young lady the other, thinking what had happened during the day, and wondering what dreadful things would come next.

"She had helped me bury three boxes of silver in the cellar. The soldiers were all around them, and afterwards I found one of the boxes sticking out; but they did n't find them. When they asked me for my silver I thought I'd lie once, and I told them I had none. 'It's a lie,' says one. Then the old cook's son spoke up, 'Take the word of a slave; she's nothing buried.' On that they stopped looking.

"Some of the officers had colored girls with them. One stopped over night with his miss at the house of one of our neighbors. When they came down stairs in the morning, she was dressed up magnificently in Mrs. J——'s best clothes.

They ordered breakfast; while they were eating, the last of the army passed on, and they were left behind. ' Captain,' says she, ' aint ye wery wentur'some ? '

"When one division was plundering us, the men would say, ' We 're nothing; but if such a division comes along, you 're gone up.'

" Besides the fifty bushels of corn the lieutenant left us, I don't think there were fifty bushels in the whole district. Our neighbors were jealous because we had been treated so much better than they. The Yankees did n't leave enough for the children to eat, nor dishes to eat off of. Those who managed to save a little corn or a few potatoes, shared with the rest.

" We thought we were served badly enough. Of all my bedding, I had but two sheets and a pillow-case left. The Yankees did n't spare us a hat or a coat. They even took the children's clothes. We had n't a comb or a brush for our heads the next day, nor a towel for our hands. But, after all is said about Sherman's army, I confess some of our own soldiers, especially Wheeler's men, were about as bad.

" I never gave the negroes a single order, but they went to work, after the Yankees had passed, and cleared up the whole place. They took corn and ground it; and they went to the Yankee camp for meat, and cooked it for us. Our horses were taken, but they planted rice and corn with their hoes. There were scarcely any white men in the country. Most were in the army ; and the Yankees took prisoners all who came under the conscript act. They carried some away who have never been heard from since.

" My husband was in Charleston, and for weeks neither of us knew if the other was alive. I walked seventeen miles to mail a letter to him. The old cook went with me and carried my child. From seven in the morning until dark, the first day, I walked twelve miles; and five the next. The old cook did n't feel tired a bit, though she carried the baby ; but she kept saying to me, ' Do don't set down dar, missus ; we 'll neber git dar ! ' We were two days coming home again."

CHAPTER LXXVII.

THE BURNING OF COLUMBIA.

"It has pleased God," says the writer in the "Daily Phœnix," already quoted, " to visit our beautiful city with the most cruel fate which can ever befall states or cities. He has permitted an invading army to penetrate our country almost without impediment; to rob and ravage our dwellings, and to commit three fifths of our city to the flames. Eighty-four squares, out of one hundred and twenty-four which the city contains, have been destroyed, with scarcely the exception of a single house. The ancient capitol building of the State — that venerable structure, which, for seventy years, has echoed with the eloquence and wisdom of the most famous statesmen — is laid in ashes; six temples of the Most High God have shared the same fate; eleven banking establishments; the schools of learning, the shops of art and trade, of invention and manufacture; shrines equally of religion, benevolence, and industry; are all buried together, in one congregated ruin. Humiliation spreads her ashes over our homes and garments, and the universal wreck exhibits only one common aspect of despair."

Columbia, the proud capital of the proudest State in the Union, — who ever supposed that *she* could be destined to such a fate? Who ever imagined that in *this* way that fine bird, secession, would come home to roost?

Almost until the last moment the people of South Carolina, relying upon the immense prestige of their little State sovereignty, even after the State was invaded, believed that the capital was safe. Already, during the war, thousands of citizens from Charleston and other places, in order to avoid the possibility of danger, had sought the retirement of its beautiful shady streets and supposed impregnable walls. The population of Columbia had thus increased, in two or three years, from fourteen thousand to thirty-seven thousand. Then Sherman appeared, driving clouds of fugitives before him into the city. Still the inhabitants cherished their delusion, until it was dispelled by the sound of the Federal cannon at their gates. The Confederate troops fell back into the city, followed by bursting shells.

Then commenced the usual scenes of panic. " Terrible was the press, the shock, the rush, the hurry, the universal confusion — such as might naturally be looked for, in the circumstances of a city from which thousands were preparing to fly, without previous preparations for flight, burdened with pale and trembling women, their children and portable chattels, trunks and jewels, family Bibles and the *lares familiares*. The railroad depot for Charlotte was crowded with anxious waiters upon the train, with a wilderness of luggage, millions, perhaps, in value, much of which was left finally and lost. Throughout Tuesday, Wednesday, and Thursday, these scenes of struggle were in constant performance. The citizens fared badly. The Governments of the State and of the Confederacy absorbed all the modes of conveyance. Transportation about the city could not be had, save by a rich or favored few. No love could persuade where money failed to convince, and SELF, growing bloated in its dimensions, stared from every hurrying aspect, as you traversed the excited and crowded streets. In numerous instances, those who succeeded in getting away, did so at the cost of trunks and luggage ; and, under what discomfort they departed, no one who did not see can readily conceive."[1]

Numbers of the poorer classes took advantage of this confusion to plunder the city. On Friday morning, they broke into the South Carolina Railroad Depot, which was " crowded with the stores of merchants and planters, trunks of treasure, innumerable wares and goods of fugitives, all of great value. It appears that among its contents were some kegs of powder. The plunderers paid, and suddenly, the penalties of their crime.

[1] *Daily Phœnix.*

Using their lights freely and hurriedly, they fired a train of powder leading to the kegs." A fearful explosion followed, destructive to property and life.[1]

Early on Friday the Confederate quartermaster and commissary stores were thrown open to the people. Old men, women, children, and negroes, loaded themselves with plunder. Wheeler's cavalry rushed in for their share, and several troopers were seen riding off " with huge bales of cotton on their saddles." [1]

The same day — Friday, February 17th — Sherman entered Columbia. To the anxious mayor he said : "Not a finger's breadth of your city shall be harmed. You may lie down and sleep, satisfied that your town will be as safe in my hands as in your own." That night Columbia was destroyed.

It is still a question, who is responsible for this calamity. General Sherman denies that he authorized it, and we are bound to believe him. But did he not permit it ? or was it not in his power at least to have prevented it ? General Howard is reported to have said to a clergyman of the place, that no orders were given to burn Columbia, but the soldiers had got the impression that its destruction would be acceptable at head-quarters. Were the soldiers correct in their impression ?

A member of General Sherman's staff speaks thus of the origin of the fire : —

" I am quite sure that it originated in sparks flying from the hundreds of bales of cotton which the Rebels had placed along the middle of the main street, and fired as they left the city. Fire from a tightly compressed bale of cotton is unlike that of a more open material, which burns itself out. The fire lies smouldering in a bale of cotton long after it appears to be extinguished; and in this instance, when our soldiers supposed they had extinguished the fire, it suddenly broke out again with the most disastrous effect.

" There were fires, however, which must have been started independent of the above-named cause. The source of these

[1] *Daily Phœnix.*

is ascribed to the desire for revenge from some two hundred of our prisoners, who had escaped from the cars as they were being conveyed from this city to Charlotte, and with the memories of long sufferings in the miserable pens I visited yesterday on the other side of the river, sought this means of retaliation. Again it is said that the soldiers who first entered the town, intoxicated with success and a liberal supply of bad liquor, which was freely distributed among them by designing citizens, in an insanity of exhilaration set fire to unoccupied houses." [1]

It is also probable that fires were set by citizen marauders. But is this the whole truth with regard to the burning of Columbia?

I visited the place nearly a year after its great disaster, when the passions of men had had time to cool a little. Through the courtesy of Governor Orr I made acquaintance with prominent and responsible citizens. To these gentlemen — especially to Mr. J. G. Gibbes, the present mayor of the city — I am indebted for the following statements and anecdotes.

Early in the evening, as the inhabitants, quieted by General Sherman's assurance, were about retiring to their beds, a rocket went up in the lower part of the city. Another in the centre, and a third in the upper part of the town, succeeded. Dr. R. W. Gibbes, father of the present mayor, was in the street talking, near one of the Federal guards, who exclaimed, on seeing the signals, "My God! I pity your city!" Mr. Goodwyn, who was mayor at the time, reports a similar remark from an Iowa soldier. "Your city is doomed! These rockets are the signal!" Immediately afterwards fires broke out in twenty different places.

The dwellings of Secretary Trenholm and General Wade Hampton were among the first to burst into flames. Soldiers went from house to house, spreading the conflagration. Fireballs, composed of cotton saturated with turpentine, were thrown in at doors and windows. Many houses were entered,

[1] Nichols's *Story of the Great March.*

and fired by means of combustible liquids poured upon beds and clothing, and ignited by wads of burning cotton, or matches from a soldier's pocket. The fire department came out in force, but the hose-pipes were cut to pieces and the men driven from the streets. At the same time universal plundering and robbery began.

The burning of the house of Dr. R. W. Gibbes, — an eminent physician, well-known to the scientific world, — was thus described to me by his son: —

"He had a guard at the front door; but some soldiers climbed in at the rear of the house, got into the parlor, heaped together sheets poured turpentine over them, piled chairs on them, and set them on fire. As he remonstrated with them, they laughed at him. The guard at the front door could do nothing, for if he left his post, other soldiers would come in that way.

"The guard had a disabled foot, and my father had dressed it for him. He appeared very grateful for the favor, and earnestly advised my father to save his valuables. The house was full of costly paintings, and curiosities of art and natural history, and my father did not know what to save and what to leave behind. He finally tied up in a bedquilt a quantity of silver and gems. As he was going out of the door, — the house was already on fire behind him, — the guard said, 'Is that all you can save?' 'It is all I can well carry,' said my father. 'Leave that with me,' said the guard; 'I will take charge of it, while you go back and get another bundle.' My father thought he was very kind. He went back for another bundle, and while he was gone, the guard ran off with his lame leg and all the gems and silver."

One of Mr. Gibbes's neighbors, a widow lady, had an equally conscientious guard. He said to her, "I can guard the front of the house, but not the rear; and if you have anything valuable buried you had better look after it." She threw up her hands and exclaimed, "O, my silver and my fine old wine, buried under that peach-tree!" The guard immediately called a squad of men, and told them to respect the widow lady's wine and silver, buried under that peach-tree. He went with them, and they dug a little to see if the treasures were safe. Finding the wine, they tasted it to see if it merited the epithet "fine old." Discovering that it did, they showed their approbation of her good sense and truthfulness by drinking it up. They then carried off the silver.

The soldiers, in their march through Georgia, and thus far into South Carolina, had acquired a wonderful skill in finding treasures. They had two kinds of "divining-rods," negroes, and bayonets. What the unfaithful servants of the rich failed to reveal, the other instruments, by thorough and constant practice, were generally able to discover. On the night of the fire, a thousand men could be seen, in the yards and gardens of Columbia, by the glare of the flames, probing the earth with bayonets. " Not one twentieth part of the articles buried in this city escaped them," Mr. Gibbes assured me.

The fire was• seen at immense distances. A gentleman living eighty-five miles north of Columbia, told me he could see to read in his garden that night by the light it gave.

The dismay and terror of the inhabitants can scarcely be conceived. They had two enemies, the fire in their houses and the soldiery without. Many who attempted to bear away portions of their goods were robbed by the way. Trunks and bundles were snatched from the hands of hurrying fugitives, broken open, rifled, and then hurled into the flames. Ornaments were plucked from the necks and arms of ladies, and caskets from their hands. Even children and negroes were robbed.

Fortunately the streets of Columbia were broad, else many of the fugitives must have perished in the flames which met them on all sides. The exodus of homeless families, flying between walls of fire, was a terrible and piteous spectacle. I have already described a similar scene in a Reminiscence of Chambersburg, and shall not dwell upon this. The fact that these were the wives and children and flaming homes of our enemies, does not lessen the feeling of sympathy for the sufferers. Some fled to the parks; others to the open ground without the city ; numbers sought refuge in the graveyards. Isolated and unburned dwellings were crowded to excess with fugitives. "On Saturday morning," said Mayor Gibbes, "there were two hundred women and children in this house."

Three fifths of the city in bulk, and four fifths in value, were destroyed. The loss of property is estimated at thirty millions. No more respect seems to have been shown for buildings commonly deemed sacred, than for any others. The churches were pillaged, and afterwards burned. St. Mary's College, a Catholic institution, shared their fate. The Catholic Convent, to which had been confided for safety many young ladies, not nuns, and stores of treasure, was ruthlessly sacked. The soldiers drank the sacramental wine, and profaned with fiery draughts of vulgar whiskey the goblets of the communion service. Some went off reeling under the weight of priestly robes, holy vessels, and candlesticks.

Not even the Masonic and Odd Fellow lodges were spared. Afterwards tipsy soldiers were seen about the streets dressed up in the regalias of these orders. The sword of state, belonging to the Grand Lodge of South Carolina, a massy, curious, two-edged weapon, of considerable antiquity, was among the objects stolen.

The buildings and library of South Carolina College were saved.

Not much drunkenness was observed among the soldiers until after the sacking of the city had been some time in progress. Then the stores of liquors consumed exhibited their natural effect ; and it is stated that many perished in fires of their own kindling.

Yet the army of Sherman did not, in its wildest orgies, forget its splendid discipline. "When will these horrors cease ?" asked a lady of an officer at her house. "You will hear the bugles at sunrise," he replied ; "then they will cease, and not till then." He prophesied truly. "At daybreak, on Saturday morning," said Mayor Gibbes, "I saw two men galloping through the streets, blowing horns. Not a dwelling was fired after that ; immediately the town became quiet."

Robberies, however, did not cease with the night. Watches and money continued to be in demand. A soldier would ask a citizen the time. If the latter was so imprudent as to produce his watch, it was instantly snatched. " A very pretty watch that; I 'll take it, if you please," was the usual remark accompanying the act.

One old gentleman who had purchased two watches for his grandchildren, lost one in this way. In his rage and grief he exclaimed, " You may as well take the other ! " And his suggestion was cheerfully complied with.

Another sufferer said, " That watch will be good for nothing without the key. Won't you stop and take it ? " " Thank you," said the soldier ; and he went off, proudly winding his new chronometer.

A few saved their watches by the use of a little artifice. " What 's the time ? " cried a soldier, stopping a ready-witted gentleman. " You 're too late ; I was just asked that question," was the opportune reply. Another looked up where the city hall clock stood until brought down by the fire, and replied to the question of time, " The clock has been burned, you see."

The women of Columbia have the credit of exhibiting great courage and presence of mind, under these trying circumstances. Occasionally, however, they were taken by surprise. I have related how one lady lost her silver and fine old wine. Another was suddenly accosted by a soldier who thrust his revolver under her bonnet : " Your money ! your watch ! " " O, my soul ! " she exclaimed, " I have no watch, no money, except what 's tied 'round my waist ! " " I 'll relieve you of that," said the soldier, ripping up her stays with his knife.

The soldiers were full of cheerful remarks about the fire. " What curious people you are ! " said one, looking at the ruins. " You run up your chimneys before you build your houses."

Although some of the guards were faithless, others — and I hope a majority of them — executed their trust with fidelity.

Some curious incidents occurred. One man's treasure, concealed by his garden fence, escaped the soldiers' divining-rods, but was afterwards discovered by a hitched horse pawing the earth from the buried box. Some hidden guns had defied the most diligent search, until a chicken, chased by a soldier, ran into a hole beneath a house. The soldier, crawling after, and putting in his hand for the chicken, found the guns.

A soldier, passing in the streets, and seeing some children playing with a beautiful little greyhound, amused himself by beating its brains out. Another soldier with a kinder heart, to comfort them, told them not to cry, and proposed to have a funeral over the remains of their little favorite. He put it in a box, and went to bury it in the garden, directly *on the spot where the family treasures were concealed.* The proprietor, in great distress of mind, watched the proceedings, fearful of exciting suspicion if he opposed it, and trembling lest each thrust of the spade should reveal the secret. A corner of the box was actually laid bare, when, kicking some dirt over it, he said, "There, that will do, children!" and hastened the burial. The soldier no doubt thought he betrayed a good deal of emotion at the grave of a lap-dog. The hole was filled up, but the danger was not yet over, for there was a chance that the next soldier who came that way might be attracted by the fresh-looking earth, and go to digging.

Some treasures were buried in cemeteries, but they did not always escape the search of the soldiers, who showed a strong mistrust of new-made graves.

It is curious to consider what has become of all the jewels and finery of which our armies robbed the people of the South. On two or three occasions gentlemen of respectability have shown me, with considerably more pride than I could have felt under the circumstances, vases and trinkets which they "picked up when they were in the army." Some of these curiosities have been heard from by their rightful owners. A ring, worn by a lady of Philadelphia, was last summer recognized by a Southern gentleman, who remarked that he thought he had seen it before. " Very possibly," was the reply ; " it was given me by Captain ——, of General Sherman's staff;

36

and it was presented to him by a lady of Columbia for his efforts in saving her property." But the lady of Columbia, who knew nothing of any such efforts in her behalf, avers that the gallant captain stole the ring.[1]

Mrs. Minegault, daughter of the late Judge Huger, of Charleston, — the same gentleman who was associated with Dr. Bollmann in the attempted rescue of Lafayette from the dungeons of Olmütz, — while on a visit to New York last summer, was one Sunday morning kneeling in Grace Church, when she saw upon the fair shoulders of a lady kneeling before her, a shawl which had been lost when her plantation, between Charleston and Savannah, was plundered by the Federals. Her attention being thus singularly attracted, she next observed on the lady's arm a bracelet which was taken from her at the same time. This was to her a very precious souvenir, for it had been presented to her by her father, and it contained his picture. The services ended, she followed the lady home, and rang at the door immediately after she had entered. Asking to see the lady of the house, she was shown into the parlor, and presently the lady appeared, with the shawl upon her shoulders and the bracelet on her arm. Frankly the visitor related the story of the bracelet, and at once the wearer restored it to her with ample apologies and regrets. The visitor, quite overcome by this generosity, and delighted beyond meas-

---

[1] An officer taking his punch (they drink punch in the army when the coffee ration is exhausted) from an elegantly-chased silver cup, was saluted thus: —

" Halloa, captain, that 's a gem of a cup. No mark on it; why, where did you get it? "

" Ye-e-s! that cup? Oh, that was given me by a lady in Columbia for saving her households gods from destruction."

An enterprising officer in charge of a foraging party would return to camp with a substantial family coach, well filled with hams, meal, etc.

" How are you, captain? Where did you pick up that carriage? "

" Elegant vehicle, is n't it? " was the reply; " that was a gift from a lady out here whose mansion was in flames. Arrived at the nick of time — good thing — she said she did n't need the carriage any longer — answer for an ambulance one of these days."

After a while this joke came to be repeated so often that it was dangerous for any one to exhibit a gold watch, a tobacco-box, any uncommon utensil of kitchen ware, a new pipe, a guard-chain, or a ring, without being asked if " a lady at Columbia had presented that article to him for saving her house from burning." — *Story of the Great March.*

ure at the recovery of the bracelet, had not the heart to say a word about the shawl, but left it in the possession of the innocent wearer.

I talked with some good Columbians who expressed the most violent hatred of the Yankees, for the ruin of their homes. Others took a more philosophical view of the subject. This difference was thus explained to me by Governor Orr's private secretary, an intelligent young man, who had been an officer in the Confederate service : —

" People who were not in the war cannot understand or forgive these things. But those who have been in the army know what armies are ; they know that, under the same circumstances, they would have done the same things." [1]

I also observed that those whose losses were greatest were seldom those who complained most. Mayor Gibbes lost more cotton than any other individual in the Confederacy. Sherman burned for him two thousand and seven hundred bales, besides mills and other property. Yet he spoke of these results of the war without a murmur.

He censured Sherman severely, however, for the destitution in which he left the people of Columbia. " I called on him to relieve the starving inhabitants he had burned out of their homes. He gave us four hundred head of refuse cattle, but he gave us nothing to feed them, and a hundred and sixty of them died of starvation before they could be killed. For five weeks afterwards, twenty-five hundred people around Columbia lived upon nothing but loose grain picked up about the camps, where the Federal horses had been fed. A stranger," he added, " cannot be made to understand the continued destitution and poverty of the people of this district. If a tax should now be assessed upon them of three dollars per head, there would not be money enough in the district to pay it. Ordi-

[1] " The grass will grow in the Northern cities, where the pavements have been worn off by the tread of commerce. We will carry war where it is easy to advance — where food for the *sword* and *torch* await our armies in the densely populated cities; and though they (the enemy) may come and spoil our crops, we can raise them as before, while they cannot rear the cities which took years of industry and millions of money to build." — *Jeff Davis in 1861 — Speech at Stevenson, Ala.*

narily, our annual taxes in this city have been forty thousand dollars. This year they have dropped down to eighteen hundred dollars."

South Carolina College is a striking illustration of the effect the war has had upon the institutions of learning at the South. Formerly it had about two hundred and fifty students; it has now but eighteen. The State appropriated annually sixty-five thousand dollars for its benefit; this year a nominal appropriation of eight thousand dollars was made, to pay the salaries of the professors, but when I was in Columbia they had not been able to get that. One, a gentleman of distinguished learning, said he had not had ten dollars in his possession since Sherman visited them.

Of the desolation and horrors our army left behind it, no description can be given. Here is a single instance. At a factory on the Congaree, just out of Columbia, there remained, for six weeks, a pile of sixty-five dead horses and mules, shot by Sherman's men. It was impossible to bury them, all the shovels, spades, and other farming implements of the kind having been carried off or destroyed.

Columbia must have been a beautiful city, judged by its ruins. The streets were broad and well shaded. Many fine residences still remain on the outskirts, but the entire heart of the city, within their circuit, is a wilderness of crumbling walls, naked chimneys, and trees killed by the flames. The fountains of the desolated gardens are dry, the basins cracked; the pillars of the houses are dismantled, or overthrown; the marble steps are broken; but all these attest the wealth and elegance which one night of fire and orgies sufficed to destroy. Fortunately the unfinished new State House, one of the handsomest public edifices in the whole country, received but trifling injury.

Not much was doing to rebuild any but the business portion of the city. Only on Main Street were there many stores or shanties going up.

CHAPTER LXXVIII.

NOTES ON SOUTH CAROLINA.

AT a distance from the Sea Islands, the free-labor system in South Carolina, was fast settling down upon a satisfactory basis. General Richardson, commanding the Eastern District of the State, — comprising all the districts east of the Wateree and Santee, except Georgetown and Horry, on the coast, — assured me that there was going to be more cotton raised in those districts this year than ever before.

In the districts west of the Wateree, the soil is not so well adapted to cotton, and the country abounds in ignorant small planters and poor whites. A planter of the average class, in York District, said to me: " The people of this country formerly lived on nigger-raising. That was the crap we depended on. If we could raise corn and pork enough to feed the niggers, we did well. Now this great staple is tuk from us."

The planters here love to dwell upon the advantages they derived from that crop. One said to me ; " Let a young man take three likely gals, set 'em to breedin' right away, and he mought make a fortune out, on 'em, 'fore he was old. But them times is past."

The winds of freedom had scarcely reached the more remote western districts. A planter of Union District told me that he was hiring good men for twenty-five dollars a year. " Heap on 'em, round here, just works for their victuals and clothes, like they always did. I reckon they 'll all be back whar they was, in a few years."

The South Carolina lands and modes of culture are not well adapted to corn. A rotation of crops is deemed necessary to keep the soil in a condition to raise it successfully.

The decay of cotton seed and waste cotton is its best fertilizer. During the war, when little cotton was raised, planters became alarmed at the yearly decrease of the corn crop. The average yield, throughout the State, the first year, was fifteen bushels to the acre; the second, twelve bushels; the third, nine bush-' els; and the fourth, six bushels.

Before the war, the city of Charleston exported annually one hundred and twenty-five thousand tierces of rice. This year, it is *importing* rice of an inferior quality from the West Indies. This fact indicates the condition of that culture. Yet in the face of it, rice-planters were raising the price of their lands from fifty dollars an acre, for which they could be bought before the war, to one hundred dollars.

As the rice plantations are confined to the tide-water region, where the fields can be flooded after sowing, their present prospects were more or less embarrassed by the knotty Sea-Island question. "If our people this year make one sixth of an average rice-crop," said Governor Orr, "they will be fortunate, and they will be doing well. In old times, our annual crop brought upwards of three and a half million dollars, when rice was only five cents a pound."

The railroads of South Carolina were nearly worn out during the war. All sorts of iron were used to keep them in repair; and the old rolling-stock was kept running until it was ready to fall to pieces. Then Sherman came. The South Carolina Road, wealthy before the war, was relaying its torn-up track and rebuilding its extensive trestle-work and bridges, as fast as its earnings would permit. The branch to Columbia was once more in operation; but, on the main road to Augusta, travel was eked out by a night of terribly rough staging.

The finances of South Carolina were at a low ebb. Governor Orr told me that there had not been a dollar in the State treasury since his inauguration. The current expenses of the war were mostly met by taxation; and the annual interest on the foreign debt of two and a half millions had been promptly paid, up to July, 1865, by the exportation of cotton.

The State bank was obliged to suspend its operations, but the faith of the State was pledged for the redemption of the bills. The other banks had been ruined by loans made to the Confederate government. Their stock had been considered the safest in the market, and the property of widows and orphans was largely invested in it. The estates of the stockholders, liable for double the amount of the bills issued, were insufficient to redeem them. In January, 1866, two National Banks had been organized in the State.

The aggregate of debts, old and new, in South Carolina, were estimated to be worth not more than twenty-five per cent. of their par value.

South Carolina had suffered more than any other State by the sale of lands for United States taxes, during the war. I heard of one estate, worth fifteen thousand dollars, which had been sold for three hundred dollars. Governor Orr instanced another, the market value of which was twenty-four thousand dollars, which was bought in by the government for eighty dollars. Such was the fate of abandoned coast lands held by the United States forces. Their owners, absent in the interior, were in most instances ignorant even of the proceedings by which their estates were sacrificed. In this way, according to the governor, "the entire parish of St. Helena, and a portion of St. Luke's, have completely changed hands, and passed either into the possession of the government, or of third parties."

The prevalence of crime in remote districts was alarming. I was assured by General Sickles that the perpetrators were in most cases outlaws from other States, to which they dared not return. Union soldiers and negroes were their favorite victims. They rode in armed bands through the country, defying the military authorities. The people would not inform against them for fear of their vengeance. Many robberies and murders of soldiers and freedmen, however, were unmistakably committed by citizens.

Much ill-feeling had been kept alive by United States treasury agents, searching the country for Confederate cotton and branded mules and horses.   Many of these agents, as far as I could learn, both in this and in other States, were mere rogues and fortune-hunters.   They would propose to seize a man's property in the name of the United States, but abandon the claim on the payment of heavy bribes, which of course went into their own pockets.   Sometimes, having seized " C. S. A." cotton, they would have the marks on the bales changed, get some man to claim it, and divide with him the profits.   Such practices had a pernicious effect, engendering a contempt for the government, and a murderous ill-will which too commonly vented itself upon soldiers and negroes.

I found in South Carolina a more virulent animosity existing in the minds of the common people, against the government and people of the North, than in any other State I visited. Only in South Carolina was I treated with gross personal insults on account of my Northern origin.

There is notwithstanding in this State a class of men whom I remember with admiration for their courteous hospitality and liberal views.   Instead of insulting and repelling Northern men, they invite them, and seem eager to learn of them the secret of Northern enterprise and prosperity.   Their ideas, although not those of New-England radicals, are hopeful and progressive.   Considering that they have advanced from the Southern side of the national question, their position is notable and praiseworthy.   This class is small, but it possesses a vital energy of which great results may be predicted.   From it the freedmen have much to hope and little to fear.   It is not so far in advance of the people that it cannot lead them ; nor so far behind the most advanced sentiment of the times that we may not expect them soon to come up to it.

Foremost among this class is Governor Orr, — almost the only man in South Carolina who seemed to me prepared to consider dispassionately the subject of universal suffrage.   The color of the negro's skin, he said, was no good reason for keep- ing the ballot out of his hand.   " In this country, suffrage is progressive ; and when the colored people are prepared for it, they will have it."   A large proportion of the freedmen, he felt sure, would become industrious and respectable citizens. As an instance of the capacity and fidelity shown by many of their race, he gave an account of one of his own slaves.

"He is by trade a carpenter, and a first-class workman. He was the son of his original owner, who emancipated him by his will, and gave him, with his liberty, a mule, a saddle, a set of tools, and some money. One of the heirs of the estate was the executor of the will. Finding Henry a very valuable man, he looked for some legal flaw by which the will could be broken. There was a law of South Carolina designed to prevent slave-owners from emancipating old worn-out servants, and thus converting them into public paupers. It required the master, before freeing his servant, to make a certain statement, under oath, that the said servant was capable of self-support. This formality had been neglected in Henry's case; and the court decided that he must remain a slave. When the fact was made known to him, he said to the executor, 'If the court has so decided, I suppose I must abide by the decision. It is unjust, but I submit to it. But I will never serve you. I have lost all confidence in you, and all respect for you; and the best thing you can do is to sell me.' The executor was so impressed by this declaration, that he told him to go and choose his future master. He came to me, and entreated me to buy him. I finally consented to do so, and paid his price, — fifteen hundred dollars.

"He lived as my slave until the close of the war; and all the time his patience under his great wrong was wonderful. He never complained; and he served me with the most conscientious fidelity. By overwork, he earned two hundred dollars a year, which he spent upon his family. I had bought him a set of tools worth five hundred dollars, and scientific books worth one hundred, which I gave him when we parted. He has wit and education enough to understand the books, I assure you. He is now doing business in Columbia. He might become wealthy, but he is too generous. He will not spend his earnings foolishly, but he will share whatever he has with his people. If I was in want, he would give me his last dollar."

There were in January fifty freedmen's schools in operation in South Carolina, with one hundred and twenty teachers, and ten thousand pupils. The New-England Freedmen's Aid, and the National Freedmen's Association, had each about fifty teachers in the field. The Boston teachers in Charleston get forty-five dollars a month, and pay their own expenses. At other points, where expenses are less, they get thirty-five dollars. * The average yearly cost of each teacher to the associations is six hundred dollars.

The American Missionary Association, the Pennsylvania Freedmen's Relief, and the Friends' Freedmen's Association, had also teachers in the field.

The State superintendent of freedmen's schools spoke in high praise of the school in the Normal school building, at Charleston. The principal was a colored man who had been educated at his own expense at the University of Glasgow. Another teacher was a colored girl, who had taught a free colored school in Charleston during the war, — paying half her income to a white woman for sitting and sewing in the school-room, and appearing as the teacher, when it was visited by the police. "This woman's pupils," said Mr. Tomlinson, "draw maps, and do everything white girls of twelve and sixteen years do, in ordinary advanced schools." General Richardson of the Eastern District, had set a number of old soldiers, unfit for military duty, to teaching the freedmen.

There was not much active opposition shown to the schools in the State, nor yet much encouragement. Only here and there an enlightened planter saw the necessity of education for the negroes, and favored it.

CHAPTER LXXIX.

THE RIDE TO WINNSBORO'.

For a distance of thirty miles north of Columbia, I had an interesting experience of staging over that portion of the Charlotte and South Carolina Railroad destroyed by Sherman. Much of the way the stage route ran beside or near the track. Gangs of laborers were engaged in putting down new ties and rails, but most of the old iron lay where our boys left it.

It was the Seventeenth Corps that did this little job, and it did it well. It was curious to note the different styles of the destroying parties. The point where one detail appeared to have left off and another to have begun was generally unmistakable. For a mile or two you would see nothing but hairpins, and bars wound around telegraph posts and trees. Then you would have corkscrews and twists for about the same distance. Then came a party that gave each heated rail one sharp wrench in the middle, and left it perhaps nearly straight, but facing both ways. Here was a plain business method, and there a fantastic style, which showed that its authors took a wild delight in their work.

Early in the morning I rode with the driver, in the hope of learning something of him with regard to the country. But he proved to be a refugee from East Tennessee, where he said a rope-noose was waiting for him. An active Rebel, he had been guilty of some offences which the Union men there could not forgive.

Finding him as ignorant of the country as myself, I got down, and took a seat inside the coach. Within, an animated political discussion was at its height. Two South Carolinians and a planter from Arkansas were dissecting the Yankees in liveliest fashion ; while a bitter South Carolina lady and a good-natured Virginian occasionally put in a word.

It was some time before I was recognized as a representative of all that was mean and criminal in the world. At length something I said seemed to excite suspicion; and the Arkansan wrote something on a card, which was passed to every one of the company except me. An alarming hush of several minutes ensued. It was as if a skeleton had appeared at a banquet. The abuse of the Yankees was the banquet; and I was perfectly well aware that I was the skeleton. At last the awful silence was broken by the Arkansan.

" What is thought of negro suffrage at the North ? "

The question was addressed to me. I replied that opinion was divided on that subject; but that many people believed some such security was necessary for the freedmen's rights. " They do not think it quite safe," I said, " to leave him without any voice in making the laws by which he is to be governed, — subject entirely to the legislation of a class that cannot forget that he was born a slave."

" I believe," said one of the South Carolinians, " all that is owing to the lies of the newspaper correspondents travelling through the South, and writing home whatever they think will injure us. I wish every one of 'em was killed off. If it was n't for them, we should be left to attend to our own business, instead of being ridden to death by our Yankee masters. It is n't fair to take solitary instances reported by them, as representing the condition of the niggers and the disposition of the whites. Some impudent darkey, who deserves it, gets a knock on the head, or a white man speaks his mind rather too freely to some Yankee who has purposely provoked him, and a long newspaper story is made out of it, showing that every nigger in the South is in danger of being killed, and every white man is disloyal."

" Certainly," .I said, " isolated cases do not represent a whole people. But the acts of a legislative body may be supposed to represent the spirit and wishes of its constituents. We consider the negro code enacted by your special legislature simply abominable. It is enough of itself to show that you are not quite ready to do the freedmen justice. Your present governor appears to be of the same opinion, judged by his veto of the act to amend the patrol laws, and his excellent advice to your representatives who passed it. You are wholly mistaken, my friend, in supposing that the people of the North wish anything of you that is unnecessary, unreasonable, or unjust. They may be mistaken with regard to what is necessary, but they are honest in their intentions."

"All we want," said the South Carolinian, " is that our Yankee rulers should give us the same privileges with regard to the control of labor which they themselves have."

" Very well ; what privileges have they which you have not ? "

" In Massachusetts, a laborer is obliged by law to make a contract for a year. If he leaves his employer without his consent, or before the term of his contract expires, he can be put in jail. And if another man hires him, he can be fined. It is not lawful there to hire a laborer who does not bring a certificate from his last employer. All we want is the same or a similar code of laws here."

" My dear sir," said I, " all any man could wish is that you might have just such laws here as they have in Massachusetts. But with regard to the code you speak of, it does not exist there, and it does not exist in any Northern State with which I am acquainted. There is nothing like it anywhere."

" How do you manage without such laws ? How can you get work out of a man unless you *compel* him in some way ? "

" Natural laws compel him ; we need no others. A man must work if he would eat. A faithful laborer is soon discovered, and he commands the best wages. An idle fellow is detected quite as soon ; and if he will not do the work he has agreed to do, he is discharged. Thus the system regulates itself."

" You can't do that way with niggers."

" Have you ever tried ? Have you ever called your freedmen together and explained to them their new condition ? A planter I saw in Alabama told me how he managed this thing. He said to his people, ' If you do well, I shall want you another year. The man who does best will be worth the most to me. But if you are lazy and unfaithful, I shall dismiss you when your contracts are ended, and hire better men. Do you know why some overseers are always wandering about in search of a situation?' 'Because nobody wants 'em,' said the negroes. 'Why not?' 'Because they a'n't good for their business.' 'Why did I keep John Bird only one year?' 'Because, soon as your back was turned, he slipped off to a grocery, or went a-fishing.' 'And why did I keep William Hooker eight years, and increase his salary every year?' 'Because he stuck by and always looked after your interest.' 'Now,' said the planter, 'you are in the condition of these overseers. You can always have good situations, and your prospects will be continually improving, if you do well. Or you may soon be going about the country with bundles on your backs, miserable low-down niggers that nobody will hire.' In this way he instructed and encouraged the freedmen; and he assured me they were working better than ever. But by your serf-codes you would crush all hope and manhood out of them."

"Well, there may be something in all that. I can't say, for I never thought of trying but one way with a nigger. But nigger suffrage the South a'n't going to stand anyhow. We 've already got a class of voters that 's enough to corrupt the politics of any country. I used to think the nigger was the meanest of God's creatures. But I 've found a meaner brute than he; and that 's the low-down white man. If a respectable man hires a nigger for wages, one of those low-down cusses will offer him twice as much, to get him away. They want him to prowl for them. A heap of these no-account whites are getting rich, stealing cotton; they 're too lazy or cowardly to do it themselves, so they get the niggers to do it for 'em. These very men hold the balance of political power in this district. They 'll vote for the man who gives 'em the most whiskey. Just before the war, at an election in Columbia, over a hundred sand-hillers sold their votes beforehand, and were put into jail till the polls opened, and then marched out to vote."

" By what right were they put in jail ? "

" It was in the bargain. They knew they could n't be trusted not to sell their votes to the next man that offered more whiskey, and they like going to jail well enough, if they can go drunk. Make the niggers voters, and you 'll have just such another class to be bought up with whiskey."

" It seems to me more reasonable," I replied, " to suppose that the franchise will elevate the negro ; and by elevating him you will elevate the white man who has been degraded by the negro's degradation. Some of both races will no doubt be found willing to sell their votes, as well as their souls, for whiskey ; but that is no more a reason why all blacks should be deprived of the right of suffrage, than that all whites should be."

This is a specimen of the talk that was kept up during the day.

We stopped to dine at a house, where I was told by a young lady that the Yankees were the greatest set of rogues, and that some passed there every day.

" Is it possible ! " I said. " Are you not afraid of them ? "

" I have nothing whatever to do with them. I should be ashamed to be seen talking with one."

" Then be careful that no one sees you now."

" *You* are not a Yankee ! " she exclaimed.

" Yes," said I, " I am one of that set of rogues."

" I am very sorry to hear it, for I had formed a more favorable opinion of you."

Only the good-natured Virginian went in with me to the dining-room. The lady of the house, sitting at the table with us, soon began to talk about the Yankees. " They often dine here," she said. " But I have nothing to say to them. As soon as I know who they are, I go out of the room." She was very sociable ; and when I informed her at parting that she had been entertaining a Yankee, she appeared confused and incredulous.

Such was the spirit commonly shown by the middle class of South Carolinians. But I remember some marked exceptions.

Late in the afternoon we stopped at a place which a sturdy old farmer said was Ridgeway before Sherman came there: " I don't know what you 'd call it now."

" If the devil don't get old Sherman," said one of my travelling companions, " there a'n't no use having a devil."

" We did it ourselves," said the farmer. " We druv the nail and the Yankees clinched it."

In the coach, the South Carolinians had just been denying that any outrages were committed on the freedmen in that part of the country. So I asked this man if he had heard of any such.

" Heard of 'em ? I hear of 'em every day. I 'm going to Columbia to-night to attend the trial of one of my neighbors for shooting a negro woman."

" You must expect such things to happen when the niggers are impudent," observed one of my companions.

" The niggers a'n't to blame," said the farmer. " They 're never impudent, unless they 're trifled with or imposed on. Only two days ago a nigger was walking along this road, as peaceably as any man you ever saw. He met a white man right here, who asked him who he belonged to. ' I don't belong to anybody now,' he says ; ' I 'm a free man.' ' Sass me ? you black devil ! ' says the white fellow ; and he pitched into him, and cut him in four or five places with his knife. I heard and saw the whole of it, and I say the nigger was respectful, and that the white fellow was the only one to blame."

" What became of the negro ? "

" I don't know ; he went off to some of his people."

" And what was done with the white man ? "

" Nothing. There 's nobody to do anything in such cases, unless the nigger goes all the way to the Freedmen's Bureau and makes a complaint. Then there 's little chance of getting the fellow that cut him."

Three miles further on, we reached a point to which the railroad had been repaired, and took the cars for Winnsboro'. While we were waiting by moonlight in the shelterless and stumpy camping-ground which served as a station, one of my

South Carolina friends said to me: "We may as well tell the whole truth as half. The Yankees treated us mighty badly; but a heap of our own people followed in their track and robbed on their credit."

On the train I found a hotel-keeper from Winnsboro' drumming for customers. He was abusing the Yankees with great violence and passion until he found that I was one. After that he kept remarkably quiet, and even apologized to me for his remarks, until I told him I had concluded to go to the house of a rival runner. Thereupon he broke forth again.

"They've left me one inestimable privilege — to hate 'em. I git up at half-past four in the morning, and sit up till twelve at night, to hate 'em. Talk about Union! They had no object in coming down here, but just to steal. I'm like a whipped cur; I have to cave in; but that don't say I shall love 'em. I owned my own house, my own servants, my own garden, and in one night they reduced me to poverty. My house was near the State House in Columbia. It was occupied by Howard's head-quarters. When they left, they just poured camphene over the beds, set 'em afire, locked up the house, and threw away the key. That was after the burning of the town, and that's what made it so hard. Some one had told 'em I was one of the worst Rebels in the world, and that's the only truth I reckon, that was told. I brought up seven boys, and what they had n't killed was fighting against 'em then. Now I have to keep a boarding-house in Winnsboro' to support my wife and children."

At Winnsboro' I passed the night. A portion of that town also had been destroyed; and there too Sherman's "bummers" were said to have behaved very naughtily. For instance: "When the Episcopal church was burning, they took out the melodeon, and played the devil's tunes on it till the house was well burned down; then they threw on the melodeon."

37

CHAPTER LXXX.

A GLIMPSE OF THE OLD NORTH STATE.

THE next day I entered North Carolina.

Almost immediately on crossing the State line, a change of scene was perceptible. The natural features of the country improved; the appearance of its farms improved still more. North Carolina farmers use manures, and work with their own hands. They treat the soil more generously than their South Carolina neighbors, and it repays them.

That night I passed at the house of a Connecticut man, in a country village, — a warm and comfortable New-England home transported to a southern community, — and went on the next day to Raleigh.

At Raleigh I found the Legislature, — composed mostly of a respectable and worthy-looking yeomanry — battling over the question of negro testimony in the civil courts ; spending day after day in the discussion of a subject which could be settled in only one way, and which ought to have been settled at once. One member remarked outside : " I 'll never vote for that bill unless driven to it by the bayonet." Another said : " I 'm opposed to giving niggers *any* privileges." These men represent a large class of North Carolina farmers ; but fortunately there is another class of more progressive and liberal ideas, which are sure at last to prevail.

The business of Raleigh was dull, the money in the country being exhausted. A few Northern men, who had gone into trade there, were discouraged, and anxious to get away.

" So great is the impoverishment of our State," Governor Worth said to me, " that a tax of any considerable amount would bring real estate at once into the market." Among other causes, the repudiation of the entire State debt con-

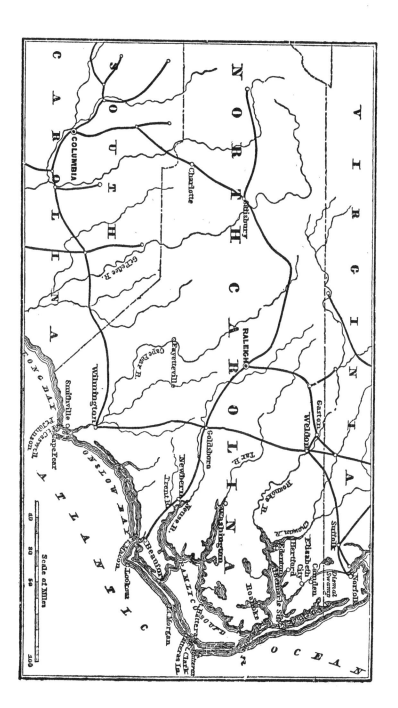

tracted during the war, had contributed to destroy the resources of the people. The middling and poorer classes had invested nearly all their surplus means in State treasury notes, which became worthless. The cause of education suffered with everything else. The University of North Carolina had all its funds invested in the banks; "Repudiation killed the banks," said Governor Worth, "and the banks killed the University." A million dollars of the common-school fund went the same way.

North Carolina, like several of her Southern sisters, had passed a stay law, which threatened a serious injury to her interests. By preventing the collection of debts, it destroyed credit, of which the people, in their present condition, stand so much in need. Although unconstitutional and impolitic, so great was the popularity of this law, that the ablest politicians feared to make an effort for its repeal.

By one of its provisions, a mortgage inures to the benefit of all the creditors of the mortgagor. Many large estates were, necessarily, to be broken up; and the best thing that could happen, for them and for the community, was, that they should fall into the hands of small farmers; but, in consequence of this curious law, the owners would not sell to these men, except for cash, which was lacking.

These Southern stay laws, I may here mention, do not touch the rights of a Northern creditor, who can bring his suit in United States courts, which ignore them.

The Northern men in the State were mostly settled on cotton plantations in the eastern counties. There were also many engaged in the turpentine and lumber business in the southern part, and along the coast. In the central and western parts there were almost none.

Of the extensive rice plantations of the tide-water region, but few were in operation, owing to the great outlay of capital necessary to carry them on. To seed them alone involves an expense of ten dollars an acre. Yet, from the representations of Northern men who had gone to rice planting, I am satisfied that here is an opening for very profitable investments.

The small farmers of North Carolina are a plain, old-fashioned, upright, ignorant class of men. Mr. Best, Secretary of State, told me that forty-five per cent. of those who took the oath of allegiance in Green County, where he administered it, made their marks. " Yet many of these are men of as strong sense as any in the State," he added ; " and they were generally Union men."

The freedmen throughout the central and northern part of the State, had very generally made contracts, and were at work. In the southern part, fewer contracts had been made, in consequence of the inability of the large planters to pay promptly. " When paid promptly, the freedmen are everywhere working well," I was assured by the officers of the Bureau. The rate of wages varied from five to ten dollars a month.

There were in the State one hundred teachers, supplied by the benevolent societies of the North. Their schools, scattered throughout the State, were attended by eight thousand five hundred colored pupils.

Cases of robberies, frauds, assaults, and even murders, in which white persons were the agents and freed people the sufferers, had been so numerous, according to the State Commissioner, " that no record of them could be kept ; one officer reporting that he had heard and disposed of as many as a hundred and eighty complaints in one day." Owing to the efforts of the Bureau, however, the number was fast decreasing.

From Governor Worth, I received a rather sorry account of the doings of Sherman's " bummers " in this State. Even after the pacification they continued their lawless marauding. " They visited my place, near Raleigh, and drove off a fine flock of ewes and lambs. I was State Treasurer at the time, and having to go away on public business, I gave my negroes their bacon, which they hid behind the ceiling of the house. The Yankees came, and held an axe over the head of one of the negroes, and by threats compelled him to tell where it was. They tore off the ceiling, and stole all the bacon. They took all my cows. Three cows afterwards came back; but they recently disappeared again, and I found them in the possession of a man who says he bought them of these bummers. I had a grindstone, and as they could n't carry it off, they smashed it. There was on my place a poor, old, blind negro woman, — the last creature in the world against whom I should suppose any person would have wished to commit a wrong. She had a new dress; and they stole even that.

"I was known as a peace man," said the Governor, "and for that reason I did not suffer as heavily as my neighbors." He gave this testimony with regard to that class which served, but did not honor, our cause: "Of all the malignant wretches that ever cursed the earth, the hangers-on of Sherman's army were the worst;" adding: "It can't be expected that the people should love a government that has subjugated them in this way."

CHAPTER LXXXI.

CONCLUSIONS.

I MADE but a brief stay in North Carolina, but passed on homeward, and reached the beautiful snowy hills and frosted forests of New England early in February.

It now only remains for me to sum up briefly my answers to certain questions which are constantly put to me, regarding Southern emigration, the loyalty of the people, and the future of the country.

The South is in the condition of a man recovering from a dangerous malady : the crisis is past, appetite is boundless, and only sustenance and purifying air are needed to bring health and life in fresh waves. The exhausted country calls for supplies. It has been drained of its wealth, and of its young men. Capital is eagerly welcomed and absorbed. Labor is also needed. There is much shallow talk about getting rid of the negroes, and of filling their places with foreigners. But war and disease have already removed more of the colored race than can be well spared ; and I am confident that, for the next five or ten years, leaving the blacks where they are, the strongest tide of emigration that can be poured into the country will be insufficient to meet the increasing demand for labor.

Northern enterprise, emancipation, improved modes of culture, and the high prices of cotton, rice, sugar, and tobacco, cannot fail to bring about this result. The cotton crop, if no accident happens to it, will this year reach, I am well satisfied, not less than two million bales, and bring something like two hundred and fifty million dollars, — as much as the five million bales of 1859 produced. Next year it will approximate to its old average standard in bulk, and greatly exceed it in value ; and the year after we shall have the largest cotton crop ever known. Meanwhile the culture of rice and sugar will have fully revived, and become enormously profitable. Nor will planting alone flourish. Burned cities and plantation-buildings must be restored, new towns and villages will spring up, old losses must be repaired, and a thousand new wants supplied. Trade, manufactures, the mechanic arts, all are invited to share in this teeming activity.

Particular location the emigrant must select for himself, according to his own judgment, tastes, and means. Just now I should not advise Northern men to settle far back from the main routes of travel, unless they go in communities, purchasing and dividing large plantations, and forming societies independent of any hostile sentiment that may be shown by the native inhabitants. But I trust that in a year or two all danger of discomfort or disturbance arising from this source will have mostly passed by.

The loyalty of the people is generally of a negative sort: it is simply disloyalty subdued. They submit to the power which has mastered them, but they do not love it ; nor is it reasonable to expect that they should. Many of them lately in rebellion, are, I think, honestly convinced that secession was a great mistake, and that the preservation of the Union, even with the loss of slavery, is better for them than any such separate government as that of which they had a bitter taste. Yet they do not feel much affection for the hand which corrected their error. They acquiesce quietly in what cannot be helped, and sincerely desire to make the best of their altered circumstances.

There is another class which would still be glad to dismember the country, and whose hatred of the government is radical and intense. But this class is small.

The poor whites may be divided into three classes : those who, to their hatred of the negro, join a hatred of the government that has set him free ; those who associate with the negro, and care nothing for any government ; and those who, cherishing more or less Union sentiment, rejoice to see the old aristocracy overthrown.

Except in certain localities, like East Tennessee, positive unconditional Union men are an exceedingly small minority. But they are a leaven which, properly encouraged, should leaven the whole lump of Southern society. Upon the close of hostilities, these men who, for near five years suffered unrelenting persecution, rose temporarily to a position of influence which their conduct had earned. Secession saw with dismay that to this class the first place in the future government of the country rightfully belonged. Their old neighbors, who had so long done evil to them continually, or given them only dark looks, now shrank sullenly out of their sight, or openly courted their smiles. A professed Union sentiment blossomed everywhere ; lives, that had all along been thistles, now bore a plentiful harvest of figs. This was a hopeful state of things. It is better, as an example to a community, that goodness should receive insincere homage, than none at all ; and that men should assume a virtue if they have it not. But as soon as it was seen that the muttering thunder-cloud of retribution was passing by with nothing but sound, and that loyal men were not to have the first, nor even the second or third or fourth place, in the government of the lately rebellious States, they sank to their former position. What is needed now is to cause this class, and the principles they represent, to be permanently respected.

The mere utterance of disloyal sentiments need not alarm any one. It is often sincere ; but it is sometimes mere cant, easily kept in vogue, by newspapers and politicians, among a people who delight in vehement and minatory talk, for the mere talk's sake.

Of another armed rebellion not the least apprehension need be entertained. The South has had enough of war for a long time to come ; it has supped full of horrors. The habiliments of mourning, which one sees everywhere in its towns and cities, will cast their dark shadow upon any future attempt at secession, long after they have been put away in the silent wardrobes of the past. Only in the case of a foreign war might we expect to see a party of malignant ma·ontents go over to the side of the enemy. They would doubtless endeavor to drag their States with them, but they would not succeed. Fortunately those who are still so anxious to see the old issue fought out, are not themselves fighting men, and are dangerous only with their tongues.

Of *unarmed* rebellion, of continued sectional strife, stirred up by Southern politicians, there exists very great danger. Their aims are distinct, and they command the sympathy of the Southern people. To obtain the exclusive control of the freedmen, and to make such laws for them as shall embody the prejudices of a late slave-holding society; to govern not only their own States, but to regain their forfeited leadership in the affairs of the nation; to effect the repudiation of the national debt, or to get the Confederate debt and the Rebel State debts assumed by the whole country; to secure payment for their slaves, and for all injuries and losses occasioned by the war; these are among the chief designs of a class who will pursue them with what recklessness and persistency we know.

How to prevent them from agitating the nation in the future as in the past, and from destroying its prosperity, is become the most serious of questions. If you succeed in capturing an antagonist who has made a murderous assault upon you, common sense, and a regard for your own safety and the peace of society, require at least that his weapons, or the power of using them, should be taken from him. These perilous schemes are the present weapons of the nation's conquered enemy; and does not prudent statesmanship demand that they should be laid forever at rest before he walks again at large in the pride of his power?

All that just and good men can ask, is this security. Vindictiveness, or a wish to hold the rebellious States under an iron rule, should have no place in our hearts. But if the blood of our brothers was shed in a righteous cause, — if for four years we poured out lives and treasures to purchase a reality, and no mere mockery and shadow,—let us honor our brothers and the ca_se by seeing that reality established. If treason is a crime surely it can receive no more fitting or merciful

punishment than to be deprived of its power to do more mischief.   Let peace, founded upon true principles, be the only
retribution we demand.   Let justice be our vengeance.

It was my original intention to speak of the various schemes
of reconstruction claiming the consideration of the country.
But they have become too numerous, and are generally too
well known, to be detailed here.   The Southern plan is simple ; it is this : that the States, lately so eager to destroy the
Union, are now entitled to all their former rights and privileges in that Union.   Their haste to withdraw their representatives from Congress, is more than equalled by their anxiety
to get them back in their seats.   They consider it hard that,
at the end of the most stupendous rebellion and the bloodiest
civil war that ever shook the planet, they cannot quietly slip
back in their places, and, the sword having failed, take up
once more the sceptre of political power they so rashly flung
down.   Often, in conversation with candid Southern men,
impatient for this result, I was able to convince them that it
was hardly to be expected, that the government, emerging
victorious from the dust of such a struggle, and finding its
foot on that sceptre, should take it off with very great alacrity.
And they were forced to acknowledge that, had the South
proved victorious, its enemies would not have escaped so
easily.

This plan does not tolerate the impediment of any Congressional test oath.   When I said to my Southern friends
that I should be glad to see those representatives, who could
take the test oath, admitted to Congress, this was the usual
reply : —

" We would not vote for such men.   We had rather have
no representatives at all.   We want representatives to *represent* us, and no man *represents* us who can take your test oath.
We are Rebels, if you choose to call us so, and only a good
Rebel can properly represent us."

This is the strongest argument I have heard against the
admission of loyal Southern members to Congress.   And if
the white masses of the lately rebellious States are alone, and

indiscriminately, to be recognized as the people of those States, it is certainly a valid argument.

" It is enough," they maintained, " that a representative in Congress takes the ordinary oath to support the government; *that* is a sufficient test of his loyalty ; " — forgetting that, at the outbreak of the rebellion, this proved no test at all.

Such is the Southern plan of reconstruction. Opposed to it is the plan on which I believe a majority of the people of the loyal States are agreed, namely, that certain guaranties of future national tranquillity should be required of those who have caused so great a national convulsion. But as to what those guaranties should be, opinions are divided, and a hundred conflicting measures are proposed for the settlement of the difficulty.

For my own part, I see but one plain rule by which our troubles can be finally and satisfactorily adjusted ; and that is, the enactment of simple justice for all men. Anything that falls short of this falls short of the solution of the problem.

The " Civil Rights Bill," — enacted since the greater portion of these pages were written, — is a step in the direction in which this country is inevitably moving. The principles of the Declaration of Independence, supposed to be our starting-point in history, are in reality the goal towards which we are tending. Far in advance of our actual civilization, the pioneers of the Republic set up those shining pillars. Not until all men are equal before the law, and none is hindered from rising or from sinking by any impediment which does not exist in his own constitution and private circumstances, will that goal be reached.

Soon or late the next step is surely coming. That step is universal suffrage. It may be wise to make some moral or intellectual qualification a test of a man's fitness for the franchise ; but anything which does not apply alike to all classes, and which all are not invited to attain, is inconsistent with the spirit of American nationality.

But will the Southern people ever submit to negro suffrage ? They will submit to it quite as willingly as they submitted to negro emancipation. They fought against that as long as any power of resistance was in them ; then they accepted it; they are now becoming reconciled to it ; and soon they will rejoice over it. Such is always the history of progressive ideas. The first advance is opposed with all the 'might of the world until its triumph is achieved ; then the world says, " Very well," and employs all its arts and energies to defeat the next movement, which triumphs and is finally welcomed in its turn.

At the close of the war, the South was ready to accept any terms which the victorious government might have seen fit to enforce. The ground was thoroughly broken ; it was fresh from the harrow ; and then was the time for the sowing of the new seed, before delay had given encouragement and opportunity to the old rank weeds. The States had practically dissolved their relations to the general government. Their chief men were traitors, their governors and legislators were entitled to no recognition, and a new class of free citizens, composing near half the population, had been created. If, in these changed circumstances, all the people of those States had been called upon to unite in restoring their respective governments, and their relations to the general government, we should have had a simple and easy solution of the main question at issue. Our allies on the battle-field would have become our allies at the ballot-box, and by doing justice to them we should have gained security for ourselves.

But are the lately emancipated blacks prepared for the franchise ? They are, by all moral and intellectual qualifications, as well prepared for it as the mass of poor whites in the South. Although ignorant, they possess, as has been said, a strong instinct which stands them in the place of actual knowledge. That instinct inspires them with loyalty to the government, and it will never permit them to vote so unwisely and mischievously as the white people of the South voted in the days of secession. Moreover, there are among them men of fine intelligence and leading influence, by whom, and not by their old masters, as has been claimed, they will be instructed in their duty at the polls. And this fact is most certain, — that they are far better prepared to have a hand in making the laws by which they are to be governed, than the whites are to make those laws for them.

How this step is now to be brought about, is not easy to determine ; and it may not be brought about for some time to come. In the mean while it is neither wise nor just to allow the representation of the Southern States in Congress to be increased by the emancipation of a race that has no voice in that representation ; and some constitutional remedy against this evil is required. And in the mean while the protection of the government must be continued to the race to which its faith is pledged. Let us hope not long.

The present high price of cotton, and the extraordinary demand for labor, seem providential circumstances, designed to teach both races a great lesson. The freedmen are fast learning the responsibilities of their new situation, and gaining a position from which they cannot easily be displaced. Their eagerness to acquire knowledge is a bright sign of hope for their future. By degrees the dominant class must learn to respect those who, as chattels, could only be despised. Respect for labor rises with the condition of the laborer. The whites of the South are not by choice ignorant or unjust, but circumstances have made them so. Teach them that the laborer is a man, and that labor is manly, — a truth that is now dawning upon them, — and the necessity of mediation between the two races will no longer exist.

Then the institutions of the South will spontaneously assimilate to our own. Then we shall have a Union of States, not in form only, but in spirit also. Then shall we see established the reality of the cause that has cost so many priceless lives and such lavish outpouring of treasure. Then will disloyalty die of inanition, and its deeds live only in legend and in story. Then breaks upon America the morning glory of that future which shall behold it the Home of Man, and the Lawgiver among the nations.